The Rules and Politics of American Primaries

The Rules and Politics of American Primaries

A State-by-State Guide to Republican and Democratic Primaries and Caucuses

Andrew E. Busch, Editor

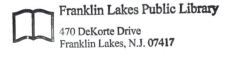

ABC-CLIO®

An Imprint of ABC-CLIO, LLC
Santa Barbara, California • Denver, Colorado

Library of Congress Cataloging-in-Publication Data

Names: Busch, Andrew, editor.
Title: The rules and politics of American primaries : a state-by-state guide to
    Republican and Democratic primaries and caucuses / Andrew E. Busch, Editor.
Description: Santa Barbara : ABC-CLIO, 2019. | Includes bibliographical
    references and index.
Identifiers: LCCN 2019026778 (print) | LCCN 2019026779 (ebook) |
    ISBN 9781440859038 (cloth) | ISBN 9781440859045 (ebook)
Subjects: LCSH: Primaries—United States—States.
Classification: LCC JK2071 .R85 2019 (print) | LCC JK2071 (ebook) |
    DDC 324.273/154—dc23
LC record available at https://lccn.loc.gov/2019026778
LC ebook record available at https://lccn.loc.gov/2019026779

ISBN: 978-1-4408-5903-8 (print)
       978-1-4408-5904-5 (ebook)

24 23 22 21 20   1 2 3 4 5

This book is also available as an eBook.

ABC-CLIO
An Imprint of ABC-CLIO, LLC

ABC-CLIO, LLC
147 Castilian Drive
Santa Barbara, California 93117
www.abc-clio.com

This book is printed on acid-free paper ♾

Manufactured in the United States of America

To Jim, who could not have been a better teacher, mentor, and friend, and whose fault it is that I study presidential primaries

Contents

Introduction

This volume aims to provide a wide-ranging overview of the presidential nominating process in the United States. The presidential nominating process, unlike the general election, is almost entirely extraconstitutional. It has developed in several stages since the formation of political parties in the 1790s and consists of elements found in state law, federal law, national party rules, state party rules, and federal court decisions. Despite its extraconstitutional status, as a practical matter no one can become president without being nominated first by the Democratic or Republican Party or (at least in theory) by a third party or independent movement of citizens.

Part I consists of 14 concise chapters examining the most important concepts regarding that process. These chapters provide historical background, information about current workings, and arguments in today's debates about varying aspects of the nominating system (such as: Are open primaries a good or bad thing? Should we have more caucuses or fewer? What are the arguments for and against a national primary?). Altogether, Part I features the following framework:

- Chapter 1 provides a historical summary of the development of the process in broad strokes.

- Chapters 2 and 3 examine in turn how the two major components of the nominating system (caucuses and primaries) work, while Chapter 4 explores more closely the crucial distinction between open and closed primaries and caucuses.

- Chapter 5 discusses the nomination calendar, in particular the development of primary "front-loading" and efforts by the parties to combat it. On a related topic, the importance of early contests such as the Iowa caucuses and New Hampshire primary is the subject of Chapter 6.

- The next set of chapters focuses on important aspects of the politics of the nomination race. Chapter 7 looks at the history and role of candidate debates held before and during the primary season, Chapter 8 examines campaign finance during the nomination stage of the presidential campaign, and Chapter 9 explores voting behavior in presidential primaries.

- Then follows a series of chapters on delegates and the national convention. Chapter 10 takes a detailed look at the varying methods used to award delegates on the basis of primary and caucus results. Chapter 11 reviews the selection of the actual individuals chosen to serve as national convention delegates, as well as their rights and responsibilities in that position. The party convention has changed considerably since its 19th-century beginnings, but it remains important and is the subject of Chapter 12.

- Chapter 13 catalogues the wide range of proposals for reforming the presidential nominating process, from establishment of a national primary or regional primaries to more incremental steps designed to extend the nomination race.

- Finally, Chapter 14 surveys a variety of non–major party forces and the mechanisms they have used to nominate candidates for president, from the "Dixiecrats" of 1948 to the Libertarians and Greens of 2016.

Part II provides entries detailing primary or caucus processes used by Democrats and Republicans in each state. Each entry contains the following components:

- A brief overview of the state's political culture, political history, and recent voting tendencies;

- An overview of how delegate selection has evolved in the state since 1912, when the first presidential primaries were held, including the state's choices about when to schedule its event and whether to use caucuses or primaries;

- A catalogue and summary of notable primaries or caucuses held in the state over time, as well as (in caucus states) key votes cast by the state's delegations to the national convention;

- Detailed election results of the state's primaries or caucuses from 2000 to 2016, including all candidates who received at least 1 percent of the vote;

- Information about delegate selection in that state in 2020, including primary or caucus dates (as of September 1, 2019) and the key rules governing the contest in each party.

Finally, an appendix provides a chronological calendar of key primary, caucus, and national convention dates.

A note about sources is in order at this point. Many sources are utilized in the state entries, but a few stand out as helpful beyond what specific citations may indicate. Attempts to provide general background on each state frequently leaned on observations found in the invaluable *Almanac of American Politics*, especially its 2014, 2016, and 2018 editions. Information regarding primary dates was harvested from the Congressional Quarterly *Guide to U.S. Elections*, 7th edition (Volume I). Because caucuses are more informal, party-run affairs, the results of which are usually not certified by state officials, information on caucus dates and results are not as easy to come by. As noted in the results section, much information on the 2000–2016 caucuses can be located in the online source The Green Papers, which also served as the main source for data on the 2020 nominating process.

Accounts of historical primary and caucus results depended on *The Guide to U.S. Elections*, a number of historical and journalistic sources that are cited, and, not infrequently, 30 years of my own study of presidential nominations and elections, which have produced authored or co-authored books on the elections of 1948, 1980, and 1992–2016.

A word of caution is also in order. Everything that is possible has been done to provide the best information regarding the 2020 process, but last-minute changes of event date or even mode of delegate selection after publication cannot be ruled out.

Finally, a word about the students who assisted on this project. My co-authors, Richard C. ("Skip") Wiltshire-Gordon, Jacob S. Leischner, and Nandeeni K. Patel, student research assistants at the Rose Institute of State and Local Government at Claremont McKenna College, were deeply involved in Part II. Skip led the student team and was responsible for the initial drafting of eight state narratives; Jake drafted eight, and Nandeeni six. I added necessary material, edited, and harmonized the drafts with the remainder of the entries. In Part I, Skip and Caroline Peck assisted with research on several chapters. It was a pleasure working with them all, and they deserve the credit that goes with their contributions, which are noted at the end of entries.

It is our hope that you will find this volume both interesting and useful.

PART 1

Foundations of the Presidential Nominating System

CHAPTER ONE

Historical Overview

The system for nominating presidential candidates in the United States is one of the most important features of the American political system, yet it is almost entirely extraconstitutional in nature. It is not quite accurate to even call it a system, as if it were deliberately designed to form a coherent whole. Rather, the American way of nominating presidential candidates is better understood as an agglomeration of features arrived at more or less independently by the national political parties, state parties, state legislators, and federal legislators, with some federal court decisions added to the mix. Sometimes, these actors truly proceed as disconnected forces; sometimes they operate in greater concert, moved by broad trends in public sentiment, intellectual direction, and policy experimentation. But they always represent separate institutions.

The party nominating system is extraconstitutional for the simple reason that the parties are extraconstitutional. While provisions in the Bill of Rights guaranteeing freedom of speech, freedom of the press, and the right to assemble and petition government for the redress of grievances made possible the existence of parties, they are nowhere explicitly mentioned in the Constitution. Fearing that political parties could divide the nation, distract officeholders from pursuing the common good, and perhaps even lead to civil conflict, the Founders were not inclined to build them into the constitutional structure. George Washington famously included a warning against the "spirit of party" in his Farewell Address, and not until the 1830s did the argument gain currency that a competitive two-party system was good for the country (Washington 1796; Ceaser 1979).

In the meantime, parties arose anyway. Disputes in George Washington's first cabinet between Alexander Hamilton and Thomas Jefferson over constitutional interpretation, political economy, and foreign policy quickly spread to Congress, and then to the country. Hamilton stood for broader constitutional interpretation, more expansive federal power, manufacturing, and a tilt toward Britain; Jefferson favored strict construction of the Constitution, states' rights, agrarianism, and France. By the nation's third presidential election in 1796, the Federalist Party of Hamilton and John Adams was squaring off against the Jeffersonian Republicans (or, sometimes, Democratic-Republicans). By the fourth presidential election both parties grasped the importance of concentrating their strength behind a single contender for the presidency. In 1788, 1792, and 1796, the "nomination" of candidates for the presidency was coterminous with the operation of the Electoral College. In 1800, the idea of a separate nominating process controlled by the parties and prior to the selection of the Electoral College was born.

From 1800 to 1824, this system took the form of the "congressional caucus," in which each party's members of Congress met and designated their party's preferred candidates for president and vice president (at the same time, most states used a legislative caucus to nominate candidates for state executive). The system had the benefit of simplicity, and guaranteed that each party's nominee for president had the stamp of approval of federal officeholders with whom they may have worked already and certainly would have to work in the future if elected. The candidates chosen to run under this arrangement were typically federal officeholders themselves, including a string of secretaries of state. The disadvantages of this arrangement, however, soon began to outweigh the advantages. For one, the congressional caucus undermined separation of powers by giving members of Congress, if not Congress as an institution, control over the president's nomination and renomination. The Federal Convention of 1787 ultimately selected the Electoral College as a means of electing the president, rejecting proposals for Congress to elect the executive because of its potentially deleterious effect on executive independence. Yet, through the back door of party nomination, the congressional caucus had put that control over presidential selection right back in the hands of the legislative branch. The dangers involved were real, and not merely hypothetical; James Madison's willingness to go to war with Britain in 1812, for example, may have been influenced by the control the congressional "war hawks" in his party exerted over his nomination (Menon 2016).

Moreover, in a rapidly democratizing America, the congressional caucus was not very mindful of desires for popular influence. To many, it looked like a top-down process in which the nation's political elite hand-picked another branch of the political elite from a pool consisting of the political elite. Of course, it could also be argued that the process was broadly representative, resting ultimately on the foundation of popular control. The people, after all, selected both the House of Representatives and the state legislatures that elected the Senate. However, that influence on presidential nomination was highly attenuated, and was only even theoretically possible when a voter's congressional representatives were of his own party. A Republican voter in a district represented by a Federalist member of Congress, for example, was not even indirectly connected to the process.

With the collapse of the Federalist Party after 1816, the nation temporarily reverted to a one-party system. The discipline exerted by two-party competition ceased to operate, and the congressional caucus began to lose its force as a means of making nominations that members of the party accepted. And, in a free country, a one-party system merely meant that the multitude of disputes and factions in American politics were housed under the umbrella of a single party. When the congressional caucus met in 1824, fewer than half of the members of Congress attended, and the person designated as the presidential nominee—William Crawford of Georgia—was widely ignored. Four other candidates, all claiming the same party label, ran despite the caucus's decision. Split among five candidates, the Electoral College vote produced no majority, throwing the election back to the House of Representatives, which chose John Quincy Adams. Andrew Jackson, who had won more popular votes in those states (18 of 24) that utilized popular votes to choose electors, was outraged. He spent the next four years building the Democratic Party, running against "King Caucus," and alleging that a "Corrupt Bargain" in the House between Adams and Henry Clay was responsible for Adams's victory. In the words of one analyst, "the people discovered that they had no voice in the nomination, and thereafter the system was doomed" (Dallinger 1897, 20). The congressional caucus was never used again.

The Rise of the National Convention

Following a chaotic election of 1828 in which candidates were "nominated" by electors, state legislatures, and others, a new system for party nomination was in place by 1832. Used for nominations for statewide office in Pennsylvania from 1788 to 1792 and pioneered for presidential nominations in 1831 by a third party, the Anti-Masonic Party, the national party convention dominated the scene for the better part of the next century. In the national convention system, state and local parties sent delegates to a national convention held solely for the purpose of nominating the party's presidential and vice presidential candidates and (starting in 1840) writing the party's "platform"—a statement of party principles for the upcoming election campaign.

The operation of the national convention differed significantly from the congressional caucus. For one thing, it was a bottom-up process, starting with local party meetings that sent delegates to local conventions, which then selected delegates to state conventions, which then selected delegates to the national conventions. Overall, the system was characterized by "party-activist control of nominations and platforms through the convention"

(Burnham 1970, 72). State and local party leaders held considerable influence at the convention, and the delegates were not generally beholden to any candidate in advance. The system accentuated federalism, as state and local party leaders were the key players. Because delegates were free agents and candidates did not generally run openly in advance of the convention, nomination outcomes were unpredictable. The Whigs, and then the Republicans who took their place, made nominations by the majority of the delegate votes. Democrats, meanwhile, utilized a two-thirds majority rule, giving the South an effective veto over nominations. In both major parties, conventions rarely concluded their business on the first ballot. Frequently, many ballots would be required, as delegates and party leaders shifted from one candidate to another until someone obtained sufficient momentum to break away from the pack.

The convention system was also more representative than the congressional caucus, since every state was represented in each party whether it had voted for or against the party in recent elections. Where the congressional caucus had demonstrated the more aristocratic tendencies of the early republic, the convention system manifested the rough-and-tumble democratic ethos of the Jacksonian era and beyond. Hence, the convention solved both the problem of the congressional caucus's unrepresentativeness and the loss of party coherence that followed the caucus's collapse (Roseboom 1970, 106). From 1832 until 1912 the national convention system dominated American politics.

But, like the congressional caucus before it, the national convention system had its weaknesses. Among other things, because it was largely under the grip of party bosses, critics accused it of corruption (heard in complaints about "smoke-filled rooms" where politicians and rich supporters secretly orchestrated nominations) and said it was too closed off to popular forces—the same criticisms raised against the congressional caucus, but for different reasons. One modern critic of the convention system called the state and local party meetings that served as the foundation for the system "undemocratic exercises in the unrestrained use of power" (Crotty 1977, 200). Some critics also intimated that the bosses, concerned above all with obtaining victory for their patronage offerings, cared more about winning than about putting forward coherent principles for the party or obtaining high-quality nominees. This phenomenon led the British observer Lord James Bryce to blame the party nominating system for why "great men are not elected president" (Bryce 1891, 73–80). And, indeed, the system produced a series of nondescript and not particularly effective presidents—figures such as Franklin Pierce, James Buchanan, Rutherford B. Hayes, and Benjamin Harrison. Defenders of the system could point out that the presidency itself was a more modest office then—possibly to the good—and that when the nation most needed presidential leadership, the system produced Abraham Lincoln.

The Rise of Primaries and the "Mixed System"

The convention system's complete reliance on state and local party leaders and the freedom of the delegates from direct control by popular opinion did not survive the rise of the Progressive Movement, an early 20th-century movement determined to introduce greater direct democracy. Many Progressives, including Woodrow Wilson and George Norris, hoped to sweep away the mediating power of the party organizations; on the other hand, Robert La Follette of Wisconsin hoped to purify and strengthen the parties (Ranney 1975, 124–25; Ceaser 1979, chapter 4). The great Progressive innovation was the direct primary, which allowed party voters to bypass the party institutions by voting directly for their preferred candidates (or, in presidential nominations, voting directly for delegates to the national convention).

In 1904, Florida held the first direct primary for national convention delegates, though there was no presidential preference vote attached. In 1910, Oregon passed the first law creating a direct primary for national convention delegates that included a presidential preference vote. Direct primaries were first used in presidential nominations in 1912, when 13 states held primaries. The number of primaries grew to 23 in 1916, but then fell back again. The Progressives altered the system, but fell well short of their ideal of a national primary or state primaries in every state. By around 1920 the so-called "mixed system" had stabilized; about one-third of states used primaries, while the other two-thirds continued using traditional methods of delegate selection.

For most of the period of the mixed system (1912–1968) the national convention remained the decisive moment, and most delegates retained freedom of action. As one political scientist describes it, "despite the widespread use of primaries, party leaders retained control of presidential nominations" (Geer 1989, 2). The primaries, however, introduced an element of popular opinion as an important factor. Because only one-third of states used primaries, it was not possible to win a nomination by concentrating only on primaries, though candidates occasionally tried. In 1952, for example, Estes Kefauver ran successfully in every primary and still did not receive the nomination. (Adlai Stevenson was selected by the convention.) Instead, candidates selected which primaries to enter based on their strategic needs—particularly the need to demonstrate their voter appeal to the party bosses who continued to influence the decisive remainder of delegates. Thus, in any given year, only a handful of primaries held real significance. Perhaps the best example was in 1960, when John F. Kennedy, a Catholic, chose to compete with labor favorite Hubert Humphrey in the heavily unionized and heavily Protestant state of West Virginia. After beating Humphrey in the Mountain State, Kennedy was able to secure support from Chicago's legendary Mayor Richard Daley and other machine mayors. He had proven that he too could win the support of union voters and, even more important, that his Catholicism would not be an insuperable obstacle to election (White 1961).

Unlike in the pure convention system, candidates in the mixed system openly ran for their party's nomination prior to the convention, though drafts of candidates at the convention were still possible (as Stevenson showed in 1952). The Democrats abandoned their two-thirds rule after 1932, but multi-ballot conventions also remained possible. Twelve years before the rule change, the Democratic national convention set a record by not settling on its nominee (John W. Davis) until the 103rd ballot.

The mixed system displayed some obvious strengths. It retained the stability of a system heavily influenced by mediating institutions while giving an advantage to candidates who could also appeal successfully to the voting public. It retained a substantial degree of "peer review." At the same time, it provided avenues of entry to well-organized and enduring political movements, such as the conservative movement in the Republican Party in 1964, while retaining barriers against movements driven by short-term passions and potentially demagogic outsiders.

However, some of these advantages were only obvious in retrospect. In 1968, many Americans called for fundamental reform of the nominating system. They complained that the mixed system remained too wedded to the party organizations and insufficiently hospitable to popular forces. The triggering event came in 1968 with the Democratic nomination of Hubert H. Humphrey. Initially, the Democratic nomination race featured President Lyndon Johnson, in the throes of commanding the Vietnam War, against antiwar U.S. senator Eugene McCarthy. Emboldened by Johnson's slow start in the primaries, U.S. senator Robert F. Kennedy, brother of slain president John F. Kennedy, entered the fray. Facing a tough battle for renomination and preoccupied with the war that seemed to be tearing American society apart, Johnson removed himself from the race. He was quickly replaced by his vice president, Hubert Humphrey, who was widely regarded as representative of the pro-administration "regular" Democrats. From that point, McCarthy and Kennedy battled it out in the primary states, swapping wins in states such as Wisconsin, Nebraska, Indiana, and Oregon. But in the nonprimary states, Humphrey, with the backing of the party organizations, cleaned up. McCarthy organizer Ben Stavis later admitted that as the primary season came to a close, "we suddenly realized, the number of delegate votes determined by these contests was actually quite low" (Stavis 1968, 150). On the last night of primaries, Kennedy won California, but was shot and killed at the Ambassador Hotel in Los Angeles. His shocking assassination left Humphrey, McCarthy, and South Dakota's Senator George McGovern, who threw his hat in the ring after Kennedy's death, the lone contenders for the Democratic presidential nomination.

In the end, the Chicago convention nominated Humphrey even though he had run in no primaries—a fact that enraged the insurgents within the party. The result was not as divorced from public opinion as critics suggested, however. A Gallup poll conducted two weeks before the convention showed Humphrey leading McCarthy by 53–39 percent among Democrats nationwide. Nevertheless, seeking intraparty peace, the nominee supported creation after the election of a party commission to reform the nominating rules. Had he won the fall election against Richard Nixon, he would have controlled the Democratic National Committee (DNC), and through it the commission.

He lost.

The McGovern-Fraser Reforms and Beyond

What followed was perhaps the most dramatic top-down change in the presidential nominating process in U.S. history. Freed by Humphrey's loss from presidential control, the Democratic National Committee selected pro-reform U.S. senator Fred Harris of Oklahoma as its chair. Harris then appointed a commission chaired initially by George McGovern and stacked with other individuals favoring significant reforms. Once his next presidential campaign began in earnest, McGovern handed over the chairmanship to Congressman Donald Fraser.

The McGovern-Fraser Commission, officially known as the Commission on Delegate Selection and Party Structure, declared that its aim was to emphasize "full, meaningful, and timely participation" by Democratic voters in the nominating process. To that end, it proposed that the DNC adopt 18 rules that would then be enforced on state parties. Through a variety of means, the commission aimed to make it more difficult for the party organization to control or influence delegate selection processes. It also sought to create a tighter connection between public opinion and delegate outcomes—or to put it another way, make it unlikely that delegates could be selected as free agents unpledged to a candidate. Overall, the guidelines banned two of the five methods used for delegate selection in 1968—the pure delegate primary and the party caucus (a meeting limited to party officials). A third method of delegate selection—appointment by party committees—was limited to no more than 10 percent of a state's delegation. The guidelines also required that meeting times and rules be publicized, and banned a number of mechanisms that had long been used to enforce party control of primaries and caucuses (Democratic National Committee 1970). On balance, the reforms meant that "the official party had been erased from what was still nominally the party's nomination process" (Shafer 1983, 6).

The McGovern-Fraser Commission fell one vote short of requiring proportional representation (a system in which delegates would be dispersed to candidates roughly in proportion to how many votes they received), but urged that states adopt it. It did require that in caucus-convention states at least three-quarters of a state delegation be selected at the congressional district level or lower. Four years later, the New Delegate Selection Commission (or Mikulski Commission, named after commission chair Barbara Mikulski) required proportional representation in caucuses and mandated that caucus participants declare a presidential candidate preference. Winner-take-all primaries were banned, and proportional representation preferred (though party rules continued to permit primaries in which at least 75 percent of delegates were chosen at the congressional district level). Open primaries, in which non-Democrats were allowed to vote, were banned on the grounds that they diluted the votes of Democrats.

Another hugely significant change flowed from the reforms, even though the reforms themselves did not call for it and some members of the commission later professed surprise at the result: the number of states using primaries increased dramatically, from 16 in 1968 to 23 in 1972 to 35 by 1980. Since then, the number has remained in the 35 to 40 states range. Some reform enthusiasts took seriously the commission's call for "full, meaningful, and timely participation," and concluded that primaries were the best method to achieve that goal. Others, fearful of how the reforms might open the caucuses or party committees to greater influence by radical political movements, actually adopted primaries as a *defense* against extremism. Finally, some states, driven by bureaucratic considerations, thought that the new rules made primaries less likely to be subject to a credentials challenge (Fraser 1980, 123; Polsby 1983, 59; Ranney 1978, 3; McGovern 1977, 153).

When McGovern won the Democratic presidential nomination in 1972, many analysts credited (or blamed) the new system for the success of his insurgent candidacy. And there was some truth to the claim. He knew the new rules better than anyone in the field, and the obstacles to party control of the process certainly helped him. The picture, however, was more complicated than that. McGovern actually did better in the old primaries than in the ones created after 1968, and did better in the caucuses than the primaries. He also benefited greatly from victories in states that were, for the moment, defying the reform ethos: Wisconsin's open primary gave him his first win, and he racked up huge delegate wins in California's winner-take-all primary and New York's delegate primary (Busch 1997, ch. 4).

It took a few election cycles for the McGovern-Fraser reforms to become fully implemented, but Democratic control of most state legislatures, combined with a Republican desire not to be left behind in the race for openness, meant that many features of what one might call the "reform system" were ultimately implemented by both parties. Most importantly, the growth of primaries affected both parties equally. Because the new system was dominated by primaries, it was no longer possible for candidates to avoid all or most primaries and seek victory by another route. Most delegates were bound by the results of their primaries or caucus processes, so the convention changed from a venue for decision making to a coronation of a predetermined nominee. Candidates had to run openly from the start of the primary season, and the earlier the better; once the primaries started, one could track with much greater confidence the progress (or lack thereof) of those candidates. Moreover, because candidates had to run in all the primaries, because there were many more primaries, and because primaries cost much more than nonprimary processes, the cost of running for president exploded. These changes coincided with the 1974 Federal Election Campaign Act amendments, which put a relatively low cap on individual contributions to federal candidates but offered presidential candidates federal matching funds for small donations. Other aspects of the reforms, such as proportional representation and rules limiting party influence in caucuses, were not adopted by the Republicans.

In one sense, the new system was simply a continuation of the drive away from mediating representative processes and toward more directly "democratic" ones that began with the collapse of the congressional caucus. In each transition, greater openness to popular opinion was one of the motivations. As political scientist Edward Banfield noted, "The 'reforms' of the late 1960s and early 1970s were the culmination of more than a century of efforts to bring party politics into correspondence with the democratic ideal" (Banfield 1980, 30). Indeed, primary elections among rank-and-file party voters has become increasingly common internationally in the last few decades (McCann 2004, 265–293). However, the McGovern-Fraser reforms—and the explosion of primaries that followed from them—proved more controversial and more subject to tinkering than earlier changes.

Defenders of the reforms saw them as necessary for securing the legitimacy of the presidential nominating system and perhaps of the parties themselves. McGovern himself declared in his 1972 nomination acceptance speech that "My nomination is all the more precious in that it is a gift of the most open political process in all of our political history" (McGovern 1972). Political scientists such as William Crotty concurred that the pre-reform system had been unacceptably undemocratic, "arcane . . . indefensible . . . an unpleasant mix of unresponsive, outdated, and arbitrary practices . . . biased and repressive" (Crotty 1977, 47).

Critics argued, however, that the reforms opened up the system to victory by candidates who were either extremists (McGovern in 1972) or unqualified outsiders unvetted by the political establishment with which he or she would have to work after the election (1976 Democratic presidential nominee Jimmy Carter was most frequently cited as an example of the latter). The organizational vacuum left by the diminished power of the parties was filled by interest groups and news media, which was embraced by ordinary primary voters who lacked both information and partisan cues by which to judge candidates (Farnsworth and Lichter 2008, 75–98). Elevated as well was the candidate himself. The reversal seemed complete from the pure national convention system, in which broad-based federal parties selected a candidate to represent them, to a new day in which ambitious candidates sought to remake the party in their own image. Some political scientists, such as James W. Ceaser and Nelson Polsby, feared that the new system might open the road to demagogues and instability (Ceaser 1982; Polsby 1983).

Within a few years, a more practical sort of critic emerged within the Democratic Party. These detractors became convinced that the reforms had put Democrats at a disadvantage and contributed to a string of losses in presidential elections between 1968 and 1988, broken only by Carter's very narrow (and perhaps Pyrrhic) victory in 1976. Thus, after every nomination contest from 1976 through 1992, Democrats altered their nominating rules. At first, the aim was to complete the reform impulse, finishing the work of the McGovern-Fraser Commission. As with many revolutions, the revolutionaries were never quite certain they were done. Then, the aim became to mitigate the reforms by reinjecting elected officials who could exercise some kind of "peer review" and limit the influence of fringe candidates who had been empowered by innovations such as proportional representation. From these efforts were born the Democratic "superdelegates," delegates to Democratic conventions from 1984 on who were appointed on the basis of the party or elected offices they held.

Another unanticipated consequence of the reforms, in combination with the 1974 campaign finance rules, was to alter significantly the nomination calendar. Prior to the reforms, the delegate selection calendar was heavily "back-loaded." Because most delegates were unpledged and the national convention was the decisive moment, most states considered it advantageous to hold their primaries relatively close to the convention. Once most delegates were pledged to candidates up front, and candidates who were unsuccessful in early primaries were forced to drop out of contention, the calculation for states shifted dramatically. Now, if a state held its primary too late, the nomination contest might effectively be over before it reached that state. Primary front-loading began, and became self-perpetuating. The national parties have been attempting to deal with front-loading in one fashion or another since the 1980s, but with only limited success. The importance of the earliest contests in Iowa and New Hampshire steadily grew, despite criticism from other states and from academic and journalistic analysts (Mayer and Busch, 2004).

From the 1990s until 2008, concerns grew that the heavily front-loaded and costly system that had developed had inadvertently brought presidential nominations full circle. Perhaps, some analysts suggested, the insiders were back in control, and only well-funded candidates with deep "establishment" support could be competitive (Cohen, Karol, Noel, and Zaller 2008). Then came the nominations of unlikely outsiders in 2008 (Democratic nominee Barack Obama) and 2016 (Republican nominee Donald Trump). It seemed that another rethinking was in order. Perhaps the reforms had worked as intended after all. And the debate was rekindled whether that outcome was good or bad for the country, a victory for the people or the demagogues.

Sources

Arizona Republic. 1968. "Rank-and-File Favor HHH." August 7.

Banfield, Edward. 1980. "Party 'Reform' in Retrospect." In Robert A. Goldwin, ed., *Political Parties in the Eighties.* Washington, DC: American Enterprise Institute.

Bryce, James. 1891. *The American Commonwealth,* Vol. I. Chicago: Charles H. Sergel.

Burnham, Walter Dean. 1970. *Critical Elections and the Mainsprings of American Politics.* New York: W. W. Norton.

Busch, Andrew E. 1997. *Outsiders and Openness in the Presidential Nominating System.* Pittsburgh: University of Pittsburgh Press.

Ceaser, James W. 1979. *Presidential Selection.* Princeton: Princeton University Press.

Ceaser, James. 1982. *Reforming the Reforms: A Critical Analysis of the Presidential Selection Process.* Boston: Ballinger.

Cohen, Marty, David Karol, Hans Noel, and John Zaller. 2008. *The Party Decides: Presidential Nominations Before and After Reform.* Chicago: University of Chicago Press.

Crotty, William J. 1977. *Political Reform and the American Experiment.* New York: Thomas Y. Crowell.

Dallinger, Frederick. 1897. *Nominations for Elective Office in the United States.* Cambridge, MA: Harvard University Press.

Democratic National Committee. 1970. *Mandate for Reform: A Report on the Commission on Party Structure and Delegate Selection to the Democratic National Committee.* Washington, DC: Democratic National Committee.

Farnsworth, Stephen J., and S. Robert Lichter. 2008. "How Television Covers the Presidential Nomination Process." In William G. Mayer, ed., *The Making of the Presidential Candidates 2008.* Lanham, MD: Rowman & Littlefield.

Fraser, Donald M. 1980. "Democratizing the Democratic Party." In Robert A. Goldwin, ed., *Political Parties in the Eighties.* Washington, DC: American Enterprise Institute.

Geer, John G. 1989. *Nominating Presidents.* Westport, CT: Greenwood Press.

Marshall, Thomas R. 1981. *Presidential Nominations in a Reform Age.* New York: Praeger.

Mayer, William G., and Andrew E. Busch. 2004. *The Front-Loading Problem in Presidential Nominations.* Washington, DC: Brookings Institution.

McCann, James A. 2004. "The Emergent International Trend Toward Open Presidential Primaries: The American Presidential Nomination Process in Comparative Perspective." In William G. Mayer, ed., *The Making of the Presidential Candidates 2004.* Lanham, MD: Rowman & Littlefield.

McGovern, George. 1972. "Address Accepting the Presidential Nomination at the Democratic National Convention in Miami Beach, Florida." July 14. Online by Gerhard Peters and John T. Woolley, The American Presidency Project. https://www.presidency.ucsb.edu/node/216662.

McGovern, George. 1977. *Grassroots*. New York: Random House.

Menon, Varun K. 2016. "The War That Congress Waged." *Penn History Review* 23, no. 1 (Spring).

Ostrogorski, M. 1908. *Democracy and the Organization of Political Parties (vol. II)*. New York: Macmillan.

Polsby, Nelson. 1983. *Consequences of Party Reform*. New York: Oxford University Press.

Pomper, Gerald. 1963. *Nominating the President*. Chicago: Northwestern University Press.

Ranney, Austin. 1975. *Curing the Mischiefs of Faction: Party Reform in America*. Berkeley: University of California Press.

Ranney, Austin. 1978. *The Federalization of Presidential Primaries*. Washington, DC: American Enterprise Institute.

Roseboom, Eugene H. 1970. *A History of Presidential Elections*. New York: Macmillan.

Shafer, Byron. 1983. *Quiet Revolution: The Struggle for the Democratic Party and the Shaping of Post-Reform Politics*. New York: Russell Sage Foundation.

Stavis, Ben. 1968. *We Were the Campaign: New Hampshire to Chicago for McCarthy*. Boston: Beacon.

Thompson, C. S. 1974. "The Rise and Fall of the Congressional Caucus as a Machine for Nominating Candidates for Presidency." Reprinted in Leon Stein, ed., *The Caucus System in American Politics*. New York: Arno.

Washington, George. 1796. "Washington's Farewell Address 1796." The Avalon Project, http://avalon.law.yale.edu/18th_century/washing.asp.

White, Theodore. 1961. *The Making of the President 1960*. New York: Atheneum Books.

Whittridge, Frederick W. 1974. "Caucus System (1883)." Reprinted in Leon Stein, ed., *The Caucus System in American Politics*. New York: Arno.

CHAPTER TWO

How Caucuses Work

Most states use either "caucuses" or "primaries" as the starting point for the selection of delegates to the national convention. "Caucuses" are the older method, reaching deep into the 19th century, though how they operate has changed significantly over that time. Also changing over time has been the terminology used: originally, what we now call caucuses were called "primaries"—because they were the first or primary step in the process of delegate selection—and what we call "primaries" did not exist. When the Progressives began securing adoption of an alternative method in the early 20th century, they were initially called "direct primaries," to distinguish them from traditional primaries. Over time, "direct primaries" simply became "primaries" and "primaries" became "caucuses," which also means small meetings. For the sake of clarity, from here forward the contemporary designations will be used.

A History of Caucuses

Caucuses are small local meetings of party members or supporters who form the base of a representational pyramid that ends at the national convention. The 19th-century political party had three key components—the caucuses, party committees, and nominating conventions—and, in theory, all party power flowed from the caucuses. Party voters attended the caucuses, at which they elected the party committees (the leadership of the parties) and delegates to the next level of nominating convention (for instance, the county). The county conventions then elected delegates to the state convention, which subsequently elected delegates to the national convention, which in turn selected the party's nominee for president. In some states, national convention delegates were selected by the party committees or by caucuses limited to party leaders, but those committees and leaders traced their power back to the local party meetings.

In reality, especially in urban areas, the party committees controlled the process most of the time. Frequently, in the days before state-sponsored voter registration, admission to the caucuses depended on one's inclusion on the "party list," the informal catalogue of the party's members in that area. Because the parties were treated legally as private associations, the party committees could include or exclude whomever they wanted on the party lists. By some estimates, in places where the party lists were commonly used, three-fourths to four-fifths of the party's actual supporters were excluded from the lists. Moreover, the local party committee usually put forward a slate of candidates for delegates, which usually won (Bryce 1889, 78–85, 93–101; Ostrogorski 1908, 211).

Nevertheless, the process was a bottom-up one from the local level to the national level with several intermediate steps along the way. As a general rule, people were not selected as delegates to a higher level because of their preexisting support for a particular candidate (or, more likely, potential candidate). They were free agents in that respect, although they might have been selected for their loyalty to a particular local officeholder, boss, or faction. In rural areas, where people knew each other better, the party lists were often not used. In addition, even in places where the local bosses kept a tight grip on the process, there is evidence that they were generally sensitive to shifts in public opinion (Bryce 1889, 179–195).

In the late 19th century, criticism of the way caucuses were run intensified and states began regulating them. From 1890 to 1920 significant changes were imposed on caucuses. At first, some states cautiously enacted small, often voluntary, reforms to limit abuse. Then, as states adopted the Australian (or secret) ballot, they considered it necessary to impose stricter rules on party nomination procedures, especially including opening up the party lists. By 1897, one observer held that "the honest enforcement of such laws has accomplished much" (Dallinger 1897, 197). Around the same time, some states began establishing direct primaries as an alternative method to caucuses for nomination to lower offices.

Within the mixed system, about two-thirds of states continued using caucuses, conventions, or selection by party committees. To the extent they were regulated by 1920, they remained regulated. Highly restricted party lists were supplanted by state voter registration, but party organizations still retained significant control over caucus processes. Party committees scheduled the caucuses (sometimes a year or more before election day), advertised the caucuses to voters (or not), and otherwise exerted organizational control under most circumstances. Delegates were not expected, let alone required, to announce their support of a particular candidate.

Even in the mixed system, however, candidates supported by large and durable political movements could sometimes break through. Barry Goldwater, for example, largely owed his 1964 nomination to the success of his well-organized supporters in the Republican caucuses of that year. Four years later, Democratic nominee Eugene McCarthy did well in caucuses in which his supporters fought vigorously (Busch 1997). In both cases, the insurgent forces defied the norm of the unpledged caucus delegate and mobilized to elect delegates who were committed from the outset to the insurgent candidate. It turned out that the caucuses gave an advantage not to the party organization per se, but to the well organized in general. Usually that meant the party, but it could also mean a political movement.

The McGovern-Fraser reforms adopted by the Democratic National Committee prior to the 1972 nomination race aimed, among other things, to further open the caucuses to popular influences and to formally draw a tighter connection between candidates and delegates. The reforms required delegate selection processes to begin within the calendar year of the election, required caucuses to be adequately advertised, and prohibited proxy voting and use of ex officio delegates, two mechanisms the official party had long used to retain control of local party meetings. The McGovern-Fraser Commission also established complex slate-making rules that encouraged the selection of pledged delegates (Democratic National Committee 1970). Four years later, Democratic rule-makers required caucus delegates to declare a presidential preference. The tools the local party organizations had used to influence caucuses had been taken away; barriers to access had been lowered. At the same time these reforms were being implemented, however, many states shifted from caucuses to primaries.

Republicans were impacted by the shift away from caucuses just as much as Democrats, but the GOP caucuses that remain have been subject to fewer changes than in Democratic politics. Some of the McGovern-Fraser reforms were adopted by Republicans as "suggestions," but have not been strictly enforced (Ranney 1975, 2–3; Crotty 1977, 256–257; Polsby 1983, 54). Others were never adopted. For example, Republicans permit state parties to limit caucuses or conventions to party officials, though it is now quite unusual for them to do so.

The number of caucus states has varied from 1972 to 2016. In 2016, 13 states used caucuses for delegate allocation in the Democratic Party and 12 in the Republican Party. (See Table 2.1.) Responding to supporters of Hillary Clinton, who argued that the Democratic caucuses were too easily controlled by groups who were not representative of party voters in general, Democrats decided to cut the number of caucuses by at least one-third in 2020, and remaining caucus states have been encouraged to make absentee ballots available in order to broaden participation. Ultimately, at least 10 of 13 Democratic caucus states announced a move to primaries in 2020 (Theobold, 2019). The reduction of caucuses was part of a package that included reduced power for superdelegates, a goal of Bernie Sanders.

Table 2.1   Number of States Using Caucuses as a Mode of Delegate Allocation in Democratic and Republican Parties, 1972–2016

Year	Republican Party	Democratic Party
1972	29	28
1976	23	22
1980	18	21
1984	23	27
1988	17	18*
1992	13	15*
1996	10	17*
2000	8	13*
2004	18	14*
2008	12	14*
2012	12	18
2016	12	13

* Figure does not include Texas and the Texas "Two-Step" system toward the state count.

Sources: The Green Papers, U.S. Election Atlas, Frontloading HQ, National Conference of State Legislatures, and the University of Virginia Center for Politics.

How a Modern Caucus Works

As in the 19th and 20th centuries, caucuses today represent the first, most local level of delegate selection. That level may be the precinct, the county, or the legislative district, depending on the state. The party holding the caucus selects a venue, most commonly a public building but also sometimes a private home or business. Voters arrive at the location at the scheduled time, and party officials verify that they are eligible to vote. By national Democratic rules, participation in Democratic caucuses is supposed to be "open to all voters who wish to participate as Democrats"; Republicans limit caucus participation to "legal and qualified voters who are deemed to be Republicans" and allow state party committees to establish further restrictions on eligibility. In some states these additional restrictions take the form of limiting caucus participation to people holding party office, such as members of precinct committees.

Caucus meetings typically begin with election of a temporary chair of the meeting, followed by election of a permanent chair (often the person selected as the temporary chair). Speeches by representatives of the party, representatives of the candidates, and voters follow. The caucuses then elect delegates to the next level of party meeting (possibly county, congressional district, or state convention). Here, again, Republican and Democratic rules diverge. Democrats require that caucus attendees divide themselves into groups on the basis of their declared candidate preference. The votes received this way are translated into a proportional number of delegates for every candidate who gets at least 15 percent of the overall vote. (If a candidate receives less than 15 percent, his or her voters are released so that they can attach themselves to another candidate.) After officials determine how many delegates to the next level each candidate will receive, the groups supporting each candidate select the actual individuals who will attend the next level as delegates (Mayer 1996).

Republicans have fewer rules. They now require caucuses held between March 1 and March 15 to use proportional representation, and any caucuses using proportional representation to elect pledged delegates. However, there is no proportional rule starting March 15, and caucuses may elect unbound, unpledged delegates. Nevertheless, there are some standard practices and patterns to GOP caucuses. The caucus elects delegates to the next level. Candidates for delegate may or may not identify themselves as supporters of a particular presidential candidate. Because there is no proportionality requirement, a majority in the caucus can easily translate into a delegation made up entirely of supporters of a single candidate—if they are well organized and know for whom to vote. On the other hand, groups of voters supporting different candidates have been known to divide up delegate positions based on mutual agreement, and delegations elected by caucuses are also sometimes uncommitted or unknown in their presidential preferences. To satisfy the media's desire to be able to declare a "winner," Republican caucuses will often hold a straw vote or nonbinding presidential preference poll. These results are reported to the media and can take on a symbolic importance out of proportion to their tangible significance.

In both parties, caucuses usually have a function beyond the selection of delegates to a higher-level party meeting; they also select party officials at the local level. In both parties the occasion will typically last longer than an hour. In both parties—but more so with the Republicans—the actual distribution of national convention delegates produced at the end of the caucus process is not necessarily closely related to the disparity between candidate supporters reported at the caucuses weeks or months before (for example, see the data on Iowa in Winebrenner 1987).

Although most states using party caucuses for delegate allocation use them as the sole delegate selection process, they are sometimes used as part of a hybrid system. In particular, there were a number of states in 2016 that held a presidential primary to determine how many delegates each candidate would receive but that also used caucuses to determine which individuals would be named as delegates. For many years, Texas Democrats selected about two-thirds of their delegates in a primary and the remainder in caucuses (though they discontinued the practice in 2016). Finally, over the past four decades, a few states have held a purely advisory presidential primary and held caucuses to allocate delegates. Wisconsin Democrats, for example, did this during the 1980s in order to comply with the national party's ban on delegate selection in open primaries.

More generally, a number of things can be said about the features of caucuses in the modern presidential nominating system.

The first is that they cost less both to operate and to run in as a candidate than do primary elections. They cost less to operate because they are conducted by the party (rather than the state), sometimes in private homes and always without the use of costly voting equipment or state election judges. They are, so to speak, "old school," with operating costs to go along.

It typically costs less to run a campaign in a caucus state because caucuses typically draw a much smaller turnout than primary elections. Caucuses, which can take several hours to conduct, require a significantly greater time commitment by voters, and the more personal, interactive character of the caucus may also discourage voters who are not comfortable in that setting. The smaller turnout means that highly motivated voters—usually party activists, ideological movement supporters, or single-issue enthusiasts—dominate the caucuses. That the electorate is effectively smaller and motivated by well-organized, targeted appeals means that it costs less to campaign—by some estimates, four times less (Cronin and Loevy 1983, 53; Witcover 1999, 42; Foley, Britton, and Everett Jr., 1980, 43; Mayer and Busch 2004, 32). Indeed, a broad-based, expensive media campaign is not only not necessary to win in most caucus circumstances, it may not even be possible to win a caucus that way. Publisher Steve Forbes spent $4 million running in Iowa's Republican caucuses in 1996 ($6.1 million in 2016 terms), and finished in fifth place. Thus, caucuses still provide an advantage to the well organized and intensely motivated, though the organizational threshold of entry might be lower than it used to be.

Several presidential candidates since the 1980s have demonstrated this point:

- In 1988, Pat Robertson, standard-bearer of much of the Christian Right movement, excelled in caucuses. On the other hand, prior to the Ohio Republican primary, one of his campaign organizers predicted a possible pickup of no more than 15–18 delegates (out of 88), saying, "This would have to be a caucus state for us to win it" (*National Journal* 1988, 617).

- The Republican candidates most closely aligned with the Christian Right movement in 2008 and 2012 (Mike Huckabee and Rick Santorum, respectively) also performed their best in caucus states.

- The 2008 Democratic insurgent from the left, Barack Obama, won the presidential nomination for his party largely because he built a lead in caucus states that Hillary Clinton could not overcome in primary states. Obama gained nearly twice as many delegates as Clinton in caucus states, while slightly trailing Clinton's delegate haul in contested primaries (Sizemore 2008). Clinton's supporters responded by attempting unsuccessfully to convince the 2008 Democratic platform committee to endorse a ban on caucuses in the future (Nicholas 2008).

- In 2016 insurgent Democratic candidate Bernie Sanders rode a wave of ideological mobilization among young people on the left to win a number of caucus states. If Sanders had done as well in primaries as he did in caucuses, he would have won the Democratic presidential nomination (Enten 2016).

- On the Republican side that same year, Ted Cruz from the right did best in caucus states, winning six caucuses to Donald Trump's two. For his part, Trump called the caucuses "dangerous" (Trudo 2016).

The Debate over Caucuses

Since it is one of two delegate selection methods widely used today, it is difficult to assess the pros and cons of caucuses without considering them relative to the pros and cons of primaries. Also, the same feature may be seen as an advantage by one person but a disadvantage by another.

For example, even after McGovern-Fraser, many observers believe that caucuses continue to give relatively more influence to the local parties than primaries do. This is true especially in the Republican Party, where the caucuses have undergone fewer reforms. If the official party has lost most of its influence, the party activists remain a disproportionately large faction of the caucus electorate. And, even today, caucuses are more likely than primaries to elect uncommitted delegates who can go to the convention and use their best judgment. For some, this is an advantage of the caucus method; for others, a disadvantage.

Similarly, as noted above, caucuses also provide an avenue for well-organized, politically intense but cash-strapped movements to have access to the presidential nominating system. Arguably, they are more effective at providing openness for such popular forces than are primaries, and have been since before the McGovern-Fraser reforms. On the other hand, the very same fact means that caucuses have been accused of providing extremists and single-issue voters with the means to have a disproportionate impact on the nomination process.

More generally, caucuses offer an opportunity for little-known candidates with few resources to get noticed and gain a foothold in the early stages of a presidential nominating contest. Perhaps the best example is Jimmy Carter, who began his long climb to the presidency by prevailing over a crowded Democratic field in the 1976 Iowa caucuses. Instantly, Carter went from "Jimmy Who?" to a top contender. The declining strength of local party organization has meant that movement candidates and lesser-knowns in general have fewer obstacles in the caucuses than they used to.

For those concerned with the negative effects of front-loading of the delegate selection calendar, caucuses offer something of a remedy. Because caucuses are only the first step in the delegate selection process, months can elapse between the caucuses and determination of the final outcome of delegate allocation in a state. This extended period of indeterminacy could conceivably mute the stampeding impact of early delegate selection contests by extending somewhat the period before the de facto winner of the nomination is known. If a larger number of states used caucuses, it could change the entire psychology of the race. However, given the plebiscitary ethos, or deference to the commands of unmediated public opinion, that dominates modern American politics, this seems unlikely to occur. Indeed, Democrats moved after 2016 to reduce the number of caucuses. Moreover, that same plebiscitary ethos leads the media interpretation of caucuses to emphasize the popular vote results on caucus day rather than the long-term delegate selection process.

Finally, defenders of the caucus often tout it for the civic engagement it fosters. In a caucus, voters must be highly committed and engage in extended deliberation with their neighbors. The caucus, from this point of view, is a qualitatively superior form of voting. Perhaps fewer citizens go to a caucus, but those who do go participate more fully in self-government. Moreover, before caucus day arrives, campaigns in a caucus state are more likely to be retail affairs. Because big media buys have limited utility in such an environment, candidates and their campaigns are more likely to engage personally with voters.

Critics argue that this description is an idealized version of the caucus. In reality, they say, caucuses often feature not debate and dialogue but a simple division of who supports whom—not unlike a regular election, but more time-consuming and with lower rates of participation (Mayer 1996, 129). Nor is there any guarantee of retail politicking by the candidates. Early caucuses might feature more personal campaigning, but once the delegate selection calendar heats up and candidates must compete in multiple contests every week, such an approach becomes much more difficult. Other critics emphasize the small, unrepresentative caucus electorate, the very low turnout, and the danger of empowering extreme candidates and groups (Norrander 2010, 70; Wang 2007).

Not least, some critics of caucuses note that they are not conducted by state-appointed election officials but by the party organizations, which may not have the same level of professional competence and which can still bend the rules in ways that may seem unfair to disfavored candidates. In 2012, pro-Romney state party officials in Iowa were slow to reveal that rather than registering a narrow victory over Rick Santorum in that state caucus, as had been initially reported, Mitt Romney had actually lost to Santorum. By the time that news broke, nearly two weeks after the caucuses and one week after the New Hampshire primary, the public impression of a Romney win had been cemented and the news cycle had moved on (Farenthold and Wilgoren 2012). In 2016, in another close race, pro-Clinton Iowa officials were accused of bungling the tabulation and reporting of caucus results in a way that enhanced the appearance of a Clinton win over Bernie Sanders (*The Guardian* 2016).

In between the critics and the defenders of the caucus, there are a number of academic analysts who argue that the differences between caucuses and primaries are exaggerated and that neither the pros nor cons are decisive. In this view, especially after the reforms of the early 1970s, primaries and caucuses are more alike than different. Although there might be some marginal gains for the nominating system by shifting toward one mode or the other, and some marginal redistribution of benefits to particular types of candidates, no one should expect dramatic change (Mayer 1996; Panagopolous 2010).

Skip Wiltshire-Gordon provided research assistance on this chapter.

Sources

Block, Valerie. 2019. "With a Focus on 2020, Democratic Party Aims to Satisfy Its Base and Repair the Damage of 2016." CNBC, March 14. https://www.cnbc.com/2019/03/14/as-democrats-look-to-2020-heres-how-theyre-trying-fix-2016-damage.html.

Bryce, James. 1889. *The American Commonwealth*, Vol. II. Chicago: Sergel.

Busch, Andrew E. 1997. *Outsiders and Openness in the Presidential Nominating System*. Pittsburgh: University Press of Pittsburgh.

Cronin, Thomas, and Robert Loevy. 1983. "The Case for a National Pre-Primary Convention Plan." *Public Opinion* 5 (December–January).

Crotty, William J. 1977. *Political Reform and the American Experiment*. New York: Thomas Y. Crowell.

Dallinger, Frederick A. 1897. *Nominations for Elective Office in the United States*. Cambridge, MA: Harvard University Press.

Democratic National Committee. 1970. *Mandate for Reform: A Report of the Committee on Party Structure and Delegate Selection to the Democratic National Committee*. Washington, DC: Democratic National Committee.

Enten, Harry. 2016. "Bernie Sanders Continues to Dominate Caucuses, But He's About to Run Out of Them." *FiveThirtyEight*, March 27. https://fivethirtyeight.com/features/bernie-sanders-continues-to-dominate-caucuses-but-hes-about-to-run-out-of-them/.

Fahrenthold, David A., and Debbi Wilgoren. 2012. "Santorum Finished 34 Votes Ahead of Romney in New Iowa Tally; Votes from 8 Precincts Missing." *Washington Post,* January 19. https://www.washingtonpost.com/politics

/report-santorum-finished-34-votes-ahead-of-romney-in-new-iowa-tally
-votes-from-8-precincts-missing/2012/01/19/gIQAJGuRAQ_story.html.

Foley, John, Dennis A. Britton, and Eugene B. Everett Jr., eds. 1980. *Nominating a President: The Processs and the Press.* New York: Praeger.

The Guardian. 2016. "Iowa Democratic Party Altered Precinct's Caucus Results During Chaotic Night." February 5. https://www.theguardian.com/us-news/2016/feb/05/iowa-democratic-party-altered-precinct-caucus-results-clinton-sanders.

Mayer, William G. 1996. "Caucuses: How They Work: What Difference They Make." In William G. Mayer, ed., *In Pursuit of the White House: How We Choose Our Presidential Nominees.* Chatham, NJ: Chatham House.

Mayer, William G., and Andrew E. Busch. 2004. *The Front-Loading Problem in Presidential Nominations.* Washington, DC: Brookings Institution.

National Journal. 1988. "Robertson Backers Hooked on Politics in Buckeye State." March 5.

Nicholas, Peter. 2008. "Clinton Loyalists Fail in Bid to End Caucuses." *Los Angeles Times,* August 10. http://articles.latimes.com/2008/aug/10/nation/na-campaign10.

Norrander, Barbara. 2010. *The Imperfect Primary: Oddities, Biases, and Strengths of U.S. Presidential Nomination Politics.* New York: Routledge.

Ostrogorski, M. 1908. *Democracy and the Organization of Political Parties,* Vol. II. New York: Macmillan.

Panagopoulos, Costas. 2010. "Are Caucuses Bad for Democracy?" *Political Science Quarterly* 125, no. 3, 425–442.

Polsby, Nelson. 1983. *Consequences of Party Reform.* New York: Oxford University Press.

Ranney, Austin. 1975. *Curing the Mischiefs of Faction: Party Reform in America.* Berkeley: University of California Press.

Sizemore, Justin M. 2008. "How Obama Did It." *Sabato's Crystal Ball,* June 5. http://www.centerforpolitics.org/crystalball/articles/jms2008060501.

Theobold, Bill. 2019. "Who Knew? Ranked-Choice Voting Is Coming to the Presidential Election." *The Fulcrum,* June 12. https://thefulcrum.us/voting/iowa-virtual-caucus.

Trudo, Hannah. 2016. "Trump Trashes 'Dangerous' Caucus System." *Politico,* February 23. https://www.politico.com/story/2016/02/donald-trump-nevada-caucuses-219654.

Wang, Tova. 2007. "Has America Outgrown the Caucus? Some Thoughts on Reshaping the Nomination Contest." New York: The Century Foundation.

Winebrenner, Hugo. 1987. *The Iowa Precinct Caucuses: The Making of a Media Event.* Ames, IA: Iowa State University Press.

Witcover, Jules. 1999. *No Way to Pick a President.* New York: Farrar, Straus, and Giroux.

CHAPTER THREE

How Primaries Work

If caucuses can trace their lineage deep into the 19th century, presidential primaries are a newer innovation, brought into existence in the early 20th. They arose as a proposal by reformers who wanted to reduce the power of the party organizations and empower ordinary voters. First demanded by the populists in the 1890s, the primary (then called the "direct primary") was endorsed by the progressives and then actually implemented in states where progressives had sufficient political influence.

The idea behind the primary was that voters should be given a means of bypassing the party organizations, which were deemed by the progressives to be corrupt and an obstacle to change. Instead of attending local meetings (if they were fortunate enough to be on the "party list") where multiple rounds of delegate selection would take place in a winnowing process—all through the filter of the party leaders—voters would elect delegates to the national convention directly.

From 13 states with presidential primaries in 1912, the number grew to 23 in 1916. Then, a backlash took hold. By 1924, the number had fallen back to 17. States using primaries remained around that number until 1972.

Primaries in the "Mixed System"

Although primaries were intended to undercut the power of the parties, their effect during the period of the "mixed system" was muted. For one thing, only about one-third of the states, with about 40 percent of the delegates, held primaries. This state of affairs meant that no one could win through primaries alone. In the big picture, the road to the nomination still ran through the parties.

Moreover, there were many variations in the states that held primaries, and most of the variants diluted the plebiscitary impact of the primary. One variant was the "pure delegate" primary, in which voters selected the national convention delegates but with no connection to presidential candidates. These delegates were generally uncommitted, and the party organization was usually strong enough to dominate the results. Another variant was the "beauty contest" primary, or nonbinding presidential preference poll, in which voters indicated which presidential candidate they preferred, while actual delegate selection took place in other ways unconnected to the preference vote. A third common variant was the tactical device of the "favorite son" candidate. In these cases, some popular officeholder from a primary state—usually a governor or U.S. senator—would run in the primary and lock up the state's delegation as a means of gaining leverage over the process, not with any intention of seriously pursuing the presidential nomination. With his home state's delegate votes in hand, the "favorite son" positioned himself to deliver his state to his preferred candidate. All of these mechanisms disconnected the public vote from ultimate delegate outcomes. As political scientists John S. Jackson and William Crotty note, during this era:

> [T]he primaries could be used to attract attention to a candidate and to help create an image. The primaries could be used to prove a point about the perceived popularity of a candidate. The point was made for the benefit of party leaders who had the power, through their endorsements and their actions at the national conventions, to bargain for a candidate and to form coalitions which ultimately selected the presidential nominee. . . . [I]f a candidate wanted to prove that he could organize an effective campaign and could campaign well and appeal to certain types of voters, the primaries were ideal. The primaries were also important for gaining media attention. (Jackson and Crotty 2001, 45)

The McGovern-Fraser reforms in the Democratic Party, adopted after the 1968 election in response to criticisms by Eugene McCarthy's supporters that they had been unfairly shut out of the process, had as a chief objective promoting "full, meaningful, and timely participation" by party voters. The rules had two effects. First, primaries that existed were reformed to assure a more direct correlation between the presidential candidate preferences of Democratic voters and delegate outcomes. Pure delegate primaries were banned, delegates were required to declare a preference, and winner-take-all primaries were banned. Proportional representation was encouraged. To prevent non-Democrats from influencing the outcome, open primaries allowing them to vote were also banned for a time. For a few elections in the 1980s, nonproportional primaries at the congressional district level were an option again, but not statewide winner-take-all. Since 1992, proportional representation has been required in Democratic primaries. In 2012 and 2016, Republicans also required proportional representation, but only between March 1 and April 1 (2012) or between March 1 and March 14 (2016).

Second, the number of primaries exploded. From 17 Democratic primaries in 1968, the number grew to 30 in 1980. Although the number of primaries has ebbed and flowed since then, it has averaged 36 Republican and 38 Democratic primaries since 1988. Some reformers claimed that the growth in primaries was an unintended and unanticipated by-product of the McGovern-Fraser Commission's reforms (Fraser 1980, 123; Ranney 1975, 205–206; Bode and Casey 1980, 16–18). McGovern himself noted, "This quantum leap in primary contests was part of a reform tide that has swept the Democratic Party since 1968" (McGovern 1977, 153).

Because primaries are largely controlled by state law and Democrats controlled most state governments in 1972, Republicans were pulled along into many of these changes. Most importantly, they have closely tracked the number of Democratic primaries. (See Table 3.1.)

On the other hand, Republicans resisted some of the moves toward a more plebiscitary system. They never banned statewide winner-take-all primaries, and are still less likely than Democrats to use proportional representation. They also never banned pure delegate primaries. Additionally, they did not attempt, as Democrats did, to prohibit open primaries. They have generally left greater discretion in the hands of the state parties.

How Primaries Work Today

The growth in primaries and the more direct connection that they provide between voter preferences and delegate outcomes has meant that primaries play a fundamentally different role in the modern system than before. Candidates do not have the luxury of concentrating on a few primaries and ignoring the rest. They are in those races for the delegates, as well as legitimacy and momentum; no one can win a nomination without prevailing in the primaries.

Indeed, in contrast to systems that had fewer or no primaries, candidates have little choice but to announce their candidacies and begin campaigning long before the first primary votes are cast. Political scientists have long noted the existence of the so-called "invisible primary" (sometimes also called the "money primary"), the period of months or years before the first primary and caucus when candidates are raising money, building organizations, seeking endorsements from respected party leaders, competing in straw polls of party faithful around the country, and jockeying for position in national polls. Poor performance in the "invisible primary" can end a

Table 3.1   Number of Democratic and Republican Primaries, 1952 to 2016

Year	Democratic	Republican
1952	18	14
1956	20	19
1960	18	16
1964	18	17
1968	17	16
1972	23	23
1976	29	28
1980	30	33
1984	24	28
1988	33	34
1992	35	38
1996	34	41
2000	37	42
2004	35	30
2008	38	38
2012	39	38
2016	38	39

Sources: For 1952–2008, Alan Silverleib and William G. Mayer, "By the Numbers: A Statistical Guide to the Presidential Nomination Process," in William G. Mayer, ed., *The Making of the Presidential Candidates 2012* (Lanham, MD: Rowman & Littlefield, 2012), p. 219; 2012 found in NCSL, "2012 Presidential Primary and Caucus Calendar"; 2016 found in NPR, "Election 2016 Calendar: Primaries and Caucuses."

campaign before a single ballot is cast. In the 2016 presidential contest, two of five Democratic candidates and five of 17 initial Republican candidates had dropped out of contention before the Iowa caucuses.

Primary elections today, as in the past, are a matter of state law elaborated on by state and national party rules. They are, first and foremost, state-run elections. The state usually sets the date, often determines the electorate (whether open or closed), selects the polling places, hires and trains election judges, prints the ballots, provides the voting equipment, and counts the votes. The parties determine how delegates will be chosen and how they will be allocated to candidates on the basis of the voting results. Where state law does not dictate, the state parties can also decide when to hold their primary and whether to allow independents or voters from the opposite party to vote in their primary.

Table 3.2   Presidential Primary Ballot Access by Method and Number of States (2016)

Placement by election officials OR petition	13
Petition	8
Petition OR filing fee	4
Petition AND filing fee	3
Filing fee	3
Placement by party officials	2
Petition OR proof of candidacy in two other states	1
Candidate files notice of intent	1
Varies by party	2

Source: "Ballot Access for Presidential Candidates," Ballotpedia, https://ballotpedia.org /Ballot_access_for_presidential_candidates.

Ballot Access

Because the state prints the primary ballots, it also has to establish rules for ballot access. Consequently, each state sets requirements for what candidates must do in order to appear on the ballot. There are a wide variety of requirements established by states for presidential primary ballot access. The single most common mode, used by around a dozen states, is for the secretary of state or other designated election officials to determine who will be placed on the ballot, but with an alternate option for candidates of submitting a specified number of petition signatures. Other states require some combination of petition signatures, filing fees, submission by party officials, or some other means (see Table 3.2). New Hampshire, for example, requires a $1,000 filing fee; in Alabama, candidates must pay a filing fee set by the party and submit 500 petition signatures; Indiana requires 4,500 petition signatures, at least 500 from each congressional district; in North Carolina, state election officials and party leaders determine who is to appear on the ballot, though ballot access can also be achieved through the collection of 10,000 signatures (Ballotpedia 2016). This maze of varying state ballot regulations means that one of the first organizational tests of a serious presidential campaign is understanding and complying with those regulations in order to get on the ballot.

Voting

Every state enforces certain common baseline standards for eligibility to vote based on the U.S. Constitution and federal law, sometimes as interpreted by the U.S. Supreme Court. On account of the Fifteenth, Nineteenth, and

Twenty-Sixth Amendments, no one may be denied the right to vote on the basis of race, sex, or age above the age of 18. The so-called "white primary," in which voting in Democratic primaries was limited to whites, was common in the South for several decades as a means of evading the intent of the Fifteenth Amendment guaranteeing blacks the right to vote, but was declared unconstitutional in 1947 in the U.S. Supreme Court case *Rice v. Elmore*. The white primary's defenders argued that it did not run afoul of the Fifteenth Amendment because parties were private associations; the Court held that the primary election was a quasi-public event, made so both by its public purpose (nominating candidates for public office) and its status as a government-run event. In 1962, the Twenty-Fourth Amendment banned the use of the poll tax, which applied a tax to voters exercising their franchise, and the Voting Rights Act of 1965 also provided a variety of protections to assure that citizens could exercise their right to vote. These measures apply in both primary and general elections. The National Voter Registration Act of 1993 also established national rules facilitating easier voter registration (such as the requirement that voters be allowed to register at state DMV offices, the so-called "motor-voter" law). Similarly, the Helping Americans Vote Act of 2002 (HAVA) made mandatory the use of provisional ballots when voters seek to vote in precincts in which they are not found on the official voter rolls.

There are other qualifications for voters that are decided on a state-by-state basis. For example, there are residency rules requiring voters to have resided at their address for various periods of time prior to election day. Perhaps most importantly, varying by the state, voters may or may not be eligible to vote in a party primary depending on their party registration or self-identification.

Those voters who are eligible vote in a variety of ways depending on the state. Traditionally, the entire election was held on election day; voters either showed up at the polls on that day or did not vote. Today, there are a number of variants that allow voters to cast their ballots days or weeks before the official election day (NCSL 2017). In 27 states and the District of Columbia, voters may request a "no-excuses" absentee ballot for any reason. The ballot is then sent to their home, marked by (presumably) the voter, and returned. In seven states and DC, voters can even put their names on a list that automatically receives an absentee ballot for each election with no reason given; another 10 states offer permanent absentee ballot status to specified subsets of voters (usually disabled voters or rural voters far from polling places). In the 2016 California primary, 58.9 percent of votes cast were by absentee ballot, a typical number for that state (California Secretary of State 2018). In all of the no-excuses absentee states and seven additional states, voters may vote early in person at local elections offices or satellite voting centers. The early voting period averages 22 days prior to election day. In three states, every voter receives a mail ballot, which can be returned by mail or to specified collection stations, and there are no regular election day polling places at all.

These varying forms of "early voting" have changed campaign dynamics, certainly requiring earlier and more sustained campaigns and possibly limiting the benefits of unexpected early victories in the primary season. To put it another way, there is some evidence that early voting works to the benefit of the preprimary front-runners (Fullmer 2015).

One key question is who actually turns out to vote in primaries. Except for the first-in-the-nation primary in New Hampshire and an occasional particularly pivotal primary, voter turnout in presidential primaries is significantly lower than in the general elections (though significantly higher than in caucuses). From 1980 to 2016, presidential primary turnout averaged 21.7 percent of eligible voters; in 2016 alone it was 28.5, about half the turnout rate in the general election (Desilver 2016). Earlier primaries tend to have higher voter turnout than primaries scheduled toward the end of the nominating contest, when the race has often already been effectively decided. However, studies tend not to support widespread assumptions that primary voters are more ideologically extreme than members of their party who do not vote in primaries (Norrander 2010).

After the Vote

Once the primary votes are cast, the vote totals must somehow be turned into delegates. This step is accomplished through a combination of national party rules, state party rules, and state law. In a few states, the presidential primary vote is totally disconnected from delegate selection; occasionally, for example, states will hold a nonbinding presidential preference primary but delegates will be allocated by a caucus procedure. In some other states, the primaries determine how many delegates each candidate receives, but a caucus and convention procedure is used to select which actual individuals will fill those delegate positions.

The Debate over Presidential Primaries

When primaries were first proposed around the turn of the 20th century, supporters claimed they were necessary to assure popular control of parties and elected officials. Skeptics worried about the possible ill effects of popular control in what was, by their lights, supposed to be a Madisonian republic of representative institutions and mediated politics. Some expressed fear of empowering extremists or demagogues. For decades after adoption of primaries, concerns have been raised that they often "produced disorderly scrambles for office by self-seekers" (David, Goldman, and Bain 1964, 328).

That debate has remained much the same over the past century or more. One key dividing line over primaries is whether increased direct popular participation is a benefit or a disadvantage. This debate flared anew with the explosion of primaries after 1968. Defenders of the post-1968 system touted its openness, while critics again cited dangers of extremism and demagoguery.

However, the full scope of the debate over primaries is much broader than this. For example, there are some analysts who argue that primaries are not only *not* prone to extremism, but positively inoculate against it. Ideological movements such as those that supported Barry Goldwater, George McGovern, and Pat Robertson did best in caucuses; primaries actually hindered them in many ways. Defenders of primaries note that primaries widen the field of competition, making it more difficult for candidates with narrow bases of support to succeed. Another way of seeing this issue is that because turnout in primaries is typically higher than in alternative forms of delegate selection, they confer a greater level of legitimacy on the winner. As political scientists note, recent Democratic and Republican nominees have consistently won about 90 percent of their party's voters in the general election, indicating that there has been a wide acceptance of the primary results by party voters (Norrander 2010, 57). An alternative explanation would be that the highly polarized national political atmosphere, rather than perceptions of the legitimacy of the primary system, accounts for high levels of party voting in the general election.

Critics note that, if movement supporters are limited by primaries, outsiders without a basis of organized support, who rely disproportionately on mass media, are empowered by them. The big winner from the new, reformed Democratic primaries in 1972 was not McGovern but George Wallace, the demagogic segregationist. In 2016, had the system been dominated by caucuses, Bernie Sanders would have won the Democratic nomination—but Donald Trump would likely have lost the Republican nomination.

Another positive for primaries is that they provide a greater test than caucuses of the broad appeal and suitability of a candidate. Not only do primary competitors have to win large numbers of votes across the country, they have to develop a national fundraising capacity that is demonstrated by raising millions of dollars. At a very basic level, the physical, mental, and emotional stresses of a nationwide primary campaign approximate the sort of stresses faced by the president while serving. If a candidate can show endurance in the primaries, the reasoning goes, he can endure the trials of the presidency.

These same points are sometimes turned against primaries, however. For example, the dramatically rising costs of campaigns for party nomination since 1972 are largely a result of the rise of primaries. To put it simply, it costs much more to run in the average primary than the average caucus state, because of the interconnected facts that the electorate is typically much larger and that more mass media presence is required. This arguably means that candidates with deep pockets are favored and candidates who might make very good presidents but do not have the same fundraising prowess (or personal resources) are disadvantaged.

There are other possible disadvantages to the expanded electorate of the primary. The need to appeal to a large electorate, some argue, leads to a more superficial campaign, especially after the first few contests. Once the campaign calendar begins to be filled with several primaries in the same week, or even the same day, candidates are forced to turn to the "tarmac campaign"—making stops at airports, descending to give a speech, then returning to their airplane to fly to the next airport in the next state. Voters have little opportunity to observe or interact with candidates; the increase in quantity of participation in primaries may be more than overshadowed by the loss in quality of participation.

Another objection raised by skeptics of the primary points to another cost of widespread direct popular participation. That objection is that the reformed primary system has displaced the party organization as a dispenser of nominations, quite deliberately. There are costs in both what has been prevented and what has been advanced. While progressives saw the party as a corrupt machine, others have seen it as a great synthesizing force in American politics, a force that brokered compromise among the many disparate factions in American society. The party also had a long-term reputation to uphold, and because it included large numbers of officeholders, it exerted a certain degree of "peer review" over presidential aspirants. According to critics, that function has now almost entirely disappeared (Shafer 1983).

Others have countered that, most of the time, the party still decides. Though it has lost the formal control over nominations it once exerted, informal networks of party activists and donors often (perhaps usually) coalesce behind a candidate acceptable to the party establishment, adding their power to that of party officeholders whose endorsements are still coveted by candidates and respected by voters (Cohen, Karol, Noel, and Zaller 2008). In this view, the nominations of candidates such as Walter Mondale, George H. W. and George W. Bush, Bob Dole, Al Gore, John Kerry, Mitt Romney, and Hillary Clinton are not terribly different from what one would have expected in an earlier system; Jimmy Carter, Barack Obama, and Donald Trump are the outliers.

One other matter of debate among political scientists is whether primaries damage parties by dividing them (the "divisive primary" thesis) or whether primaries help build parties by drawing in enthusiasts for the primary candidates, even those who do not win their party's nomination. One argument is that primaries are necessarily divisive because they invite candidates to appeal to some subset of factions within the party (Polsby 1983). Certainly, some primary fights seem to have been internally destructive, including Democrats in 1968 and 1980 and Republicans in 1976. On the other hand, much evidence compiled across many elections suggests that supporters of primary candidates, including losing candidates and candidates widely deemed "outsiders," frequently continue working for the party in the general election and beyond (Stone, Atkeson, and Rapoport 1992). Skeptics of the "divisive primary" thesis also argue that intraparty conflict that is visibly manifested through the primary system is often already present; primary struggles are the effect of party division, not the cause. In this view, incumbent presidents, for example, whose performance is widely deemed unsatisfactory face difficulty because of that fact; if they face a primary contest, it is the result of their vulnerability more than the cause of it.

Regardless, it is clear that the individual candidate plays a bigger role in the reformed primary system than before, as does the media, which now has power to advance or inhibit candidates depending on how it reports early polling and fundraising, as well as primary results in relation to expectations. The "candidate-centered" modern primary system revolves around the individuals seeking their party's nomination. Whether this "plebiscite" is good or bad for American politics remains a source of contention.

Sources

Ballotpedia. 2016. "Ballot Access for Presidential Candidates." https://ballotpedia .org/Ballot_access_for_presidential_candidates.

Bode, Kenneth A., and Carol F. Casey. 1980. "Party Reform: Revisionism Revised." In Robert A. Goldwin, ed., *Political Parties in the Eighties*. Washington, DC: American Enterprise Institute.

California Secretary of State. 2018. "Historical Vote-by-Mail (Absentee) Ballot Use in California." http://www.sos.ca.gov/elections/historical-absentee/.

Cohen, Marty, David Karol, Hans Noel, and John Zaller. 2008. *The Party Decides: Presidential Nominations Before and After Reform*. Chicago: University of Chicago Press.

David, Paul T., Ralph M. Goldman, and Richard C. Bain. 1964. *The Politics of National Party Conventions*, rev. ed. New York: Vintage Books.

Desilver, Drew. 2016. "Turnout Was High in the 2016 Primary Season, But Just Short of 2008 Record." Pew Research, June 10. http://www.pewresearch .org/fact-tank/2016/06/10/turnout-was-high-in-the-2016-primary -season-but-just-short-of-2008-record/.

Fraser, Donald M. 1980. "Democratizing the Democratic Party." In Robert A. Goldwin, ed., *Political Parties in the Eighties*. Washington, DC: American Enterprise Institute.

Fullmer, Elliott B. 2015. "Early Voting and Presidential Nominations: A New Advantage for Front-Runners?" *Presidential Studies Quarterly* 45, no. 3 (September): 425–444.

Jackson, John S., III, and William Crotty. 2001. *The Politics of Presidential Selection*, 2nd edition. New York: Longman.

McGovern, George. 1977. *Grassroots*. New York: Random House.

NCSL. 2017. "Absentee and Early Voting." August 17. http://www.ncsl.org /research/elections-and-campaigns/absentee-and-early-voting.aspx.

Norrander, Barbara. 2010. *The Imperfect Primary: Oddities, Biases, and Strengths of U.S. Presidential Nomination Politics.* New York: Routledge.

Polsby, Nelson W. 1983. *Consequences of Party Reform.* New York: Oxford University Press.

Ranney, Austin. 1975. *Curing the Mischiefs of Faction: Party Reform in America.* Berkeley: University of California Press.

Rice v. Elmore, 165 F.2d 387 (4th Cir. 1947).

Shafer, Byron E. 1983. *Quiet Revolution: The Struggle for the Democratic Party and the Shaping of Post-reform Politics.* New York: Russell Sage Foundation.

Stone, Walter J., Lonna Rae Atkeson, and Ronald B. Rapoport. 1992. "Turning On or Turning Off? Mobilization and Demobilization Effects of Participation in Presidential Nomination Campaigns." *American Journal of Political Science* 36 (1992): 665–691.

CHAPTER FOUR

Open vs. Closed Primaries

A key question in every primary (or caucus) is: Who is allowed to vote? In particular, are voters only allowed to vote in their own party's primary, or in the other party's? In relation to this question, primaries are usually sorted into three types:

1. Closed, in which voters can only vote in the primary of their party. If they are unaffiliated ("independent"), they cannot vote. In other words, only Democrats can vote in the Democratic primary, only Republicans in the Republican primary. In closed-primary states, it is usual for fewer people to register as independents.
2. Open, in which voters can vote in either primary as they wish. Democrats, Republicans, and independents can all vote in either the Republican or Democratic primary.
3. Semiopen (or semiclosed), in which both a party's voters and unaffiliated voters can vote in a party's primary, but voters from the opposite party cannot. Democrats and unaffiliated can vote in the Democratic primary; Republicans and unaffiliated can vote in the Republican primary.

A fourth type of primary is technically closed but in reality operates like an open primary. This takes place when a state utilizes "same-day declaration," which allows voters to declare their party registration preference at the polls on election day. Although they are then required to vote in the primary of their declared party, there is arguably no meaningful difference between being able to vote for whichever party you want regardless of registration (an open primary) and being able to register for whichever party you want on election day (same-day declaration). In many states, state law leaves that question up to the state parties. In those states, it is possible for one party's primary to be open but the other party's to be closed.

In 2016, open primaries or same-day declaration arrangements were used by Democrats in 23 states and Republicans in 19 states. Twenty-seven Republican primaries and caucuses were closed, as were Democratic contests in 22 states. Semiopen/semiclosed processes were used by Democrats in six states and Republicans in four states (Ballotpedia 2016).

The earliest primaries were usually open. The progressives who enacted the first primaries tended to favor open primaries as an additional means of undermining the traditional party structure. Wisconsin, for example, was an open primary and has remained so for the last century. One of the more striking indications of how open primaries might be used to upset the established parties came in 1964, when Alabama's segregationist governor George C. Wallace ran in three open Democratic primaries and shocked the Democratic establishment by garnering one-third of the vote in Wisconsin, just short of 30 percent in Indiana, and 43 percent in Maryland, all with substantial crossover votes (Busch 1997, 135–136). These strong showings, won with minimal formal campaigning, contributed heavily to Wallace's decision to briefly leave the Democratic Party in 1968 and run as an independent. In 1972, Wallace returned to the Democratic fold and showed strongly in open primaries before being severely wounded by a would-be assassin while campaigning in Maryland; an estimated one-half of Wallace votes in Wisconsin and Michigan came from crossovers (*New York Times* 1972a; *New York Times* 1972b; Rosenthal 1972). Eugene McCarthy also benefited heavily from crossover votes in the 1968 Michigan and Wisconsin primaries (Price 1984, 131).

The Democratic Party's so-called "McGovern-Fraser reforms" of 1971 included a call for the end of open primaries in the Democratic Party on the grounds that they diluted the influence of Democratic voters. The reform commission undoubtedly had Wallace's unwanted success in mind. The ban on open primaries was not formally adopted, however, until the Mikulski Commission prior to the 1976 election. Ironically, George McGovern's first primary win in 1972—which launched his campaign on the path toward the nomination—came in Wisconsin's open primary. Wisconsin subsequently became the chief battleground over the reform rule.

In the late 1970s and early 1980s, the Democratic National Committee wrestled with the state legislatures of Wisconsin and other open-primary states. In some states with open primaries, state law shifted to a "same-day declaration" system, which was permitted by Democratic rules but was only a half-step away from an open primary (Price 1984, 130). In Wisconsin, the legislature, though controlled by Democrats, refused to conform to national party rules and retained the state's traditional open primary. In response, the DNC threatened to refuse to seat the delegates chosen in the Wisconsin primary at the national convention. A legal battle ensued, which was resolved in the Supreme Court case *Democratic Party of the United States v. Wisconsin* (1981).

Relying on a key precedent in *Cousins v. Wigoda* (1975), the Court ruled that the party had associational rights to set rules for its own convention. It could not, however, dictate or override state law. In other words, the Wisconsin legislature retained the right to hold an open primary if it chose, while the DNC retained the right not to seat delegates chosen that way. The practical resolution was that the open primary remained, but only as a nonbinding preference poll; delegate allocation and selection were carried out through caucuses that were closed to all but Democratic voters. The national party's legal victory was Pyrrhic, however; the battle was so politically counterproductive—Democrats vs. Democrats, as one account of the dispute framed it—that national Democrats gave up the battle against the open primary after 1984 (Wekkin 1984).

Over the next few years, the Supreme Court elaborated on its reasoning in Wisconsin. In the 1986 case *Tashjian v. Republican Party of Connecticut*, the Court reaffirmed that parties could not be forced by state law to open their primaries to nonparty voters. In a case pushing back against a system used in California and Washington state, the Court ruled against the "blanket primary," which allowed voters to vote in one party's primary for one office and the other party's primary for another office (*California Democratic Party v. Jones* 2000). However, the Court has declined to act against the creation of California's top-two or "jungle" state primary, in which all voters choose from among all candidates and the top two advance to the general election regardless of party. The top-two primary calls into question the earlier line of cases, though they have not been formally overturned; in any event, California has retained its traditional party primary for delegate selection to the national party conventions. In contrast to the Democrats, the national Republican Party never attempted to ban open primaries. In keeping with a model of federalism, Republicans have left the choice of open versus closed primaries up to each state.

In both parties, open primaries have often worked to benefit relative outsiders and mavericks, while closed primaries have tended to bolster "establishment" candidates. Republican Ronald Reagan benefited from crossover votes in 1976, as did Pat Robertson, Pat Buchanan, and John McCain in later contests; Democrats Gary Hart, Bill Bradley, Barack Obama, and Bernie Sanders likewise benefited from crossover votes in open primaries. In 2016, it was widely assumed that Donald Trump was helped by the votes of independents and even Democrats in open primaries. In actuality, exit polls showed he did better among Republican voters than among non-Republicans in 17 of 26 open contests that were polled; in another three, he did equally well. Every time Trump won a particularly crucial open primary, he won among Republicans as well as among Democrats or independents. Perhaps he gained only modest benefit from open primaries because he was far from the only "outsider" running that year (Ceaser, Busch, and Pitney 2017, 93–94). Sanders, however, bitterly complained during the 2016 campaign about the large number of closed primaries on the Democratic side, and he repeatedly criticized the exclusion of independent voters from the New York Democratic primary.

Following the 2016 Democratic primaries, Sanders endorsed a petition directed to the Democratic National Committee Rules Committee and ultimately signed by 42,000 people calling for a rule mandating open primaries in 2020. An examination of the question of open primaries was incorporated into the charge of the Democratic Party Unity Reform Commission approved by the national convention to consider the reform of caucuses, primaries, and superdelegates (Opdycke 2017). Observers note, though, that a national open-primaries-only rule could have an effect similar to the national no-open-primaries rule. Because in most states it is state law, not state party rules, that control the decision over whether to hold an open or closed primary, many state Democratic parties were forced to shift from primaries to caucuses in the 1980s in order to bring their delegate selection into line with national party requirements. One might anticipate a similar trend in response to a national open-primary rule.

The call of Sanders and the petition-signers for an open primary rule represented a dramatic turnaround in progressive opinion, which once had been expressed in the McGovern-Fraser and Mikulski Commission reports calling for closed primaries in order to avoid diluting the participation of Democratic voters. In another sense, the progressives have returned to their roots, which began with support for open primaries; in this view, it was Democratic reformers in the 1970s who deviated from the original progressive perspective.

Debating the Merits of Open and Closed Primaries

Originally, supporters of open primaries contended that, like the primary itself, open primaries ensured greater popular control of the nominating process by undercutting the power of the party establishments. This argument still resonates with many. For example, progressive activist Tim Canova, who ran in the 2016 Democratic congressional primary in Florida against former Democratic National Committee chair Debbie Wasserman-Schultz, argues:

> Open primaries are good for democracy because they encourage full citizen participation in our elections. Since both Democrats and Republicans often need independent voters to win at the general election stage, they should stop making it so difficult for such voters to join the electoral

process. They should welcome open primaries, which will allow each party to address the issues that matter to all the voters. (Opdycke 2017)

Proponents of this argument often frame their position as one based on concern for democratic justice. As one commentator contends, "We have set up a system in which certain voters are allowed to vote in the first round of the publicly funded election process, and others are not. It's wrong. It's unfair" (Opdycke 2017).

Additional arguments have emerged. One key argument is that open primaries serve an important function by giving an electoral advantage to candidates who have broad, cross-partisan voter appeal. Indeed, sometimes parties have deliberately sought to broaden their base by adopting open primaries. Perhaps the best example is the Republican Party in the South, which sought to use the open presidential primary as a mechanism to gradually move conservative Democrats and independents into the Republican Party. Finally, some advocates of open primaries contend that closed primaries contribute to partisan polarization by limiting each party's primary electorate to its hard-core partisan identifiers, who tend to be more ideologically extreme than the average American (Norrander 2010, 65).

On the other hand, Democratic reformers in the 1970s criticized the open primary for diluting the influence of loyal party voters. If you are a registered Democratic voter, they reasoned, why should you allow an independent or even Republican voter an equal share in the selection of what is, after all, your party's presidential nominee?

Two other arguments amplify this contention. In some ways, they are simply different versions of the same concern. One looks at the issue more institutionally and less from the perspective of individual participation. From this perspective, the open primary takes away the right of the party to control its own nominations. This, of course, is the flip side of the original progressive goal, which was to end the party organization's ability to control its own nominations. Critics of the progressives note that one of the most important functions of political parties is that of nominating candidates; to take away that function, in this view, is to largely negate the relevance of the political party.

A related fear is that open primaries allow hostile voters—that is, voters who are loyal to the opposite party—to tip the scales in favor of the weakest candidate that might represent your party. During the 2016 campaign, rumors were rife that Democratic voters were flooding open Republican primaries in order to support Donald Trump in the belief that he would be the weakest candidate Republicans could run (Lind 2016). Similarly, some argued in 1972 that Republican crossover voters deliberately supported George McGovern because they perceived him to be the weakest possible Democratic opponent to Richard M. Nixon. In 2008 conservative radio personality Rush Limbaugh urged his listeners to vote for Hillary Clinton in open Democratic primaries to keep the nomination fight with Obama going longer in hopes of undermining the Democratic cause in the general election. Despite anecdotal evidence, there is little systematic scholarly evidence to support the prevalence of deliberately mischievous strategic voting actually taking place in open primaries (Norrander 2010, 66).

However, as one scholar notes, even if they are not deliberately obtuse, crossover voters may have different preferences than party voters, and may saddle the loyal voters of a party with a nominee not to their liking (Norrander 2010, 65–66). In 2008, John McCain won Michigan's open Republican primary on the strength of support from Democrats and independents; George W. Bush won two-thirds of Republican voters, but lost the primary anyway. In 2016, liberal commentator Peter Beinart suggested that like-minded Democrats in open primary states should use their votes to try to block the nomination of Donald Trump on sincere substantive grounds— that is, not because he calculated Trump would be the weakest nominee but because he believed that Trump would be the most destructive nominee and president. As Beinart wrote in the *Atlantic*,

> [I]f I lived in any of the nine Super Tuesday states that allow non-Republicans to vote in their GOP presidential primary, I would cross over—forfeiting my chance to cast a ballot for Hillary Clinton or Bernie Sanders—and vote for [Marco] Rubio. Other liberals should do the same. Those who can should write him checks. Whatever it takes to stop the nomination of Donald Trump. (Beinart 2016)

Though Limbaugh's and Beinart's appeals demonstrated the potential for the other party's members to invade an open primary for either mischievous or sincere reasons, the outcomes also demonstrated the limited effectiveness of such strategies. In 2008, it was Obama who actually benefited a bit from open primaries, and in 2016 Rubio lost the open primaries on Super Tuesday to Donald Trump. In neither case did the openness of a primary seem to affect the ultimate primary outcomes. The probability of voters crossing over just because they find the other party's contest or candidates more compelling rises in years when one party's voters have no serious race (perhaps because a popular incumbent is running unopposed for renomination) and are free to indulge in participation in their rivals' contest, or when their race effectively ends sooner than that of the other party.

To summarize the case against the open primary, political scientist and former Democratic congressman David E. Price argues:

> Open primaries dilute the impact of the parties' core constituencies and substantially reduce the role and influence of party leaders and organizations.

Although they have a superficial "democratic" appeal—allowing individuals to vote for anyone they please at every electoral stage—they make the party label less significant for voters and candidates alike. The primary loses its character as a party nomination and becomes little more than the first round of the general election. This may make individual voters feel less restricted, but insofar as it reduces the meaning of the party label and weakens the party ties of elected officials, the result hardly enhances the functioning of democracy. (Price 1984)

Price adds that closed primaries "help preserve the integrity of the party system" and make the nomination process "less vulnerable to freewheeling candidate and issue appeals based outside the parties" (Price 1984, 132).

At its essence, the debate over open vs. closed primaries is a debate over the proper understanding of political parties and democracy itself. Should the parties be seen as associations of like-minded people who should be able to select their own nominees for office? Or are they, in some sense, public utilities, whose nominations are so important that they should be accessible to any voter? Unless public officials and party leaders reach consensus on that question, there will continue to be a mixture of open, semiopen, and closed presidential primaries.

Sources

Ballotpedia. 2016. "Open Primaries," "Closed Primaries," and "Semi-Closed Primaries." https://ballotpedia.org/Open_primary; https://ballotpedia.org /Closed_primary; https://ballotpedia.org/Semi-closed_primary.

Beinart, Peter. 2016. "Why Liberals Should Vote for Marco Rubio." *The Atlantic*, February 29. https://www.theatlantic.com/politics/archive/2016/02/why -liberals-should-vote-for-marco-rubio/471444/.

Busch, Andrew E. 1997. *Outsiders and Openness in the Presidential Nominating System*. Pittsburgh: University of Pittsburgh Press.

California Democratic Party v. Jones, 530 U.S. 567 (2000).

Ceaser, James W., Andrew E. Busch, and John J. Pitney. 2017. *Defying the Odds: The 2016 Elections and American Politics*. Lanham, MD: Rowman & Littlefield.

Cousins et al. v. Wigoda et al., 419 U.S. 477 (1975).

Democratic Party of U.S. v. Wisconsin, 450 U.S. 107 (1981).

Lind, Dara. 2016. "Trying to Sabotage Republicans by Supporting Trump Is a Very Bad Idea." *Vox*, March 1. https://www.vox.com/2016/3/1/11135388 /trump-general-election.

New York Times. 1972a. "Cross-Over a Key Factor." April 5, p. 1.

New York Times. 1972b. "Times Study Finds Voters Liked McGovern on Taxes." April 6, p. 1.

Norrander, Barbara. 2010. *The Imperfect Primary: Oddities, Biases, and Strengths of U.S. Presidential Nomination Politics.* New York: Routledge.

Opdycke, John. 2017. "Open Primaries Are the Answer to America's Election Woes—So What Are We Waiting For?" *The Hill*, April 5. http://thehill .com/blogs/pundits-blog/lawmaker-news/327297-open-primaries -are-the-answer-to-americas-election-woes-so.

Price, David E. 1984. *Bringing Back the Parties.* Washington, DC: Congressional Quarterly Press.

Rosenthal, Jack. 1972. "Survey Ties Issues, Not Shooting, to Wallace Victory." *New York Times*, May 17, p. 30.

Tashjian v. Republican Party of Connecticut, 479 U.S. 208 (1986).

Wekkin, Gary. 1984. *Democrat vs. Democrat: The National Party's Campaign to Close the Wisconsin Primary.* Columbia: University of Missouri Press.

CHAPTER FIVE

The Nomination Calendar

Because the presidential nomination system consists of delegate selection processes in 57 separate states and territories, each of which schedule their own (sometimes multistage) events—and because earlier primaries and caucuses can impact later ones—the nomination calendar is constantly shifting and is important to both candidate strategies and nomination outcomes.

Under the congressional caucus system of presidential nomination, the calendar was quite simple. On a chosen day, the party's members in Congress would meet and designate presidential and vice presidential nominees. Under the 19th-century convention system, there were no primaries in advance of the convention, no open campaigns in advance of the convention, and no pledged delegates. So, in one sense, the nominations again took place in one stretch of a few days during the conventions. However, selection of delegates stretched over a period of many months prior to the convention. In many states, the key moment was the state convention or state party committee meeting that selected national convention delegates. These state events were scheduled on a decentralized basis, state by state. Even these were preceded by local meetings or caucuses and local conventions. Sometimes, the first, most local stage of the delegate selection process began a year before (or even, in unusual cases, two years before) the national convention and presidential election.

With the advent of primaries, a new element was added to the nomination calendar: the sequence and timing of the primaries. That portion of the delegate selection process was more open to public view than the caucus/ convention/party committee process, at least until the point of the state conventions. In 1912, the first primary was North Dakota's on March 19 and the last was South Dakota's on June 4. In between, another 11 primaries took place, approximately one per week (only on April 19 did two states— Nebraska and Oregon—hold their primaries on the same day) (*Congressional*

Quarterly 1975, 313–314). However, the nonprimary states continued in the traditional way, and some began their processes before or concluded after the primary season. For the duration of the "mixed system," the nomination calendar worked about the same way. Some delegate selection processes started before the primaries or continued after them; the primary season, affecting about one-third of the states, lasted from March to early June; and the nomination process ended not only nominally but in reality with the convention.

The timing of the primaries within the March–June window tended to be heavily "back-loaded" under the mixed system. That is to say, the sequence of primaries got off to a slow start and a heavy preponderance of primary delegates were chosen in the last half of the window. In 1960, for example, the New Hampshire primary kicked off the primary season on March 8. The next primary was in Wisconsin nearly a month later, on April 5. The following three weeks saw one, one, and two primaries. In a primary season that had 14 weeks from beginning to end, only four primaries were held in the first seven weeks. The other 14 primaries, selecting 80 percent of the primary delegates, were held in the final seven weeks. Over one-fourth of primary delegates were chosen in primaries held in week 14 (Mayer and Busch 2004, 5–6).

The Nomination Calendar in the Reform System

The nominating reforms of the 1970s had a profound effect on the nomination calendar. For one thing, the McGovern-Fraser reforms in the Democratic Party, adopted after the contentious 1968 nomination contest to meet concerns that the process was too heavily controlled by party officials, prohibited delegate selection prior to the calendar year of the presidential election. Caucuses or other party meetings that might have been held in the year (or two) before the election now had to be held during the election year. At the other end, for reasons described in earlier chapters, nominations came to be effectively decided prior to the national convention, which became the ornamental rather than real end of the process. The number of primaries doubled or more, making the primary portion of the nomination calendar much more important. At the same time, reformed caucuses became more transparent, and some caucuses became an object of media attention not unlike a primary.

One important change in the postreform calendar was the earlier start date. In 1968, the New Hampshire primary was held on March 12. In 1976, the Iowa caucuses, which Jimmy Carter successfully turned into the big opening contest of the year, were held on January 24. Iowa kept moving earlier, holding its caucuses on January 3 in 2008 before moving back again. In 2016, the Iowa caucuses were held February 1, with the New Hampshire primary February 9. A second crucial postreform change in the primary calendar, though related to the first, was the rise of primary "front-loading"—the increasing tendency of states to schedule their primaries early in the primary calendar. This tendency grew gradually at first, then became more pronounced starting in 1988. By 1996, both parties had elected more than three-fourths of their national convention delegates by week 6 of 16 (Mayer and Busch 2004, 6). A number of factors led to this phenomenon.

The essential cause of front-loading was that the new rules led to early decisions in the nominating contests. The rise of primaries and pledged delegates meant that leading candidates were much more likely to collect sufficient delegates to get nominated before the convention began. New campaign finance rules made it less likely that candidates could find sources to fund their campaigns if they got off to a slow start. The combination of these things led to early departures from the race by candidates who did not win early contests. Under the old rules, when nominations were not decided until or shortly before the convention, states that went late had extra leverage in the system. Under the new circumstances, states that scheduled their primaries late in the calendar could easily find themselves voting after the race had already been decided. In addition to that general concern, states observed and envied the advantages enjoyed by the states hosting the first two contests, Iowa and New Hampshire. Those advantages include greater influence over the outcome of the contest, more campaign and media resources poured into the state, and sometimes greater leverage over candidates' policy commitments, such as the success of Iowa, a state with many farmers, in obtaining commitments to federal spending on corn-based ethanol. Of course, as states moved their primaries earlier in the schedule, it became even more likely that the race would be decided early. The earlier the race was decided, the more states wanted to move up their primary dates, creating a self-perpetuating cycle. A similar phenomenon took place in caucus states. Of the 23 Democratic caucus states in 1976, only 10 first-round caucuses were held in the first half of the caucus calendar, fewer than 50 percent of the total. By 1996, however, the terrain was much different. Of the 18 Democratic caucus states that year, 16 of them held their first-round caucuses in the first half of the schedule (Mayer and Busch 2004, 21).

Despite the self-reinforcing pressures for front-loading, not every state has tried to move toward the front of the pack, and some (like California) have moved forward and back several times. Traditionally holding its primary on the first Tuesday of June, California moved to early February in 2008, back to June in 2012 and 2016, and up to early March in 2020. There are a variety of factors motivating state decisions about when to hold a primary or caucus. One powerful set of factors that sometimes works against the front-loading pressure is a combination of cost and the self-interest of local politicians. When political leaders in a state have their own reasons for wanting a later primary for state elected officials, a state can only move its primary up if it either disregards the interests of its own elected officials (the same ones who have to enact the change) or decouples its state primary from its presidential primary, which is a very costly proposition. Many states prefer to keep their state and presidential primaries together, even if it means continuing to hold the primary later.

Concerns with Front-Loading

Some analysts have argued that the unintended and decentralized development of front-loading should not worry the parties. The advantage of front-loading is that it usually leads to fast, decisive wins by the ultimate party nominee, who is thus able to avoid long, drawn-out, and bitterly divisive contests. A Democratic Party subcommittee charged with examining front-loading in 2000 argued:

> The most important part of any primary/caucus schedule is that it needs to identify a strong Democratic nominee early and lead to a Democratic victory in the general election. . . . In the last few cycles, the current system has allowed the Democratic Party to identify its presumptive nominee early. As a result, the process has helped the party unify behind its nominee and focus its resources on the general election. (Rules and Bylaws Committee 2000, 11)

Some scholars affirm that there is a benefit for a party to decide its nominating contest early. Otherwise, parties risk a "divisive primary" that can hinder its chances in November by damaging party unity (Wattenberg 1991). Moreover, because the front-loaded system requires candidates to acquire substantial organizational and financial resources up front, it establishes a test of seriousness and breadth of support that is useful in weeding out fringe figures.

Others, however, argue that front-loading is problematic. The very things its defenders praise are cause for concern, assert some critics. For example, critics contend that front-loading produces such quick and decisive victories that there is little opportunity for voters to exercise second thoughts. If weaknesses emerge in a candidate that show him or her to be unfit, they might well appear too late. And the high threshold of organizational and fundraising capacity that constitute the "entry fee" into the front-loaded system might shut out not only "fringe" candidates but also well-qualified candidates who would make excellent presidents but did not start the campaign season with a large reservoir of resources (Mayer and Busch 2004, 66–88). By the early 21st century, some analysts were arguing that front-loading had put the party establishment back in charge of nominations practically, if not on paper (Cohen, Karol, Noel, and Zaller 2008a). (Of course, from the perspective of someone advocating strong parties, this might be an advantage.)

Another problem with front-loading noted by some is that voters in later-voting states could be effectively disenfranchised in the party nomination process. If the primary was held after the nomination was already determined, it would be essentially meaningless. Understandably, this reality also led to a sharp drop-off in voting turnout in late-voting primary states. All of this brought into question whether the front-loaded system had achieved the "full, meaningful and timely participation" promised by the McGovern-Fraser reforms.

The Parties Fight Back

In recent elections, front-loading receded a bit due to a combination of a concerted effort by party rules-makers and the natural effects of some races that lasted longer than anticipated. Concerns about the negative effects of increasingly early starts and heavy front-loading led both parties to make efforts, sometimes in unison, to push back against the trend. To combat the early starts, both parties attempted to institute "windows" for their delegate selection contests. Democrats began instituting a delegate selection "window" when the 1978 Commission on Presidential Nomination and Party Structure (or Winograd Commission) approved a rule restricting delegate selection events to the period from the second Tuesday of March to the second Tuesday of June, though exceptions were made for states governed by state law where the state party could show it made an effort to have the date of the event moved to be in conformity with the rule. In 1980, the first year of operation of the window, exceptions were made for two primaries and three caucuses (Price 1984, 154). Republicans established their own window in 2008, banning delegate selection before February 5. For 2012, Republicans and Democrats agreed to allow no delegate selection events prior to the first Tuesday of March except in Iowa, New Hampshire, Nevada, and South Carolina, which were permitted to hold caucuses or primaries in February. The windows have frequently been ignored by states in both parties, however. In 2008, Michigan and Florida Democrats defied party rules to hold their primaries in January, prior to their party's February 1 window that year. Although national Democrats threatened to refuse to seat their delegations to the national convention, one half of the delegates representing each state were restored after presumptive nominee Barack Obama intervened on their behalf. A number of states in 2008 also defied the Republican scheduling rule—Wyoming, New Hampshire, Michigan, South Carolina, and Florida—and consequently were stripped of half of their delegates. These states did not attempt to hold their primaries in the restricted primary window after 2008. In 2012, three of the four states Republicans allowed to vote in February jumped ahead to January instead.

To address front-loading, the 1996 Republican National Convention adopted rules for the 2000 race that included a provision offering bonus delegates to states that would vote later in the calendar. The bonus ranged from 5 percent to 10 percent depending on the date. However, the GOP incentive plan failed to achieve its objective; of 12 states that changed their primary date between 1996 and 2000, eight moved earlier. Twenty-eight states remained where they were on the calendar. Ultimately, most states calculated that the benefit of gaining a few extra delegates was not worth the cost if they voted after the nominee was effectively decided. Prior to the 2000 contest, Democrats banned delegate selection except for Iowa and New Hampshire until March 1, meaning a month elapsed between the New Hampshire primary and the next contest. However, 14 primaries were then held on March 1.

Republicans came back in 2000, apparently more serious about their desire to reverse front-loading. The convention Rules Committee voted to approve for floor consideration a scheme known as the "Delaware Plan," or "Small States First" plan. The Delaware Plan would have required states to hold their primaries in one of four groupings based on ascending population, with the smallest states first and the most populous states last. The Delaware Plan might not have worked as planned—the national party could not force states to change their primary dates, it could only threaten to refuse to seat delegates chosen contrary to the plan—but Republicans never found out. Under pressure from the George W. Bush campaign, the Delaware Plan was withdrawn from consideration and never voted on by the convention (Clymer 2000).

For 2012, Republicans adopted rules requiring proportional representation be used in primaries held before April 1; starting April 1 states could use winner-take-all rules. This rule was intended to prevent knockout blows by candidates who win early contests. (It also provided an incentive for states that wanted to maximize their importance in the process to move their contest later than March 31.) In 2016, the rule was modified to require proportional representation through March 14.

Political events have also contributed to some reversal of front-loading; most notably, a number of closely fought nomination races starting with the Democratic contest of 2008. In that race, Barack Obama and Hillary Clinton fought tooth-and-nail for four months, with Obama not winning the final delegates needed to clinch the nomination until the last week of primaries. Some California officials, who had moved their primary up to March 1, suddenly envied the position of pivotal Pennsylvania, voting in late April (Busch 2009). Four years later, eventual GOP nominee Mitt Romney was dogged by several opponents in the Republican primaries; his closest rival, Rick Santorum, did not leave the race until April 10. Then, in 2016, both parties faced drawn-out contests, with Donald Trump not dispatching his toughest opponents until the May 3 Indiana primary and Hillary Clinton not acquiring the delegates needed for nomination until the eve of the California primary in early June.

Just as early nomination decisions produced front-loading by states not wanting to be left out, later nomination decisions have undoubtedly contributed to some unwinding of front-loading as states saw that there are sometimes advantages in voting later. The self-perpetuating cycle that contributed to front-loading may have been reversed for a time, partially unwinding front-loading. From 2012 to 2016, 17 states moved the date of their primary or caucus earlier, but 23 states moved theirs later (FrontloadingHQ.com 2016).

The changing campaign finance environment may be part of the interconnected picture, too. The Federal Election Campaign Act Amendments of 1974 probably contributed significantly to front-loading by making it very difficult for candidates to raise sufficient funds if they were unsuccessful early. This feature of campaign finance law led many candidates to leave the race after a few early losses (or sometimes even before the actual voting started, if they were struggling in the polls). That still happens to some candidates, and will undoubtedly continue to occur. However, the development of Super PACs after the *Citizens United* and *Speech Now* federal court decisions probably had some effect in delaying candidate departures. With Super PACs able to raise and spend unlimited amounts on behalf of presidential candidates, some candidates are able to better weather the storm of early losses. Races are consequently extended, and states have less incentive to schedule their primaries early.

Overall, in 2016, the primary season stretched 19 weeks, from New Hampshire on February 9 to the District of Columbia Democratic primary on June 14. (See Table 5.1.) In the first half of the primary season, Republicans held 25 primaries, accounting for 63.9 percent of primary delegates; Democrats held 24 primaries, accounting for 52.0 percent of primary delegates. In the last half of the primary season, Democrats held 17 primaries, Republicans 16. The percentage of primary delegates chosen in the first half of the primary season in 2016 was thus much higher than in 1960 (when it was about 20 percent), but lower (and on the Democratic side, much lower) than in 1996 (when it was about 75 percent).

Although the trend toward primary front-loading receded significantly in recent election cycles, it seems to have regained some momentum in 2020. At least four states moved their contests up into the first two weeks of March, including giant California, which announced a shift from early June to March 3 (Frontloading HQ 2019). In 2016, 13 Democratic and 13 Republican contests were held on Super Tuesday, the first primary date after the parties' windows opened for most states (March 1); a few months before voting was set to begin, 16 Democratic and 14 Republican contests had been scheduled for Super Tuesday 2020 (March 3).

The "Invisible Primary" and Interregnum

Aside from the front-loading of primaries and the end of the convention as the actual point of decision, the reform system has spawned two other unique features of the nomination calendar.

Table 5.1 2016 Democratic and Republican Delegate Selection Calendar

Date	State	Contest(s)
Feb 1	Iowa	D and R caucuses
Feb 9	New Hampshire	D and R primaries
Feb 20	Nevada	D caucuses
	South Carolina	R primary
Feb 23	Nevada	R caucuses
Feb 27	South Carolina	D primary
March 1	Alabama	D and R primaries
	Alaska	R caucuses
	Arkansas	D and R primaries
	Colorado	D and R caucuses
	Georgia	D and R primaries
	Massachusetts	D and R primaries
	Minnesota	D and R caucuses
	Oklahoma	D and R primaries
	Tennessee	D and R primaries
	Texas	D and R primaries
	Vermont	D and R primaries
	Virginia	D and R primaries
	Wyoming	R caucuses
	American Samoa	D caucuses
	Dems Abroad	D primary
March 5	Kansas	D and R caucuses
	Kentucky	R caucuses
	Louisiana	D and R primaries
	Maine	R caucuses
	Nebraska	D caucuses
March 6	Maine	D caucuses
	Puerto Rico	R primary
March 8	Hawaii	R caucuses
	Idaho	R primary
	Michigan	D and R primaries
	Mississippi	D and R primaries
March 10	Virgin Islands	R caucuses

(continued)

Table 5.1 *(continued)*

Date	State	Contest(s)
March 12	District of Columbia	R convention
	Wyoming	R county conventions
	Guam	R convention
	N. Mariana Islands	D caucuses
March 15	Florida	D and R primaries
	Illinois	D and R primaries
	Missouri	D and R primaries
	North Carolina	D and R primaries
	Ohio	D and R primaries
	N. Mariana Islands	R caucuses
March 22	Arizona	D and R primaries
	Idaho	D caucuses
	Utah	D and R caucuses
	American Samoa	R caucuses
March 26	Alaska	D caucuses
	Hawaii	D caucuses
	Washington	D caucuses
April 5	Wisconsin	D and R primaries
April 19	New York	D and R primaries
April 26	Connecticut	D and R primaries
	Delaware	D and R primaries
	Maryland	D and R primaries
	Pennsylvania	D and R primaries
	Rhode Island	D and R primaries
May 3	Indiana	D and R primaries
May 7	Guam	D caucuses
May 10	Nebraska	D and R primaries
	West Virginia	D and R primaries
May 17	Kentucky	D primary
	Oregon	D and R primaries
May 24	Washington	D and R primaries
June 4	Virgin Islands	D caucuses
June 5	Puerto Rico	D caucuses

June 7	California	D and R primaries
	Montana	D and R primaries
	New Jersey	D and R primaries
	New Mexico	D and R primaries
	North Dakota	D caucuses
	South Dakota	D and R primaries
June 14	District of Columbia	D primary

Source: "Election 2016 Calendar: Primaries and Caucuses." National Public Radio, February 17, 2016. https://www.npr.org/2016/01/26/464430411/election-2016-calendar -primaries-and-caucuses.

One, frequently dubbed the "invisible primary," comes before the voting begins in Iowa. It is the period that begins when potential candidates for nomination create their exploratory committees and begin raising money, recruiting an organization, making visits to Iowa and New Hampshire, and laying the groundwork for endorsements. When Jimmy Carter announced his campaign for president on January 3, 1975—22 months before election day 1976—it was considered absurdly early by most observers. Such early entry into a presidential race, whether by way of formal announcement or exploratory preparation, is now the rule rather than the exception.

Factors driving the rise of the "invisible primary" include the high cost and organizational demands of the expanded number of primaries; the even higher financial and organizational costs of competing in a heavily front-loaded system; and the positive examples of candidates such as Carter who started early and won. Objectives of the candidates in this period include increasing their national visibility and poll standings, acquiring the necessary resources to conduct a successful campaign, building support within the party, and winning some tests of strength such as straw polls held at party dinners, conventions of allied organizations, or other public events. Although "invisible primary" is the term widely used by political scientists to describe this period of campaign activity before actual voting begins, the goal of the candidates is to escape invisibility well enough to put themselves in a position to win the earliest contests and beyond. The importance of the invisible primary can be seen in the fact that nearly every presidential nominee of the modern era entered the primary and caucus season leading in the national polls, fundraising race, or both (Mayer 1996). Winning the invisible primary is usually the route to winning the real primaries.

On the other side of the primaries and caucuses lies the "interregnum." This is the period between one candidate effectively securing the nomination, either because he or she has won enough delegates to be nominated or because all of his or her viable rivals have ended their campaigns, and the time of formal nomination by the convention. It is a part of the nomination calendar that shifts, since the moment of effective nomination varies from year to year and from party to party. It is also a feature of the calendar that did not exist until nominations ceased to be effectively decided at the convention.

Because each party's contest may end at a different time, the interregnum can pose complicated strategic issues for a candidate. For example, in 2016, Donald Trump had effectively vanquished his Republican foes by May 3, while Hillary Clinton did not secure the Democratic nomination until a month later. This left Trump free to pivot to his general election strategy and to focus on attacking Clinton. Clinton then had to decide how much to return fire and how much to remain concentrated on her intraparty fight with Bernie Sanders for the Democratic nomination.

Prior to 2008, when candidates were still likely to accept federal funds for the general election, they could not do so until they were officially nominated at the national convention. Before then, they were still bound by the spending limits they had agreed to when they had accepted federal matching funds in the primaries. This situation led to great difficulty for some campaigns during the interregnum. In 1996, for example, Bob Dole wrapped up the Republican nomination, for all practical purposes, in early March. He had used most of his FECA-imposed spending limit winning the nomination, but was immediately engaged in general election skirmishing with Bill Clinton, who had spent almost none of his primary limit in his uncontested renomination race. Dole was not officially nominated (and given a new reserve of funds) until four months later, during which Clinton attacked him frequently and effectively. The Republican National Committee stepped in and funded some ads defending Dole, but he was badly hurt (Ceaser and Busch 1997).

Because no nominee since Dole has accepted federal primary funds, this situation has not been repeated in the interregnum. Indeed, Dole's predicament was one reason candidates subsequently began refusing federal funds. Nevertheless, the period of being the nominee in substance but not officially remains awkward.

Sources

Busch, Andrew E. 2009. "Assumptions and Realities of Presidential Primary Front-loading." In Jack Citrin, David Karol, et al., eds., *Nominating the President: Evolution and Revolution in 2008 and Beyond*. Lanham, MD: Rowman & Littlefield.

Ceaser, James W., and Andrew E. Busch. 1997. *Losing to Win: The 1996 Elections and American Politics*. Lanham, MD: Rowman & Littlefield.

Clymer, Adam. 2000. "A G.O.P. Overhaul of Primary Season Is Killed by Bush." *New York Times*, July 29, p. A1.

Cohen, Marty, David Karol, Hans Noel, and John Zaller. 2008a. *The Party Decides: Presidential Nominations Before and After Reform*. Chicago: University of Chicago Press.

Cohen, Marty, David Karol, Hans Noel, and John Zaller. 2008b. "The Invisible Primary in General Elections." In William G. Mayer, ed., *The Making of the Presidential Candidates 2008*. Lanham, MD: Rowman & Littlefield, pp. 1–38.

Congressional Quarterly. 1975. *Guide to U.S. Elections*. Washington, DC: Congressional Quarterly.

FrontloadingHQ.com. 2016. "The 2016 Presidential Primary Calendar." http://frontloading.blogspot.com/p/2016-presidential-primary-calendar.html.

FrontloadingHQ. 2019. "The 2020 Presidential Primary Calendar," May 2. http://frontloading.blogspot.com/p/2020-presidential-primary-calendar.html.

Mayer, William G. 1996. "Forecasting Presidential Nominations." In William G. Mayer, ed., *In Pursuit of the White House: How We Choose Our Presidential Nominees*. Chatham, NJ: Chatham House, pp. 44–71.

Mayer, William G., and Andrew E. Busch. 2004. *The Front-Loading Problem in Presidential Nominations*. Washington, DC: Brookings Institution.

Price, David E. 1984. *Bringing Back the Parties*. Washington, DC: Congressional Quarterly.

Rules and Bylaws Committee of the Democratic National Committee. 2000. *Beyond 2000: The Scheduling of Future Democratic Presidential Primaries and Caucuses*. Washington, DC: Democratic National Committee.

Wattenberg, Martin P. 1991. "The Republican Presidential Advantage in the Age of Party Disunity." In Gary W. Cox and Samuel Kernel, eds., *The Politics of Divided Government*. Boulder: Westview.

CHAPTER SIX

The Importance of Iowa, New Hampshire, and Other Early Contests

In theory, every national convention delegate from every state has an equal vote. In reality, primaries and caucuses held early in the process exert outsized influence. Sometimes they propel a single candidate to the nomination by providing him or her with unstoppable momentum. More often, they thin the field dramatically, driving unsuccessful candidates out of the race and establishing which two or three contenders will have a serious chance.

The ability of the early contests to shape the nomination contest in this way is highly controversial. The very earliest contests—the Iowa caucuses and the New Hampshire primary—are held in small, disproportionately rural states. Demographically, few racial minorities live in either state, and the average age of residents is above the national average. (See Table 6.1.) Some critics focus on the unrepresentative character of Iowa and New Hampshire, arguing that they should not have gatekeeping power over presidential nominations. Other critics are less concerned about the specific peculiarities of the two states, arguing instead that no two states should hold such power in every election (Flanagin 2016).

However, Iowa and New Hampshire have their defenders, too. Because they are small and voters take pride in their gatekeeping role, candidates have to engage in "retail" politics—extensive personal interactions with individual voters and small groups—if they hope to do well. Voters thus get an opportunity to study the candidates up close and interact with them, forming judgments over a period of months (or even years). After the first few contests, the

Table 6.1 **Demographics of Iowa, New Hampshire, and United States 2016**

	Iowa	N.H.	U.S.
White, non-Hispanic	86.2	90.8	61.3
Black	3.7	1.5	13.3
Hispanic	5.8	3.5	17.8
Asian	2.5	2.7	5.7
Persons age 65 and over	16.4	17.0	15.2
Median household income	$54,570	$68,485	$55,322
Population per square mile	54.5	147.0	87.4

Source: U.S. Census Bureau, https://www.census.gov/quickfacts/fact/table/NH,IA,US
/PST045216.

race devolves into "wholesale" politics, in which most voters' exposure to the candidates comes through television advertising or other mass media. Consequently, some argue that the overall process would lose an important qualitative element without Iowa and New Hampshire (Loebsack 2016).

Whether good or bad, it is clear that much of the message sent by early contests has to do with performance relative to expectations rather than performance in any absolute sense. Those expectations are largely formed by the news media on the basis of poll standings, fundraising, crowd reactions, endorsements, straw votes, and other traditional measures of campaign strength.

What Are the Earliest Contests?

New Hampshire has held the nation's first primary since 1920. It was noticed as important in 1948, but came into its own as an early test of strength in 1952, when it first instituted a presidential preference poll. Its "First in the Nation" status is so important to New Hampshire that state law requires that it remain first; the secretary of state is empowered to move the date of the primary to remain at least one week ahead of any other primary. Though it had already attained an important position prior to the McGovern-Fraser reforms, adopted by the Democratic Party prior to the 1972 election with the aim of increasing the power of ordinary voters in the nominating process, the reformed system accentuated its influence by inflating the power of the primaries in general. New Hampshire is a semiopen primary state in which independents may vote in either party primary, and they are a large and highly prized bloc. Partly for this reason, New Hampshire has a reputation for volatility and for supporting mavericks and underdogs, although in reality it usually supports the national front-runner.

The reforms also had the effect of inflating the importance of being early, and another early contest that quickly came into view was Iowa. There, the state Democratic Party had decided after 1968 to move its caucuses up in the calendar to make it easier to comply with the reforms. State law required 30 days between each stage of the delegate selection process, and the arithmetic in 1972 required the caucuses to be moved to January 24, earlier than any other state. Four years later, the presidential campaign of Jimmy Carter, a little-known one-term governor of Georgia, noticed Iowa's new spot in the calendar and fixed on it as an opportunity to score an influential early win. The success of Carter's strategy in 1976 led to the Iowa caucuses, now typically held eight days before the New Hampshire primary, becoming recognized as the other key gatekeeper in the presidential nominating system.

Since 1976, other states have occasionally tried to leapfrog in front of Iowa and New Hampshire with early caucuses. Michigan Republicans in 1986, Hawaii and Kansas Republicans in January 1988, and Louisiana Republicans in 1996 all held caucuses earlier than Iowa, and in 2000, Alaska Republicans held their caucuses on the same day as Iowa. However, Iowa and New Hampshire's role in the system is supported by nearly automatic media coverage, and the upstarts never received the attention that their established rivals did. Moreover, because Democratic rules forbade contests before Iowa, these early contests were only held on the Republican side, further diminishing public and media interest. By the next election cycle, these states had each abandoned their efforts.

Where these freelance efforts to go early failed, a handful of other states have succeeded in receiving special dispensation from both parties to hold their contests in close proximity to (though after) Iowa and New Hampshire. In 2012 and 2016, Nevada caucuses and the South Carolina primary followed the traditional first two in the first month of contests. South Carolina had inched forward for years, becoming a crucial gateway to the southern primaries that followed, until national party rules formally gave it a place. South Carolina Republicans are so protective of their role that they have adopted a state party rule requiring that the South Carolina GOP primary be held no more than two weeks following the New Hampshire primary, and earlier if necessary to preserve their "First in the South" status. Nevada, for its part, gave the West a voice in the early weeding out of candidates. For the time being, the first five weeks of the nomination contest features one midwestern, one northeastern, one southern, and one western state. Supporters of the addition of South Carolina and Nevada to the set of earliest contests note that they offset the perceived unrepresentativeness of Iowa and New Hampshire. South Carolina has the fifth largest percentages of African Americans of any state (27.5 percent in 2016), and Nevada has the fifth largest Hispanic population by percentage (28.5 percent in 2016).

Development and History of the Earliest Contests

A history of key contests in New Hampshire, Iowa, and other early states follows. That history really starts in 1952, when New Hampshire held a presidential preference primary for the first time, unseated a president, and helped pick his successor. By examining important races, one can see how the significance of early states has grown.

New Hampshire 1952–1972

1952: In the Democratic primary, President Harry Truman lost against Senator Estes Kefauver 55 percent to 44 percent, driving Truman out of the race for another term. Robert Taft lost the Republican primary to Dwight D. Eisenhower despite spending several days in the state campaigning; Eisenhower was in Paris serving as top military commander of NATO. Eisenhower's win put him on the road to the GOP presidential nomination.

1964: Barry Goldwater had been expected to win the Republican primary, but lost to U.S. ambassador to South Vietnam Henry Cabot Lodge, whose supporters ran a write-in campaign. Although Goldwater ultimately won the Republican nomination, New Hampshire set him back and exposed weaknesses, including politically unwise statements about nuclear weapons and Social Security, that Democratic president Lyndon Johnson would later exploit fully in the November general election.

1968: Like Truman before him, President Lyndon Johnson was challenged from within his own party in the New Hampshire primary. Johnson's challenger, antiwar senator Eugene McCarthy, outperformed expectations, losing to the incumbent only 49.6 percent to 41.9 percent. New Hampshire put Johnson on notice that his renomination was not assured. A few weeks later, facing probable defeat in the next primary in Wisconsin, Johnson bowed out of the race.

1972: Democratic front-runner Senator Edmund Muskie won New Hampshire—but was held below 50 percent, a surprise since he hailed from neighboring Maine. George McGovern, on the other hand, exceeded expectations and finished a strong second. Having established himself as a serious candidate, McGovern gradually built support until his win in Wisconsin on April 4 propelled him toward the nomination.

Iowa, New Hampshire, and Other Early Contests, 1976–2016

1976: Jimmy Carter was the first to recognize the potential for an underdog candidate to use the Iowa caucuses to propel himself to a nomination. Having focused unprecedented time and organizational energy on Iowa, Carter outpolled his Democratic rivals (though "uncommitted" ran ahead of Carter).

In New Hampshire five weeks later, Carter again defeated a bevy of more experienced and better-known contenders, including Senators Hubert Humphrey and Fred Harris and Congressman Morris Udall. There is no question that Carter's success in Iowa improved his standing in New Hampshire. In combination with his victory in Iowa a week before, New Hampshire put Carter on the road to the presidency (Zelizer 2016). This one-two punch became the goal of many subsequent campaigns, though it has proven difficult to carry out.

On the Republican side, Iowa was a nonfactor. It was not yet seen as important, and most delegates selected were uncommitted. In New Hampshire, President Gerald Ford came from behind in the polls to narrowly defeat challenger Ronald Reagan. Leveraging his New Hampshire win, Ford took control of the early portion of the race and barely held on to win renomination in a see-saw contest with Reagan.

1980: After trailing in the polls through most of 1979, Jimmy Carter came storming back against challenger Senator Edward M. Kennedy with the aid of the Iranian hostage crisis and the Soviet invasion of Afghanistan. Carter crushed Kennedy 59–31 percent in Iowa, followed by a 47–37 percent win in New Hampshire. He was never really seriously threatened thereafter.

In the Republican race, Ronald Reagan was stung by George H. W. Bush's Iowa upset, which established Bush as the Californian's main rival. Reagan regained the initiative in two New Hampshire debates and won the Granite State primary by a 2–1 margin. Having righted his campaign ship, neither Bush nor his other rivals could catch him, though Bush wound up with the vice presidential nomination. For the first time, South Carolina played an important role in the Republican nomination; there, Reagan dispatched former Texas governor and treasury secretary John Connally, who had spent large sums of money in the state and staked his campaign on a South Carolina win (Busch 2005).

1984: Walter Mondale, widely expected to be the Democratic nominee, won as expected in Iowa but suffered an embarrassing upset in New Hampshire to Colorado senator Gary Hart, who campaigned on a theme of "new ideas." Mondale would recover to fight his way to the Democratic nomination, but went on to lose to Ronald Reagan in one of the biggest landslides in U.S. history.

1988: Vice President George H. W. Bush placed third in the Iowa caucuses behind Senator Bob Dole and religious leader Marion "Pat" Robertson. Many analysts saw New Hampshire as a key test of whether Bush would remain a viable candidate. Bush came back in New Hampshire by emphasizing that he had signed a "No New Taxes" pledge but Dole had not. In New Hampshire, a strongly antitax state, the pledge was decisive, and Bush won. South Carolina was the next stop, and Bush's win there established unstoppable momentum. By March 29, Dole had withdrawn and Bush had wrapped up the nomination.

1992: In both parties, Iowa played a lesser role. The Democratic caucuses were won by home-state senator Tom Harkin, as expected. Incumbent president George H. W. Bush won the Republican caucuses against little organized opposition.

However, considerable drama attended the New Hampshire Democratic primary as scandal broke around front-runner Bill Clinton. Clinton found himself battling allegations of marital infidelity as well as evidence that he had evaded the draft as a young man. After dropping precipitously in the polls, Clinton fought back with the help of a pre–Super Bowl *60 Minutes* interview of himself and wife, Hillary. He finished a respectable second to Paul Tsongas in New Hampshire, with 25 percent to Tsongas's 33 percent, and built on a reputation as the "comeback kid." He went on to win the Democratic nomination.

Bush won New Hampshire by a surprisingly close 53–38 percent margin against challenger Patrick J. Buchanan. Buchanan, who had never held elective office, hammered Bush for breaking his 1988 No New Taxes pledge and for various other violations of conservative principle on issues including affirmative action and taxpayer funding of obscene art. (Buchanan also anticipated both Ross Perot and Donald Trump by attacking free trade agreements as giveaways hurting American workers.) New Hampshire was the closest Buchanan came to beating Bush in any primary, as Bush turned the tide with a decisive win in South Carolina. Bush's relatively weak showing in New Hampshire, though, was a sign of his vulnerability in November.

1996: As in 1988, the Kansan Bob Dole won the caucuses in his neighboring state of Iowa, though Pat Buchanan scored a surprising second-place finish. In New Hampshire, Buchanan built on his strong 1992 showing to actually win the primary against the heavily favored Dole. Lamar Alexander of Tennessee, who finished third in Iowa, also threatened to overtake Dole. However, Buchanan had a relatively low ceiling in the national Republican primary electorate, so Dole's last-minute decision to attack Alexander, who was gaining fast, may have saved his nomination. While Dole lost New Hampshire to Buchanan, he beat Alexander for second place, preventing the rival with greater potential appeal from establishing himself. Dole declared South Carolina to be his "firewall," and won there decisively. Having failed to make his mark in New Hampshire or his home region of the South, Alexander faded, while Buchanan hit his ceiling in South Carolina and lost the nomination to Dole.

2000: With no incumbent running for reelection for the first time since 1988, both parties entered the primary season with a contest between an "establishment" front-runner and a "maverick" challenger. The front-runners were Vice President Al Gore and Texas governor George W. Bush; the self-styled mavericks were former New Jersey senator Bill Bradley and Arizona senator John McCain. Iowa was easily won by the front-runners.

New Hampshire, on the other hand, lived up to its reputation as a state hospitable to outsiders. Given that independents could vote in either primary, a major contest under the surface was the cross-party competition between Bradley and McCain for independent voters. McCain won the independents, and thus his primary against Bush. Bradley lost the independents to McCain, and thus lost his primary against Gore. Bush regained momentum by winning a high-stakes primary in South Carolina two and a half weeks later, while Democrats had no primaries or caucuses for nearly a month, giving Bradley no opportunities to recover. When Democrats resumed voting, Gore swept the remaining primaries (Ceaser and Busch 2001).

2004: Democrat John Kerry, senator from Massachusetts, fell from apparent front-runner status to fifth place in some Democratic polls at the end of 2003. However, he recovered by January, won in Iowa, then prevailed in New Hampshire against Vermont governor Howard Dean. Kerry went on to win the nomination.

2008: The Democratic race between front-runner Hillary Clinton, Illinois senator Barack Obama, and North Carolina senator and 2004 Democratic vice presidential nominee John Edwards produced a big surprise in Iowa, where Clinton finished third behind Obama and Edwards. With a chance to put Clinton on the ropes, though, Obama faltered in New Hampshire. Clinton's win there assured that the race would not end soon; Obama's win in South Carolina, which came up next, put him in the driver's seat and knocked Edwards out of the race.

On the Republican side, John McCain, like Kerry in 2004, had slipped from the lead to fifth place but had come back in late 2007. He did not seriously contest Iowa, which was won by Arkansas governor Mike Huckabee. He focused instead on New Hampshire, where he had had great success eight years before. McCain won New Hampshire again with a solid victory against his main competitor there, Massachusetts governor Mitt Romney. This win reestablished him as the man to beat, after which he went on to win South Carolina and Florida, which also voted in the first month of Republican primaries (Ceaser, Busch, and Pitney 2009).

2012: Mitt Romney came into the Republican primaries as the expected favorite. In the initial count, he seemed to have barely held off former Pennsylvania senator Rick Santorum in the Iowa caucuses. He then went on to win the New Hampshire primary with 39 percent; Ron Paul came in second with 23 percent. Only after New Hampshire was it revealed that a recount had shown that Santorum, rather than Romney, had won Iowa. Eleven days later, former House Speaker Newt Gingrich denied Romney what might have been a clinching victory in South Carolina. However, Romney's strong start, combined with his formidable fundraising capacity, eventually won him the nomination (Ceaser, Busch, and Pitney 2013).

2016: Hillary Clinton was determined not to lose the Iowa caucuses again, but her contest with Bernie Sanders led to a near tie in delegates from Iowa. No vote results by caucus attendees was available, but Clinton led the county delegate counts by 49.9 to 49.6 percent. Sanders, who hailed from neighboring Vermont, went on to crush Clinton 60.4 to 38.0 percent in the New Hampshire primary. Not until South Carolina and Nevada did Clinton regain her footing. As in 2008, Clinton found herself in a two-person race with a closely matched opponent, exemplified by splitting the first few contests. In the end, she won the nomination, but did not clinch it until the final week of primaries.

Throughout the last half of 2015, Republicans were transfixed by the sight of billionaire real estate developer and reality TV personality Donald J. Trump rising in the polls. However, Texas senator Ted Cruz out-organized Trump in Iowa, beating him in the caucuses. Trump finished second, and Florida senator Marco Rubio came in a close third. Rubio's campaign had banked on a 3-2-1 strategy—third in Iowa, second in New Hampshire, building to first in South Carolina. However, Trump recovered to win handily in New Hampshire. Rubio, who had been rising in the New Hampshire polls after his strong Iowa showing, was hurt by a poor debate performance on the weekend before the vote and dropped to fifth place. Cruz was never a factor and finished third with 11.6 percent. These jumbled results set up South Carolina as a key test. Rubio came back from his New Hampshire debacle, edging out Cruz for second place. But Trump finished first there, then posted another first-place finish a week later in Nevada. With wins in three of the first four contests, the New Yorker was well on his way to the nomination (Ceaser, Busch, and Pitney 2017).

What Effects Do the Earliest Contests Have?

One consistent impact of Iowa and New Hampshire is that the winner usually gains ground in subsequent national polls. In Iowa, for example, Walter Mondale in 1984 gained 14 percentage points from the last pre-Iowa poll to polling between Iowa and New Hampshire; Richard Gephardt gained 11 points in 1988; Bob Dole gained 8 points in 1988; Al Gore gained 7 points in 2000; George W. Bush gained 2 points in 2000; and John Kerry gained 22 points in 2004 (Busch 2008, 64). Sometimes candidates even parlay a strong third-place Iowa finish in a large field with an unsatisfactory front-runner into some momentum that gives them a shot at New Hampshire. Both Lamar Alexander in 1996 and Marco Rubio in 2016 finished third in Iowa and immediately jumped in the New Hampshire polls; in both cases, their momentum broke just a few days too soon, and they fell back into the pack.

A similar effect can be seen following the New Hampshire primary. In New Hampshire, Henry Cabot Lodge rocketed from 12 percent in the last pre–New Hampshire Gallup Poll to 42 percent in the first postprimary poll in 1964, Jimmy Carter went from 4 percent to 16 percent, Gary Hart jumped from 3 percent to 30 percent, Paul Tsongas climbed from 5 percent to 31 percent, and Pat Buchanan went from 7 percent to 27 percent. Even better-known winners, like incumbent Jimmy Carter and Ronald Reagan in 1980, gained 5 points and 8 points respectively (Buell 2000, 105). Of course, in most of these cases, the winners only added to their national lead (or reduced the front-runner's lead but did not overcome it).

These polling gains come about largely because of the enormous attention showered on the Iowa and New Hampshire contests by the national media. One study showed that ABC, CBS, CNN, and NBC devoted 74 stories to the 1996 Iowa caucuses and 101 stories to the New Hampshire primary, in comparison with 35 stories about the 14 Super Tuesday primaries together, which included such major states as Florida, Texas, Illinois, Ohio, Michigan, and California. Coverage of New Hampshire accounted for 42.5 percent of all broadcast seconds spent on the 1996 primaries and caucuses by the four networks, and Iowa accounted for another 34.4 percent (Buell 2000, 102–103). Other studies show similar results for both television and newspaper coverage (Mayer and Busch 2004, 24–25).

The earliest contests not only give a bump to the winner's national standing, they play a major role in shaping the field. Overall, in the 18 contested nomination races since 1976, the candidate who ultimately won the nomination won Iowa and/or New Hampshire 17 times. Only on the Democratic side in 1992 did a candidate—Bill Clinton—win the nomination after losing both Iowa and New Hampshire. Even that case might be deceiving, though, as Iowa was essentially uncontested and won by its home-state senator (Tom Harkin) and Clinton's second-place finish in New Hampshire was widely seen as a victory against expectations. On only six occasions, though, did the ultimate winner prevail in both Iowa and New Hampshire. In the 11 cases of split winners, there was no clear advantage to either of the first two contests. The New Hampshire winner got the nomination six times and the Iowa winner five times. Although Jimmy Carter blazed the trail of the unknown candidate using a win in Iowa to win New Hampshire and go on to the nomination, his trail has been followed successfully by few, if any. Most of the candidates who won both of the early contests and then the nomination were the race's established front-runners already.

Interestingly, the early state that is less talked about, South Carolina, is more clearly decisive—in the nine cases of split Iowa–New Hampshire winners that featured a South Carolina primary as an early contest, too, the winner of the South Carolina primary went on to win the nomination eight times. Since becoming an early primary, South Carolina has usually been the tie-breaker. (See Table 6.2.)

Table 6.2   Iowa, New Hampshire, Early South Carolina, and Nomination Winners in Contested Races 1976–2016

Year	Iowa	N.H.	S.C.	Nominee
1976D	Carter	Carter		Carter
1976R	Ford	Ford		Ford
1980D	Carter	Carter		Carter
1980R	Bush	Reagan	Reagan	Reagan
1984D	Mondale	Hart		Mondale
1988D	Gephardt	Dukakis		Dukakis
1988R	Dole	Bush	Bush	Bush
1992D	Harkin	Tsongas		Clinton
1992R	Bush	Bush		Bush
1996R	Dole	Buchanan	Dole	Dole
2000D	Gore	Gore		Gore
2000R	Bush	McCain	Bush	Bush
2004D	Kerry	Kerry		Kerry
2008D	Obama	Clinton	Obama	Obama
2008R	Huckabee	McCain	McCain	McCain
2012R	Santorum	Romney	Gingrich	Romney
2016D	Clinton	Sanders	Clinton	Clinton
2016R	Cruz	Trump	Trump	Trump

Political observers agree that results in Iowa and New Hampshire work together to weed out a large number of the weaker contenders, setting the field and the choices for subsequent primary voters. In 2016, for example, Democrats entered the Iowa caucuses with three candidates, but emerged with only two because former Maryland governor Martin O'Malley dropped out immediately after the votes were counted. There were 12 Republican candidates still active when the Iowa caucuses opened. Of those, three (Huckabee, Paul, and Santorum) dropped out after Iowa, another three (Christie, Fiorina, and Gilmore) after New Hampshire, and Jeb Bush after South Carolina. At that point, the Republican field had resolved itself to Trump, Cruz, Rubio, John Kasich, who finished second in New Hampshire, and Ben Carson. Every subsequent Republican contest in 2016 was won by a candidate who had finished in the top three in Iowa or the top two in New Hampshire. Overall, since 1952, no candidate has ever finished lower than second in the New Hampshire primary and gone on to win the nomination.

The importance of the earliest contests to the outcome of the race means that before the votes are cast, Iowa, New Hampshire, and now sometimes South Carolina play a major role in campaign strategy and devotion of campaign resources, including both campaign spending and candidate time. Almost every campaign strategy looks for a way to make it to the top of at least one of the earliest states. In a rare exception, in 2008, Republican Rudy Giuliani decided to bypass Iowa and New Hampshire, focusing his attention on the Florida primary as his breakthrough opportunity; by the time the race got to Florida, three weeks after New Hampshire, John McCain had already established himself as the front-runner and could not be dislodged (Norrander 2010, 93). To carry out their strategies, campaigns will often spend much more in Iowa and New Hampshire than in larger states later in the nomination calendar. Candidates will also spend a disproportionate amount of time campaigning in the earliest states. For instance, prior to the 1988 primaries and caucuses, the seven major Democratic candidates campaigned 546 days in Iowa, 288 days in New Hampshire, and 441 days in the 14 states voting on Super Tuesday combined. The six major Republican contenders spent 300 days campaigning in Iowa, 367 days in New Hampshire, and 396 days in the entire South (Norrander 1992, 94). Observers noted that top-tier Republican candidates in 2015 spent less time in New Hampshire than in past years, refocusing some of their energy on subsequent contests, especially in the South (Johnson 2015).

However they were distributed, early contests remained a disproportionate focus of campaign resources. In 2016, presidential campaigns and outside groups spent more than $70 million in Iowa and more than $100 million in New Hampshire on political ads (Murray 2016). Not least, the states with the earliest contests sometimes have sufficient leverage to be able to extract policy pledges from the candidates in a way that other states cannot. Candidates in both parties traveling to Iowa find it hard to resist calls for increased aid to agriculture and subsidies for ethanol (though Texas senator Ted Cruz did so and managed to win in 2016); Republicans campaigning in antitax New Hampshire rarely decline to sign the No New Taxes pledge circulated quadrennially by activist Grover Norquist. When they do, as Bob Dole did in 1988, they run the risk of a rebuke from the voters that they can ill afford.

Sources

Buell, Emmet. 2000. "The Changing Face of the New Hampshire Primary." In William G. Mayer, ed., *In Pursuit of the White House 2000: How We Choose Our Presidential Nominees*. Chatham, NJ: Chatham House.

Busch, Andrew E. 2005. *Reagan's Victory: The 1980 Elections and the Rise of the Right*. Lawrence: University Press of Kansas.

Busch, Andrew E. 2008. "The Re-emergence of the Iowa Caucuses: A New Trend, an Aberration, or a Useful Reminder?" In William G. Mayer, ed., *The Making of the Presidential Candidates 2008*. Lanham, MD: Rowman & Littlefield.

Ceaser, James W., and Andrew E. Busch. 2001. *The Perfect Tie: The True Story of the 2000 Presidential Election*. Lanham, MD: Rowman & Littlefield.

Ceaser, James W., Andrew E. Busch, and John J. Pitney Jr. 2009. *Epic Journey: The 2008 Elections and American Politics*. Lanham, MD: Rowman & Littlefield.

Ceaser, James W., Andrew E. Busch, and John J. Pitney Jr. 2013. *After Hope and Change: The 2012 Elections and American Politics*. Lanham, MD: Rowman & Littlefield.

Ceaser, James W., Andrew E. Busch, and John J. Pitney Jr. 2017. *Defying the Odds: The 2016 Elections and American Politics*. Lanham, MD: Rowman & Littlefield.

Flanagin, Jake. 2016. "Iowa and New Hampshire Wield Too Much Influence. The US Needs a National Primary." *Quartz*, January 28. https://qz.com/602487/iowa-and-new-hampshire-wield-too-much-influence-the-us-needs-a-national-primary/.

Higgins, Tim. "New Hampshire Flooded by $100 Million in Political Ads." Bloomberg, February 3. https://www.bloomberg.com/news/articles/2016-02-03/new-hampshire-flooded-by-100-million-in-political-ads.

Johnson, Jenna. 2015. "Many Top Republican Candidates Are Spending Less Time in New Hampshire." *Washington Post*, August 4. https://www.washingtonpost.com/politics/many-top-gop-candidates-are-spending-less-time-in-new-hampshire/2015/08/04/9afcc226-3aa9-11e5-9c2d-ed991d848c48_story.html.

Loebsack, David. 2016. "Rep. Loebsack: Iowa, Grassroots Politics at Its Finest." *USA Today*, January 31. https://www.usatoday.com/story/opinion/2016/01/31/iowa-caucuses-rotating-primary-2016-presidential-election-editorials-debates/79610382/.

Mayer, William G., and Andrew E. Busch. 2004. *The Front-Loading Problem in Presidential Nominations*. Washington, DC: Brookings Institution.

Murray, Mark. 2016. "And the Total Amount Spent on Campaign Ads in Iowa Is . . . ," MSNBC, January 26, 2016. http://www.msnbc.com/msnbc/and-the-total-amount-spent-campaign-ads-iowa.

Norrander, Barbara. 1992. *Super Tuesday: Regional Politics and Presidential Primaries*. Lexington: University Press of Kentucky.

Norrander, Barbara. 2010. *The Imperfect Primary: Oddities, Biases, and Strengths of U.S. Nomination Politics*. New York: Routledge.

Zelizer, Julian. 2016. "How Jimmy Carter Revolutionized the Iowa Caucuses." *The Atlantic*, January 25. https://www.theatlantic.com/politics/archive/2016/01/jimmy-carter-iowa-caucuses/426729/.

CHAPTER SEVEN

Candidate Debates During the Primary Season

Debates between presidential candidates of the same party either before or during the primary season have become an increasingly important part of the nominating contest. In recent years, there have not only been more primary debates than general election debates, they have tended to have different themes and different effects than general election debates. In many cases, debates have been a focus of media coverage and have contributed key moments in the contests.

History of Candidate Debates in the Nomination Contest

Prior to the introduction of primaries and open preconvention campaigns for nomination, a preconvention debate between candidates was unimaginable. Not until 36 years after the first presidential primaries did one occur. The first broadcast debate between primary candidates took place in 1948, 12 years before the first broadcast general election debate, when the president of Reed College sent telegrams inviting Republicans Thomas E. Dewey and Harold O. Stassen to debate one another in Portland prior to the Oregon primary. A week later, Dewey, the governor of New York, and Stassen, governor of Minnesota, held a radio debate on a single question, whether the Communist Party should be banned in the United States. Stassen argued yes, Dewey no, on the grounds that communism would be easier contained if it was out in the open than if it was driven underground (Elving 2015). The first Democratic debate—and the first televised primary debate in either party—took place on ABC in 1956 between Estes Kefauver and Adlai

Stevenson. Through 2000, there were a total of 59 Democratic and 34 Republican debates (Benoit et al. 2002, 133).

There were another 16 Democratic debates in 2004, 19 in 2008, and 9 in 2016 (10 if one includes a January 25 CNN "Town Hall" event in Iowa). Republicans held another 19 debates in 2008, 20 in 2012, and 12 in 2016 (Kondik and Skelley 2015; Election Central 2018a; Election Central 2018b). As time passed, however, each party came to feel that they needed to reduce the number of debates they were holding. Both Democrats (after 2008) and Republicans (after 2012) became anxious that the number of debates was growing out of control and threatening to overwhelm other aspects of the campaign, not to mention exhausting the candidates. After 2008, the Democratic National Committee began sanctioning specific debates and encouraging candidates to participate only in sanctioned debates. In 2012, some Republicans feared that an excess of debates had hurt Mitt Romney's general election prospects. Some members of the GOP also asserted that the debates were too often moderated by hostile media forces who were all too happy to make Republicans look bad (Gibson 2015). Consequently, Republicans established a shorter list of RNC-sanctioned debates in 2016.

Even taking into account a reduction in the number of primary debates in 2016, however, the overall trajectory since the mid-20th century has been upward, with a sharp increase starting in the 1980s. According to political scientists Samuel J. Best and Clark Hubbard, "The most likely explanation for the increasing number of these events lies in the populist impulses expressed by the McGovern-Fraser Commission reforms. . . . As more states hold primaries, debates become relevant for the various state primary electorates, providing an impetus for debate sponsorship that was largely absent when caucuses were the principal mechanism for selecting delegates" (Best and Hubbard 2000, 257).

Since 1956, candidate debates prior to the formal party nominations have been sponsored by media organizations. This is in contrast to the general election debates, which since 1988 have been organized by the Commission on Presidential Debates. For primary debates, media organizations have usually established their own debate formats and their own criteria for inviting candidates. In earlier debates, the media organization used its judgment to assess which were the most viable competitors based on prior primary results; more recently, participation has usually been based on polling results for the candidates. For example, in 2016, debates sponsored by Fox News used the average of five recent national polls—surveys from Fox News, CBS News, Bloomberg News, Monmouth University, and Quinnipiac University (Miller 2015). The Fox Business Network, on the other hand, used averages from recent national polls as well as recent Iowa or New Hampshire polls. To be invited to the FBN debate, candidates had to be among the top six candidates in the national polls or the top five in the Iowa or New Hampshire polls

(Fox News Politics 2016). In 2016, there were so many candidates vying for the Republican nomination that on several occasions a debate was split into two parts. First came the "undercard" debate among candidates who were lower in the polls, followed by a primetime debate among the main contenders. The largest number of candidates to participate in a single nomination debate has been 10 (Kondik and Skelley 2015). As researchers have noted, debate sponsors often face a "powerful tension between the competing values of inclusiveness and coherence." The scramble resulting from a large number of debate participants "has tended to produce dueling sound bites and mock dramatics better suited to professional wrestling than to political discourse" (Campaign Reform 1998, 28). When debate sponsors exclude candidates, the excluded often complain bitterly. In 1996, Alan Keyes, after being left out of Republican primary debates, engaged in a hunger strike in protest and was handcuffed by police after repeatedly charging the doors trying to gain entry (Sack 1996).

The wide variety of sponsors and formats has led to unusual situations. For example, in 2012 Donald Trump offered to moderate and co-host a Republican debate. This proposition was viewed with suspicion by some Republicans who feared that Trump intended to use the platform to launch a third-party bid that he would announced shortly after the debate. In the end, the Trump debate did not happen and Trump did not run as an independent (Haberman 2011; Burns 2011). In 1980, a New Hampshire Republican primary debate to be sponsored by a newspaper in Nashua was declared outside the bounds of federal campaign finance regulations. Candidate Ronald Reagan's campaign provided funding so the debate could go on.

Although most debates since 1956 have had a media sponsor that has been responsible for inviting participants, some debates have featured a particular set of rivals rather than the full complement of candidates. Moreover, sometimes the candidates themselves have initiated or requested debates. In May 1968, Eugene McCarthy challenged Robert F. Kennedy to a debate prior to the Oregon primary, but Kennedy refused. In July 1968, McCarthy challenged Hubert H. Humphrey, Lyndon B. Johnson's vice president and the Democratic front-runner for the nomination at that time, to a debate. A debate between Humphrey, McCarthy, and George McGovern finally occurred shortly before the Democratic National Convention in late August (Dallos 1968; Turner 1968). In several other cases, challengers unsuccessfully demanded debates with presidential incumbents. Ronald Reagan in 1976 against Gerald Ford, Edward M. Kennedy in 1980 against Jimmy Carter, and Patrick Buchanan in 1992 against George H. W. Bush all failed to secure desired debates with the president. Instead, those presidents were able to deflect the calls for debate by emphasizing their presidential duties; Carter, for example, was in the throes of the Iranian hostage crisis and crafting a response to the Soviet invasion of Afghanistan when Kennedy issued his challenge. Carter developed a "Rose

Garden strategy" of ignoring his Democratic rival and focusing on his crisis leadership (Busch 2005).

Historically, most primary debates have corresponded to important primaries and caucuses on the election calendar. As noted above, the first radio broadcast debate, in 1948, took place in Oregon just before the pivotal Oregon primary. The largest number have taken place in Iowa or New Hampshire. South Carolina and Florida have also been popular venues for Republicans, as have New York and California for Democrats (Kondik and Skelley 2015). In recent years the range of venues has broadened. Some primary debate locations have special symbolic importance. For example, some Republican debates, including the second debate of the 2016 cycle, have taken place at the Ronald Reagan Presidential Library in Simi Valley, California.

For many years, no debates took place prior to the calendar year of the election. In 1988, however, that began to change. Now, a majority of debates usually take place prior to the calendar year of the election (though in 2016 it was eight of 21) (Kondik and Skelley 2015). The debates have become much more clearly a portion of the "invisible primary," the period of preparation and preliminary combat before voting begins in actual delegate selection contests. They offer a rare opportunity for lesser-known candidates to receive attention and build national support.

There has also been a significant change in the formatting of the debates over time. In keeping with the declining length of television news sound bites and candidate advertisements on television, debates have been reformatted to drastically reduce the length of candidate answers. In the first debate, Dewey and Stassen were each allowed 20 minutes to speak and 8 minutes for rebuttal on the single question of whether the CPUSA should be banned (Davies 1948). Modern debates typically allow candidates one to two minutes for statements and less for rebuttals. For example, in the first Democratic debate on October 15, 2015, each candidate had one minute to answer questions and 30 seconds for follow-ups and rebuttals ("Presidential Debates" 2018).

Content and Consequences of Primary Debates

The first debate in 1948 addressed policy and character in equal measures, but studies have found that in a typical primary debate approximately two-thirds of primary debate material addresses policy questions while one-third addresses character (Benoit et al. 2002, 19, 118). However, this ratio varies from year to year. In 1980, for example, Republican debates hewed to the typical ratio. In 2000, Republican debates were tilted slightly in the direction of policy, while Democratic debates even more heavily favored policy (Benoit et al. 2002, 39). Studies by the same authors indicate that policy is a bigger portion—and issues of character a lesser portion—of general election presidential debates than primary debates (Benoit et al. 2002, 123). There is a certain logic to this pattern: debates among only Democrats or only Republicans are less likely to involve policy disputes because there is much greater difference on policy between the parties than within them. As the *New York Times* noted in a front-page story about the first televised debate between Stevenson and Kefauver in 1956:

> Senator Estes Kefauver and Adlai E. Stevenson canvassed their political differences for an hour on television tonight and found very little to disagree about. The nationally televised "debate" found the two chief contenders for the Democratic Presidential nomination taking virtually identical positions on almost every issue discussed. (Baker 1956)

Aside from providing insights into policy and character, primary debates help voters form views about two additional questions: the capacity of the candidates to actually obtain their party's nomination ("viability") and the candidates' capacity to win the general election against the other party's nominee ("electability").

Overall, primary debates seem to have a greater influence on voter choice than do general election debates. General election voters viewing a debate tend to be already decided because of party loyalty and because by the general election they have been inundated with information. On the other hand, primary voters cannot fall back on party cues and sometimes have much less prior information about the candidates. As a consequence, they are more open to being swayed by the information they receive in or about a debate (Yawn, Ellsworth, Beatty, and Kahn 1998; Lanoue and Schrott 1989). More generally, studies have indicated that information received earlier in the election process is more likely to alter opinions than information received later, when a large amount of information has already been compiled. Debates in the primary season thus have more impact on voters than those held in the general election phase (Best and Hubbard 2000, 264–268). Experimental studies of primary debates have shown that they can have considerable effect in altering viewers' levels of participation in the nomination race, their evaluations of candidates, and their own policy agendas (Best and Hubbard 2000, 270–276).

Media coverage of primary debates frequently focuses more on the negative, emphasizing attacks, rebuttals, and counterattacks. Coverage gives relatively short shrift to candidate attempts to stake out a positive platform. In a related vein, this coverage may overemphasize the amount of attention paid in debates to character questions, consequently understating the attention paid to policy. This coverage emphasis by newspapers and other media may particularly impact voters who did not see the debate firsthand (Benoit, Hansen, and Stein 2003).

There have been some particularly notable examples of debates affecting the course of a nomination contest, or even a subsequent presidency.

- When the Dewey-Stassen debate took place in 1948, Stassen had seized the lead in national polls and seemed the front-runner for the Republican nomination. The debate was broadcast to 900 stations nationwide and one of the largest radio audiences in history. Most analysts concluded that Dewey had gotten the better of the exchange, and voters apparently agreed. The Oregon primary was held four days after the debate, and Dewey prevailed 52 to 47 percent, winning all 12 delegates at stake. He quickly regained his national polling lead and went on to win the Republican nomination (Busch 2012, 90–91).

- The May 1960 debate between John F. Kennedy and Hubert H. Humphrey was noted by journalists as a turning point in the Democratic race. Pointing out that Kennedy was an underdog versus Humphrey before the debate and probably remained so after, *New York Times* reporter James Reston argued that "the consensus of the reporters covering the Humphrey-Kennedy debate" was that Kennedy "gained by the encounter" and that he "made a more vivid and effective presentation of his case" than Humphrey (Best and Hubbard 2000, 262).

- In perhaps the best known case, in 1980 Ronald Reagan took control of the debate in Nashua, New Hampshire, when the moderator tried to shut him down. Although chief rival George H. W. Bush had thought the debate would be limited to himself and Reagan, Reagan's campaign had invited the rest of the candidates. Reagan himself defended inclusion of the additional candidates, and when moderator Jon Breen ordered the technical crew to cut off Reagan's microphone, the Californian responded by saying, "I'm paying for this microphone, Mr. Green [*sic*]." In the eyes of many New Hampshire voters, Reagan's firmness and fairness contrasted with George H. W. Bush, who had appeared content to allow other candidates to be excluded. Though less well-known than this episode, Reagan's pollster Richard Wirthlin later contended that his comeback in New Hampshire really started at the Manchester debate a few days earlier, when Reagan scored points for his strong antitaxation stand (Busch 2005).

- In 1984, Democratic candidate Walter Mondale fended off a challenge from Senator Gary Hart with the help of a strong primary debate performance in Atlanta. Hart repeated his campaign mantra of "new ideas," and Mondale responded by referring to an iconic ad being run at the time by Wendy's hamburger chain. "When I hear your new ideas," Mondale said, "I'm reminded of that ad: 'Where's the beef?'"

- In 1988 in New Hampshire, George H. W. Bush started his comeback against early front-runner Bob Dole by challenging Dole in a debate to sign the No New Taxes pledge, which Dole declined to do. Months later, in a key debate prior to the New York primary, Senator Al Gore attacked Massachusetts governor Michael Dukakis on the issue of Willie Horton, a prison inmate who went on a violent rampage while on a furlough granted by the state of Massachusetts. Gore lost the primary anyway, but the issue was later revived by the Republicans in the general election campaign to considerable effect against Dukakis. The No New Taxes pledge, which Bush broke in 1990, came back to haunt Bush in the 1992 election, when both his primary challenger and Democratic nominee Bill Clinton brought it up time and time again.

- In a 1992 Democratic primary debate against Jerry Brown, Bill Clinton admitted marijuana use while in college in England but insisted that he had "not inhaled." Clinton's defense exposed him to ridicule and contributed to his image, which endured throughout and beyond his presidency, of someone who was not entirely truthful with voters. His later troubles in the White House, including the scandal that led to his 1998 impeachment by the House of Representatives, were partially framed by this debate comment.

- Mitt Romney's general election effort was almost certainly hurt by a number of statements he made under pressure during the Republican primary debates in 2012. These included calling for "self-deportation" of illegal immigrants and descriptions of himself as "severely conservative," a description that may have made him less appealing to voters across the political spectrum. Moderates and liberals were not attracted to a "severe conservative," and many conservatives doubted that a real conservative would describe himself that way.

The 2016 Debates

In 2016, there were 12 sanctioned Republican debates and 9 sanctioned Democratic debates. The first Democratic debate was held in Las Vegas on October 13, 2015; the final debate was held in Brooklyn on April 14, 2016, days before the New York primary. Republicans kicked off their debate schedule on August 6, 2015, in Cleveland and held their last debate in Miami on March 10, 2016. (See Table 7.1.) Seven of 12 Republican debates, and 5 of 9 Democratic debates, were held prior to voting in the first caucuses in Iowa.

There were notable moments in both parties' debates. On the Democratic side, former Virginia senator Jim Webb withdrew from the race when he received negative commentary on his October 2015 debate statement that the enemy he was proudest of was the North Vietnamese soldier he killed during his service in the Vietnam War (other candidates declared they were proudest of enemies such as the NRA). The negative reaction he received from the left wing of the Democratic Party convinced him he was not a fit for that party. Bernie Sanders gave up a potentially powerful issue against former secretary of state Hillary Clinton when he declared in the first Democratic

Table 7.1   Schedule of 2016 Democratic and Republic Presidential Primary Debates

Democrats	Republicans
October 13, 2015 Las Vegas, NV	August 6, 2015 Cleveland, OH
November 14, 2015 Des Moines, IA	September 16, 2015 Simi Valley, CA
December 19, 2015 Manchester, NH	October 28, 2015 Boulder, CO
January 17, 2016 Charleston, SC	November 10, 2015 Milwaukee, WI
January 25, 2016 Des Moines, IA	December 15, 2015 Las Vegas, NV
February 4, 2016 Durham, NH	January 14, 2016 North Charleston, SC
February 11, 2016 Milwaukee, WI	January 28, 2016 Des Moines, IA
March 6, 2016 Flint, MI	February 6, 2016 Manchester, NH
March 9, 2016 Miami, FL	February 13, 2016 Greenville, SC
April 14, 2016 Brooklyn, NY	February 25, 2016 Houston, TX
	March 3, 2016 Detroit, MI
	March 10, 2016 Miami, FL
	March 21, 2016 Salt Lake City, UT (cancelled)

Sources: See https://www.uspresidentialelectionnews.com/2016-debate-schedule/2016
-democratic-primary-debate-schedule/; https://www.uspresidentialelectionnews.com
/2016-debate-schedule/.

debate, "I think the secretary is right . . . the American people are sick and tired of hearing about your damn emails," referring to the use by Clinton of a potentially illegal private email server that led to an FBI investigation and clearly damaged her prospects in the general election (CNN 2015).

For his part, Donald Trump used the debates effectively to distinguish himself in a large Republican field. This was often done by making outlandish statements, as in the first Republican debate when he attacked Fox News moderator Megyn Kelly, claiming her tough questions were the result of her menstrual cycle (he later refused to participate in the final pre-Iowa caucuses debate in Des Moines because Kelly was scheduled to moderate again). He frequently belittled his opponents, who struggled to find an effective way to respond. Florida senator Marco Rubio, one of Trump's stronger rivals, arguably hurt himself significantly at two critical junctures of the race. After finishing a strong third in Iowa and gaining in the polls in New Hampshire, Rubio failed to respond effectively to a sustained attack by New Jersey governor Chris Christie, who complained that Rubio was too scripted and robotic. Rubio fell to fifth place in the New Hampshire results. Later, Rubio engaged with Trump on the latter's preferred terrain of personal insults. Rubio ridiculed Trump for having small hands, a reference to an old wives' tale alleging that small hands were indicative of a small sex organ. Trump responded in the next debate by boasting about his size, the first instance in American debate history in which a presidential contender made reference to his private parts. The exchange was out of character for Rubio and contributed to impressions that he had no effective strategy for countering Trump (Ceaser, Busch, and Pitney 2017, ch. 3). The final scheduled Republican debate of 2016 was cancelled when Trump backed out and John Kasich refused to debate without Trump present (Collins and Cheney 2016).

Because so many candidates were competing for the Republican nomination at the outset of the campaign, the first seven Republican debates were split into an "undercard" debate for lower-polling candidates and a primetime debate for the stronger candidates. Senator Rand Paul of Kentucky ultimately refused to participate in the undercard debate to which he was invited and held a virtual Twitter town hall meeting during the primetime debate instead.

Looking to 2020

For the 2020 nomination race, the Democratic Party planned on holding six candidate debates in 2019 (with the first on June 26–27) and another six in early 2020. Like Republicans in 2016, Democrats in 2020 had a surfeit of contenders. In order to accommodate all the people running, the Democrats announced that the first three debates would rely on a split format (Election Central 2019). To be eligible to participate in the first Democratic debate, candidates had to have received at least 1 percent support in three national polls or at least 65,000 individual donations. Eligibility requirements would become more stringent in subsequent debates. The Republican National Committee, on the other hand, voted to disband its primary debates committee and did not plan to officially sanction any primary debates for 2020. The decision recognized the strong support President Donald Trump enjoyed among Republican activists, but also made an uphill climb even harder for any Republican who might decide to challenge the incumbent (Berg 2018).

Caroline Peck provided research assistance on this chapter.

Sources

Baker, Russell. 1956. "Stevenson, Kefauver Find Agreement in TV Debate." *New York Times*, May 22, p. 1.

Benoit, William L., Glenn J. Hansen, and Kevin A. Stein. 2003. "Newspaper Coverage of Presidential Primary Debates." *Argumentation and Advocacy* 40, no. 4: 246–258. https://doi.org/10.1080/00028533.2004.11821610.

Benoit, William L., P. M. Pier, LeAnn M. Brazeal, John P. McHale, Andrew Klyukovski, and David Airne. 2002. *Primary Decision: A Functional Analysis of Debates in Presidential Primaries*. ProQuest Ebook Central. Westport, CT: Greenwood Publishing Group.

Berg, Rebecca. 2018. "Republican Party Nixes Debate Committee Ahead of 2020," CNN, May 3. https://www.cnn.com/2018/05/03/politics/rnc-2020-debates/index.html.

Best, Samuel J., and Clark Hubbard. 2000. "The Role of Televised Debates in the Presidential Nominating Process." In William G. Mayer, ed., *In Pursuit of the White House 2000: How We Choose Our Presidential Nominees*. Chatham, NJ: Chatham House, 2000.

Burns, Alexander. 2011. "Trump Debate Appearance Canceled." *Politico*, December 13. https://www.politico.com/blogs/burns-haberman/2011/12/trump-debate-appearance-canceled-107281.

Busch, Andrew E. 2005. *Reagan's Victory: The 1980 Elections and the Rise of the Right*. Lawrence: University Press of Kansas.

Busch, Andrew E. 2012. *Truman's Triumphs: The 1948 Election and the Making of Postwar America*. Lawrence: University Press of Kansas.

Campaign Reform: Insights and Evidence. 1998. Report of the Task Force on Campaign Reform. Princeton, NJ: Woodrow Wilson School of Public and International Affairs, Princeton University.

Ceaser, James W., Andrew E. Busch, and John J. Pitney, Jr. 2017. *Defying the Odds: The 2016 Elections and American Politics*. Lanham, MD: Rowman & Littlefield.

CNN. 2015. "Transcript of Democratic Debate." Las Vegas, October 13. http://cnnpressroom.blogs.cnn.com/2015/10/13/cnn-democratic-debate-full-transcript/.

Collins, Eliza, and Kyle Cheney. 2016. "GOP Debate Canceled after Trump, Kasich Pull Out." *Politico*, March 16. https://www.politico.com/story/2016/03 /politico-breaking-news-trump-says-he-will-skip-mondays-fox-news -debate-220854.

Dallos, Robert E. 1968. "McCarthy Challenges Humphrey to Debate Now." *New York Times,* July 22. https://timesmachine.nytimes.com/timesmachine /1968/07/22/76954058.pdf.

Davies, Lawrence E. 1948. "Candidates Work on Debate Plans." *New York Times*, May 17. https://timesmachine.nytimes.com/timesmachine/1948/05/17/88 120229.pdf.

Election Central. 2018a. "Republican Debate Schedule (2016 Primary Debates)." https://www.uspresidentialelectionnews.com/2016-debate-schedule /2016-republican-primary-debate-schedule/.

Election Central. 2018b. "Democratic Debate Schedule (2016 Primary Debates)." https://www.uspresidentialelectionnews.com/2016-debate-schedule /2016-democratic-primary-debate-schedule/.

Election Central. 2019. "2020 Democratic Debate Schedule (Primary Debates)." https://www.uspresidentialelectionnews.com/2020-debate-schedule /2020-democratic-debate-schedule/.

Elving, Ron. 2015. "Before Bright Lights and Rapid Fire, There Was 1948 and One Question." NPR, November 10. https://www.npr.org/2015/11/10/455 399441/before-bright-lights-and-rapid-fire-there-was-1948-and-one -question.

Fox News Politics. 2016. "GOP Candidate Lineup Announced for Fox Business Network Debate." January 11. http://www.foxnews.com/politics/2016/01/11 /gop-candidate-line-up-announced-for-fox-business-network-debate.html.

Gibson, Ginger. 2015. "Election 2016: GOP Announces Fewer Debates." *International Business Times*, January 16. http://www.ibtimes.com/election-2016 -gop-announces-fewer-debates-1786250.

Haberman, Maggie. 2011. "Trump to Moderate Newsmax-Sponsored Debate." *Politico*, December 2. https://www.politico.com/story/2011/12/trump-to -moderate-newsmax-sponsored-debate-069636.

Haberman, Maggie, and Nick Corasaniti. 2016. "Donald Trump, in Feud with Fox News, Shuns Debate." *New York Times*, January 26. https://www.ny times.com/2016/01/27/us/politics/trump-feud-fox-debate.html.

Kondik, Kyle, and Geoffrey Skelley. 2015. "Eight Decades of Debate: A Brief History of Presidential Primary Clashes." Sabato's Crystal Ball. University of Virginia Center for Politics. July 30. http://www.centerforpolitics.org /crystalball/articles/eight-decades-of-debate/.

Lanoue, David J., and Peter R. Schrott. 1989. "The Effects of Primary Season Debates on Public Opinion." *Political Behavior* 11, no. 3: 289–306. http:// www.jstor.org/stable/586156.

Miller, Jake. 2015. "Fox News Announces Participants in First 2016 GOP Debate." CBS News, August 4. https://www.cbsnews.com/news/fox-news-anno unces-participants-in-first-2016-gop-debate/.

"Presidential Debates." *The American Presidency Project.* http://www.presidency
.ucsb.edu/ws/index.php?pid=110903.

Sack, Kevin. 1996. "Atlanta Officials Abashed at the Arrest of a Candidate." *New York Times*, March 5, p. B8.

Turner, Wallace. 1968. "3 Rivals Meet in Debate; McGovern Wins Ovations." *New York Times*, August 27. https://timesmachine.nytimes.com/timesma chine/1968/07/22/76954058.pdf.

White, Daniel. 2016. "What Rand Paul Was Doing During the Republican Debate." *Time*, January 15. http://time.com/4181893/republican-debate -rand-paul-twitter-rally/.

Yawn, Mike, Kevin Ellsworth, Bob Beatty, and Kim Fridkin Kahn. 1998. "How a Presidential Primary Debate Changed Attitudes of Audience Members." *Political Behavior* 20, no. 2: 155–81. http://www.jstor.org/stable/586580.

CHAPTER EIGHT

Campaign Finance

For as long as there have been competitive electoral campaigns, there has been campaign spending. Candidates who are serious about winning have to pay for travel, for a staff to help them, and for varying means of communicating with voters. And for as long as there have been parties and candidates, there have been individuals and organizations eager to fund them, for reasons of either principle or self-interest.

Under the convention system, the cost of nomination campaigns was quite small. There were generally not open campaigns prior to the convention, so the bulk of the cost consisted of expenses connected with the convention itself. For the ambitious leading candidates, these might include the cost of hiring managers to corral votes or printing materials. Many candidates were not even aware that they would be considered until the convention itself, and spent nothing. If money was spent, it was raised from supportive benefactors with no limits on the size of donations and no requirement that donors be publicly identified.

Once primaries became part of the landscape in 1912, the campaign finance picture in presidential nominations changed considerably. Although candidates could still be drafted by the convention—and, as late as 1952, were—candidates could also run campaigns in one or more primaries. This required much greater expenditures of money, though, so campaign fundraising became a much higher priority. The demand for resources grew, but the supply of funds remained essentially unregulated (though there were a few rules in place from the early 20th century).

In the mid-1970s, the campaign finance situation changed dramatically again. This time the change affected both the demand for campaign spending and the supply of funds. The reforms of the early 1970s led to an explosion in the number of primaries and greater openness in many caucuses, thus again driving up the cost of a nomination campaign substantially. At the same time, the Federal Election Campaign Act Amendments of 1974 fundamentally altered the way candidates could raise money for a nomination campaign (as well as for a general election campaign). Since that time, the combination of a set of Supreme Court cases and practice by campaigns has shifted the landscape once again. This chapter will examine both the changing legal framework of nomination campaign finance and the costs of campaigning in the primaries and caucuses.

The Legal Framework of Campaign Finance

Prior to the early 20th century, there was essentially no regulation of campaign finance in either the nomination or general election stage. The first effort at federal campaign finance regulation focused on preventing contributions from certain types of organizations. In 1907 Congress passed the Tillman Act, which prohibited contributions to candidates for federal office by corporations and interstate banks. The Smith-Connally Act of 1943 and the Taft-Hartley Act of 1947 established an equal prohibition on contributions by labor unions. On the spending side, the Corrupt Practices Act of 1910, as amended in 1911 and 1925, put a limit on political party expenditures and on expenditures for U.S. House and U.S. Senate races, but did not affect presidential campaigns.

Those campaign finance rules stood alone until 1971, when the Federal Election Campaign Act was enacted. FECA required quarterly fundraising and expenditure disclosures and also established the legal framework for the creation of political action committees (or PACs). The legislation also established a voluntary $1 check-off on income tax forms to create a presidential election campaign fund. (In 1993, this amount was raised to $3.) Following revelations of underhanded campaign fundraising tactics in the 1972 campaign, Congress passed the Federal Election Campaign Act Amendments in 1974. This legislation was the most important and substantial campaign finance legislation to that point, and it remains a key part of the legal framework today. The FECA Amendments of 1974 included a number of elements:

- In order to encourage candidates to emphasize grassroots fundraising from small donors, candidates for a presidential nomination could receive 1–1 matching federal funds for the first $250 per donation. In order to be eligible for the matching funds, candidates had to raise at least $100,000—at least $5,000 in amounts of $250 or less from at least 20 states. Disbursement of federal matching funds were cut off if a candidate failed to win at least 10 percent of the vote in a primary on two consecutive primary dates.

- Candidates who accepted the federal funds had to accept spending limits. These spending limits were set state by state. There was also an aggregate national spending limit, which was an amount less than the sum of the state spending limits. Consequently, candidates had to set priorities; they could not spend up to the limit in every state without exceeding the national limit. Alternately, candidates could refuse federal funds, in which case they were not bound by the spending limits.

- Candidates could accept a contribution up to $1,000 for the nomination phase from any eligible individual.
- In the nomination phase, candidates could accept up to $5,000 from a political committee. However, unlike individual contributions, donations from PACs were not eligible for matching funds.
- Campaign contributions and expenditures had to be reported by the campaign quarterly.
- The Federal Election Commission was established to oversee the law and receive campaign reports.

In 1976, the Supreme Court issued a landmark decision in *Buckley v. Valeo*, a case brought by a plaintiff challenging several portions of the FECA Amendments. Though the case related specifically to the legislation's treatment of congressional elections, it had implications for presidential elections as well. The two most important findings in *Buckley v. Valeo* as they related to presidential nominations were these:

- Federal contribution limits could not be applied to the candidates themselves, who on free speech grounds had to be free to loan or give their campaigns an unlimited amount of their own money.
- Outside individuals or political committees had the right, also on free speech grounds, to spend unlimited amounts supporting or opposing a candidate as long as the spending was not coordinated with any campaign. On the other hand, direct contributions to candidates' campaigns could be limited in order to prevent corruption or the appearance of corruption.

The next major campaign finance legislation was the Bipartisan Campaign Reform Act (BCRA) of 2002. The background to BCRA was that the political parties had taken advantage of a loophole in the 1974 legislation to raise unlimited amounts of money from donors, including individuals, political committees, corporations, and labor unions, for "party building" reasons. This so-called "soft money" was channeled into "educational" television ads that attacked or praised a candidate but fell just outside the definition of a campaign ad because the words "vote for" or "vote against" were not used. BCRA banned unlimited soft money donations. It also established windows outside of which "issue advertising" by outside groups including a for-profit or nonprofit corporation or a group using corporate or union treasury funds was prohibited (30 days prior to a primary election and 60 days prior to a general election). To redirect some money back toward candidate campaigns, BCRA increased the individual contribution limit, which had been fixed at $1,000 since 1974, to $2,000 and adjusted it to inflation every two years.

Since BCRA, several controversial Supreme Court decisions have bolstered the power of outside groups and individuals to spend money to affect presidential nomination races. These decisions included:

- *FEC v. Wisconsin Right-to-Life Inc.* (2007): The Supreme Court ruled that BCRA's prohibition of issue advertising within 30 days of a primary or caucus was an unconstitutional infringement on free speech unless the advertising was engaged in explicit electioneering urging voters to vote for or against a particular candidate (*FEC v. Wisconsin Right-to-Life* 2007).

- *Citizens United v. Federal Election Commission* (2010): Prior to the 2008 Democratic primaries, a nonprofit corporation called Citizens United produced an anti–Hillary Clinton video, which it aired on television. The Federal Election Commission ruled that the video constituted illegal campaign spending, as corporations were prohibited from spending money on federal races. Citizens United challenged the FEC decision in court. The Supreme Court ruling overturned the FEC judgment by invalidating the federal law prohibiting corporations or labor unions from making independent expenditures in federal races. The ruling let stand the ban on direct corporate or labor contributions to campaigns (*Citizens United v. FEC* 2010).

  The *Citizens United* decision was condemned by President Barack Obama, and Democrats in the Senate voted in favor of a constitutional amendment that would overturn the decision. Critics saw the decision as opening the floodgates to unlimited corporate spending on federal races. They particularly objected to the Court's willingness to afford corporations free speech rights (though the fact that labor unions were also freed to spend was rarely mentioned). Defenders of the decision, including the American Civil Liberties Union, applauded the broadening of free speech rights and warned that the proposed constitutional amendment could easily be abused to inhibit speech by disfavored groups or the press. The *New York Times*, they noted, was also a corporation (ACLU 2014).

- In *SpeechNOW.org v. Federal Election Commission*, a federal appellate court drew on the rulings in *Buckley v. Valeo* and *Citizens United* to conclude that an outside group could accept unlimited donations as long as all of its spending went for independent expenditures (*SpeechNOW.org v. FEC* 2010). The decision was not reviewed by the Supreme Court, and so it stands as the relevant precedent as of mid-2019. Between them, *Citizens United* and *SpeechNOW* launched the phenomenon of "Super PACs," political action committees that could accept unlimited donations and spend unlimited funds because they engaged in independent expenditures only.

Overall, since the point of maximum regulation by Congress in 1974, the Supreme Court has made it easier for groups or individuals to spend large amounts of money supporting or opposing candidates, as long as those expenditures are not made in coordination with the campaign.

Nomination Campaign Finances

Prior to the 1974 FECA Amendments, it was common for candidates to receive large donations from supportive benefactors. In 1968, Robert F. Kennedy raised and spent $11 million in 11 weeks, a feat made possible by some very large contributions. In 1972, in the crucial days between his Wisconsin win and the California primary, George McGovern received donations ranging from $10,000 to $300,000, while a pledge of matching funds from Stewart Mott of the General Motors fortune brought McGovern a total of $400,000 (Busch 1997, 103).

The capacity of candidates to raise funds for their campaigns has long served as an early test of the campaign's viability. This has especially been true since the 1970s, since the cost of campaigning has risen dramatically and since the FECA requires periodic disclosure of how much money campaigns have raised. Today, political scientist Stephen J. Wayne notes that "the amount of money donated to a campaign's war chest and Super PACs supporting that candidate is frequently viewed by the press as a harbinger of their future success or failure" (Wayne 2016, 120). As Wayne notes, fundraising success leads to other benefits, including endorsements from public officials and interest groups and enhanced news media visibility.

Even before 1974, some campaigns had experimented with a new form of fundraising: direct mail aimed at small donors. Barry Goldwater pioneered this form, raising a record amount from small contributors in 1964 (Alexander 1966, 179–180). McGovern, alongside his mammoth take from Stewart Mott and others, also utilized direct mail to great effect, raising $5 million from 100,000 donors prior to the Democratic convention (Schlesinger 1975, 195–199). However, the 1974 legislation, with its promise of matching federal funds for small contributions, accelerated the trend toward direct mail. In the heyday of utilization of the matching funds provision, nearly all candidates tapped into federal matching funds and almost all made at least a serious effort to raise money by direct mail. Candidates perceived as antiestablishment outsiders, including George Wallace and Ronald Reagan, tended to be among the most successful at direct mail. From 1976 until 1996, every candidate for major party nomination accepted federal matching funds except for one: former Texas governor and Treasury secretary John Connally, who sought the Republican nomination in 1980. Connally, who was a prolific fundraiser, set the dubious record of spending more money per delegate won than any other contender in 1980 (Busch 2005).

However, the matching funds system had a great weakness, which was that candidates had to commit themselves to spending limits that, by the turn of the century, they could easily exceed by raising money on their own. Moreover, since *Buckley v. Valeo* in 1976, wealthy candidates had had the capacity to spend unlimited amounts of their own money on their own campaigns. There were ways of evading the spending limits in some cases; campaigns were notorious for renting their cars for New Hampshire campaigning or purchasing some of their ads designed for the New Hampshire primary in Boston, where the spending would legally apply to the Massachusetts spending limit (Norrander 2010, 36). Nevertheless, the spending limits proved too constricting and other fundraising opportunities too enticing.

The first crack in the system appeared in 1996, when wealthy publisher Steve Forbes ran for the Republican presidential nomination. Forbes chose to forego federal matching funds and self-finance his primary campaign so he would not be bound by the spending limits. He spent upward of $4 million in Iowa, leading in polls there for a time before falling back into fifth place. Overall, Forbes spent $37 million of his own money in his unsuccessful 1996 bid for the Republican nomination, and another $32 million when he ran again in 2000 (Wayne 2000).

Kansas senator Bob Dole won the Republican nomination in 1996, but reached his spending limit two months before the Republican convention. Incumbent president Bill Clinton, having spent very little in his uncontested renomination race, was able to concentrate his fire on Dole with little response. Having observed both Forbes's expensive and briefly successful gambit in Iowa and Dole's underfinanced struggles at the end of the primary season, Republican George W. Bush decided in 2000 to follow Forbes's path. Bush also declined the matching funds, freeing him to spend as much as he could raise. Unlike Forbes, Bush did not self-finance, but he did prove highly successful at raising money from large donors who could "max out" their $1,000 contributions. In the Republican nomination race of that year, Bush raised $60 million. That year, it was Democratic nominee Al Gore, who had accepted federal funds and spending limits in his nomination race, who had to cope for several months of the general election campaign with insufficient funds.

The 2000 campaign was important for another reason too, as John McCain successfully pioneered the use of the Internet to raise money (Glasser 2000). The Internet quickly supplanted direct mail as the most effective and important way to raise small contributions in large numbers. Candidates including McCain, Howard Dean, Barack Obama, Ron Paul, Bernie Sanders, and Donald Trump were particularly successful at this strategy. In January 2008, Obama raised an estimated 87 percent of his funds online; in February, he raised another $55 million without holding a single fundraiser (Steger, Dowdle, and Adkins 2012, 16; Corrado 2012). In 2016, Trump and Sanders were the two leaders in small contributions, with Trump setting new records (Sherfinsky 2017; Megerian 2016).

In 2004, the first election after BCRA, it was even easier to raise money from large donors, as the contribution limit had doubled to $2,000. Bush and Democrats John Kerry and Howard Dean all declined the matching funds, bringing closer the collapse of the matching funds system. Four years later, only three candidates in both parties combined accepted matching funds. No major party nominees, and almost no other candidates for nomination, have accepted the matching funds since then. In 2016, Democrat Martin O'Malley was the only one of 23 major-party presidential aspirants to accept matching funds (Scott-Sheets 2016). (Not until 2008 did a candidate—Barack Obama—turn down the federal general election funds, the other part of the 1974 FECA Amendments funding system.)

Thus, since 2008, candidates for nomination have nearly all eschewed the federal matching funds, believing (in most cases, correctly) that they could raise and spend more without them. No longer constrained by federal spending limits, campaign spending on primaries and caucuses took an upward course. Shortly thereafter, the *Citizens United* and *SpeechNOW* court decisions led to the creation of Super PACs that could raise and spend unlimited amounts of money on independent expenditures.

The result was a rapid growth of outside spending on presidential nomination races. Two types of Super PACs emerged. Some Super PACs were just like regular political action committees—groups with an issue agenda that supported candidates at several levels—except limited to independent expenditures. Examples included Americans for Prosperity, founded by the libertarian-leaning Koch brothers, and Next Gen Climate Action Committee, funded by liberal Tom Steyer. Other Super PACs were a reincarnation of the benefactors of old—groups organized with the sole purpose of supporting a particular candidate for president.

In 2012, Mitt Romney and Barack Obama benefited most from Super PACs that were formed on their behalf, often by wealthy supporters. Although most Republican aspirants enjoyed the support of a single-candidate Super PAC, only those supporting three candidates spent more than a million dollars: Newt Gingrich ($17 million), Rick Perry ($4 million), and Jon Huntsman ($2.8 million) (OpenSecrets 2012). Sheldon Adelson and his wife drew attention when they formed the Super PAC for Gingrich and contributed $10 million to it.

In 2016, the phenomenon grew tremendously in importance. Among Republicans, Jeb Bush, Marco Rubio, Chris Christie, Lindsey Graham, Carly Fiorina, Ben Carson, Mike Huckabee, Bobby Jindal, Scott Walker, and Rick Perry each had a Super PAC devoted to their cause. John Kasich and Rand Paul benefited from two Super PACs, while Ted Cruz had four. A Super PAC was formed by supporters of Donald Trump, but he asked them to desist and

Table 8.1   Spending by Campaigns and Outside Groups in 2016 Presidential Nomination Campaign

"Also-ran" Candidates Totaling More Than $10 Million (in millions of dollars)			
Candidate	Campaign	Outside Groups	Total
Bernie Sanders D	228.1	.9	229.0
Marco Rubio R	52.3	110.5	162.8
Jeb Bush R	34.1	121.8	155.9
Ted Cruz R	89.5	53.7	143.2
Ben Carson R	63.3	19.1	82.4
John Kasich R	18.9	15.6	34.5
Scott Walker R	8.5	25.2	33.7
Chris Christie R	8.4	23.9	32.3
Carly Fiorina R	12.0	14.6	26.6
Rand Paul R	12.1	11.8	23.9
Rick Perry R	1.4	15.2	16.6
Lindsey Graham R	5.9	5.2	11.1
Mike Huckabee R	4.3	6.1	10.4

Source: OpenSecrets, "Also-rans: 2016 Presidential Race." http://www.opensecrets.org /pres16/also-rans.

they spent a minimal amount of money. Like Trump, Bernie Sanders rejected Super PAC help and raised a large amount for his own campaign in small donations (though a national nurses PAC wound up spending a modest amount on his behalf). Hillary Clinton had the substantial support of at least three Super PACs (Ready PAC, Priorities USA Action, and Correct the Record), but her own campaign raised and spent much more. Overall levels of funding by the candidates' own campaign and outside spending—both by Super PACs devoted to a candidate and others—can be seen in Table 8.1. Among 7 of the 13 candidates who fell short of the nomination, the candidates' own campaign spent less than outside groups spent on their behalf, though that was true of neither of the winners.

Aside from Super PACs, which must report donations they receive in excess of $200, outside groups organized in different legal forms have also played an increasing role in presidential nominations, elections, and other American elections. So-called 527 groups first filled the vacuum left by BCRA's prohibition on soft money donations to the parties. These groups, named after Section 527 of the U.S. Internal Revenue Code, are political organizations organized for the purpose of influencing elections. They can raise and spend unlimited amounts, but are required to disclose their donors and expenditures. They first gained prominence in 2004, when George Soros and the Swift Boat Veterans for Truth organized 527s on opposite sides of that year's presidential elections. Other groups operate under Internal Revenue Code Section 501(C)(4) ("social welfare" organizations), Section 501(C)(5) (labor organizations), or as 501(C)(6) organizations. The major purpose of these groups is to promote policy or educate the public on policy issues. These nonprofit organizations are allowed to accept donations that are not disclosed—so-called "dark money"—and to engage in politics, as long as less than 50 percent of their expenditures are political in nature. Total election spending by nondisclosing groups rose from $2.35 million in 2010 to $27.0 million in 2016 (OpenSecrets 2018). Connected with these groups, the phenomenon of "dark money" has drawn attention, as groups organized this way can raise money without disclosures and then donate it to Super PACs.

These trends in campaign finance have spawned an intense debate. Some analysts are deeply troubled by the large infusion of outside money into the nomination races. To these analysts, the return of big money into the process marks a blow against democracy because that big money threatens to drown out the voices of the majority of Americans with modest means. Noting that about half of the $181 million raised by Super PACs in the 2012 election cycle came from 200 very wealthy people, Fred Wertheimer, former head of the group Common Cause, contended:

> Super PACs are a game for millionaires and billionaires. They are a game for corporations and other wealthy interests. Meanwhile, citizens are pushed to the sidelines to watch the corruption of our democracy. (Wertheimer 2012)

Some observers also suggested that the infusion of big money made it less likely that ordinary Americans would make small contributions to presidential candidates in the future, and some linked it to the decline in public participation in the federal campaign funding tax check-off, which fell from 29 percent of taxpayers in 1980 to 6 percent in 2013 (Overby 2015). Critics questioned whether it was realistic to expect that candidate Super PACs would actually remain independent from the candidates they were seeking to aid, a presumption underlying federal court decisions including *Buckley v. Valeo*, *Citizens United*, and *SpeechNOW*. In the view of some, "In practice, the independence is fiction. Super PACs are typically run by a candidate's close aides, but it's hard to prove illegal coordination" (*USA Today* 2015). Even if they were not somehow influenced or instructed by the candidates, critics think it unlikely that the candidates themselves will not be influenced by the agenda of the Super PAC's founders. Opponents of Super PACs also assert that most Super PAC independent expenditures are devoted to negative advertising that attacks opposing candidates rather than positive advertising touting preferred candidates (Sonmez 2012). This trend, say critics, has contributed to the ugliness of contemporary American politics. Focusing on 501(C) groups, others have criticized the lack of transparency.

Other analysts are untroubled, pointing out that little correlation could be found between the money spent on candidates' behalf by Super PACs and the ultimate outcomes of primary races. On the Republican side in 2016, of the five major candidates—Trump, Bush, Cruz, Kasich, and Rubio—Bush had the most Super PAC support and Trump the least. Yet Trump won the nomination and Bush was the first of the five to drop out of the race after disappointing finishes in Iowa, New Hampshire, and South Carolina. Sanders had no Super PAC operating on his behalf, yet he nearly matched Clinton in overall fundraising in the primaries, and Clinton did not clinch the nomination until the final week of primaries. And, despite concerns to the contrary, it does not seem that Super PACs have discouraged individual contributions in reality: two of the top three record hauls of contributions from small donors have occurred after the rise of Super PACs (Obama in 2008 and 2012 and Trump in 2016) (Campaign Finance Institute 2017).

Another argument could be made that Super PACs actually have a positive role. They could play much the same role as major donors did for Robert Kennedy, Eugene McCarthy, and George McGovern, keeping a candidate afloat to continue campaigning even after setbacks in early primaries and caucuses. Though Super PACs did not fulfill this role for Bush, whose failure at the polls was too complete to be salvaged, they may well have contributed to the capacity of candidates like Cruz, Rubio, and Kasich in 2016 and Newt Gingrich in 2012 to carry on the fight when 20 years before they might have been forced from the field much earlier. As Bradley A. Smith, chair of the Center for Competitive Politics, argues,

> Before super PACs, if a presidential candidate didn't do well in Iowa and New Hampshire, his campaign typically ended for lack of money. In 2012, however, super PACs kept campaigns of candidates such as Newt Gingrich and Rick Santorum alive. They didn't ultimately win, but they did win primaries and millions of votes, and, more important, gave Americans more time to consider and debate the candidates and issues. (Smith 2015)

To the extent that is true, Super PACs have contributed to mitigating the ill effects of front-loading, and may even have contributed to the partial unwinding of front-loading that has taken place since 2008. As evidence that they have made American elections more competitive all the way down the ballot, one can observe that incumbent reelection rates in congressional elections have also fallen since Super PACs began operating in 2010. According to the defenders of Super PACs, they have an additional benefit: they contribute to voter knowledge and allow candidates to spend more time meeting with voters rather than fundraising (Smith 2015).

Sources

ACLU. 2014. Statement for Senate Hearing on Udall Amendment. June 3. https://www.aclu.org/other/aclu-statement-senate-hearing-udall-amendment.

Alexander, Herbert E. 1966. "Financing the Parties and Campaigns." In Milton C. Cummings Jr., ed., *The National Election of 1964*. Washington, DC: Brookings Institution.

Buckley v. Valeo, 424 U.S. 1 (1976).

Busch, Andrew E. 1997. *Outsiders and Openness in the Presidential Nominating System*. Pittsburgh: University of Pittsburgh Press.

Busch, Andrew E. 2005. *Reagan's Victory: The 1980 Elections and the Rise of the Right*. Lawrence: University Press of Kansas.

Campaign Finance Institute. 2017. "President Trump, with RNC Help, Raised More Small Donor Money Than President Obama; As Much As Clinton and Sanders Combined." February 21. http://www.cfinst.org/Press/PRe leases/17-02-21/President_Trump_with_RNC_Help_Raised_More _Small_Donor_Money_than_President_Obama_As_Much_As_Clinton _and_Sanders_Combined.aspx.

Citizens United v. Federal Election Commission, 558 U.S. 310 (2010).

Corrado, Anthony. 2012. "Financing Presidential Nominations in the Post-Public Funding Era." In William G. Mayer and Jonathan Bernstein, eds., *The Making of the Presidential Candidates 2012*. Lanham, MD: Rowman & Littlefield.

Federal Election Commission v. Wisconsin Right to Life, Inc., 551 U.S. 449 (2007).

Glasser, Jeff. 2000. "Virtual Campaign Pays Off." *U.S. News & World Report*, March 6, p. 22.

Megerian, Chris. 2016. "Bernie Sanders Rode Wave of Small Donations in Democratic Primary." *Los Angeles Times*, July 12. http://www.latimes.com /politics/la-na-trailguide-updates-bernie-sanders-rode-wave-of-small -1468337592-htmlstory.html.

Norrander, Barbara. 2010. *The Imperfect Primary: Oddities, Biases, and Strengths of U.S. Presidential Nomination Politics*. New York: Routledge.

OpenSecrets. 2012. "2012 Outside Spending by Single-Candidate Super PACs." https://www.opensecrets.org/outsidespending/summ.php?cycle=2012&c hrt=V&disp=O&type=C.

OpenSecrets. 2018. "Dark Money Basics." OpenSecrets.org. https://www.open secrets.org/dark-money/basics.

Overby, Peter. 2015. "You Didn't Check the 'Presidential Election Campaign' Box on Your Taxes, Did You?" NPR, April 15. https://www.npr.org/sections /itsallpolitics/2015/04/15/399699566/you-didnt-check-the-presidential -election-campaign-box-on-your-taxes-did-you.

Schlesinger, Stephen C., Jr. 1975. *The New Reformers.* Boston: Houghton Mifflin.

Scott-Sheets, Jason. 2016. "Public Financing Is Available for Presidential Candidates. So What's Not to Like About Free Money?" Open Secrets, April 14, 2016. https://www.opensecrets.org/news/2016/04/public-financing-is-available-for-presidential-candidates-so-whats-not-to-like-about-free-money/.

Sherfinsky, David. 2017. "Trump Smashes Obama's Small-Donor Fundraising Pace, Bests Clinton, Sanders Combined." *Washington Times*, February 21. https://www.washingtontimes.com/news/2017/feb/21/trump-smashes-obamas-small-donor-fundraising-pace/.

Smith, Bradley A. 2015. "Super PACs Are Not the Problem: Opposing View." *USA Today*, May 25. https://www.usatoday.com/story/opinion/2015/05/25/super-pacs-center-for-competitive-politics-editorials-debates/27928735/.

Sonmez, Felicia. 2012. "Negative Ads: Is It the Campaigns, or the Super PACs?" *Washington Post*, March 22. https://www.washingtonpost.com/blogs/election-2012/post/negative-ads-is-it-the-campaigns-or-the-super-pacs-thursdays-trail-mix/2012/03/22/gIQAOf8VTS_blog.html.

SpeechNOW.org v. Federal Election Commission, 599 F.3d 686 (D.C. Cir. 2010).

Steger, Wayne P., Andrew J. Dowdle, and Randall E. Adkins. 2012. "Why Are Presidential Nomination Races So Difficult to Forecast?" In William G. Mayer and Jonathan Bernstein, eds., *The Making of the Presidential Candidates 2012*. Lanham, MD: Rowman & Littlefield.

USA Today. 2015. "2016 Presidential Campaigns Chase Money, with No Cop on the Beat: Our View." May 25. https://www.usatoday.com/story/opinion/2015/05/25/campaign-finance-super-pacs-federal-election-commission-editorials-debates/27928689/.

Wayne, Leslie. 2000. "The 2000 Campaign: The End; Forbes Spent Millions, But for Little Gain." *New York Times*, February 10. https://www.nytimes.com/2000/02/10/us/the-2000-campaign-the-end-forbes-spent-millions-but-for-little-gain.html.

Wayne, Stephen J. 2016. *The Road to the White House 2016.* New York: Cengage.

Wertheimer, Fred. 2012. "Super PACs a Disaster for Democracy." CNN, February 12. https://www.cnn.com/2012/02/15/opinion/wertheimer-super-pacs/index.html.

CHAPTER NINE

Voting Behavior

As in general elections for president, voters in presidential primaries and caucuses demonstrate certain voting patterns. The sum of these patterns is what political scientists call "voting behavior." There are some commonalities between voting behavior in general elections and nomination contests, but there are also significant differences. The first question is who actually votes.

Who Votes in Primaries and Caucuses

In general, many more voters vote for president in general elections than in primaries, and many more vote in primaries than in caucuses. In the four presidential general elections from 2004 to 2016, the average estimated turnout of the voting-eligible population was 60.4 percent; in 2016, it was 60.2 percent (United States Elections Project 2018a). On the other hand, the average turnout in presidential primaries in 2016 was 27.4 percent of eligible voters, and the average turnout in the caucus states that calculated participation was 7.4 percent. The highest primary and caucus turnouts in 2016 were recorded in the first two contests, 15.7 percent in the Iowa caucuses and 52.4 percent in the New Hampshire primary. No other caucus in 2016 recorded turnout above 8.2 percent, while no other primary had better than a 39.8 percent turnout of eligible voters (United States Elections Project 2018b). Turnout patterns in 2016 were typical of previous years.

The group of Americans who turn out for primaries and caucuses are also not simple microcosms of the general election electorate. Although it is frequently assumed that primary voters distort the nominating process, scholar Barbara Norrander notes:

> In most years, the presidential primary electorate is composed of those who are slightly older, slightly more partisan, more interested in politics,

and more aware of the candidates and the issues. Most scholarly studies find few differences between presidential primary voters and nonvoting members of their party on issues positions or candidate preferences. Nor are presidential primary voters distinctive in their ideological positions. Rather than being a more ideologically extreme proportion of the electorate, presidential primary voters are more aptly described as the slightly more interested and knowledgeable segment of the electorate. (Norrander 2010, 63)

On the other hand, as one might expect with a much smaller turnout, there is evidence that caucus-goers are more significantly unrepresentative. Whether compared with primary voters, the party's general election voters, or party identifiers as a whole, caucus participants have been shown to have much higher incomes, much higher levels of education, much more pronounced levels of ideological commitment, and much stronger party attachment (Mayer 1996, 129–136). As discussed in Chapter 4, some primaries and caucuses limit the electorate to members of the party, while others allow both members of the party and independents, or even any voter, to vote.

How Primary and Caucus Voters Decide

General election voters take into account a number of factors when making their choice among candidates. Those factors include party, specific issue positions, general philosophy of government, experience, character, and retrospective evaluations of performance in office by the candidates or their parties. These all come into play in primary and caucus voter choice, as well, but usually in different degrees than in the general election. There are also some additional factors that affect vote choice during the nomination contest, but are essentially absent in the general election.

One important difference from the outset is that, for most voters, the general election contest resolves itself to a binary choice between the Democratic and Republican nominees. Of course, other choices exist, including third-party or independent candidates and the ever-present and frequently utilized option of not voting. However, for those who choose to vote, the two major party candidates are usually seen as the only ones who might possibly win. Nomination contests are much different, frequently featuring many more than two viable choices available to voters. In the early stages of the 2016 Republican contest, for example, there were 17 presidential aspirants. Twelve of them were still in contention when voters attended the first caucuses in Iowa. Democrats had a simpler affair, which was quickly reduced to a choice between Hillary Clinton and Bernie Sanders, but even there the initial field consisted of five candidates. In the early months of the 2020 Democratic nomination race, there were as many as 26 candidates.

Connected with this lack of a binary structure is the fact that party plays a significantly different role in primary vote choice than during the general election. In November, party identification is the single best predictor of the vote. According to CNN exit polls in the last four elections, Democrats voted for the Democratic nominee 89 (2004), 89 (2008), 92 (2012), and 89 (2016) percent of the time. Likewise, Republicans in the electorate voted for the Republican presidential candidate 93, 90, 93, and 88 percent of the time. Because the primaries feature intraparty contests among Republicans and among Democrats, party plays less role in guiding vote choice. In other words, the dominant cue for voters in the general election is largely absent in the primaries and caucuses.

However, as scholar William G. Mayer has shown, it would be mistaken to say that party plays no role. Indeed, under certain circumstances, party can be a surprisingly large factor. Because many states hold open or semiopen primaries or caucuses, the electorate includes many nonparty members, usually independents, comprising around one-fourth of all primary voters. Sometimes those nonparty voters have significantly different preferences than party identifiers in the same primary. The usual condition under which this difference becomes evident is when one candidate in the field seems to be the representative of the "regular" party while another is widely understood to be an outsider or party nonconformist. In that case, non-Republicans voting in a Republican primary might be drawn rather intentionally toward the banner of the candidate they perceive as least like a "standard" Republican. Similarly, non-Democrats voting in a Democratic primary might be more likely to vote for the Democratic candidate they see as most different from a traditional or establishment Democrat in some way. In 2016, this phenomenon took the form of independent voters in open primaries voting for Bernie Sanders at much higher rates than registered Democrats did. Other striking examples of this phenomenon came in 2000, when John McCain won 60 percent of the independent vote in the Republican primaries while gaining only 31 percent of the Republican vote. In the same year Bill Bradley won 43 percent of the independent vote but only 22 percent of votes cast by Democrats (Mayer 2008).

Another unique feature of primary election voting behavior that results from the multicandidate, same-party nomination field is that "strategic voting" plays a much larger role than in the general election. Strategic voting is "a decision by a voter to cast a ballot for a less preferred candidate who has a better chance of winning an election than marking the ballot for the most preferred candidate with a lesser chance of winning the election" (Norrander 2010, 107). In the general election, strategic voting is a factor for voters who might be attracted to a third-party or independent candidate, but who ultimately choose to vote for a major party candidate to avoid "wasting their vote" on a likely loser. In the primaries the bulk of voters are not locked into a vote choice by party loyalty, so there is much broader scope for strategic voting.

This might take the form of voters choosing a candidate they consider more "viable" than their sincere preference—that is, more likely to have a chance to win the nomination—or the candidate they consider more "electable"—that is, more likely to be able to win the general election.

In particular, concern with electability is a factor only in primary voting. The purpose of the primaries and caucuses is to nominate the party's candidate for president, and it is natural that many party voters will take into consideration not only which candidate they like best on the merits but which candidate has the best chance to win the general election. Although there is debate over the exact mechanism, there is strong scholarly evidence that the average primary voter puts a significant weight on electability.

In the general election, perceptions of performance in office by the incumbent or incumbent's party—especially as regards the economy—is the second most critical factor driving vote choice behind simple party identification. If the economy is going well, the president and his or her party generally benefits at the ballot box; if not, the president and his or her party suffers. Again, in the primaries, intraparty contests scramble this common device for vote choice (Steger, Dowdle, and Adkins 2012, 11). However, approval of the president's job performance remains an important factor in primaries featuring an incumbent running for renomination, especially if the incumbent is facing a serious challenger, as well as in primaries in which a sitting vice president is seeking nomination. Primary voters who approved of Ronald Reagan and Bill Clinton were much more likely to vote for the vice presidents in their administrations—George H. W. Bush in 1988 and Al Gore in 2000— than voters who did not. Support for Clinton was the single strongest variable explaining a primary vote for Gore (Mayer 2008, 179–183).

Issues and general philosophy or orientation toward government can also play a part in voter choice in the primaries, as in the general election. On the Democratic side, the issue of the Vietnam War in 1968 and 1972 and the Iraq War in 2008 played an important part in the campaigns and voter choice. On the Republican side in 1988, taxes and the Intermediate Nuclear Forces (INF) Treaty with the Soviet Union were major issues emphasized by the candidates and taken into account by the voters.

Likewise, some voters look for "centrists," while others press the lever for the "true conservative" or "authentic progressive." For many years in Republican nomination contests, the winning candidate was the one who successfully put together a coalition of self-described "very conservative" and "somewhat conservative" primary voters. In 2016, Donald Trump upended that pattern, building over time a coalition of "somewhat conservative" and "moderate" voters, while the "very conservative" were more likely to gravitate toward rival Ted Cruz. In most of the crucial primaries, Hillary Clinton did 10 to 15 percentage points better among self-described "moderate" voters than among the "very liberal" (CNN 2016a).

While important, the impact of issues and governing philosophy is mixed. On one hand, the voters who participate in primaries and (especially) in caucuses are more likely than the average voter to be knowledgeable about issues and to have a coherent ideological framework for understanding politics. For these reasons, such factors may be more important in certain primary contests. On the other hand, there is usually less difference in a primary between the candidates on these dimensions. In most nomination contests, one is hard-pressed to find a Democratic aspirant who touts his support from the National Rifle Association, who contends that the rich are already taxed enough, or who questions abortion rights. Republican candidates who oppose tax cuts, call for stronger gun control, or endorse *Roe v. Wade* are equally scarce. Candidates who try to break out of the mold, like former Pennsylvania senator Arlen Specter, who ran for the 2000 Republican nomination on a vehemently pro-choice platform, or former Virginia senator Jim Webb, who told a Democratic debate audience in late 2015 that he was proud of his lethal action against the enemy during the Vietnam War, do not typically remain in the race for long. Counterexamples can be found—including Donald Trump, who deviated from GOP orthodoxy in several ways—but only under certain favorable circumstances.

What party voters are sometimes willing to tolerate for the sake of electability is a deviation from a losing script, as long as key positional and coalitional commitments of the party are preserved. Hence, Bill Clinton in 1992 and George W. Bush in 2000 were able to attract a winning collection of their party's primary voters by offering a "New Democrat" approach (in the former case) or a "compassionate conservatism" (in the latter) that seemed to build out from their party's traditions without repudiating them. Without attaching a label to his effort, Donald Trump in 2016 also discarded part of his party's longstanding issue checklist, while maintaining core Republican commitments on abortion, guns, tax cuts, and judicial conservatism. In any event, the evidence is that ideology has the greatest effect on the vote for second- or third-tier candidates who fill an ideological niche (Mayer 2008, 191).

Experience is another candidate attribute that can affect vote choice in the primaries. Indeed, since party is usually not a cue and issues and ideology usually do not divide the candidates as much in the primaries as in the general election, factors such as experience, character, and temperament can become more decisive for voters. Character has traditionally included perceptions of honesty and integrity, courage, strength, and dependability. In recent decades it has broadened to include softer character traits such as compassion and empathy; Bill Clinton's famous declaration "I feel your pain" was aimed at voters looking for empathy in their candidate, as was George H. W. Bush's much-ridiculed "Message: I care." Temperament refers to the ability to withstand the pressures of the office without losing composure or abusing power.

While most voters value good character in a presidential candidate, the character trait they value most can shift depending on circumstances. In 2016, a plurality of Republican primary voters supported Donald Trump despite evidence that he did not possess many of the character traits that would once have been expected. However, their assessment was that the circumstances most called for a certain pugnaciousness, authenticity, and candor (if not always honesty), which they attributed to Trump.

Experience by a candidate also factors into vote choice in a more complex way than might be assumed. If every voter wants good character but agreement on what that means is elusive, past political experience is a complicated candidate trait because not everyone wants it. To the contrary, moments arise in which a large proportion of the electorate deliberately prefers candidates who are not tainted by long association with the political "establishment."

In those moments, one can say that a spirit of "outsiderism" is ascendant. Experience in Washington loses its luster for many voters, and independence from the establishment becomes the dominant desire. In 1992, the nation experienced a moment of outsiderism. Pat Buchanan challenged President George H. W. Bush in the Republican primaries, giving the incumbent a scare in New Hampshire before fading, while Arkansas governor Bill Clinton offered a relatively moderate form of outsiderism—outside of the Washington establishment, but not devoid of substantial political experience (Ceaser and Busch 1993). (This trend toward outsiderism was also evident in the general election that year, when independent Ross Perot won nearly one in five votes nationwide.) Voters were again in a mood of outsiderism in 2008, when Hillary Clinton's supposedly inevitable campaign march to the Democratic nomination was upended by Barack Obama, who had served only three years in the U.S. Senate at the time of the Iowa caucuses. (Gallup polls in the fall of 2007 anticipated Clinton's difficulty when they showed that nearly three-fourths of Democratic voters preferred change to experience [Jones 2007]). And in the outsider year of 2016, Clinton managed with difficulty to hold on to the Democratic nomination against Bernie Sanders, who had not even been a registered Democrat, only to lose in the end to Donald Trump, who, without any political or military experience, had seized the GOP nomination against 16 more experienced rivals.

One additional, largely subconscious, factor influencing vote choice in primaries but not general elections is "momentum." Although there is certainly the potential for general election candidates to develop an intangible momentum due to events in the campaign such as a successful convention or debate, there is still only one election. The results of the general election cannot affect a subsequent election. The nomination contest, on the other hand, consists of a sequence of state primaries or caucuses starting in Iowa and stretching over several months. The sequential nature of the nomination process means that voters in later contests can be influenced by results of earlier contests. When the relatively unknown Jimmy Carter came in first among Democratic candidates in Iowa and then won the New Hampshire primary, his momentum carried him to the 1976 Democratic nomination. Since then, many underdogs have sought to emulate Carter's success. Some, like Gary Hart in 1984, have had qualified success, enjoying a brief momentum-driven surge before falling to the front-runner's superior resources. Another form of momentum is frequently observable in which the front-runner briefly falters, reestablishes himself, then wins a crucial primary and sets things right, after which party voters move decisively in his or her direction. At the very least, early contests establish the field of viable options for later voters. (For varying scholarly views on the role of momentum, see Bartels 1988; Mayer 2004.)

Voting Blocs and Primary Voting Behavior

Although voters in general utilize the factors discussed above to form their vote choice, it is a truism of voting behavior that different groups of voters often process those factors differently. In the general election electorate, white voters tend to lean Republican, while racial minorities lean more heavily Democratic; women are more likely to vote Democratic than men; evangelical Protestants vote heavily Republican, while agnostics and atheists are heavily Democratic; urbanites and self-described liberals normally vote Democratic, and small-town voters and self-described conservatives usually vote Republican.

In the primaries, these rules are useless. Groups such as evangelicals and African Americans, who overwhelmingly vote for Republicans or Democrats in the general election, frequently splinter and support a variety of candidates. The shifting landscape of bloc voting in the primaries depends on the quadrennially shifting lineup of candidates, as well as the strategic calculations of key opinion leaders within the groups. Moreover, "the turnout of various constituency groups in one party's primaries can change across nomination races as the party coalitions evolve" (Steger, Dowdle, and Adkins 2012, 11).

On the Democratic side, virtually every candidate engages in aggressive outreach to the party's key constituencies, such as minorities, unions, and liberal activist groups. On the Republican side, virtually every candidate fashions an appeal to social conservatives, businesspeople, and gun owners. Some are more effective than others, and the groups themselves are often divided. In 1988, when religious right leader Pat Robertson was a candidate for the Republican nomination, most other candidates, including George H. W. Bush and Jack Kemp, also sought the votes of religious conservatives. Jerry Falwell, founder of the Moral Majority, shunned Robertson and endorsed Bush. Although African American voters overwhelmingly supported black candidates Jesse Jackson and Barack Obama, in other years they are frequently quite divided. In 1980, for example, Senator Edward M. Kennedy won 50 percent of the black vote in Democratic primaries, while President Jimmy Carter won 45 percent. In 2004, John Kerry won 56 percent of the black vote, while three other candidates reached into double digits (Hutchings and Stephens 2008). In 2016, when Hillary Clinton was on the road to becoming the first female major party nominee, she consistently performed about 10 percentage points better than Sanders among women—hardly a blowout—but would often either win a plurality among both men and women or lose both men and women to Sanders.

Just as a gender gap has existed for 40 years in presidential general elections, there is frequently a gender gap in the primaries within each party; some candidates do better among women than men, and vice versa. In 1992, for example, George H. W. Bush did about 10 percentage points better among women than men. In other cases, gender differences are modest, such as the 1996 Republican primaries in which Pat Buchanan did about 4 percentage points better among men than women, while Bob Dole had the same advantage among women. (Both Bush in 1992 and Dole in 1996 won both the men's and women's vote, just by different margins.) In yet other cases, as among Democrats in 1992, there is no significant gender gap in primary voting. When a gender gap emerges in the primaries, its origin is often complex. In 1992, for example, men who listed the economy or immigration as top concerns gave Buchanan an edge among male voters, but that edge was reduced a bit by the advantage Buchanan achieved among those women for whom abortion was the most important issue (Norrander 2000).

A few generalizations can be made. Typically, Republican candidates widely identified as candidates of the religious right (say, in 2012, Rick Santorum) or Democratic candidates with a union focus have their greatest voting strength at the lower end of the income and education scale; Democratic candidates widely seen as representatives of the left activists (like George McGovern or Bernie Sanders) have their greatest strength among higher incomes and higher education levels, as in their party do Republican candidates generally seen as safe advocates for the business establishment (such as Mitt Romney). Overall, however, group adhesion has less predictive power regarding primary votes than general election votes.

The 2016 Primaries

Many of the points discussed above were demonstrated in the 2016 primaries and caucuses. For evidence, one can examine exit poll data from Democratic and Republican primaries.

In the crucial New Hampshire primary, the top five Republican candidates split the vote in interesting ways (see Table 9.1). Although Trump won most categories of voters, he did so by often dramatically different margins depending on the category. Among demographic groups, he did better among men than among women, among lower income than higher income voters, and among those with high school education or less. Kasich and Cruz did about equally well among men and women, while Bush and Rubio did best among women.

Trump won both Republicans and independents with 36 percent, while Kasich—widely perceived as the most moderate and heterodox Republican—did twice as well among independents as among Republicans. Cruz, widely perceived as the most conservative, did slightly better among Republicans as among independents. Though his share of the moderate vote grew after New Hampshire, in the nation's first primary Trump did slightly better among the self-described very conservative voters.

Trump did significantly better among voters who were not evangelical Christians, while Cruz nearly tied him among evangelicals. On issues, Trump did best among those who identified immigration as their top concern, and he was challenged most closely on issues of economy and jobs. However, the story of New Hampshire, the Republican primaries overall, and ultimately the November election was captured most dramatically in the exit poll questions that showed Trump running away among voters who said they most wanted a candidate who "tells it like it is," who "can bring change," and who is "outside the establishment" (the preference of 50 percent of voters, as opposed to 44 percent who said it was more important for the next president to have experience in government). Rubio challenged Trump among voters who said electability was their chief concern, while Trump was at the bottom of the pack among voters who said they most wanted a nominee who shared their values (CNN 2016b). Although there was some shifting throughout the Republican primaries, the New Hampshire patterns largely held.

In the Democratic South Carolina primary, the first in the nation featuring a large proportion of nonwhites in the electorate, there were also some notable differences among subgroups of voters (Table 9.2). Like Trump in New Hampshire, Clinton won nearly every category, but important distinctions emerged nonetheless. The most obvious was that Clinton won Democratic voters by a 4–1 margin while narrowly losing independents. She did 11 percentage points better among women than among men. Otherwise, the pattern of the vote when a left activist candidate is a major part of the field continued to hold. Bernie Sanders, though losing every category but independents, did better among the white, the highly educated, the affluent, the liberal, and the less religious than among the nonwhite, less affluent and educated, more religiously observant, and the moderate-to-conservative. Additionally, voters who cared most about electability or experience overwhelmingly favored Clinton, and a total of 85 percent said they wanted a candidate with experience while only 11 percent preferred someone "outside

Table 9.1 2016 New Hampshire Republican Primary Vote by Group (in percentages)

	Trump	Kasich	Cruz	Bush	Rubio
Men	38	16	12	8	9
Women	33	16	11	14	12
Age 18–44	37	12	14	9	15
Age 45+	35	19	11	12	9
Income under $50k	40	11	13	11	8
Income $50k+	34	18	11	11	12
High school or less	47	8	13	11	8
College grad.	33	18	12	11	11
Postgrad.	25	22	9	15	13
Republicans	36	13	12	10	12
Independents	36	18	11	11	9
Very conservative	36	6	23	9	13
Somewhat cons.	38	14	9	11	11
Moderate	32	27	4	14	8
Evangelical	27	11	23	10	13
Not	38	18	8	11	10
Key issue is:					
Immigration	53	5	21	6	8
Economy/jobs	32	24	6	12	12
Terrorism	29	15	12	14	13
Govt. spending	34	15	13	10	8
Most important:					
Electability	33	16	6	9	29
Shares values	13	20	21	16	13
Tells it like it is	66	7	3	2	4
Can bring change	37	20	10	13	5
Most important:					
Experience	6	27	14	21	17
Outside establish.	62	6	10	4	5

Source: CNN 2016 New Hampshire Republican Primary Exit Poll.

Table 9.2   2016 South Carolina Democratic Primary Vote by Group (in percentages)

	Clinton	Sanders
Men	68	32
Women	79	21
Age 17–44	63	37
Age 45+	81	19
White	54	46
Nonwhite	85	14
High school or less	86	14
College graduate	70	30
Postgrad.	70	30
Income under $50k	76	23
Income $50k+	68	32
Democrats	80	20
Independents	46	53
Liberal	70	30
Moderate/conserv.	77	23
Relig. services wkly	86	14
Occasionally	69	30
Key issue is:		
Health care	79	21
Economy/jobs	75	25
Terrorism	82	17
Income inequality	63	37
Most important:		
Electability	82	18
Cares	68	31
Honest	51	49
Experience	94	6
Next pres. should:		
Continue Obama	81	19
Be more liberal	45	55

Source: CNN 2016 South Carolina Democratic Primary Exit Poll.

the establishment." However, she split evenly with Sanders the votes of those for whom an honest candidate was most important. On issues, Clinton did best among those for whom terrorism was the biggest issue; in comparison with terrorism, Sanders more than doubled his percentage among those who said income inequality was their chief concern. Approval of the president's policies also played a role, as Clinton won 81 percent of South Carolina primary voters who said they wanted to continue Barack Obama's policies and Sanders won a 10 percentage point margin among those who said they wanted more liberal policies than Obama's (CNN 2016c). Here, too, although there were some ups and downs through the primary season, the pattern laid down by Democrats (and independents) in South Carolina remained throughout the primary season.

In both parties, the key variable from primary to primary was less a change in the percentages given by each group than a change in turnout by each group. Where affluent whites were a higher percentage of the Democratic electorate, Sanders's vote totals went up; where there were fewer evangelicals or fewer college-educated whites in the Republican electorate, Trump's totals would grow. And, in the contest between experience and change, through the course of the 2016 primaries, Democrats chose experience, Republicans change—preferences that would have enormous implications for the November election.

Sources

Bartels, Larry. 1988. *Presidential Primaries and the Dynamics of Public Choice.* Princeton, NJ: Princeton University Press.

Ceaser, James W., and Andrew E. Busch. 1993. *Upside Down and Inside Out: The 1992 Elections and American Politics.* Lanham, MD: Rowman & Littlefield.

CNN. 2016a. Presidential Primary Exit Polls. https://www.cnn.com/election /2016/primaries/polls.

CNN. 2016b. Presidential Primary Exit Polls. https://www.cnn.com/election /2016/primaries/polls/NH/Rep.

CNN. 2016c. Presidential Primary Exit Polls. https://www.cnn.com/election /2016/primaries/polls/SC/Dem.

Hutchings, Vincent L., and LaFleur Stephens. 2008. "African American Voters and the Presidential Nomination Process." In William G. Mayer, ed., *The Making of the Presidential Candidates 2008.* Lanham, MD: Rowman & Littlefield.

Jones, Jeffrey M. 2007. "Democrats Express Decided Preference for Change over Experience." Gallup, September 4. https://news.gallup.com/poll/28591 /democrats-express-decided-preference-change-over-experience.aspx.

Mayer, William G. 1996. "Caucuses: How they Work, What Difference They Make." In William G. Mayer, ed., *In Pursuit of the White House: How We Choose Our Presidential Nominees.* Chatham, NJ: Chatham House.

Mayer, William G. 2004. "The Basic Dynamics of the Contemporary Nominating Process: An Expanded View." In William G. Mayer, ed., *The Making of the Presidential Candidates 2004.* Lanham, MD: Rowman & Littlefield.

Mayer, William G. 2008. "Voting in Presidential Primaries." In William G. Mayer, ed., *The Making of the Presidential Candidates 2008.* Lanham, MD: Rowman & Littlefield.

Norrander, Barbara. 2000. "The Gender Gap in Presidential Nominations." In William G. Mayer, ed., *In Pursuit of the White House 2000: How We Choose Our Presidential Nominees.* Chatham, NJ: Chatham House.

Norrander, Barbara. 2010. *The Imperfect Primary: Oddities, Biases, and Strengths of U.S. Presidential Nomination Politics.* New York: Routledge.

Steger, Wayne P., Andrew J. Dowdle, and Randall E. Adkins. 2012. "Why Are Presidential Nomination Races So Difficult to Predict?" In William G. Mayer, ed., *The Making of the Presidential Candidates 2012.* Lanham, MD: Rowman & Littlefield.

United States Elections Project. 2018a. "Voter Turnout." http://www.electproject .org/home/voter-turnout/voter-turnout-data.

United States Elections Project. 2018b. "2016 Presidential Nomination Contest Turnout Rates." http://www.electproject.org/2016P.

CHAPTER TEN

Methods of Awarding Delegates

A wide variety of methods have been used for awarding national convention delegates. The choice determines both how the underlying allocation of delegates to states is made and how those delegates are allocated among candidates on the basis of caucus or primary voting results.

Allocation of Delegates to States

Allocation of delegates to states is determined by national party rules. Each party has a formula for determining the number of delegates that each state receives before the automatic delegates are added. The formulas are different and lead to about twice as many Democratic delegates as Republican delegates, but both are based on electoral votes and feature bonuses for varying measures of party success in that state.

In the very first national conventions, delegations were sent by state parties in rather haphazard fashion. However, by the late 1800s both Democrats and Republicans allocated delegates to each state based on a standard formula built around the number of electoral votes each state possessed. In 1884, by way of example, both parties allocated to each state a number of national convention delegates equal to two times its number of electoral votes. They also afforded two delegates per territory. In the 20th century the parties diverged both from this formula and from each other. Formulas tended to be based on population while adding bonus delegates for the party's performance in the state, national committee officials, or other factors.

Democrats now start with a base of 3,200 delegate votes, which they assign to states on the basis of a formula that takes account of the state's vote for the Democratic nominee for president in the previous three elections and the state's number of electoral votes divided by the national totals. This percentage, or "allocation factor," is applied to the 3,200 base delegates to produce a base number of state delegates. One-fourth of those delegates are allocated statewide, the other three-fourths by district (usually congressional district, though in some states state legislative districts are used). To the base number, states are given an additional 15 percent as "add-ons." These "add-ons" are local party officials and elected officials. Unlike the "superdelegates," the add-ons are pledged and are elected and allocated in the same way as the at-large delegates.

Republicans give each state 10 at-large delegates and three delegates per congressional district. Republicans also assign one bonus at-large delegate to states that gave the majority of their electoral votes to the Republican candidate for president in the most recent election, and another one bonus at-large delegate for states that elected a Republican to any one of the following: governor, at least half of the state's seats in the U.S. House, a majority of members in the state house or state senate (if the presiding officer is a Republican), a majority of members of all chambers of the state legislature (if the presiding officers are Republicans), or a U.S. Senate seat (Coleman 2015, 11–12).

Not counting territories, Republicans in 2016 gave between 16 delegates in Vermont and 172 delegates in California. Democrats assigned a low of 14 delegates to Wyoming and a high of 475 to California, not including superdelegates. The overall number of delegates was 4,763 Democratic delegates (including 4,051 elected delegates and 712 superdelegates) and 2,472 Republican delegates.

Delegate apportionment formulas rarely make news, but they are important and can affect the geographical and political balance within a party. Conservative control of the Republican Party, for example, was aided by a delegate apportionment formula that disproportionately benefited small, conservative states (Busch 1997, 71–73). A liberal Republican organization called the Ripon Society has twice sued in court to force a change in the Republican delegate apportionment formula, but neither effort was successful (Wayne 2016, 107).

Allocation to Candidates

Once a state is allocated a certain number of delegates, the next question is how to award those delegates to candidates. That is determined by a combination of national party rules and state party rules. National Democrats since the 1970s have tended to be more prescriptive, leaving fewer options to state parties; Republicans, in keeping with their general leanings toward federalism, have left more discretion to state parties. Altogether, there are a large number of possible means of awarding delegates that have been used and continue to be used by one or both parties, often in some combination. Those methods include:

Winner-Take-All by State

In this case, whichever candidate receives a plurality of votes statewide receives all of the state's delegates. This method has been banned by Democratic rules since the 1970s. Republicans continue to allow it, but the number of states using it has declined. Prior to 1976, the big prize in both parties was California, which allocated its entire haul of delegates to the statewide winner, leading to dramatic primary contests such as Goldwater vs. Rockefeller in the 1964 Republican primary and McGovern vs. Humphrey in the 1972 Democratic primary.

States have often seen an advantage in this method, insofar as their influence in the nominating process is maximized. On a more abstract level, some have favored these rules because they allow the candidate with the most support to wrap up the nomination quickly and decisively. On the other hand, some (including Democratic reformers) have criticized the method for providing no representation to supporters of the minority candidates, even when they might be a majority or plurality in certain regions of the state.

A variant of winner-take-all by state is the "unit rule." In states that use the unit rule, delegates become committed to candidates in a variety of ways, and the state delegation may arrive at the national convention divided in their commitments. However, prior to the roll call vote, the state delegation meets and votes for the candidates. If a candidate receives the majority of votes, the state casts all of its delegate votes for that candidate. From 1832 forward, the unit rule was a common device in the Democratic Party and was generally allowed whenever a state convention instructed its delegation to the national convention to vote as a unit. It was banned, however, by the 1968 Democratic national convention as a precursor to broader reforms that followed. In the late 1800s, there were a few attempts to enforce a unit rule on certain state delegations to the Republican national convention, but these were overruled from the floor and Republicans never actually used the unit rule. Both the unit rule and statewide winner-take-all rules have been defended as expressions of federalism.

Winner-Take-All by District

An alternative or complement to statewide winner-take-all is a system in which delegates are allocated on a district basis and votes are tabulated by district—usually congressional district—with the plurality leader in each district awarded all of its delegates. This system has consistently been allowed on the Republican side and is widely used, generally to complement a certain number of delegates selected at-large. However, it is not allowed by current Democratic rules. It, too, gives an edge to candidates who can place first and shuts out those who cannot, but potentially on a regionally varied basis within states.

Proportional Representation by State

A third method of awarding delegates is proportional representation (PR) by state. In this case, votes for candidates are counted statewide and delegates are awarded to candidates in proportion to the votes they won. However, determining the number of delegates produced for each candidate in a proportional representation system is not as simple as it seems, and depends on a number of questions. Most notably, there is typically a threshold percentage of the vote that candidates must reach before winning any delegates in order to avoid splitting the delegation among nonviable candidates with very little voter support. The higher the threshold, the greater the advantage to the leading candidate. The Democratic threshold percentage since the 1970s has typically been 15 percent. Proportional representation was encouraged in the McGovern-Fraser report, was required by the Mikulski Commission (with a 15 percent threshold) though with exceptions, and has been required by Democrats since 1992.

Until recently, Republicans left the option of proportional representation strictly up to each state. In an attempt to reverse primary front-loading and extend the nomination race, however, Republicans in 2012 required states holding primaries before April 1 to use proportional representation. Starting April 1, they were permitted to use winner-take-all allocation. In 2016 Republicans modified the 2012 rule to require proportional representation through March 14. No specific threshold percentage was mandated by the national party, though the threshold cannot be higher than 20 percent (Coleman 2015, 10). Actual thresholds on the Republican side vary considerably. In 2016, many states used the maximum 20 percent threshold. Others used a 15 percent threshold, while some established no explicit threshold; in those states, the practical threshold was 100 percent divided by however many delegates there were.

At least three other considerations can affect delegate allocation in a proportional representation system. One is the rounding rule that is used. Another is the question of how to distribute the delegates left over by candidates who failed to meet the threshold. For example, in a state with 20 delegates at stake and a 15 percent threshold, what if there are four candidates who split the vote 40 percent, 30 percent, 20 percent, and 10 percent? Proportionally, candidate A would get 8 delegates, candidate B 6 delegates, and candidate C 4 delegates, but what would happen to the 2 leftover delegates? Some states divide them proportionally among the top three, while others give them as a bonus to the plurality winner. A third question is what happens in a large field if only one candidate reaches the threshold? Some would give all the delegates to that candidate, producing a "back-door" winner-take-all outcome. Others would divide the delegates proportionately among the top three or use some other mechanism to spread them out.

The arguments for and against proportional representation are essentially a mirror image of the arguments for and against winner-take-all rules. Supporters of proportional representation argue that it more faithfully reflects voter preferences and provides a voice to most candidates. Opponents fear it gives too great a voice to fringe groups and makes it too hard for the party to unify behind a decisive winner. Supporters point out that proportional representation might succeed in extending the race, but critics also note that if voters have second thoughts about a candidate who won early contests, proportional representation in later contests makes it very difficult mathematically for trailing candidates to catch up.

Proportional Representation by District

A variation of statewide proportional representation is proportional representation by district, again usually congressional district. In this case, delegates are allocated by district and votes are tabulated by district, with delegates awarded proportionately (with a percentage threshold). Because there are always many fewer delegates awarded in a district than in the entire state, attempting to apply proportional representation at the district level can lead to delegate totals that are less congruent with actual vote totals than one would find with statewide proportional representation. For example, Republicans typically assign three delegates for each congressional district, and there are a very limited number of ways three delegates can be divided. A contest with serious competition could deliver two delegates to the winner and one to the loser, even if the actual vote totals were 53–47 percent (or, on the other hand, 80–20 percent).

Direct Election of Delegates

A traditional form of presidential primary is the direct delegate primary. Direct delegate primaries are primaries in which individual delegates appear on the primary ballot and are elected to the national convention without attachment to a candidate. They have been banned statewide in the Democratic Party since the 1970s, but Democrats allowed it at the district level in 1976 as an alternative to proportional representation (if at least 75 percent of a state's delegates were chosen by district), and again in 1984 and 1988. When Democrats used it, it has been called a "loophole primary." Direct election of delegates is permitted by Republicans. In pure delegate primaries, a couple of outcomes are possible. The delegates who are elected may be uncommitted as to candidate, and they often obtain their position by virtue of their long service to the party. Delegates may also be elected because they support a particular candidate whose campaign is well organized enough to mobilize its supporters to vote and educate them about who to vote for. In neither case do rules regarding awarding of delegates come into play, as there is no explicit vote for candidates to use as a basis for either winner-take-all or proportional allocation of delegates. However, in practice, they are the practical equivalent of winner-take-all. A version of direct delegate election can be said to take place in some Republican caucuses, where unbound delegates are selected by state or congressional district (CD) conventions.

Hybrid Systems

There are a number of ways states might combine these building blocks to form hybrid systems.

Current Democratic rules require every state to use a hybrid system. One-quarter of Democratic elected delegates are allocated at-large on the basis of the statewide vote. The other three-fourths are allocated in units no larger than congressional districts on the basis of the vote in those units. In both cases, delegates are allocated proportionally with a 15 percent threshold. In the past, Democrats have experimented with other hybrids. These included the "loophole primary," in which winner-take-all could be used in the district-level primaries as long as three-fourths of the state's delegates were allocated at the district level. In 1984 and 1988 they also allowed the use of the "bonus primary," in which delegates were allocated by proportional representation by district but the district winner received one additional delegate over and above the proportional allotment. Since 1992, Democrats have not permitted loophole or bonus primaries.

On the Republican side, the two most common forms of hybrid combine district and statewide winner-take-all or district and statewide proportional representation with a trigger that shifts allocation to winner-take-all if the leading candidate wins above a specified percentage. A typical example of the former would allocate three delegates per congressional district, awarded winner-take-all, while the remainder of the state's delegation would be awarded statewide to the overall state winner. South Carolina, Wisconsin, and California are among states that utilize this method. The most typical form of the latter would be to trigger winner-take-all if a candidate wins an absolute majority of the votes, though some states use a supermajority trigger. In 2016, one state (Missouri) combined statewide and CD winner-take-all, but established a majority trigger at the state level that would give all the state's delegates to the statewide winner.

Some Republican states also combine proportional allocation of the at-large delegates with CD delegates chosen proportionately but with a trigger.

In 2016, one (Connecticut) allocated CD delegates on a simple winner-take-all basis and at-large delegates through PR with a trigger. Yet other GOP states use some form of proportional representation at both the statewide and CD levels, but convert to winner-take-all in any venue where the winner receives an absolute majority of the votes cast. This range of hybrids is often referred to as "winner-take-most."

Prior to the 2016 contest, the Republican National Committee counsel's office left open the possibility that states voting before March 15 could select their congressional district delegates on a winner-take-all basis as long as the at-large statewide delegates were allocated proportionally (Coleman 2015, 10–11). Such an arrangement is similar to what Democrats allowed in some years prior to 1992.

Finally, a small number of Republican primaries allow for a mix of winner-take-all at the state level for at-large delegates and direct delegate elections at the congressional district level.

"Beauty Contest" Primaries

What is described above applies to presidential primary elections or caucuses in which the awarding of delegates is directly connected to the primary or caucus vote. Sometimes, however, preference primaries are held to register public opinion regarding the presidential nomination contest—so-called "beauty contest" primaries—but the allocation of delegates depends either on caucuses or pure delegate primaries that are also taking place.

Awarding of Delegates in 2016

As noted above, in 2016, Democrats required proportional representation, with a 15 percent threshold for winning delegates. Three-fourths of state delegates were elected at the district level and one-fourth statewide. Republicans required proportional representation prior to March 15, after which states were allowed a wider range of options. Moreover, exceptions to the proportional representation rule were granted to the first four contests allowed before the general delegate selection window opened: Iowa, New Hampshire, South Carolina, and Nevada. However, all but South Carolina utilized statewide proportional representation anyway. Table 10.1 shows the distribution of systems for awarding delegates in that election year.

The Effect of Differing Rules of Delegate Allocation

It is clear that different rules regarding delegate allocation can result in significantly different outcomes. In 1976, at the dawn of the era of proportional representation, scholars noted a slight difference in outcomes in the

Table 10.1   **Number of States Using Each Method of Allocating Republican Delegates, 2016**

	Caucuses	Primaries
Statewide winner-take-all (WTA)	0	9
Statewide proportional (PR)	7	7
Direct delegate election statewide	1	0
Hybrid:		
WTA state/Cong. district	0	6*
PR state/Cong. district	1	1
PR state/PR+ trigger CD	0	3
PR + trigger statewide	2	1
PR + trigger state/CD	0	7
PR + trigger state/WTA CD	0	1
WTA state/Direct CD	0	2
Direct state/CD (or county)	2	1

*Of these states, one (Missouri) had a trigger of 50% of the statewide vote that would negate CD allocations and give all of the state's delegates to the statewide winner.

Source: "2016 Republican Delegate Allocation Rules by State." Frontloading HQ. http:// frontloading.blogspot.com/p/2016-republican-delegate-allocation-by.html.

Republican contest, which featured 16 plurality and 11 proportional primaries, between Gerald Ford and Ronald Reagan. Studies indicated that Ford would have gained 17 to 38 delegates had all primaries been conducted under proportional representation rules—a small shift but not trivial in a race Ford won by 117 delegates out of 2,257 at the convention. It turned out that he would also have gained if every state used statewide winner-take-all; Reagan benefited from the particular mix of methods used in 1976 (Pomper 1979; David and Ceaser 1980, 54–56).

It is possible to do similar analyses in subsequent races. An analysis of the 2008 Republican nomination race, for example, showed that different allocation rules would have led to significantly varying outcomes. If every state had used statewide winner-take-all, by March 4 John McCain would have led Mike Huckabee by 1,108 to 314 delegates (Mitt Romney, who had already dropped out, would have accumulated 313). If every state had used statewide proportional representation, McCain would still have led Huckabee, but by the much reduced margin of 682–416; Romney would have won 425 before bowing out. In fact, by the end of the Super Tuesday primaries on February 5, Romney would actually have led McCain by 425–422, with Huckabee at

238. Under those circumstances, it is highly unlikely that Romney would have dropped out, further scrambling the delegate totals by March 4.

Even more striking, under a system of statewide winner-take-all in every state, Hillary Clinton, not Barack Obama, would have won the 2008 Democratic presidential nomination, outgaining Obama by 272 delegates. Obama, on the other hand, would have won in a pure statewide proportional representation system. Had Democrats used the Republican rules in each state, Clinton would have led Obama by 4 delegates at the end of the primary season, and the outcome of the race would have hinged on a few state conventions in caucus states that selected their national delegates in the summer (Norrander 2010, 84–88).

In 2016, Donald Trump reached a majority of pledged delegates on June 7. Had Republicans uniformly used statewide winner-take-all rules, he would have reached a majority on April 26. On the other hand, had Republicans used statewide proportional representation only, Trump would have ended the primary season 100 delegates short of a majority (Brake and Clark 2017).

Since there is no realistic possibility that either party will adopt universal statewide proportional representation or winner-take-all, or that Democrats will adopt the Republican rules, scenarios based on such systems are only thought exercises. But they illustrate how different rules can in fact change the game, and potentially the outcome of the game.

Sources

Brake, Brittany Page, and John A. Clark. 2017. "The Rigors of a Rigged System? Delegate Allocation Rules in the 2008 and 2016 Presidential Primaries." Prepared for delivery at the 2017 State of the Parties Conference, Akron, OH, November 9–10. https://www.uakron.edu/bliss/state-of-the-parties /papers/brake+clark.pdf.

Busch, Andrew E. 1997. *Outsiders and Openness in the Presidential Nominating System*. Pittsburgh: University of Pittsburgh Press.

Coleman, Kevin J. 2015. *The Presidential Nominating Process and the National Party Conventions, 2016: Frequently Asked Questions*. Washington, DC: Congressional Research Service, December 30.

CQ Researcher, "The Two-Thirds Rule and the Unit Rule." http://library.cqpress .com/cqresearcher/document.php?id=cqresrre1926062100.

David, Paul T., and James W. Ceaser. 1980. *Proportional Representation in Presidential Nominating Politics*. Charlottesville: University Press of Virginia.

Norrander, Barbara. 2010. *The Imperfect Primary: The Oddities, Biases, and Strengths of U.S. Presidential Nomination Politics*. New York: Routledge.

Pomper, Gerald. 1979. "New Rules and New Games in Presidential Nominations." *Journal of Politics* 41.

Wayne, Stephen J. 2016. *The Road to the White House 2016*. New York: Cengage.

CHAPTER ELEVEN

Delegate Selection, Rights, and Responsibilities

Although delegate totals are awarded to candidates mostly on the basis of primary or caucus/convention results, the selection of the actual individuals who serve as delegates is a separate question. There are a number of ways that individuals become national convention delegates, with greater variation in the Republican Party than in the Democratic Party due to the greater discretion allowed to state parties in the former. Since the 1970s, Democrats have established detailed rules governing delegate selection. In 2016, these were found in the *Delegate Selection Rules for the 2016 Democratic National Convention* and the *Call for the 2016 Democratic National Convention*. As noted by a Congressional Research Service report, "State Democratic parties are required to submit delegate selection plans to the Democratic National Committee Rules and Bylaws Committee to determine compliance with national party rules and receive approval in the year before the presidential election" (Coleman 2015, 9). Republicans set general guidelines in *The Rules of the Republican Party* and *Call of the Convention*, but leave substantial discretion with the state parties. State law also plays a role, especially in primary states. In both Democratic and Republican parties, there are two types of delegates: automatic and elected. Once determined, delegates have a variety of tasks and responsibilities assigned by party rules and sometimes by state law.

Selection of Automatic Delegates

In the Republican Party, three automatic delegates from each state are added to the state delegation. These three are the three representatives from the state on the Republican National Committee: the state party chair, the national committeeman from the state, and the national committeewoman from the state. These automatic Republican delegates represented around 7 percent of the total delegates to the 2016 Republican National Convention.

In the Democratic Party, the automatic delegates have also been called "unpledged Party Leaders and Elected Officials" (PLEOs). More commonly, they are referred to as "superdelegates." Superdelegates were first introduced in 1984 and have been approximately 15–20 percent of the total number of delegates to each Democratic national convention since then. In 2016, superdelegates were about 16 percent of the delegates to the Democratic convention. The Democratic superdelegates consist of the following categories of individuals: all Democratic members of Congress, all Democratic state governors, all members of the Democratic National Committee, former chairs of the Democratic National Committee, and a group designated "distinguished party members," which includes former presidents and vice presidents and former Democratic leaders of the Senate, Speakers of the House of Representatives, and minority leaders.

Superdelegates were introduced by the Hunt Commission in 1982 to rectify a dramatic decline in the number of Democratic officeholders and party organization leaders attending the Democratic convention as delegates immediately following the McGovern-Fraser reforms prior to the 1972 election. Those reforms were largely driven by concerns by Eugene McCarthy's 1968 supporters that the nominating process was too much under the control of party insiders. However, some observers argued that the subsequent loss of influence by the official party had led to the electorally catastrophic McGovern nomination in 1972 and the 1976 nomination of Washington outsider Jimmy Carter, whose one-term presidency ended with Ronald Reagan's 1980 landslide presidential victory and a Republican takeover of the U.S. Senate.

Although Democratic superdelegates are not required to pledge support to a particular candidate prior to the convention, almost all ultimately do. In each nomination race since 1984, the majority of superdelegates have voted for the same candidate as the majority of elected delegates, so their votes have never led to a different outcome than what would have occurred otherwise. Nevertheless, in 1984, Walter Mondale only won a bare majority of elected delegates (52 percent compared with 79 percent of superdelegates), and Barack Obama in 2008 only pulled ahead of Hillary Clinton in superdelegate commitments late in the nomination race (Norrander 2010, 79–81). In 2016, Hillary Clinton outpaced Bernie Sanders among superdelegates prior to the Democratic convention by 570½ to 44½. In that contest, there was considerable controversy over whether superdelegate endorsements should be included in preliminary state delegate totals. Sanders supporters argued that they should not have been included since the superdelegates remained unbound even if they had announced an endorsement, and their inclusion "padded" Clinton's lead in media reports (Ryan 2016). More generally, throughout the race, Sanders supporters protested what they saw as the undemocratic nature of the superdelegates, even directing petitions to the superdelegates themselves urging them to follow the popular will (Strauss 2016). Sanders himself called for the abolition of superdelegates altogether.

Prior to the opening of the 2016 Democratic national convention, the Democratic National Committee Rules Committee voted 158–6 to approve a superdelegate reform package that would require two-thirds of the superdelegates to the 2020 convention to be pledged in accordance with their state's primary or caucus results (Weigel 2016). A commission headed by a Clinton supporter and a Sanders supporter was approved to work out details. Ultimately, the DNC voted that all superdelegates will remain unpledged, but may only vote on the first ballot if a candidate already has a majority of pledged delegates. If no candidate has a first-ballot majority of pledged delegates, superdelegates may vote on subsequent ballots (270 to Win 2019). The practical impact of this reform, however, may be negligible; there has not been a Democratic convention vote for the presidential nomination that has gone beyond the first ballot since 1952.

Selection of Elected Delegates

Elected or nonautomatic delegates represent the lion's share of delegates at both parties' conventions. In 2016, approximately 84 percent of Democratic delegates and 93 percent of Republican delegates were elected.

Delegate selection in primary states can take place in one of three ways. In a preference primary, voters vote just for the presidential candidate of their choice. The results of the primary determine how many delegates are allocated to each candidate, but the selection of the individuals who serve as delegates utilizes a different process. Typically, either there are slates of delegates representing each candidate selected in preprimary caucuses, and how many of each slate are elected depends on the primary results, or postprimary caucuses and conventions select the number of individuals pledged to each candidate as determined by the primary results.

In a direct election primary, there is both a presidential preference vote and a vote for individuals who will serve as delegates. The preference vote determines how many delegates each candidate will receive, while the delegate vote will determine which individuals will serve in those slots.

A third type of delegate selection in a primary is a pure delegate primary. In this method, there is no presidential preference component to the primary. Voters only vote for delegates. This mode of delegate selection was relatively common prior to 1972, but was banned in the Democratic Party by the McGovern-Fraser reforms. Republicans still permit states to use pure delegate primaries, but in 2016 only Pennsylvania and Illinois did so, and only at the congressional district level.

Delegate selection in caucuses is more complicated. Ultimately, the selection of national convention delegates in caucus states occurs at the end of a long process that begins with precinct caucuses, usually goes to local conventions, and ends with conventions at the state or congressional district level. In the Democratic Party, caucus attendees divide themselves into groups based on which candidate they support. Only groups with at least 15 percent of the caucus attendees are considered "viable," and members of non-viable groups are given an opportunity to attach themselves to a new, viable group. Once that is done, a final count of supporters in each remaining group is taken to determine how many delegates from each group will be sent to the next level. In most cases, a similar process is followed at the county level, which selects delegates to the congressional district or state convention. Those conventions then elect delegates to the national convention using similar proportional rules. At every stage, people seeking to become delegates to the next stage must pledge themselves to a presidential candidate or declare themselves uncommitted.

One of the more important Democratic reforms of the 1970s, starting with the Commission on Delegate Selection and Party Structure (Mikulski Commission) following the 1972 election, established a delegate slatemaking procedure that gave candidate organizations rather than the party control over the process of identifying delegate slates (Price 1984, 151–152, 155). Now Democratic delegates cannot be elected without the approval of the candidate to whom they have been allocated by the primary or caucus results.

Republican rules are much less prescriptive. Proportional representation is not required except in states voting between March 1 and March 14; when it is used, national Republican guidelines permit a threshold of not more than 20 percent, but do not mandate a particular percentage. In 2016, three Republican caucuses also elected unbound delegates disconnected from a presidential preference vote (Colorado, Wyoming, and North Dakota).

Overall, only about one-fourth of Republican national convention delegates are slated by the candidates. The remainder are individuals selected outside of the candidate's control by caucuses and conventions, though candidate campaigns may try to influence the delegate elections.

Characteristics of Delegates

As noted by scholars John S. Jackson III and William Crotty,

The national convention delegates are first and foremost political activists. . . . In many cases they are also recruited or encouraged to run by a candidate's organization. . . . The delegates share the usual characteristics of other party and political activists, which makes them atypical representatives of the American population as a whole . . . the delegates are better

Table 11.1　Characteristics of National Convention Delegates, 1944–2008, by Percentage

	1944		1968		1996		2008	
	D	**R**	**D**	**R**	**D**	**R**	**D**	**R**
Women	11	9	13	16	53	36	49	32
Black	–	–	5	2	17	3	23	2
Under 30	–	–	3	4	6	2	7	3
1st conv.	63	63	67	66	61	56	57	58
Lawyer	38	37	28	22	10	11	17	16

Sources: John S. Jackson III and William Crotty, *The Politics of Presidential Selection,* 2nd ed. (New York: Longman, 2001), p. 86; Karlyn Bowman and Andrew Rugg, *AEI Special Report, Delegates and National Conventions 1968–2008.* http://images.politico.com/global /2012/08/convention_delegates_survey.pdf.

educated, more affluent, and from higher-status occupations than the average American voter and they tend to be more ideological (Liberal-Conservative) and more committed on a range of policy concerns. (Jackson and Crotty 2001, 84–85)

Starting in the 1950s, the Democratic National Committee began imposing national rules on state parties to prohibit racial discrimination in selection of delegates. In 1964, the convention seated the official Democratic delegation from Mississippi despite violation of those rules, but considered seating an alternative delegation. In 1972, the Democrats adopted a variety of gender and racial quotas for state delegations as part of the McGovern-Fraser reforms. A backlash forced Democrats to ease many of these rules, but they retain an affirmative action requirement. Though they have encouraged diversification of their delegations, Republicans have opposed race or gender quotas for delegates.

Overall, the proportion of delegates in both parties who are women, minorities, or under 30 years old has grown considerably since 1968, though the median age has not changed much. The percentage of delegates attending their first convention has gone up and down, but has generally been around three in five since 1944. Interestingly, the proportion of delegates who are attorneys has declined markedly since 1944, when nearly 40 percent of delegates to both conventions were in that profession. (See Table 11.1.)

Rights and Responsibilities of Delegates

Delegates to both Democratic and Republican national conventions have the same tasks. Although since 1980 every convention has begun with the leading candidate claiming more than enough delegate support to assure nomination, the headline task for delegates remains nominating the presidential candidate of their party. They must also nominate the vice presidential candidate. In addition to these responsibilities, delegates must vote at the beginning of the convention to establish the rules under which the convention will operate. They decide credentials disputes when one faction in a state party claims members of another faction have been improperly chosen as delegates, or when (as in Mississippi in 1964) whole delegations are alleged to have been selected in a manner contrary to national party rules. The party platform, drafted by a platform committee in consultation with representatives of the presumptive nominee, must be approved or altered by the delegates. As with credentials disputes, platform disputes used to be quite common, but are now rare. In the modern convention, party leaders and the campaign of the presumptive nominee work hard to tamp down such disputes in advance in order to maintain the well-scripted convention as a showcase for the party.

Finally, delegates may be called upon to vote on delegate selection rules changes that will be implemented in the next presidential selection cycle or to establish a party commission to consider such changes. Democrats have long maintained as well the ability to adopt nomination rules changes in between conventions; reform commissions such as McGovern-Fraser recommend changes, which the Democratic National Committee can then adopt. Prior to 2008, Republicans could only make changes to their nominating rules at the national convention itself, four years before implementation. The 2008 Republican national convention agreed to allow the Republican National Committee to adopt nominating reforms in between conventions. It was on the basis of this new authority that the RNC imposed for the 2012 contest the March 1 window and the rule requiring proportional representation (PR) in primaries held before April 1. Similarly, when Republicans modified the PR rule to require PR only until March 15, it was done by the RNC in between elections. Nevertheless, both parties can also still make changes at their conventions.

An unofficial responsibility of delegates, one that they typically fulfill, is to present a colorful, positive, and patriotic portrait of their party to the American people. Even before the age of television, delegates have found interesting ways to express their partisan loyalty, their candidate preference, and their state pride. In 1948, the Republican convention witnessed a blonde woman in a sailor suit suspended over the convention hall in a rowboat with a sign saying "Man the Oars and Ride the Crest. Harold Stassen, He's the Best" (Donaldson 1999, 153). The traditional roll call of state delegations voting for the presidential nomination always featured extravagant praise for the state voting. Take, for example, the roll call declaration of Illinois casting its votes at the 1984 Republican national convention:

> Illinois, the home of great Republican presidents from Lincoln to Reagan, the home of the Illinois advantage, Charles Percy, the host to the 1985 National Young Republican Convention, and the home of the National

League and American League Champions, the Cubs and the White Sox, proudly and unanimously, without dissent cast 92 votes for the next President and Vice President of the United States, Ronald Reagan and George Bush. (Republican National Committee 1984, 398–399)

Now, as conventions revolve almost entirely around television, both delegates and convention managers are even more concerned about visual impressions. Individual delegates are known to dress in outlandish red, white, and blue outfits, wear colorful oversized hats, and wave handmade placards extolling their candidate or testing a new political slogan. As a group, the delegates are turned by convention managers into a unified prop when important speeches are delivered in primetime, especially the nominee's official acceptance speech, when the convention hall is typically flooded with color-coordinated signs or small American flags to make the most striking image for the viewing public.

Perhaps the most important question bearing on the rights and responsibilities of national convention delegates is whether and for how long they are bound to a candidate. To put it another way, are they required to be pledged to a candidate, and if so, for how many convention ballots must that pledge be honored? Fourteen states have statutes requiring delegates to honor their candidate pledges for one or two ballots, but Supreme Court jurisprudence makes it debatable whether those statutes would override state or national party rules. To the extent that party rules would prevail, the answer to the question is significantly different depending on the party.

Democratic delegates who are elected through the usual process are required to be pledged. The only unpledged Democratic delegates are the unpledged PLEOs (Party Leaders and Elected Officials). Pledged Democratic delegates are bound to vote in accordance with their pledge on the first ballot. On the Republican side, the three automatic delegates (the members of the Republican National Committee) are allocated and bound with the rest of the delegation in most states. National convention delegates selected through pure delegate primaries are unbound, and in 2016 three Republican caucus states elected unbound delegates. In other primary and caucus states, delegates are usually considered bound by their primary results. Indeed, in 2016, Republicans for the first time introduced a national rule requiring that delegates be bound to the choice of their primary or caucus voters if there was a presidential preference element to the vote. However, states differ in the length to which they bind delegates before releasing them.

Because of the fragmentation in the Republican field in 2016, it was conceivable until late in the primary season that no candidate would enter the national convention with a sufficient number of delegates to win nomination. A great deal of attention was focused on the question of how firmly bound the delegates were, and for how long. Although the significant majority of delegates were bound on the first ballot of the convention, 36 states, territories, and the District of Columbia would have released 1,335 delegates on the second ballot. Another 768 delegates in 13 states could have been unbound under special circumstances. In seven of those states, delegates would be released if their candidate received less than a specified threshold percentage of delegates on the first ballot (35 percent in four states; one-third, 20 percent, and 10 percent in one state each). If the contest continued to a third ballot, another eight states with 688 delegates would have been unbound, while 235 delegates from six states might have been released under special circumstances. At that point, only 196 delegates out of 2,473 would have been firmly locked down. Over half of those—the 99 from Florida—would be released on the next ballot (Epstein, McGill, and Rust 2016). In anticipation of the opportunities that might be presented by such a scenario, in a number of states Senator Ted Cruz's well-organized campaign secured election of Cruz supporters to serve as delegates allocated to Trump. Though they might be bound to Trump on the first ballot, Cruz could count on their support at some point after that. Of course, in actuality, Trump drove Cruz from the field and acquired a majority of pledged delegates prior to the convention, rendering Cruz's stratagem moot (Ceaser, Busch, and Pitney 2017).

Anti-Trump forces then attempted a final maneuver, proposing that a national party rule be adopted that freed all delegates from their pledges regardless of state party rules. This proposal, however, was easily defeated in the Rules Committee and did not come before the convention. This effort was a reprise of an attempt made by supporters of Senator Edward M. Kennedy in 1980 to unbind delegates to the Democratic National Convention. Kennedy's proposal did reach the floor, but was defeated (Busch 2005). In both cases, supporters of the maneuver made the argument that delegates should be free to use their judgment to save the party from what appeared to be (and, in 1980 for Democrats, actually was) impending electoral disaster; the binding rules, they complained, treated delegates as robots. Their opponents, who prevailed, made the democratic argument that losing candidates were attempting to subvert democracy by allowing delegates to betray the instructions they received from the voters. Perhaps no other episodes in contemporary times better have illustrated the shifting role of the national convention delegate and the tension between deliberation and democracy. In an earlier era, there would have been no question that delegates could exercise their independent judgment. In the current era, the suggestion of such exercise was widely seen as an unacceptable affront to democratic propriety.

Sources

Ballotpedia. 2019. "State Election Law and Delegates to National Conventions." https://ballotpedia.org/State_election_law_and_delegates_to_national _conventions.

Busch, Andrew E. 2005. *Reagan's Victory: The 1980 Elections and the Rise of the Right*. Lawrence: University Press of Kansas.

Ceaser, James W., Andrew E. Busch, and John J. Pitney Jr. 2017. *Defying the Odds: The 2016 Elections and American Politics*. Lanham, MD: Rowman & Littlefield.

Coleman, Kevin J. 2015. *The Presidential Nominating Process and the National Party Conventions, 2016: Frequently Asked Questions*. Congressional Research Service, December 30.

Donaldson, Gary A. 1999. *Truman Defeats Dewey*. Lexington: University Press of Kentucky.

Epstein, Reid J., Brian McGill, and Max Rust. 2016. "Republican Convention's Delegate Math Explained." *Wall Street Journal*, May 5. http://graphics.wsj .com/elections/2016/rnc-convention-delegates/.

Jackson, John S., III, and William Crotty. 2001. *The Politics of Presidential Selection*, 2nd ed. New York: Longman.

Norrander, Barbara. 2010. *The Imperfect Primary: Oddities, Biases, and Strengths of U.S. Presidential Nomination Politics*. New York: Routledge.

Price, David E. 1984. *Bringing Back the Parties*. Washington, DC: CQ Press.

Republican National Committee. 1984. *Official Report of the Proceedings of the Thirty-Third Republican National Convention, 1984*.

Ryan, Shane. 2016. "The AP Announcing Clinton's 'Victory' Was an Embarrassment to Journalism and U.S. Politics." *Paste Magazine*, June 7.

Strauss, Daniel. 2016. "Sanders Supporters Revolt Against Superdelegates." *Politico,* February 14. https://www.politico.com/story/2016/02/bernie-sanders -superdelegates-democrats-219286.

270 to Win. 2019. "Democratic Superdelegate Rule Changes for 2020." https:// www.270towin.com/content/superdelegate-rule-changes-for-the-2020 -democratic-nomination.

Weigel, David. 2016. "Democrats Vote to Bind Most Superdelegates to State Primary Results." *Washington Post*, July 23.

CHAPTER TWELVE

The Party Conventions

Although there was some precedent at the state level, party conventions as a mode of nominating presidential candidates were first seen prior to the 1832 presidential election. The Anti-Masonic Party, a third party focused on fighting the influence of the Masonic Order in American politics, pioneered the use of the national convention in 1831, when 116 party members met in Baltimore and nominated former attorney general William Wirt. Three months later, the National Republicans—predecessors to the Whigs—met and chose Henry Clay as their standard-bearer. Andrew Jackson's Democratic Party followed suit in 1832, nominating Jackson for reelection at its first-ever convention. Jackson had embraced the convention as a means of exerting control over his party and achieving the nomination of his preferred vice presidential candidate, Martin Van Buren. He wanted Van Buren as a replacement for the unruly South Carolinian John Calhoun, who had, to Jackson's consternation, rallied his state's attempt to "nullify" the federal tariff. The Democratic convention followed a number of procedures developed by the Anti-Masons: "each state could use its own judgment in choosing delegates; delegation votes were allotted on the electoral college basis; and a special majority—two thirds—was required for nomination" (David, Goldman, and Bain 1963, 55). An additional Anti-Masonic precedent was adopted in which failure to achieve the requisite majority on the first ballot would lead to a second ballot, with "no provision for compulsory elimination [of candidates] in run-off balloting" (David, Goldman, and Bain 1963, 55).

Over time, party conventions in the 19th century developed a number of functions, as follows.

Presidential Nomination

The chief task of the convention was to nominate a candidate for president. Potential candidates did not run open campaigns and usually did not declare themselves interested in the presidency. Rarely did they attend the convention, though occasionally a political figure in attendance would have the opportunity to speak and would impress the delegates enough to be carried into contention. Too much of an open display of ambition by potential candidates was considered unseemly and was disqualifying. The convention was usually made up of delegates who were not committed in advance to any candidate, but who were often under the influence of state and local party leaders who bargained freely among themselves.

Candidates were, with or without their prior knowledge and assent, put into nomination on the convention floor. The delegates then voted, with Democrats requiring a two-thirds vote to win nomination and Whigs and then Republicans requiring a majority. Eight of 18 times between 1832 and 1908, the Democratic convention failed to reach a decision on the first ballot; in 6 of 17 National Republican, Whig, and Republican conventions, they failed to do so (*Congressional Quarterly* 1976, 21–63). In these instances, delegates and party leaders recalibrated, voted again, and monitored results to see where the momentum (or the "bandwagon") was headed. Sometimes, a candidate opened the convention with a lead and continued to build that lead over a few additional ballots until securing enough support to claim the nomination. In other cases, the leading candidate proved unable to build support beyond a certain ceiling, and found himself overtaken by a trailing candidate. It was not uncommon for none of the initial candidates—leading or trailing—to be able to wrap up the requisite votes. In those cases, after many ballots left the initial contenders bruised and short of the requisite number of delegates, a "dark horse" candidate emerged, building a winning coalition from a position as everyone's second (or third) choice. In general, candidates played little direct role, except sometimes communicating by telegram to let the convention know they were withdrawing from contention when they were clearly stalled (or if they had no desire to run to begin with). Once a candidate reached 80 percent of the delegate votes required to nominate, he more often than not became unstoppable (Busch 2000).

Once a candidate received the requisite number of delegate votes to be nominated, the convention designated a committee to visit him and formally convey his nomination. Typically, the candidate then accepted his nomination by way of an open letter. As early as 1844, the Whig convention extended an invitation to nominee Henry Clay to address the convention, but Clay declined, citing his "sense of delicacy and propriety" (*Congressional Quarterly* 1976, 25). However, by the late 19th century some nominees began to deliver acceptance speeches several weeks after the convention. An example was the speech given by William Jennings Bryan officially accepting the 1896 Democratic nomination in Madison Square Garden over a month after the convention concluded its business.

Perhaps the key feature of the presidential nomination was that the convention was acting on behalf of the party—or to be more precise, the state and local parties—and that the parties controlled the process of nomination.

Vice Presidential Nomination

Once the presidential nomination was settled, the convention turned to the vice presidential nomination. Leaving aside the exception of 1832, when Jackson muscled aside Calhoun in favor of Van Buren, for the remainder of the 19th century the party convention made the choice of vice president without regard to the presidential candidate's preferences, which were in any case usually unknown.

The same process was used as for the presidential nomination. Party leaders put forward names of candidates to be considered by the delegates, frequently over multiple ballots. Here a critical consideration by the convention was usually "ticket-balancing." Delegates would strive to pick a vice presidential nominee who in some way balanced the features of the presidential nominee. This ticket-balancing was usually geographic or ideological. In the Democratic Party, a northern presidential nominee called for a southern vice presidential nominee (or vice-versa); Republicans tried to balance Northeast and Midwest (Devine and Kopko 2016, 2–6). On issues or philosophical dispositions that divided the party, the convention might try to find a vice presidential candidate who represented a different intraparty faction than the one represented by the presidential nominee. Overall, the aim was always to enhance the electoral appeal of the ticket. The vice presidential nominee's fitness to become president was rarely a factor. Like candidates for the presidency, candidates for the vice presidency did not openly seek the position and were often put into consideration by party leaders without their prior knowledge or intention.

Platform

A third major function of the national convention was the approval of a party platform. The platform was a statement of the party's key principles and an exposition of how those principles applied to issues of the day. The first major party platform was issued by the Democratic national convention of 1840. It was nine paragraphs long and proclaimed the Democratic Party's affinity for strict construction of the Constitution, limited government, and states' rights. The Whig Party followed with a platform issued by the convention of 1844. From that point forward, the major parties wrote plat-forms that were adopted by their conventions.

By 1900, the Democratic platform had grown to 2,580 words, the Repub-lican version to 2,299 words, and convention fights over platform language and priorities had become commonplace. How to address slavery, what tariff policy to adopt, how to approach national expansion, and whether to embrace or repudiate inflationary monetary policy were among the issues that inflamed passions and led to platform fights.

Prior to 1852, the convention typically drafted the platform after the pres-idential and vice presidential nominations were made. From 1852 forward, the platform itself was typically adopted by the convention before it made the nominations, and the candidates who were ultimately nominated were expected to run on the platform adopted by the party. If there was a doubt, they were sometimes asked to affirm that they could run on the platform before accepting the nomination.

An example of the twists and turns of the 19th-century party convention can be seen in the 1860 Republican convention that nominated Abraham Lin-coln. Held in Chicago in May 1860, the convention included delegates from all the free states; the slave states of Maryland, Delaware, Virginia, Kentucky, Missouri, and Texas; the territories of Kansas and Nebraska; and the District of Columbia. Credential disputes (over whether to reduce southern delegation voting strength) and rules disputes (over whether to require a majority of those present or a majority of all electoral votes) occupied the early portion of the convention. On the first ballot, front-runner William Seward led with 173½ votes, Lincoln had 102, and several other candidates each had the sup-port of around 50 delegates. Lincoln's convention managers had given guest passes to the hometown Chicago crowd, which demonstrated vociferously for Lincoln. On the second ballot, Seward was stalled at 184½ votes, while Lin-coln had surged to 181, peeling off votes from several lower-tier candidates. His momentum carried him to the third ballot, where Lincoln overtook Seward and won the nomination (*Congressional Quarterly* 1976, 36–37).

Twentieth-Century Transformation of the Party Convention

Each of the three key tasks of the convention were significantly trans-formed over the course of the 20th century. Gradually, the convention changed from a party event that represented the end of the nominating pro-cess to a candidate-centered event that launched the general election cam-paign. At the same time, in a bid to become more "representative," the parties significantly expanded the number of delegates and alternates attending the conventions. In 1900, there were 926 Republican and 936 Democratic con-vention delegates; in 2016, there were 4,763 Democratic and 2,472 Republican delegates.

Presidential nomination remained, officially, the fundamental purpose of the convention. However, over time that function became more nominal than real. One key change came with the origin of presidential primaries in 1912, which drove candidates to launch campaigns in advance of the convention to compete for primary votes. In the first few decades after the introduction of primaries, "dark horse" candidates or "drafts" of inactive potential candidates remained a possible feature of the system, but 1952 Democratic nominee Adlai Stevenson was the last presidential nominee to have run no preconvention campaign in primary or caucus states.

At the same time, convention delegates became increasingly likely to arrive at the convention pledged to a candidate. At first, this was a decentralized development driven by the strategies of campaigns. The 1964 Barry Goldwater campaign, for example, pioneered the strategy of identifying committed supporters in advance and working to get them elected as delegates, as opposed to attempting to persuade whoever happened to be elected as delegates (White 1967). Then, in the Democratic Party, the McGovern-Fraser reforms, adopted after the 1968 contest with the intention of interjecting voter preferences more directly into the system, required most delegates to identify their presidential preference and eliminated the delegate primary as an allowable mechanism.

The consequences of these changes were profound. Multiballot conventions became less common, then disappeared. The 1924 Democratic convention set the record in this regard, requiring 103 ballots to nominate John Davis of West Virginia. The last multi-ballot convention came in 1952, when Democrats took three ballots to nominate Adlai Stevenson; that year, Dwight D. Eisenhower won the Republican nomination on the first ballot.

An even more profound change was that, starting in the 1970s, the de facto nominee became known well in advance of the convention itself, even when the nomination was hotly contested. The last convention that opened without a candidate clearly possessing sufficient delegates to be nominated was the Republican convention in 1976, when President Gerald Ford and challenger Ronald Reagan were still jostling for the decisive few delegates as the Kansas City convention began (Ford ended up winning narrowly) (Shirley 2010). On a handful of other occasions, there seemed an outside chance that the leading candidate could lose his lead once the convention started. In 1980, President Jimmy Carter entered the Democratic convention with enough delegates to be renominated, but his main opponent, Senator Edward M. Kennedy, challenged the rule binding delegates to their primary pledge. Kennedy's forces hoped that if they succeeded in changing the rule, a large number of delegates initially pledged to Carter might switch to Kennedy, putting him over the top. The brief moment of suspense was broken when the rule change was decisively defeated (Busch 2005). In 2016, anti-Trump Republicans hoped to attempt a similar maneuver, but could not even manage to bring the proposal to the floor for a vote (Arkin 2016). Otherwise, since 1976, the party conventions have been coronations of the presidential nominee rather than the venue of fights where an uncertain outcome hung in the balance.

As in many other things in American politics, Franklin Roosevelt played an important role in the transformation of the party convention. In 1932 he contributed to the candidate-centered character of the modern convention by becoming the first candidate to travel to the convention to accept his nomination in person (Neal 2005). With that precedent set, every subsequent major party nominee has done so, and the nomination acceptance speech has become the centerpiece of the convention. Four years later, Roosevelt promoted a national party rules change that played some part in the end of the multiballot convention, at least on the Democratic side: the end of the Democratic two-thirds rule that dated back to the 1832 convention.

Vice Presidential Nomination

The vice presidential nomination function of the convention also changed significantly, though in ways consistent with changes in the presidential nomination (Mayer 2000). At the end of the 19th century, the convention remained an agent of the party, selecting vice presidential nominees according to the party's perceived needs and with little regard for the preferences of the presidential nominee. By the middle of the 20th century, the vice presidential nomination had become a decision of the presidential nominee, ratified by the convention. In 1932, Roosevelt made a deal with his rival for the presidential nomination and House Speaker John Nance Garner; Garner dropped his bid for the presidency and Roosevelt supported him for vice president. By 1940, the Texan Garner was in open revolt against the New Deal, and Roosevelt worked successfully (though with some difficulty) to have him replaced on the Democratic ticket by his hand-picked successor, Agriculture secretary Henry Wallace. However, the pro-Soviet Wallace was sufficiently worrisome to the southerners and to the big-city mayors representing large Catholic constituencies that Democratic Party leaders were able to force Roosevelt to accept the convention's decision to replace Wallace with Harry S. Truman in 1944 (Barone 1991).

In 1948, Republican nominee Thomas Dewey effectively controlled the convention's vice presidential nomination. By contrast, Democratic president Harry Truman showed little interest in the decision, which was made by the convention. The last time a nominee left the vice presidential choice up to the convention was in 1956. In that year, Senator Estes Kefauver (D-Tenn.) and Senator John F. Kennedy (D-Mass.) vied for the vice presidential position while presidential nominee Adlai Stevenson looked on as a neutral observer. Kefauver ultimately prevailed.

Since 1956, every presidential nominee has successfully dictated his choice of running mate to the convention. Although this tendency originally took the form of the nominee declaring his vice presidential preference either surreptitiously or after being officially nominated, this was only a brief stop on the road toward a more openly candidate-centered approach. By the mid-1980s, when it became common for presumptive nominees to be known long in advance of the convention, they began openly considering and vetting potential running mates and declaring their choice before the convention even opened. In recent elections, the vetting and narrowing of choices has been accomplished by a vice presidential selection team formed by the presumptive nominee. The team has collected names of potential running mates, researched and assessed those individuals, conducted preliminary interviews, and arranged for top candidates to meet with the presumptive nominee. Once, in 2000, the chair of the vice presidential search (Richard Cheney) impressed the presumptive nominee (George W. Bush) so much that Bush ditched the search and named Cheney his running mate instead. The role of the convention has been reduced here, as in the presidential nomination itself, to a rubber-stamp for decisions made earlier by others.

On two occasions, trailing candidates have attempted to bolster their chances by announcing their vice presidential intentions before compiling enough delegates to win the presidential nomination. In 1976, Ronald Reagan declared on the eve of the Republican convention that he would pick Pennsylvania senator Richard Schweiker if nominated. Reagan's hope was that he would broaden his appeal by balancing his ticket with a northeastern liberal, but the ploy backfired, costing Reagan the support of some key southern conservatives (Shirley 2010). In the other instance, Republican Ted Cruz, in a desperate primary fight against Donald Trump in 2016, named Carly Fiorina his putative running mate in late April, long before the convention. This move also failed to save his campaign (Martin, Flegenheimer, and Burns 2016).

Though it was now the presumptive presidential nominee rather than the convention who made the vice presidential decision, the traditional desideratum of enhancing electoral appeal remained, and with it a version of ticket balancing. However, the form of these considerations changed. Before, the potential ability to deliver a large state and/or the capacity to provide ideological or geographical balance to the ticket were key. In the modern era, an equal or greater consideration is the ability to balance perceived characteristics of the presidential nominee, particularly if they are seen as deficiencies. For example, Bill Clinton's choice of Al Gore in 1992 did not meet traditional criteria of ticket-balancing—Gore was from a neighboring state of the peripheral South and came from the same moderate wing of the Democratic Party. However, as was fitting in a candidate-centered system, Gore balanced many of Clinton's perceived personal and political weaknesses. Clinton had evaded the draft, was accused of marital infidelity, was distrusted by environmental-ists, and had no foreign policy experience; Gore had served in Vietnam, seemed to have an exemplary family life, was a hero of environmentalists, and, as a member of the U.S. Senate, had considerable exposure to foreign policy issues. Similarly, in 2000, George W. Bush picked Richard Cheney as his running mate, though both were conservative and Cheney offered no electoral benefit, coming from a small, solidly Republican state (Wyoming). What Cheney offered was a "gravitas" that offset Bush's greater jocularity, and experience as secretary of defense during the first Gulf War that offset Bush's domestic focus as governor of Texas. Sometimes more traditional cri-teria prevail, as in 1980 when conservative westerner Ronald Reagan chose his main primary rival, the moderate George H. W. Bush, whose greatest primary strength was in the Northeast, or 2004, when Massachusetts liberal John Kerry ran with his main primary rival, North Carolinian John Edwards. Moreover, in the nuclear era, the governing capacity of the vice presidential nominee has been given greater consideration. In every case, though, the candidate—not the party—made the choice, with the candidate's perceived needs in mind. The convention simply carried out the wishes of the candi-date. The last time there was any significant resistance to a nominee's VP choice was in 1980, when some conservative Republicans rebelled against Reagan's choice of Bush and unsuccessfully pushed for Senator Jesse Helms (R-N.C.) or Congressman Jack Kemp (R-N.Y.) instead. The last roll call vote for a vice presidential nominee was in 1984; since 1988, all vice presidential nominees have been voted by acclamation under a suspension of the rules.

Platform

Party platforms have grown tremendously in breadth and length since the first nine-paragraph Democratic platform in 1840. In 2016, the Democratic platform was 26,058 words long, the Republican platform 35,467 words.

As with the vice presidential nomination, the convention formally retains the task of writing a platform, but in reality it mostly accepts what the pre-sumptive presidential nominee and his team have decided. In advance of the convention, the national committee of each party appoints a platform com-mittee made up of convention delegates, whose job is to draft a platform. In practice, the presumptive nominee almost always controls the majority of the platform committee. In the party-centered era of conventions, the party declared its principles and insisted that its nominee adhere to them. In the candidate-centered era of conventions, the candidate largely writes the plat-form to reflect his preferences.

Having said that, the back-and-forth between party and candidate is more complicated on the platform, even today, than is their relationship when it comes to vice presidential nominations. In the latter case, the candidate simply indicates his preferred running mate and the convention complies. In the former case, varying powerful interests within the party jealously guard the platform concessions they have won in the past. If a candidate feels strongly about a platform issue, he will usually prevail, but he must pick his battles carefully. A Republican candidate who sought to reverse his party's traditional planks on guns or abortion would face a politically damaging firestorm, as would a Democrat seeking to change his party's pro-choice stance or long-term (though practically defunct) commitment to ratification of the Equal Rights Amendment. However, sometimes parties make a strategic decision to reduce their exposure to criticism by reducing the overall size of their platform. In 1988, for example, Democrats chose to drastically reduce the length of their platform from 37,000 words to fewer than 5,000, though they lost that election anyway and the platform soon grew back.

Although political cynics often presume that party platforms are meaningless verbiage, they serve the function of tying parties to a series of policy commitments that are important to elements of the coalition that make them up. Political scientists studying party platforms conclude that winning candidates make a serious effort to fulfill their campaign promises most of the time (Pomper 1967; Fishel 1985; Goldsmith 2016).

A New Function

With the personalization of the party convention and the rise of new media came a new function, that of launching the general election campaign. In one sense, it was always the case that the convention launched the general election campaign, insofar as the party identified the candidates and platform that it would take into the fall. However, this function was limited when candidates were not determined in advance and did not accept their party's nomination until days or weeks after the convention.

Several conditions were necessary before the convention could perform this task in a serious way. First, candidates had to emerge and compete before the convention, so that the convention itself was seen as the culmination of a nomination process rather than the entirety of the process. Even more, as the presumptive nominee was known before the convention, the dramatic focus of the convention had to shift. Second, it had to become acceptable for the presidential and vice presidential nominees to appear at the convention to accept nomination in person. Finally, new modes of media had to arise to convey the convention directly to the public.

Modern mass media coverage began when radio broadcast the Republican National Convention in 1924. Although the 1940 and 1948 Republican National Conventions were televised to a limited audience, in 1952 both parties' conventions were nationally televised for the first time. Cable networks began broadcasting conventions in the 1980s, with CNN covering the 1980

GOP convention just six weeks after being launched as a network; in 1984, C-SPAN offered gavel-to-gavel coverage. Bloggers were invited to party conventions for the first time in 2004, while they were live-streamed for the first time in 2012 (Bowman, Sims, and O'Neil 2016).

Together, these developments gave the parties both the opportunity and the imperative to find a new role for the conventions. Conventions would no longer determine the nominee, except nominally; that would be done earlier. But they could serve as the nominee's opening audition on the national stage. That role has affected other aspects of the convention. In general, it took several years for convention managers to adjust to the central importance of television. The 1964 Republican convention televised bitter platform arguments that contributed to public perceptions of Barry Goldwater as an extremist. The 1968 Democratic convention was marred by scenes of violence outside the convention hall between police and antiwar demonstrators, as well as strife inside it. In 1972, Democrats managed their convention so poorly that George McGovern started his acceptance speech at nearly 3 a.m. Eastern time. Now, the parties work to avoid any conflict that might produce discordant pictures that would interfere with the image they desire to project. That means a tightly scripted convention, including few if any fights over rules or platform language on the floor. In order to minimize unseemly wrangling over the nomination when it is a foregone conclusion, Republicans have adopted Rule 40, requiring that a candidate have a majority of delegates in at least eight states before his or her name can be placed into nomination.

The parties have also turned to the convention as an avenue to frame their case for the upcoming election and introduce new or rising political figures. The keynote address, the presidential and vice presidential nominating addresses, and other primetime addresses are key elements of the party's message for the electorate. Some, like then–U.S. Senate candidate Barack Obama, parlay their opportunity into a brighter political future; Obama's keynote speech at the 2004 Democratic convention launched him toward the presidency. Others stumble, though some recover; Bill Clinton's 1988 speech nominating Michael Dukakis was widely panned as overly long and boring, but bad reviews did not prevent him from winning the nomination four years later (Kornacki 2012).

Paradoxically, the new convention role as a televised general election campaign launch has made the convention less interesting and newsworthy. Television viewership of the convention has accordingly declined. Democratic and Republican conventions from 1960 to 1980 averaged a Nielsen rating of 25.9, with the highest score for any convention being 31.2 for the hotly contested 1976 Republican meeting; conventions from 1984 to 2012 averaged a Nielsen rating of only 18.6 (Sabato 2012). The decline in viewership has, in turn, caused the major networks to curtail their coverage. While cable news continues to offer gavel-to-gavel coverage of the conventions, the

"Big Three" networks (ABC, CBS, and NBC) now typically restrict live coverage to about two hours a night. This requires the convention managers to script the conventions even more closely, in order to take full advantage of the narrow window of coverage.

The Convention "Bounce"

Since the main task of the convention is now to launch the general election campaign, a key question of any given convention is how successful it is in boosting its presidential candidate's position in the contest. It is generally expected that a convention will provide some polling gain for the party's candidate, though how much depends on both contingencies such as the skill of the nominee's acceptance speech and fixed circumstances such as whether the nominee is already well known to the public, particularly an incumbent. Generally speaking, lesser-known candidates have more potential to boost their poll standings than incumbents, though both can gain.

The most dramatic convention "bounce" was seen when Bill Clinton gained 16 percentage points in 1992; in this, he was aided by Ross Perot's simultaneous (though temporary) exit from the race and semi-endorsement. Other big gainers were Jimmy Carter in 1976 and 1980, Walter Mondale in 1984, Ronald Reagan in 1980, and both George W. Bush and Al Gore in 2000 (cancelling out each other's 8-point gains). On the other hand, Mitt Romney, John Kerry, and George McGovern either made no gain or slightly lost ground. On average, since 1964, the convention bounce has averaged 5 percentage points. Of course, the bounce from the first convention is often counteracted by the bounce from the second convention. Bounces from either convention can also simply fade away as the "fundamentals" of the contest reassert themselves. On average, challengers have gotten slightly larger bounces than incumbents (5.3 percent to 4.7 percent), and bounces from 1964 to 1992 were nearly twice as large on average as those from 1996 to 2016. One possible explanation is that increased partisan polarization in the electorate has combined with reduced viewership to limit the capacity of a convention to shift views. Table 12.1 shows postconvention polling bounces since 1964.

Convention Scheduling and Location

Finally, the scheduling of modern conventions has shifted somewhat over the years. In the 1960s until the 1990s, there was an understanding between the parties that the nonincumbent party would hold its convention in July and the incumbent party would convene about a month later in August. It is still generally understood that the nonincumbent party will go first and the incumbent party second, but the exact timing has changed.

Table 12.1   Convention "Bounces" 1964–2016

Year	First Convention/Bounce	Second Convention/Bounce
1964	R/ Goldwater +5	D/Johnson +3
1968	R/Nixon +5	D/Humphrey +2
1972	D/McGovern +0	R/Nixon +7
1976	D/Carter +9	R/ Ford +5
1980	R/Reagan +8	D/Carter +10
1984	D/Mondale +9	R/ Reagan +4
1988	D/Dukakis +7	R/ Bush +6
1992	D/Clinton +16	R/ Bush +5
1996	R/Dole +3	D/Clinton +5
2000	R/Bush +8	D/ Gore +8
2004	D/Kerry -1	R/ Bush +2
2008	D/Obama +4	R/McCain +6
2012	R/Romney -1	D/ Obama +2
2016	R/Trump +3	D/Clinton +2

Source: Gerhard Peters. "The Post-Convention Bounce in Voters' Preference." *The American Presidency Project.* Ed. John T. Woolley and Gerhard Peters. Santa Barbara, CA: University of California, 1999–2016. http://www.presidency.ucsb.edu/data/convention_bounces.php.

Campaign finance rules, which restricted fundraising after the convention for candidates accepting federal funds, drove conventions into late August and early September in 2008 and 2012, but because candidates are no longer realistically expected to accept federal general election funds, this factor is no longer relevant. Both parties have also taken care to avoid scheduling their conventions at times that conflict with the Summer Olympics, which are always held in American presidential election years. Recently, a desire by incumbent parties to undercut their opponents' convention bounces has also led them to schedule their conventions only one or two weeks later. For the last three elections, only one week has separated the first and second party convention. In 2016, Republicans held their convention from July 18 to 21 and Democrats followed from July 25 to 28.

The party's decision about where to hold its convention is a strategic decision based on a number of factors. These include available convention venues, accommodations, and other logistical details; the local party's organizing capacity; and a desire to appeal to important swing states. (Studies by political scientists are divided on the question of whether parties actually gain local benefit from their conventions [Atkinson, Mann, Olivella, Simon, and

Table 12.2 Democratic and Republican National Convention Dates and Venues, 1964–2016

	First Convention	Second Convention
Year	Party/Location/Start	Party/Location/Start
1964	R/San Francisco/July 13	D/Atlantic City/August 24
1968	R/Miami/August 5	D/Chicago/August 26
1972	D/Miami/July 10	R/Miami/August 21
1976	D/New York City/July 12	R/Kansas City/August 16
1980	R/Detroit/July 14	D/New York City/August 11
1984	D/San Francisco/July 16	R/Dallas/August 20
1988	D/Atlanta/July 18	R/New Orleans/August 15
1992	D/New York City/July 13	R/Houston/August 17
1996	R/ San Diego/August 12	D/Chicago/August 26
2000	R/Philadelphia/July 31	D/Los Angeles/August 14
2004	D/Boston/July 26	R/New York City/August 30
2008	D/Denver/August 25	R/Minneapolis/September 1
2012	R/Tampa/August 27	D/Charlotte/September 3
2016	R/Cleveland/July 18	D/Philadelphia /July 25
2020	D/Milwaukee/July 13	R/Charlotte/August 24

Uscinski 2014].) Today, party conventions are much sought-after by cities, which stand to gain tens of millions of dollars from the event in the form of hotel bookings, outings to restaurants, and visits to other city attractions. Economic benefits to Cleveland from hosting the 2016 Republican national convention were estimated to be from $68 million to $110 million (Urycki 2017). In the 19th century, a handful of cities hosted the great majority of conventions: New York, Philadelphia, Baltimore, and Chicago. In the 20th century, the list of convention host cities grew considerably, though New York, Chicago, and Philadelphia remain popular choices. (In total, Chicago has hosted 25 national conventions.) Democrats will be holding their 2020 national convention in Milwaukee, Wisconsin, while Republicans will congregate in Charlotte, North Carolina, with both Wisconsin and North Carolina widely perceived to be swing states. In a departure from recent practice, the conventions will be spaced six weeks apart. Convention dates and locations from 1948 to 2020 can be seen in Table 12.2.

Party conventions have changed dramatically since the first presidential nominating convention held by the Anti-Masonic Party in 1831. However, they remain an important element of the presidential nominating system.

Party strategists will continue to try to get the most benefit from them, and cities will doubtless continue to vie to host them.

Sources

Arkin, James. 2016. "'Never Trump' Movement Dies in Committee." RealClear Politics, July 15. https://www.realclearpolitics.com/articles/2016/07/15 /never_trump_movement_dies_in_committee.html.

Atkinson, Matthew D., Christopher B. Mann, Santiago Olivella, Arthur M. Simon, and Joseph E. Uscinski. 2014. "(Where) Do Campaigns Matter? The Impact of National Party Convention Location." *Journal of Politics* 76, no. 4 (October): 1045–1058.

Barone, Michael. 1991. *Our Country: America from Roosevelt to Reagan.* New York: Free Press.

Bowman, Kathryn, Heather Sims, and Eleanor O'Neil. 2016. "How Conventions Have Been Covered, from NBC to YouTube." *Newsweek,* July 24. http:// www.newsweek.com/how-conventions-have-been-covered-nbc-you tube-482772.

Busch, Andrew E. 2000. "Momentum in the Pre-Reform Presidential Nominating Systems." Presented at the American Political Science Association, August 31–September 3.

Busch, Andrew E. 2005. *Reagan's Victory: The Presidential Election of 1980.* Lawrence: University Press of Kansas.

Congressional Quarterly. 1976. *Guide to U.S. Elections.* Washington, DC: Congressional Quarterly.

David, Paul T., Ralph M. Goldman, and Richard C. Bain. 1963. *The Politics of National Party Conventions.* Revised edition. New York: Vintage Books.

Democratic Party Platforms. 1840. "1840 Democratic Party Platform." May 6. Online by Gerhard Peters and John T. Woolley, *The American Presidency Project.* https://www.presidency.ucsb.edu/node/273160.

Devine, Christopher J., and Kyle C. Kopko. 2016. *The VP Advantage: How Running Mates Influence Home State Voting in Presidential Elections.* Manchester, UK: Manchester University Press.

Fishel, Jeff. 1985. *Presidents and Promises.* Washington, DC: CQ Press.

Goldsmith, Brian. 2016. "It Turns Out That Politicians Keep Their Word." *The Atlantic,* June 11. https://www.theatlantic.com/politics/archive/2016/06 /promises-promises/485981/.

Kornacki, Steve. 2012. "When Bill Clinton Died Onstage." *Salon,* July 30. https:// www.salon.com/2012/07/30/when_bill_clinton_died_on_stage/.

Martin, Jonathan, Matt Flegenheimer, and Alexander Burns. 2016. "Ted Cruz Names Carly Fiorina as His Running Mate, Seeking a Jolt." *New York Times,* April 27. https://www.nytimes.com/2016/04/28/us/politics/ted-cruz-carly -fiorina.html.

Mayer, William G. 2000. "A Brief History of Vice Presidential Selection." In William G. Mayer, ed., *In Pursuit of the White House 2000: How We Choose Our Presidential Nominees*. Chatham, NJ: Chatham House.

Neal, Steve. 2005. *Happy Days Are Here Again: The 1932 Democratic Convention, the Emergence of FDR—and How America Was Changed Forever*. New York: Harper.

Pomper, Gerald. 1967. "'If Elected, I Promise': American Party Platforms." *Midwest Journal of Political Science* 11, no. 3 (August 1967): 318–352.

Sabato, Larry J. 2012. "Reviewing the Convention Ratings." *Larry J. Sabato's Crystal Ball*, September 13. http://www.centerforpolitics.org/crystalball/articles/reviewing-the-convention-ratings.

Shirley, Craig. 2010. *Reagan's Revolution: The Untold Story of the Campaign That Started It All*. Nashville: Thomas Nelson.

Urycki, Mark. 2017. "How Much Did the Republican Convention Benefit Cleveland? Two Studies Disagree." WOSU, August 4. http://radio.wosu.org/post/how-much-did-republican-convention-benefit-cleveland-two-studies-disagree#stream/0.

White, F. Clifton. 1967. *Suite 3505: The Story of the Draft Goldwater Movement*. New Rochelle, NY: Arlington House.

CHAPTER THIRTEEN

National Primaries and Other Proposed Reforms

A variety of shortcomings in the presidential nominating system have led to a large number of proposals for reform. Some suggestions, like introduction of a single national primary to replace state primaries, would represent a fundamental change in the way the parties select candidates for president. Others are much more modest. Nearly all face obstacles, sometimes quite large, in the form of constitutional limits, political constrains within or between the parties, public apathy, or simple inertia in a system of federalism and separation of powers. Potential reforms also must always be weighed against the "law of unanticipated consequences," which warns that even well-intended change often brings unexpected results, some of them negative. Of possible reform proposals discussed in this chapter, four would be comprehensive reforms of the whole nominating system, while others would be more incremental.

Overall, the reformers' paradox remains: the bigger a proposed change, the less likelihood of it being adopted. Conversely, the more plausible the path to adoption, the less likely the impact will be noticeable. Although anyone can devise a perfect reform to solve the problems of the nominating system, enacting it and then seeing it perform as promised without negative unanticipated side effects is another thing altogether.

National Primary

The idea of a national primary is almost as old as the direct primary itself. The Progressive Party platform of 1912 endorsed the notion of a national primary, as did Woodrow Wilson in 1913 (Link 1979). Since then, advocates for the national primary have periodically raised the cry anew.

There are two basic versions of the national primary. In its purest form, supporters have argued that the series of state primaries and caucuses should simply be replaced by a single primary election held nationwide. Candidates would qualify for the ballot by obtaining a specified number of petition signatures—perhaps a number equal to 1 percent of the previous presidential election turnout. Votes would be tabulated across state lines, and the candidate with the most votes would win his or her party's nomination. In order to prevent a fringe candidate from winning with a plurality in a divided field, some proponents have endorsed inclusion of a run-off primary between the top two finishers if no one gains a majority in the first round. Some versions would allow independent voters to cast a ballot in the party primary of their choice, while others would close the national primary to party voters only. A national convention might still be held after the primary to designate a vice presidential nominee, approve a party platform, and attend to other party functions, but it would not have any role in the selection of the presidential candidate.

In the other version, state primaries would remain but would all be scheduled on a single day. Delegates would still be allocated state-by-state on the basis of those state primary results, and the nominee would still be determined by winning a majority of delegates. The decisive change in both cases would be that there would be no caucus procedures, only primaries, and the election(s) would take place on one day (though perhaps modified by contemporary early voting practices).

The national primary is, in certain respects, the most radical reform that is frequently proposed for the presidential nominating system. Its supporters tout its simplicity, uniformity, democratic character, and ability to remedy the disadvantages of primary front-loading. The pure form of national primary is undeniably simple, essentially undoing federalism as a factor in presidential nominations. Everyone would vote in more or less the same way, at more or less the same time. The result should be clear: Whoever receives a plurality or majority of votes wins. Straightforward majority rule is emphasized, and any residual influence by local party organizations would be further diminished. The simultaneous vote across the country would ensure that no early states (such as Iowa or New Hampshire) had outsized influence and no late-voting states would be left out as essentially irrelevant because they voted after the nomination was effectively decided (Nelson 2017).

There are, however, also a number of counterarguments raised by critics of the national primary. For one thing, simplicity is not always an advantage. Indeed, the entire American political system is built on complexity—separation of powers, checks and balances, bicameralism, and federalism all eschew simplicity in pursuit of a more complex and finely balanced democratic order. Additionally, while the national primary would combat one disadvantage of front-loading—unequal impact for state primaries depending on their place in the primary calendar—it would worsen others. Indeed, front-loading is often criticized for producing a system that is too much like a national primary. Critics of front-loading note that it raises the cost of the "entry fee" that must be raised and spent by candidates before and during the first few weeks of the primary calendar. A national primary, in which all states vote at the same time, would further raise the entry fee significantly for serious candidates. Analysts also note that front-loading gives voters little time for second thoughts about candidates who take control of the race early on; a national primary would offer no chance for second thoughts at all. In a related vein, since there would only be one stage of the vote, there would be no opportunity to gradually overcome candidates with a narrow but intense base as other candidates drop out along the way. Instead, especially without a run-off but perhaps even with one, a large group of mainstream candidates could split the vote, leaving extreme voices in command of the field. There is no guarantee against this in the current system— indeed, the primary success of Donald Trump in a fractured field would seem to show that it is possible—but it seems less likely. Finally, there would be even less opportunity for retail politicking or discussion of local issues than in the current system (Busch 2017).

Regional Primaries

Another comprehensive reform would replace the current decentralized system with a rationalized system of regional primaries that would vote in sequence. In most such proposals, the United States would be divided into four or five regions. All states in the region would vote on the same day, and the regions would take turns voting, with perhaps one month separating each vote. In most plans, the order of the regions would rotate in every election.

The first regional primary plan introduced as congressional legislation was proposed by Senator Robert Packwood (R-Ore.) in 1972. The "Packwood Plan" would have divided the country into five regions: Northeast, Midwest, South, Great Plains, and West. Seventy days prior to the first primary, to be held on the second Tuesday of March, the Federal Election Commission would select the first region by lot. The subsequent four primaries would be held at one-month intervals in an order also determined by lot (*Congressional Record* 1972; *Congressional Quarterly Weekly Report* 1972; Ranney 1978; Davis 1997).

The idea of regional primaries has been endorsed by the National Association of Secretaries of State (NASS), which has put forward its own specific plan. The NASS plan would group states into four regions—East, South, Midwest, and West. In a nod to state tradition and the benefits of ensuring at least some retail politicking, the voting would still begin with the Iowa caucuses and the New Hampshire primary, followed by one region voting on the Tuesday after the first Monday in each month from March through June. The order would rotate each election (National Association of Secretaries of State 1999).

In order to introduce more diversity into each region, a variation of the regional primary would define the regions by time zone—Eastern, Central, Mountain, and Pacific. Hence, both Massachusetts and South Carolina would share a region, as would Texas, Illinois, and South Dakota. All the states in a time zone would vote at once, followed perhaps a month later by all the states in the next time zone, and so on (Lengle 1992).

Proponents of the regional primary idea say that it would create an orderly system which would, like the national primary, end the madness of decentralized front-loading, but with less severe disruption. Unlike both the front-loaded system and the national primary, voters might have a better chance to assess candidates over time, and the pace of the campaign would be less frantic (FairVote 2018).

On the other hand, there would still be a significant probability that a presumptive nominee would emerge before the end of the primary season, meaning that many states could be left out of the decision. Detractors also say that unlike the current system, an early decision would also leave entire regions without influence. Though less problematic than the national primary in terms of the "entry fee," the regional primaries plan would not resolve that problem, either. To the contrary, since the primary season would start (or in the NASS plan, nearly start) with a large group of states voting at once, the entry fee could even be higher than in the current system.

Proponents of some form of the idea have often worked more informally to create regional coalitions of states that voluntarily adopted a uniform primary day. However, this has been done more often to advance particular regional interests than with a national system in mind. The first example came in the 1980s, when moderate and conservative southern Democrats concluded that they needed to work together to pull the Democratic Party back to the center by deliberately influencing the presidential nomination. This effort produced so-called "Super Tuesday," a primary date relatively early in the primary season when a large number of southern states vote at the same time. (It was possible for them to achieve this coordination because most southern state legislatures were still under Democratic control at the time.) The first meager attempt came in 1980, when three southern states voted together. In 1988, the southern Super Tuesday reached its peak when 14 southern and border states voted on the same day.

Although the promoters of what amounted to a regional southern primary achieved considerable success in coordinating southern primaries, the results were not what they had expected. In 1984, the chief beneficiary of Super Tuesday in the Democratic field was Minnesota liberal Walter

Mondale; in 1988, Al Gore from Tennessee won five southern or border states on Super Tuesday, but Jesse Jackson won five and Michael Dukakis of Massachusetts, the ultimate nominee, won Maryland plus the two biggest prizes, Florida and Texas (Richard Gephardt of Missouri won his home state). Moreover, seven nonsouthern states and territories also held their contests on Super Tuesday, and Dukakis won six of them. Only in 1992, when the southern primaries were divided across two days, did moderate southern Democrat Bill Clinton win the nomination (Norrander 1992).

Subsequently, other regions have tried to piece together regional primaries. The so-called "Yankee Primary" coordinated a number of New England primaries in 1996 and 2000, while there was a Great Lakes regional primary in 1996 (sometimes called the "Big Ten Primary") in which voters in Illinois, Michigan, Ohio, and Wisconsin all went to the polls on the same day. After 1996, there were also short-lived efforts to establish a "Rocky Mountain Primary," Prairie States Primary, Mid-Atlantic Primary, and Pacific Coast Primary, all of which came to naught.

In a decentralized system, coordination has proven very difficult. Differing subregional interests, partisan differences within a region, and even parochial concerns by officeholders have blocked voluntary bottom-up attempts to create regional primaries (Busch 2003). Moreover, the organizers of most voluntary regional primaries have typically aimed to increase their region's visibility by voting early in the nominating process, in contrast with a nationwide system of regional primaries, in which some regions would necessarily vote relatively late.

Small States First

A third comprehensive reform would be aimed explicitly and exclusively at reversing the front-loading in the nomination calendar. That reform, sometimes called the "Delaware Plan" or "Small States First Plan," would organize the order of primary contests so that smaller states would vote first and the largest states last. The United States would be divided into four groups of states based on population. The groups would take turns voting by month in ascending order of population, with the first group (of smallest states) voting in March; the final group, voting in June, would contain states with 60 percent of the U.S. population. This proposal was actually approved by the Republican National Committee in 2000, before being withdrawn from consideration by the convention under pressure from the George W. Bush campaign (Advisory Commission on the Presidential Nominating Process 2000). A variant of the Delaware Plan would have states vote by groups in ascending order of population, but with the weakest candidates removed from contention after each stage; another variant would allow Iowa and New Hampshire to continue voting first (Norrander 2010, 98–100).

Supporters of the Delaware Plan argue that it would promote more retail politicking by candidates in the early phase of a campaign and would extend the race, undoing the effects of front-loading. Because it would be based on population rather than region, each group of states would have representatives of each region of the nation. On the other hand, it is reasonable to wonder how much would be gained if all 13 Group 1 primaries were held on the first available date in March. The geographical dispersion of states within each group, touted as an advantage by supporters, could also be seen as a disadvantage that would require successful candidates to run what amounted to a national primary campaign four times over. Moreover, based on past experience, it seems possible that a nomination contest could effectively end with the exit of most candidates before the voting ever reached Group 4, essentially disenfranchising states with 60 percent of the population of the United States.

Other Grouped Primaries

Other proposals have advocated for different kinds of grouped primaries. The Ohio Plan would start the primary season with the small states, followed by three regional primaries (East and Midwest, South, and West) of roughly even population. Iowa, New Hampshire, Nevada, and South Carolina would be allowed to retain their early positions. Reminiscent of the fate of the Delaware Plan in 2000, a Republican committee voted to recommend that the 2008 Republican National Convention adopt the Ohio Plan for the 2012 primaries, but a second committee rejected the plan and it never reached the convention floor for a vote. Several other plans have been proposed that would create random groupings of states across regions, but none have achieved much attention or political traction (Norrander 2010, 100–103).

Preprimary Convention

Another truly radical proposal would reverse the order of the primaries and the national convention. Modeled after the system for party nomination for state offices used in Colorado and a few other states, this plan calls for holding the national convention first. The national convention, attended by delegates chosen through caucuses and local conventions, would consider and vote on the prospective candidates. Those candidates who reached a predetermined threshold of support—perhaps 20 or 30 percent—would advance to a national primary. The winner of the primary would be the party nominee. Some other states have a milder version of the preprimary convention. In California, for example, the Democratic Party holds a preprimary convention for purposes of deciding whether to endorse candidates in the primary; a candidate must receive 60 percent of the convention vote to be endorsed. This decision cannot block nonfavored candidates, but the endorsement is listed on the ballot and can benefit the candidate who receives it.

Several specific proposals have been advanced under this general rubric. The best-known may be the version proposed by political scientists Thomas Cronin and Robert Loevy. Under this plan, three-quarters of national convention delegates would be selected through state caucus-convention procedures; the other one-quarter would be party and elected officials. The national convention would hold two ballots. The first would identify the three candidates with the most support, allowing them to go on to the second ballot and eliminating the rest. Any candidate who received at least 25 or 30 percent of the votes on the second ballot would advance to the national primary (Cronin and Loevy 1982–1983; Wayne 2000).

Supporters of the preprimary convention argue that it would restore the party organization and peer review to the nominating process. The national convention would again achieve significance, but in this form might be more tolerable in a democratic age; rather than make the final nominating decision, the convention would serve to screen the candidates. Party activists would determine the first cut, but primary voters would have the final say. Moreover, because caucuses are a slow-motion process, front-loading would become irrelevant. And because caucuses cost so much less than primaries, worthy candidates with meager resources will have more of a chance to gain a foothold and become competitive. They would still ultimately have to navigate the very expensive national primary, but those that did make it past the convention as one of two or three surviving candidates would be virtually guaranteed attention and resources.

Critics respond that a candidate with broad popular support might never make it to the final round. The activists—either party regulars or movement ideologues—might so thoroughly control the front end of the process that other candidates would be shut out. Opponents of the reform raise the specter of the return of the "smoke-filled room"—a reference to political decision-making made in secret, rather than in an open and democratic fashion, by a small group of politically influential "kingmakers." Skeptics note that the cost advantage of a caucus-based system might not be fully replicated in larger, more populous states; in any event, candidates would still need to run a lengthy nationwide organizational campaign to prepare for caucus day (Mayer and Busch 2004a, 112–113). They can also point to the shortcomings of the Colorado system. Because the caucus-convention process might always be criticized as too closed and undemocratic, state lawmakers have provided a "safety valve": Candidates can choose to skip the caucus/convention process and petition directly onto the ballot. Candidates who do so are essentially negating the gatekeeping function of the preprimary convention. A national nominating system based on this premise would face a similar dilemma, either offering no roundabout and being subject to criticism as undemocratic, or providing a roundabout that would negate its purpose.

In any event, the preprimary convention as a presidential nominating mechanism is unlikely to be adopted. In certain respects, it is an even more radical reform than the national primary, since it would institute a national primary on top of a significant change in the delegate selection process, the nominating schedule, and the role of the national convention. It would require a drastic rewriting of national party rules, state law, and state party rules in both parties. The constituency for the reform is largely limited to political scientists who are searching for a way to reintroduce a strong role for the parties in the nominating process. For the time being, it represents an interesting thought exercise rather than a realistic reform option.

Incremental Reforms

If the preprimary convention and the national primary are the most extreme (though unlikely) possible reforms, there are a number of other proposed reforms that are much more incremental in character. One incremental reform would be to simply alter the balance between primaries and caucuses. Some argue for increasing the number of primaries on the grounds that caucuses are unrepresentative and provide too much opportunity for mischief by organized extremists. Others argue for increasing the number of caucuses on the grounds that primaries impose too great a cost on candidates and foster a depersonalized, media-driven campaign. The actual balance between primaries and caucuses typically shifts a bit from election to election. In 2020, the shift on the Democratic side will be more dramatic, as reforms adopted by the national Democratic Party in 2019 encouraged a move from caucuses to primaries. By summer 2019, 10 of the 13 Democratic caucus states from 2016 had declared that they would hold primaries in 2020 (Theobold 2019).

Another set of perennial proposals for primary reform revolves around the question of proportional representation. One school calls for more PR as a means of more accurately representing the views of the electorate. Another school calls for more winner-take-all rules, at least at the congressional district level, as a means of assuring that candidates who can build plurality or majority coalitions are not hamstrung by fringe candidates. Both of these questions—caucuses versus primaries and proportional representation versus winner wins more rules—are discussed at the national level, but most effective action takes place at the state level in a decentralized manner.

A third sort of incremental reforms is frequently proposed to combat the effects of primary front-loading and calendar creep. As detailed in Chapter 5, both parties have already undertaken a number of rules changes to try to prevent the nomination calendar from starting earlier and to try to reduce the compression of delegate selection in the front portion of the process. These efforts, which have included offering bonus delegates to states that go later, penalties for states that go too early, and calendar windows for contest scheduling, have yielded mixed results.

In addition, there exist some proposed political reforms that affect or could affect the primary system indirectly. Campaign finance reform is one of these. For example, the rise of Super PACs after the *Citizens United* and *SpeechNOW* court cases had the effect of providing resources to candidates who were not initially successful in early primaries, arguably elongating the nomination contests. In a sense, *Citizens United* has been a partial antidote to primary front-loading. If attempts to overturn *Citizens United* by constitutional amendment or a new Supreme Court decision ever prove successful, they could easily have the contrary effect of reinforcing front-loading.

Similarly, reforms of voting systems, whether by facilitating ease of voting through mail ballot elections or by curtailing the risk of voter fraud through voter identification laws, could impact primary processes and outcomes. Of course, they would also have an impact on the electoral system more generally, including general elections and nonpresidential primaries. Another reform of the voting mechanism is ranked-choice voting (RCV), an idea that is growing in popularity among reformers and has been adopted in general elections by Maine. At least two states (Alaska and Hawaii) have adopted ranked-choice voting for all voters in their 2020 Democratic primaries, while another two (Iowa and Nevada) proposed RCV for caucus voters who could not attend in person, but were rebuffed by the Democratic National Committee. Kansas Democrats have replaced their caucuses with an RCV primary. If a voter's first choice does not receive the necessary 15 percent to win delegates, the voter's second- or third-choice candidate will receive the vote. As of summer 2019, some other states, including Maine and New Hampshire, were considering making the move to RCV in their primaries (Eichen 2019; Theobold 2019). Proponents argue that such a system would more accurately represent voters' true preferences, especially in a large and splintered candidate field where many candidates may struggle to reach the 15 percent threshold required for delegates under Democratic rules.

Process of Reform

Procedurally, there is a valid question whether the federal government has the constitutional authority to impose a national primary, regional primaries, or other primary reforms on the states. Legislation that would establish a national primary, a system of regional primaries, or other comprehensive changes has been proposed over 300 times in Congress, but has never been approved by either chamber (Kamarck 2016). Article I, Section 4 of the Constitution gives state legislatures the authority to regulate the times, places, and manner of congressional elections, broadly subject to revision by Congress. Article II, Section 1 gives states power over the manner of election of presidential electors, while giving to Congress the authority to determine the day on which electors shall vote. In no case does the Constitution explicitly confer any authority to dictate the time or manner of presidential primaries, which are not even contemplated in the Constitution. Supporters of the national primary argue that existing language on congressional elections should be read as implicitly applying to presidential elections, including primaries. Such was the view of Justice Hugo Black in *Oregon v. Mitchell* (1970) in which he argued, "It cannot be seriously contended that Congress has less power over the conduct of presidential elections than it has over congressional elections." However, while Black voted with the majority to uphold a federal law establishing an 18-year voting age in federal elections, his opinion stood alone and was not joined by the majority, which seemingly found it to be too extreme.

Other cases have come to conflicting conclusions about whether political party primaries are essentially a public utility that is theoretically subject to nearly unlimited regulation. A series of federal court decisions that ultimately invalidated the "white primary" in the South treated the parties as a public agency, not a merely private association. In *Rice v. Elmore*, decided in the Fourth Circuit Court of Appeals in 1947, the court declared, "The party may, indeed, have been a mere private aggregation of individuals in the early days of the Republic, but with the passage of the years, political parties have become in effect state institutions, government agencies through which sovereign power is exercised by the people." Subsequent decisions beginning in the 1970s, however, at least partially returned to the view of parties as private associations with broad (though not unlimited) power to control their own nominations. In *Cousins v. Wigoda* (1975), the Court ruled that because "the National Democratic Party and its adherents enjoy a constitutionally protected right of association," its rules governing delegate selection could override contrary state law. A line of subsequent decisions have reaffirmed that general principle. In short, if Congress were ever to enact a law mandating a national primary—arguably the only realistic mode of adopting the reform—there is a good chance the law would be struck down as unconstitutional (Mayer and Busch 2004b).

There is, on the other hand, no question that the national parties have the right to impose rules for the conduct of delegate selection contests. Although the national parties were reluctant to do this before national Democrats began imposing civil rights requirements on state delegations in the 1960s, both parties have grown comfortable doing so. In contrast to Congress, which has the practical power but may lack the lawful authority, the national parties have the authority but often lack the power or will. This is because the national parties' main mechanism for enforcing delegate selection rules is to refuse to seat a state's convention delegation if the state has failed to comply with national party rules. This mechanism is a blunt instrument, which the national party is usually reluctant to utilize for political reasons. In *Democratic Party of United States v. Wisconsin* (1981), Democrats won the right to refuse to seat Wisconsin delegates who had been selected through an open primary in contravention of national party rules, but within a few years the party had given up on trying to prohibit open primaries because the political cost of doing so was too great (*Democratic Party of the United States v. Wisconsin* 1981). In 2008, Democratic rules required that delegations from Florida and Michigan be reduced in size because the states voted outside the allowed primary window, but eventual nominee Barack Obama insisted that the convention restore the delegations to full size; both states were critical to his electoral strategy in November.

Reforms also require adjustment of state law in many, or even all, states—adjustments that can only take place if both houses of the state legislature and the governor agrees. Major reforms can also require coordination of state party rules between Democrats and Republicans. This level of cooperation across institutions, states, and parties is very difficult to achieve. The fragmented and diverse character of the current American system for party nomination of presidential candidates is itself a telling example of why comprehensive reforms of the system face an uphill climb.

Sources

Advisory Commission on the Presidential Nominating Process. 2000. *Nominating Future Presidents: A Review of the Republican Process.* Washington: Republican National Committee.

Busch, Andrew E. 2003. "The Rise and Fall of the 2000 Rocky Mountain Regional Primary?" *PS: Political Science and Politics* 36 (April).

Busch, Andrew E. 2017. "National Primary—Con." In Richard J. Ellis and Michael Nelson, eds., *Debating the Presidency,* 4th ed. Washington, DC: Sage CQ Press.

Congressional Quarterly Weekly Report. 1972. "Presidential Primaries: Proposals for a New System." July 8, pp. 1650–1654.

Congressional Record. 1972. 92nd Congress, 2d session, vol. 118, pt. 12.

Cousins et al. v. Wigoda et al., 419 US 477 (1975).

Cronin, Thomas, and Robert Loevy. 1982–1983. "The Case for a National Pre-Primary Convention Plan." *Public Opinion* 5 (December–January), pp. 50–53.

Davis, James W. 1997. *U.S. Presidential Primaries and the Caucus-Convention System: A Sourcebook.* Westport, CT: Greenwood.

Democratic Party of the United States v. Wisconsin, 450 US 107 (1981).

Eichen, Adam. 2019. "The Case for Using Ranked Choice Voting in the 2020 Democratic Presidential Primaries." *In These Times*, April 1. http://inthes etimes.com/article/21814/ranked-choice-voting-2020-democratic -presidential-primary-bernie-sanders.

FairVote. 2018. "Rotating Primary Plan." http://archive.fairvote.org/index.php? page=2084&mode=showallbig&offset=9.

Kamarck, Elaine C. 2016. "Why Is the Presidential Nominating System Such a Mess?" Brookings Institution, January. https://www.brookings.edu/wp -content/uploads/2016/07/primaries.pdf.

Lengle, James I. 1992. "Reforming the Presidential Nominating Process." In Stephen J. Wayne and Clyde Wilcox, eds., *The Quest for National Office: Readings on Elections*. New York: St. Martin's.

Link, Arthur S., ed. 1979. *The Papers of Woodrow Wilson*, vol. 29. Princeton, NJ: Princeton University Press.

Mayer, William G., and Andrew E. Busch. 2004a. *The Front-Loading Problem in Presidential Nominations*. Washington, DC: Brookings Institution.

Mayer, William G., and Andrew E. Busch. 2004b. "Can the Federal Government Reform the Presidential Nomination Process?" *Election Law Journal* 3, pp. 613–625.

Minor/Third Party Platforms. 1912. "Progressive Party Platform of 1912." November 5. Online by Gerhard Peters and John T. Woolley, *The American Presidency Project*. https://www.presidency.ucsb.edu/node/273288.

National Association of Secretaries of State. 1999. "Rotating Regional Primary Plan Endorsed by National Association of Secretaries of State." Press release, February 16.

Nelson, Michael. 2017. "National Primary—Pro." In Richard J. Ellis and Michael Nelson, eds, *Debating the Presidency,* 4th ed. Washington, DC: Sage CQ Press.

Norrander, Barbara. 1992. *Super Tuesday: Regional Politics and Presidential Primaries*. Frankfort: University of Kentucky Press.

Norrander, Barbara. 2010. *The Imperfect Primary: Oddities, Biases, and Strengths of U.S. Presidential Nomination Politics*. New York: Routledge.

Oregon v. Mitchell, 400 US 112 (1970).

Ranney, Austin. 1978. *The Federalization of Presidential Primaries*. Washington, DC: American Enterprise Institute.

Rice v. Elmore, 165 F.2d 387 (4th Cir. 1947).

Theobold, Bill. 2019. "Who Knew? Ranked-Choice Voting Is Coming to the Presidential Election." *The Fulcrum*. June 12. https://thefulcrum.us/voting /iowa-virtual-caucus.

Wayne, Stephen J. 2000. "A Proposal to Reform the Presidential Nominating Process." *Nominating Future Presidents: A Review of the Republican Process*. Washington, DC: Republican National Committee, pp. 129–131.

CHAPTER FOURTEEN

Third-Party Presidential Nominations

As is well known, the American political system essentially revolves around two major parties, and since the 1850s those two parties have been the Democrats and the Republicans. There are a number of factors undergirding the two-party system in the United States. Perhaps the most important is the single-member plurality electoral system, which stipulates that each legislative district has one member elected per election, and that the candidate with the most votes (a plurality) wins. There is no benefit in finishing second or third. One way to understand how the single-member plurality system supports a two-party system is to think about how some common alternatives to it work. A single-member majority system would continue to limit the election to one winner but would require that winner to receive a majority of the vote (that is, more than half). Majority systems hold a second-round, or "run-off," election if no one receives a majority in the first round. In that situation, even small third parties can have leverage, as the top two finishers sometimes have to appeal to them in order to build a majority. Another alternative, widely used in European democracies, is proportional representation, in which multiple representatives are elected in a single electoral district, and parties win seats roughly in proportion to the votes they receive. In those cases, relatively minor parties regularly win representatives. The single-member plurality system used in the United States usually yields neither seats nor significant leverage to minor parties.

At the presidential level, the Electoral College works on similar (though not identical) principles. A candidate must win an outright majority of electoral votes to win the presidency, and there is a run-off of sorts if no one attains that. In that case, the election moves to the House of Representatives, where each state delegation gets a single vote and a majority of states are required to elect. However, the critical fact is that electoral votes are won by plurality, usually statewide (though in Maine and Nebraska, by a combination of congressional district and statewide). In other words, whichever candidate wins the most votes in California receives all 55 of the state's electoral votes. As in congressional elections, the second-place finisher receives nothing—let alone the third- or fourth-place finishers. In 1992, independent candidate Ross Perot won nearly 19 percent of the nationally aggregated popular vote but won zero electoral votes because he did not finish in first place in any state.

Along with the effects of the electoral system, other legal and cultural features in American politics discourage third parties. Since the advent of the Australian ballot, or secret ballot, in the 1890s, states have controlled ballot access. They have generally used that control to make it difficult for third parties to reach the ballot by imposing lengthy filing deadlines, high thresholds of petition signatures, and substantial fees for ballot access. On the other hand, major parties are often granted more or less automatic ballot access.

Federal campaign finance regulations since 1974 have also advantaged major parties. Although both major party candidates are given the option of accepting a large lump sum of federal funding for the general election, minor parties must win at least 5 percent of the nationally aggregated popular vote in order to receive federal matching funds after the election. (It should be noted, though, that no major party nominee has accepted the federal general election lump sum since John McCain did so in 2008.)

The framework devised by the Commission on Presidential Debates (CPD) makes it difficult, though not impossible, for minor party or independent candidates to participate in the general election debates. Since 2000, commission rules have called for non–major party candidates to be invited to join the presidential debates if candidates "appear on a sufficient number of state ballots to have a mathematical chance of winning a majority vote in the Electoral College, and have a level of support of at least 15 percent of the national electorate as determined by five selected national public opinion polling organizations, using the average of those organizations' most recently publicly reported results at the time of the determination" (Commission on Presidential Debates 2018). Among non–major party candidates, only John Anderson in 1980 and Ross Perot in 1992 participated in any presidential debate between 1960 and 2016, and both of those appearances came before the CPD's polling threshold was established (Anderson's came before the CPD even existed). Some reformers have suggested that an alternate measure be used to determine eligibility for inclusion in the presidential debates, perhaps lowering the polling threshold to 10 percent or basing eligibility only on whether the candidate is on the ballot in all 50 states or states with a majority of electoral votes (*Charlotte Observer* 2016).

Although more difficult to sort out than legal obstacles to minor parties, some also argue that there are cultural barriers in the United States. In this view, family is an important component of political socialization, and family loyalties to the two existing major parties are handed down. Major media are also socialized to focus on the two major parties.

Despite the wide range of obstacles to minor party success in American politics, there are nevertheless many examples of third-party or independent candidates. Broadly speaking, there are three types of such parties and candidates. The first category consists of rigidly ideological parties that can be quite long-lasting but tend to have limited influence. They nominate candidates for president in election after election, but garner very few votes and go largely unnoticed, appealing only to a hard core of committed supporters. The second category consists of parties or individual candidates that often have a short shelf-life, running hard in a few elections before disappearing, but that can win many votes and exert considerable influence on the major parties while they are active. These third-party or independent candidates arise to fill a gap in American politics when a major issue remains unaddressed by the major parties. The third category consists of schismatic third parties—essentially, a dissident wing of a major party that breaks off, usually temporarily, to protest the direction taken by the party's majority.

No third-party candidate has ever won the presidency; even the Republicans had established themselves by 1860 as the second major party in the wake of the total collapse of the Whigs. Only once since 1860 has a party other than Democrats or Republicans even finished as high as second in the popular vote or electoral vote. Nevertheless, third parties have significantly affected American politics on several occasions by either tilting the election to the major party farthest from them or by winning enough votes to draw one or both major parties in their preferred policy direction. The Populists, for example, won 22 electoral votes in 1892, grew in power by 1896, and drew the Democrats into their pro-regulation, free silver orbit before being in turn absorbed by the Democrats. Both Democrats and Populists nominated William Jennings Bryan, the pro-Populist Democrat from Nebraska, as their presidential candidate in 1896, essentially fusing the two parties. Ross Perot's 19 percent in 1992, holding the balance between Bill Clinton's popular vote (43 percent) and George H. W. Bush's (37 percent), subsequently drew both major parties in his direction on issues such as the federal deficit and political reform. Both major parties responded, Democrats with a tax increase and campaign finance reform and Republicans with spending cuts and term limits.

Third Parties and Their Presidential Nominations in the 19th Century

The 19th century saw its share of all three kinds of third parties. In the category of the rigidly ideological, the Prohibition Party arose in the later part of the century to push the abolition of alcohol. The category featuring short but powerful bursts by parties filling a crucial gap included the Free-Soil Party in 1848, the Republican Party of the 1850s (before becoming the second major party), and the Populist Party of the 1890s. The category of major party bolters included the Southern Democrats in 1860, Reform Republicans (or Mugwumps) of the 1880s, and the Gold Democrats and Silver Republicans in 1896 (both dissented from their respective parties' stance on currency inflation).

In every case, third parties utilized the same mechanism to nominate their presidential and vice presidential candidates as the major parties did: the national convention. Supporters of the third-party movement organized a convention, sent delegates representing local opinion, wrote a platform, and nominated candidates. In the case of party "bolts," the dissidents often walked out of their regular national convention and directly formed their own rump convention or reconvened in a different city after a short interval of time. In 1912, for example, the Progressive Party was formed by delegates supporting Theodore Roosevelt who walked out of the Republican Convention in protest of what they called the Taft "steamroller," or the ability of the Republican establishment backing Taft to control the process and secure the nomination of its candidate in defiance of the apparent preference of Republican primary voters.

Modern Third-Party Nominations

As the 20th century progressed, however, non–major party candidacies took a wider variety of routes. Because primary elections are run by the states and state laws systematically advantage major parties, third parties have usually not followed the major parties into the realm of state primaries.

A large number of third parties have retained use of the national convention to conduct their nominations. The Progressive Party of 1948 nominated former Democratic vice president Henry Wallace and running mate Gene Taylor by means of a national convention attended by 3,240 delegates. The Wallace-Taylor ticket was nominated by acclamation, and the two men accepted their nominations at an open-air rally at Shibe Park, the stadium of the Philadelphia Phillies. The party platform called for government ownership of large banks, railroads, electric power and gas, and the aircraft industry; a major expansion of the welfare state; and, as part of a broader attack on "anti-Soviet hysteria," repudiation of the Marshall Plan and the policy of containment of communism. (For balance, an earlier draft had included a condemnation of "left totalitarianism," but the reference was removed at Wallace's insistence.) A proposed platform amendment stipulating that "it is not our intention to give blanket endorsement of the foreign policy of any nation" was voted down, adding to the public perception that the Progressive Party was dominated by pro-Soviet elements (Devine 2013; MacDonald 1948; Starobin 1972; MacDougall 1965).

The same year, 13 members of the Alabama delegation and the entire Mississippi delegation walked out of the Democratic national convention in Philadelphia when it approved a platform containing a strong civil rights plank. Supporters of the protest met in Birmingham, Alabama, to launch a third party. Most established Southern politicians stayed away. Although convention organizers planned for delegates from 13 states, none came from Georgia, Kentucky, or North Carolina; only four college students and a woman traveling home from vacation represented Virginia. After more prominent leaders such as Arkansas governor Ben Laney declined to run, the convention nominated (or, as party leaders later claimed, "recommended") South Carolina governor Strom Thurmond as the presidential candidate (Busch 2012, 114–118). Unlike Wallace, who had been running for president for months before being formally nominated by the Progressive Party, Thurmond had arrived in Birmingham not knowing that he would be pressed into running by the movement's leaders. The party platform praised states' rights, condemned the Democratic civil rights plank, and warned of impending totalitarianism in America unless federal power were checked (Frederickson 2001; Cohodas 1993). In November, Thurmond's States' Rights (or Dixiecrat) ticket won 2.4 percent of the national vote and 39 electoral votes from four Southern states—Louisiana, Mississippi, Alabama, and South Carolina. Wallace won about the same number of popular votes but no states and hence no electoral votes.

The Independents

The most successful non–major party candidates since 1948 have been independents who ran with either no third-party structure or as head of a nominal party that they constructed to serve as their platform. In most of those cases, there was no party nomination; instead the candidates put their names on the ballot through extensive petition drives.

For example, the American Independent Party was contrived by segregationist George Wallace to support his run for the presidency in 1968. However, there was no party convention. Wallace wrote his own platform, named his own vice presidential running mate, and forbade the use of the AIP label by anyone running for lower office. The AIP was not a real party making a nomination so much as a convenient structure built around and for an independent candidate who had left the Democratic Party and would return to it in 1972. As one observer noted, "the AIP was not an integrated, functioning party; it existed only as a vehicle for Wallace's candidacy" (Carlson 1981). The party served as a nucleus around which volunteers could organize the petition drives necessary to put Wallace's name on the ballot. In some states, Wallace was put on the ballot as the candidate of other parties, including (in Connecticut) the "George Wallace Party" (Nelson 2014).

In that sense, George Wallace's 1968 candidacy was an example for others, pointing the way toward another model for future independent candidates. The crucial element of Wallace's "nomination" was the effort by his supporters to put his name on the ballot in 50 states. It was that element—"nomination" by ballot qualification—that some others would copy. In his fight for ballot access, Wallace successfully challenged restrictive state ballot access laws. In *Williams v. Rhodes* (1968), the Supreme Court ruled that Ohio's ballot access rule that third-party candidates had to secure around 433,000 petition signatures by February 7 of the election year posed an unconstitutionally high burden on the rights of third parties to associate and run campaigns. From then on, high petition requirements and early filing deadlines could be challenged in court, and a number of cases resulted in further loosening of ballot access restrictions (Flood and Mayer 1996).

After George Wallace, four other notable independent candidates would run without the assistance or cover of a party. In 1976, former Democratic senator and 1968 presidential aspirant Eugene McCarthy ran as a liberal independent. In 1980, Republican congressman John Anderson of Illinois ran as an independent after unsuccessfully seeking the Republican presidential nomination. Anderson appealed primarily to liberal Republicans and college-educated upscale independents; he made a point, when announcing his candidacy, of emphasizing that he was running as an independent, not for a third party (Bush 1985, 299–304). Both McCarthy and Anderson successfully challenged in court additional ballot access restrictions; Anderson's campaign brought the case *Anderson v. Celebrezze* (1983), in which the Supreme Court held Ohio's new March 20 filing deadline for petitions to still be too early. McCarthy had minimal success at the polls, winning fewer than 1 percent nationwide, but Anderson made a bigger impact. He participated in one nationally televised general election debate with Ronald Reagan and won 7 percent of the nationally aggregated popular vote in November 1980, which qualified him to receive a modest allotment of federal funds retroactively for his 1980 campaign (he would also have been eligible for federal funds in 1984 but he declined to run that year).

In February 1992, Texas businessman H. Ross Perot declared on the *Larry King Show* that he would run for president as an independent if supporters would put his name on the ballot in all 50 states. They did so under the umbrella of an organization (but not a party) called United We Stand America. Perot emphasized the federal deficit, political reform, and his opposition to trade deals such as the North American Free Trade Agreement (NAFTA). He appealed to relatively conservative independents, and according to exit polls drew roughly evenly from George H. W. Bush and Bill Clinton (Hibbitts 2012). Perot dropped out of the race in July, reentered in October, and participated in all three fall presidential debates. He won 19 percent of the nationally aggregated popular vote, the best showing by a non–major party candidate since Theodore Roosevelt in 1912. However, because his support was spread evenly around the country, Perot, like Anderson, won no states and no electoral votes. Like Anderson, though, Perot also became eligible for federal funds in the following election, and in 1996 he accepted them.

In 2016, Republican Evan McMullin left his party to run as an independent conservative against Donald Trump. McMullin, however, started his campaign late in 2016 and was on the ballot in only 11 states. In another two dozen, he ran a write-in campaign. Although he never polled well nationally, McMullin (who was Mormon) was competitive in Utah for a time in October 2016, before Trump pulled ahead. Consequently, unlike most non–major party candidates, he had a realistic shot at winning some electoral votes; some commentators even spun a scenario in which McMullin's Utah votes would prevent the major party candidates from attaining an Electoral College majority, thus throwing the election into the House of Representatives, where McMullin—who once served as policy director for the House Republican Conference—might have a chance to win (Morris 2016). In the end, McMullin lost 45 to 21 percent to Trump in Utah, and gained only half a percent nationwide.

Wallace, Anderson, and Perot each managed to achieve ballot access in all 50 states. Both Anderson and Perot attempted to build a more organized national campaign structure after their initial runs as independent candidates. Anderson announced the formation of the National Unity Party in November 1983, but the effort faced ballot access difficulties and had trouble finding a compelling rationale when Anderson's critique of the incumbent Reagan administration was nearly indistinguishable from that offered by Democrats. Ultimately, the attempt to build a National Unity Party collapsed and Anderson endorsed Walter Mondale in 1984 (Flood and Mayer 1996, 307–308).

Perot used United We Stand as the basis for the creation of a new party, the Reform Party, that would run a candidate in 1996. The Reform Party devised an innovative nomination system that combined a nationwide primary vote of party members by mail, email, or phone, followed by a convention to hear speeches by the finalists, followed by a second balloting procedure, followed by a convention in Valley Forge to announce the winner. Perot personally intervened to offer himself as a candidate, taking the nomination from former Colorado governor Richard Lamm at the last moment. Moreover, the balloting procedure was marred by breakdowns and irregularities; tens of thousands of votes cast by telephone were invalidated (Toner 1996). In the end, only about 5 percent of Reform Party members voted in the primary (Ceaser and Busch 1997, 111–112). Perot won with 65.2 percent of the vote. Facing a calmer political environment than in 1992, though,

Perot won only 8.4 percent of the nationally aggregated popular vote (and no electoral votes) as the Reform Party nominee in the general election.

Perot stepped away from the Reform Party for good after 1996. Four years later, the party used the same combination of mail ballots and convention to nominate Pat Buchanan, who had run for the Republican nomination in 1992 and 1996. (Buchanan's main rival, John Hagelin, bolted from the Reform Party after losing at the convention, rejoining the Natural Law Party from which he had come [Norrander 2010, 57].) In November, Buchanan won less than 1 percent of the vote nationally, though his vote total was larger than Al Gore's margin over George W. Bush in four states with 30 electoral votes (Ceaser and Busch 2001, 159). After 2000, however, the Reform Party slipped into obscurity.

Contemporary Ideological Parties

There also remain many small ideological parties that run every year, usually to little effect. Some that fall into this category have included several versions of socialist parties, the Constitution Party (formerly the Taxpayers Party), the Natural Law Party, and the Prohibition Party, which, to the surprise of many, still exists. These parties typically use a national convention held in the year of the presidential election, though in 2016, for the first time, the Prohibition Party was reduced to making its nomination by conference call rather than convention (Winger 2015).

There are two other long-term ideological parties that have developed nomination procedures and have actually obtained a nontrivial number of votes from time to time.

The organization with the longest history is the Libertarian Party, which was founded in 1972. The Libertarians espouse minimalist government in all realms, favoring minimal taxes and spending, decentralization of power to state and local governments, deregulation of economic activity, a loosening of restrictive drug laws, reduction of foreign aid and military intervention abroad, privatization of education and other government services, and elimination of what might be called "morals laws." They are divided on abortion, as some libertarians see it as a natural right that should be legally protected and others see it as a violation of the right to life and hence something that can legitimately be restricted. Libertarian candidates have been nominated for president in every election since 1972, finishing most strongly in 1980 (with 1 percent of the national vote won by Ed Clarke) and 2016 (when nominee Gary Johnson garnered nearly 3 percent).

Libertarians have always used a national convention to nominate their candidates. Delegates are selected by state Libertarian parties, which have wide freedom to determine their delegate selection procedures as long as they are closed to all but formal party members. Most use state conventions.

Delegates are not bound or pledged to candidates for the nomination. To be eligible for consideration by the convention, a candidate for president or vice president must collect the signatures of 30 delegates; each delegate can nominate one candidate for each office. Multiballot conventions are common, and balloting continues until a candidate receives a majority of votes. If no one receives a majority on a given ballot, the candidate with the fewest votes, as well as any candidates with less than 5 percent of the vote, is removed from future ballots (Libertarian Party 2016). Libertarian conventions required four ballots to select their 1984 presidential nominee, three ballots to select the 2004 nominee, six ballots to pick their 2008 nominee, and two ballots in 2016. In 2016, former Republican governor of New Mexico Gary Johnson was nominated for president, having won a majority of votes on the second ballot. Johnson began as one of six candidates, but after the first ballot, the candidate with the fewest votes was dropped from consideration. Former Republican governor of Massachusetts William Weld was chosen by the convention majority to run for vice president on the second ballot. Again, the weakest candidate on the first ballot was excluded from the second ballot. There were 911 delegates and 76 alternates present at the 2016 Libertarian convention, which received live coverage on C-SPAN, including coverage of a debate between the presidential candidates prior to the convention vote.

The Green Party ran its first presidential candidate in 1996 and had its greatest success in 2000, when nominee Ralph Nader won nearly 3 percent of the national vote and may have cost Al Gore the crucial state of Florida. In 2016 Green Party presidential candidate Jill Stein won 1 percent of the national vote in another exceedingly close presidential election. Like its counterparts in Europe, the Green Party in the United States focuses on environmentalism, cultural leftism, social democracy, and opposition to military spending and interventions. The Green Party also uses a convention for nomination, though in 2016 the convention delegates were chosen through a combination of state conventions, caucuses, and primaries. Most of the primaries were by mail ballot and were held privately, though a few (including California's) were conducted publicly and in conjunction with the Democratic and Republican primaries. Delegates from these state processes are allocated proportionately and are pledged. At the convention, candidates receiving less than 10 percent after two rounds of balloting are dropped from consideration (Green Party of the United States 2016).

For a summary of third-party and independent nominations procedures since World War II, see Table 14.1.

Altogether, third-party and independent candidates receive their "nominations" by a variety of means. These processes are not given succor by state and federal law to the same extent as major party nominations, but that also frees them to experiment and innovate more widely. Although the general

Table 14.1 Selected Third Party and Independent Presidential Nominations, 1948–2016

Candidate/Party	Year	Nomination Procedure
Wallace/Progressive	1948	National convention
Thurmond/States' Rights	1948	Dem convention bolt/National convention
Wallace/American Independent	1968	Ballot qualification
Schmitz/American	1972	National convention
McCarthy/independent	1976	Ballot qualification
Anderson/independent	1980	Ballot qualification
Perot/independent	1992	Ballot qualification
Perot/Reform	1996	National mail primary/National convention
Buchanan/Reform	2000	National mail primary/National convention
Nader/Green	2000	National convention
Johnson/Libertarian	2016	National convention
Stein/Green	2016	State caucuses, conventions, or primaries/National convention
McMullin/independent	2016	Ballot qualification
Constitution	2016	State caucuses/National convention
Socialist	2016	National convention
Prohibition	2016	Conference call

election system in the United States creates great obstacles to third parties, the ongoing dissatisfaction of American voters with the two major parties means we should not ignore the ways they choose their candidates.

Skip Wiltshire-Gordon provided research assistance on this chapter.

Sources

Busch, Andrew E. 2012. *Truman's Triumphs: The 1948 Elections and the Making of Postwar America*. Lawrence: University Press of Kansas.

Bush, Gregory, ed., 1985. *Campaign Speeches of American Presidential Candidates 1948–1984*. New York: Frederick Ungar.

Carlson, Jody. 1981. *George C. Wallace and the Politics of Powerlessness: The Wallace Campaigns for the Presidency, 1964–1976*. New Brunswick, NJ: Transaction.

Carter, Dan T. *The Politics of Rage: George Wallace, the Origins of the New Conserva-tism, and the Transformation of American Politics.* New York: Simon & Schuster.

Ceaser, James W., and Andrew E. Busch. 1997. *Losing to Win: The 1996 Elections and American Politics.* Lanham, MD: Rowman & Littlefield.

Ceaser, James W., and Andrew E. Busch. 2001. *The Perfect Tie: The True Story of the 2000 Presidential Election.* Lanham, MD: Rowman & Littlefield.

Charlotte Observer. 2016. "The Election Isn't Rigged, But the Presidential Debates Seem to Be." August 12. http://www.charlotteobserver.com /opinion/editorials/article95292627.html.

Cohodas, Nadine. 1993. *Strom Thurmond and the Politics of Southern Change.* New York: Simon & Schuster.

"The Commission on Presidential Debates: An Overview." http://www.debates .org/index.php?page=overview.

Devine, Thomas W. 2013. *Henry Wallace's 1948 Presidential Campaign and the Future of Postwar Liberalism.* Chapel Hill: University of North Carolina Press.

Flood, Emmet T., and William G. Mayer. 1996. "Third-Party and Independent Candidates: How They Get on the Ballot, How They Get Nominated." In William G. Mayer, ed., *In Pursuit of the White House: How We Choose Our Presidential Nominees.* Chatham, NJ: Chatham House.

Frederickson, Karl. 2001. *The Dixiecrat Revolt and the End of the Solid South 1932–1968.* Chapel Hill: University of North Carolina Press.

Green Party of the United States. "Rules of the Presidential Nominating Conven-tion of the Green Party of the United States." https://web.archive.org/web /20151020052758/http://gpus.org/national-committee/rules-of-the -presidential-nominating-convention-of-the-green-party-of-the-united -states/#01.

Hershey, Marjorie Randon. 2013. *Party Politics in America,* 15th ed. Boston: Pearson.

Hibbitts, Tim. 2012. "The Man Who Supposedly Cost George H. W. Bush the Presidency." PollingReport.com, January 30. http://www.pollingreport .com/hibbitts1202.htm.

Libertarian Party. "How the Libertarian Party Selects Its Presidential, VP Nomi-nees." https://www.lp.org/news-press-releases-how-the-libertarian-party -selects-its-presidential-vp-nominees/

MacDonald, Dwight. 1948. *Henry Wallace: The Man and the Myth.* New York: Vanguard Press.

MacDougall, Curtis. 1965. *Gideon's Army.* New York: Marzani and Munsell.

Morris, Benjamin. 2016. "How Evan McMullin Could Win Utah and the Presi-dency." FiveThirtyEight, October 13. http://fivethirtyeight.com/features /how-evan-mcmullin-could-win-utah-and-the-presidency/.

Nelson, Michael. 2014. *Resilient America: Electing Nixon in 1968, Channeling Dis-sent, and Dividing Government.* Lawrence: University Press of Kansas.

Norrander, Barbara. 2010. *The Imperfect Primary: Oddities, Biases, and Strengths of U.S. Presidential Nomination Politics.* New York: Routledge.

Starobin, Joseph R. 1972. *American Communism in Crisis: 1943–1957.* Cambridge, MA: Harvard University Press.

Toner, Robin. 1996. "Reform Party Names Perot Its Presidential Candidate; 49,000 Participated in Vote." *New York Times*, August 18. http://www.nytimes.com/1996/08/18/us/reform-party-names-perot-its-presidential-candidate-49000-participated-in-vote.html.

Winger, Richard. 2015. "Prohibition Party Cancels Presidential Convention and Instead Will Nominate by Direct Vote of Members." *Ballot Access News*, May 7. http://ballot-access.org/2015/05/07/prohibition-party-cancels-presidential-convention-and-instead-will-nominate-by-direct-vote-of-members/.

PART 2

State-by-State Guide

Primary results from 2000 to 2016 are self-explanatory. Caucus results may come in one of three forms. If labeled simply "caucus," the results are the total tabulated votes received by the candidates in the first-level caucus meetings. In some cases, however, results are reported in terms of delegates supporting each candidate at or elected to a higher-level convention in the state. These cases are labeled, as are other cases—especially when an incumbent president is running for renomination unopposed—when the only results that are available are in the form of the commitments of delegates sent to the national convention. In many of those cases, the delegates to the national convention are elected as nominally uncommitted, but almost always vote for the incumbent at the convention.

The 2020 delegate selection entries examine several factors. These include:

Number of Delegates

For Democrats, that includes a total; a number assigned to be elected at the district level (usually in congressional districts but sometimes in other districts such as state districts senate); pledged PLEOs, or Party Leader/Elected Official delegates who are pledged and allocated by the results of the primary or caucus; and automatic or unpledged PLEOs, or "superdelegates." For Republicans, delegate numbers include a total; a number of at-large delegates that includes a base number (10) given to every state, bonus delegates depending on the party's formula, and three automatic party delegates (the state party chair and the two national committee members); and three delegates per congressional district.

Date of 2020 Delegate Selection Event

Please be aware that a few of these may shift after publication.

What Week of the Delegate Selection Season

This number is measured from the date of the Iowa caucuses.

Type of Delegate Selection Event, Which Has Two Dimensions

(1) Caucus/convention or primary (see Chapters 2 and 3 in Part I). (2) Open (in which all voters can participate regardless of party); semiopen (in which the party allows independents but not members of the opposing party to participate); or closed (in which only the party's member's may participate). (See Chapter 4 in Part I.) Some GOP primaries or caucuses may be canceled in 2020.

Mode of Awarding Delegates, Possibilities for Which Differ by Party (see Chapter 10 in Part I)

Democrats mandate that proportional representation be used with a 15 percent threshold at both the district and at-large level.

Republicans permit a much broader range of options. These include pure delegate primaries or caucuses unconnected to a presidential preference vote; proportional representation with thresholds ranging up to 20 percent; winner-take-all by statewide and/or district vote; winner-take-most by statewide and/or district vote. There are many specific forms of winner-take-most, but the essence of the idea is that the vote leader can win all the delegates at stake if he or she receives a majority of the vote, but delegates will be more broadly distributed if no one attains a majority of the vote.

How Delegates Are Chosen (see Chapter 11 in Part I)

Where the mode of awarding delegates has to do with how numbers of delegates are allocated to candidates, this question has to do with how the individuals who serve as delegates are selected. In some states, the delegates appear on the ballot and are elected in the primary itself. Most states, however, choose the delegates after the primary, by convention, state party committee selection, or election of at-large delegates by those already chosen to serve as district delegates.

Bound for How Many National Convention Ballots

No convention vote for a presidential nomination has gone past the first ballot since the 1952 Democratic convention. However, it is always theoretically possible that such a scenario could be repeated someday. Democratic national rules release delegates from their pledges after the first ballot or if the candidate leaves the race. Republican rules determining binding are decided state-by-state, and most states release delegates after the first ballot.

In many states, there are additional exceptions. GOP delegates are generally released if their candidate ends his or her campaign, and in some states may be released early if their candidate does not achieve a certain level of balloting strength. In a few winner-take-all cases, after release delegates are then bound to the second-place winner. These complications are not noted in the entry here.

Alabama

Alabama was one of the first states to secede before the Civil War, and Montgomery was the capital of the Confederate States of America until Virginia left the Union and Richmond became the capital. A century later, the state was the scene of key civil rights battles such as the Montgomery bus boycott, conflicts over desegregation of schools, and strife in Selma over voting rights. Alabama has the fifth-highest proportion of African Americans of any state, and is significantly more rural than the national average, but also has a manufacturing base in Birmingham. Alabama was part of the Democratic "Solid South" for decades, and the Republican Party was a nonfactor in Alabama politics until late in the 20th century. However, no Democrat has won Alabama's presidential electors since Southerner Jimmy Carter did so in 1976. Ronald Reagan's razor-thin win over Carter in 1980—48.8 percent to 47.5 percent—started a Republican streak that continued in 2016 with Donald Trump's 62 to 34 percent defeat of Hillary Clinton.

Alabama held its first presidential primary in 1928. Initially run as a pure delegate primary, Alabama's primary typically produced unpledged delegates, though they often expressed informal preferences. After 13 of the state's unpledged but anti-Truman delegates walked out of the 1948 Democratic national convention protesting passage of a strong civil rights plank, Alabama discontinued its primary for the next four presidential elections. The primary resumed in 1968 as a delegate selection primary, and in 1980 became a binding presidential preference primary.

Scheduled in early March from 1968 to 1988, the Alabama primary was held in the first week of June in 1992–2004, then early February (2008), mid-March (2012), and back to early March (2016). On several occasions, Alabama lawmakers have added the state to a large number of Southern and other states voting on the same day; Alabama shared its primary date with 15 other primaries in 1988, 15 in 2008, and 10 in 2016, along with numerous caucuses.

Significant Alabama primaries have included:

1980: In Alabama's first binding presidential preference primary, Republican Ronald Reagan soundly defeated George H. W. Bush by 70 percent to 26 percent. Reagan won a Southern trifecta that day, prevailing by big margins in the Georgia and Florida primaries as well just days after the South Carolina primary. Democratic president Jimmy Carter won an even wider Alabama victory, with 82 percent of the vote against liberal challenger Edward Kennedy.

1984: Democrat Walter Mondale came back from a surprise loss to Gary Hart in New Hampshire to win March 13 primaries in Alabama and Georgia. Though Mondale lost three other primaries that day, his Southern wins stabilized his campaign, allowing him to go on the offensive subsequently.

1988: The first mega–Super Tuesday, with 16 primaries in early March, included Alabama. Republican George H. W. Bush won handily in the state, as he did elsewhere, helping to cement his front-running status. Democrats were more splintered. Jesse Jackson won over Al Gore by 44–37 percent, benefiting from turnout by the state's large black population. Gore's inability to capitalize in more Southern primaries on Super Tuesday helped doom his campaign.

2008: On a day when 15 other states held primaries, Republican Mike Huckabee beat ultimate nominee John McCain by 41 to 37 percent, while Barack Obama defeated Hillary Clinton 56 to 41 percent in the Democratic contest. Altogether, Huckabee won a respectable four primaries that day to McCain's nine and Mitt Romney's two. Clinton outpolled Obama in nine of 16 primaries, but Obama won the six caucuses that day.

2012: Republican Rick Santorum received a boost when he edged out former House Speaker Newt Gingrich and ultimate nominee Mitt Romney 34.5–29.3–29.0 percent.

2016: In her second try in Alabama, Hillary Clinton swamped Bernie Sanders by 78–19 percent by winning black voters by a ratio of 15:1 (Cohen 2018, 21). On the Republican side, Donald Trump beat conservative competitors Ted Cruz and Marco Rubio 43–21–19 percent. Ten other states voted.

Source

Cohen, Richard E., with James A. Barnes. 2018. *Almanac of American Politics.* Washington, DC: National Journal.

Alabama Primary Results 2000–2016

2000

Democratic primary (6/6)		Republican primary (6/6)	
Gore	77.0	Bush	84.2
Uncommitted	17.4	Keyes	11.5
LaRouche	5.65	Uncommitted	4.2

2004

Democratic primary (6/1)		Republican primary (6/1)	
Kerry	75.0	Bush	92.8
Uncommitted	17.5	Uncommitted	7.2
Kucinich	4.2		
LaRouche	3.3		

2008

Democratic primary (2/5)		Republican primary (2/5)	
Obama	56.0	Huckabee	41.3
Clinton	41.6	McCain	37.1
Edwards	1.5	Romney	17.8
		Paul	2.7

2012

Democratic primary (3/13)		Republican primary (3/13)	
Obama	84.1	Santorum	34.5
Uncommitted	15.9	Gingrich	29.3
		Romney	29.0
		Paul	5.0
		Uncommitted	1.5

2016

Democratic primary (3/1)		Republican primary (3/1)	
Clinton	77.9	Trump	43.4
Sanders	19.2	Cruz	21.1
Uncommitted	2.4	Rubio	18.7
		Carson	10.2
		Kasich	4.4

Sources: https://transition.fec.gov/pubrec/fe2000/2000presprim.htm#AL;
https://transition.fec.gov/pubrec/fe2004/federalelections2004.pdf;
https://transition.fec.gov/pubrec/fe2008/federalelections2008.pdf;
https://transition.fec.gov/pubrec/fe2012/federalelections2012.pdf;
https://transition.fec.gov/pubrec/fe2016/federalelections2016.pdf.

2020 Delegate Selection

Democratic

Number of delegates: 61 total delegate votes—34 district, 11 at-large, 7 pledged
    PLEOs, 9 unpledged PLEOs

Date of 2020 contest: March 3

What week of the delegate selection season: 5

Type of delegate selection event: Open primary

Mode of awarding delegates: Proportional representation with a 15 percent
    threshold

Mode of becoming a delegate: District delegates to the national convention are
    slated by the campaigns, appear on the ballot, and are elected in the pri-
    mary in accordance with primary results; at-large delegates and pledged
    PLEOs are elected by the state executive committee

Bound for how many national conventions ballots: One

Source: http://www.thegreenpapers.com/P20/AL-D.

Republican

Number of delegates: 50 total delegates—29 at-large (10 base, 3 party, 16 bonus),
    21 in 7 congressional districts

Date of 2020 contest: March 3

What week of the delegate selection season: 5

Type of delegate selection event: Open primary

Mode of awarding delegates: Winner-take-most: District—If a candidate for
    president wins a majority of the vote or if only one candidate receives at
    least 20 percent, he or she receives all 3 delegates; if no one receives a major-
    ity and more than one receives 20 percent, the first-place finisher receives 2
    delegates and the runner-up receives 1

At-large: If a candidate for president wins a majority of the vote or if only
    one candidate receives at least 20 percent, he or she receives all at-large del-
    egates. If no one receives a majority and more than one receives 20 percent,
    at-large delegates are allocated proportionally with a 20 percent threshold

Mode of becoming a delegate: Candidates for delegate file a declaration of candi-
    dacy that includes a pledge for a candidate; delegates are elected in the
    primary

Bound for how many national conventions ballots: All

Source: http://www.thegreenpapers.com/P20/AL-R.

—*Andrew E. Busch*

Alaska

The largest by area and one of the least populated states, Alaska truly is "The Last Frontier." An oil powerhouse since the Alaska pipeline was completed in the 1970s, the state harbors a mixture of libertarian sentiments and a tendency to keep its public officials in office for decades as long as they are "delivering the bacon." Alaska leans heavily toward Republicans but elects an occasional moderate Democrat or independent. Since becoming a state in 1959, Alaska has only voted for a Democrat for president once, in Lyndon Johnson's landslide of 1964. In 2016, the state voted for Donald Trump by a margin of 51 percent to 37 percent.

Both Democratic and Republican national conventions accepted delegates from Alaska starting in 1892, nearly seven decades before it became a state. It has always been a caucus-convention state and has never held a presidential primary. Democrats have generally used precinct caucuses, though results are sometimes reported in percentages of delegates elected to the next level. Republicans also hold caucuses and conventions. However, Democrats will be moving to a primary in 2020 to allocate and bind delegates; the caucus-convention system will still be used to select the individuals who will serve as delegates.

Historically, Democratic delegations from Alaska backed JFK in 1960, Alaska's first presidential election as a state, as well as Hubert Humphrey in 1968, Jimmy Carter in 1976 and 1980, Walter Mondale in 1984, and Bill Clinton in 1992. In 1988, the delegation was split closely between Michael Dukakis and Jesse Jackson, with Dukakis winning a slight edge. Republicans tended to support establishment moderates, backing William Scranton against Barry Goldwater in 1964, Richard Nixon in both 1960 and 1968, and Gerald Ford in the contentious 1976 race against Ronald Reagan.

In more recent elections, notable Alaska caucuses included:

1996: In an early caucus held two weeks before Iowa, Republican Pat Buchanan won with 33 percent to Steve Forbes's 31 percent and ultimate nominee Bob Dole's 17 percent. Though widely dismissed at the time, Alaska's vote provided an early glimpse of the challenge posed to Dole by Buchanan, who would go on to best the front-runner again in the much more important New Hampshire primary.

2000: George W. Bush barely edged out Steve Forbes in the Republican caucuses, held the same day as Iowa's. However, Bush's more substantial win in Iowa received the lion's share of media attention.

2004: John Kerry beat his serious competition badly in the Democratic caucuses, and was challenged most closely by gadfly Dennis Kucinich.

2008: Barack Obama swamped Hillary Clinton by a 3–1 margin in the Democratic caucuses, while Mitt Romney doubled Mike Huckabee's vote in the Republican caucuses. Both were held in early February.

2012: Returning to the scene of his 2008 victory, Republican Mitt Romney beat Rick Santorum, whose greatest strength nationwide was in caucuses, by 32 to 30 percent.

2016: In the March 1 Republican caucuses, Ted Cruz outpaced Donald Trump by 36 percent to 34 percent, one of several Cruz caucus victories. Three weeks later, in the Democratic caucuses, Bernie Sanders delivered Hillary Clinton her second Alaska trouncing, 80 percent to 20 percent. Clinton did not campaign in the state, but Sanders's wife Jane did (Kelly 2016).

Source

Kelly, Devin. 2016. "Bernie Sanders' Wife Campaigns in Anchorage as Alaska Democrats Prepare for Saturday Caucuses." *Anchorage Daily News*, March 24. https://www.adn.com/politics/article/alaska-democrats-head-caucuses -saturday/2016/03/25/.

Alaska Caucus Results 2000–2016

2000

Democratic caucuses (4/22)	Republican caucuses (1/24)	
No popular vote reported	Bush	36.3
Gore won all convention delegates	Forbes	36.2
	McCain	9.5
	Keyes	9.5
	Bauer	4.8
	Hatch	3.8

2004

Democratic caucuses (3/20) (percent delegates selected)		Republican caucuses (2/21–4/17) Delegates to national convention	
Kerry	47.8	Uncommitted	100.0
Kucinich	26.5		
Uncommitted	12.0		
Dean	11.1		
Edwards	2.6		

2008

Democratic caucuses (2/5)		Republican caucuses (2/5–2/9)	
Obama	75.2	Romney	43.7
Clinton	24.7	Huckabee	21.9
		Paul	17.2
		McCain	15.6
		Unpledged	1.6

2012

Democratic caucuses (4/10–4/14)		Republican caucuses (3/6–3/24)	
Obama	100.0	Romney	32.2
		Santorum	30.1
		Paul	24.1
		Gingrich	13.3

2016

Democratic caucuses (3/26)		Republican caucuses (3/1)	
Sanders	79.6	Cruz	36.4
Clinton	20.2	Trump	33.6
		Rubio	15.2
		Carson	10.8
		Kasich	4.0

Sources: https://www.thegreenpapers.com/P04/AK-D.phtml;
Atlas of U.S. Presidential Elections, https://uselectionatlas.org/.

2020 Delegate Selection

Democratic

Number of delegates: 18 total delegate votes—9 district, 3 at-large, 2 pledged PLEOs, 4 unpledged PLEOs

Date of 2020 contest: April 4

What week of the delegate selection season: 9

Type of delegate selection event: Closed primary

Mode of awarding delegates: Proportional representation with 15 percent threshold

How delegates are chosen: Delegates to the national convention are elected by the state convention in accordance with statewide primary results

Bound for how many national convention ballots: One

Source: The Green Papers, https://www.thegreenpapers.com/P20/AK-D.

Republican

Number of delegates: 28 total delegates—25 at-large (10 base, 3 party, 12 bonus), 3 in 1 congressional district

Date of 2020 contest: March 3

What week of the delegate selection season: 5

Type of delegate selection event: Closed caucus/convention

Mode of awarding delegates: Proportional representation with 13 percent threshold

How delegates are chosen: Delegates to the national convention are elected by the state convention in accordance with statewide caucus results

Bound for how many national convention ballots: All

Source: The Green Papers, https://www.thegreenpapers.com/P20/AK-R.

—*Andrew E. Busch*

Arizona

The 5C's of Arizona—copper, cattle, cotton, citrus, and climate—are a picture of both Arizona at statehood and ongoing reality (two-thirds of the country's copper is still mined in Arizona). Important shifts have also occurred through time: the advent of air conditioning helped pave the way for a more habitable state and an economic boom, which, in turn, attracted both large numbers of retired Americans and widespread immigration, legal and illegal (Barone and McCutcheon 2014). Arizona has been a staunch Republican stronghold for a period of time extending back decades and traceable to the rise of conservative senator Barry Goldwater in the 1950s. Arizona's electors have gone to the Republican presidential candidate in every election since 1952, save Bill Clinton's 47 to 44 percent win in 1996. The GOP hold may be slipping, though: in 2016, Donald Trump won Arizona, but only by a margin of 48 to 45 percent over Hillary Clinton.

Arizona selected its national convention delegates through a caucus-convention procedure prior to 1996. During those years, key contested races saw Democratic delegations heavily supporting FDR in 1932, JFK in 1960, Hubert Humphrey in 1968, George McGovern in 1972, Jimmy Carter in 1980,

Michael Dukakis in 1988, and Bill Clinton in 1992; delegates were roughly split between Walter Mondale and Gary Hart in 1984, with Mondale enjoying a slight edge. Republican delegations backed Robert Taft in 1952, hometown conservative hero Barry Goldwater in 1964, and Ronald Reagan in the contest of 1976.

From 1996 through 2016, Arizona held presidential primaries except when an incumbent president was running for renomination. In an attempt to increase its relevance during primary season, Arizona has consistently scheduled its primary early in the calendar. However, there will be no GOP primary in 2020. Some notable Arizona primaries have included:

1996: Arizona attempted to schedule its first primary to occur simultaneously with New Hampshire's, but the Granite State moved up a week, foiling Arizona's plan. Arizona's 1996 primary was enacted in hopes of building early momentum for Texas senator Phil Gramm's candidacy (Barone 2014). However, Gramm withdrew from the race a few days prior to New Hampshire's primary following a poor showing in Iowa. Publisher Steve Forbes won with 33 percent to Bob Dole's 30 percent and Pat Buchanan's 28 percent. Forbes subsequently won only one other state, Delaware, and dropped out of the race in March.

2000: Many of the state's Republican leaders rejected hometown hero John McCain and publicly endorsed George W. Bush's run. This move did not prevent a resounding victory by McCain, who won by nearly 25 percentage points over Bush. McCain's home state success was joined by his triumph in securing 52 of Michigan's delegates on the same day.

2004: Arizona's primary was the first in the western United States, and thus an important marker to assess candidates' relative support from Hispanic voters. Only Democrats John Kerry and Wesley Clark targeted the state, but over $2.5 million was spent over the course of the primary race for a turnout of only 240,000 people (Campaign 2004). Kerry garnered 43 percent of the vote to Clark's 27 percent. Howard Dean, who did not actively campaign, finished with 14 percent.

2008: Arizona was content with a spot as one of 16 Super Tuesday primary states. The Republican primary featured a spirited contest between McCain and Mitt Romney, which McCain won by 12 percentage points. On the Democratic side, Hillary Clinton beat Barack Obama 50 percent to 42 percent with strong support from Arizona Latinos (Barone and McCutcheon 2014).

2012: Without the obstacle of John McCain running in his home state, Mitt Romney won handily over Rick Santorum. Santorum captured only 27 percent of the vote to Romney's 47 percent.

2016: For the first time since Arizona began using primaries, the state's vote was held in March. On both sides of the aisle, the eventual nominee won. Donald Trump earned 46 percent and the next closest candidate to him, Ted Cruz, won 27 percent. Trump was awarded all 58 of Arizona's Republican delegates. Hillary Clinton again won the Democratic primary with 56 percent of the vote, while Bernie Sanders gained just over 41 percent. Because of Democratic proportional representation rules, both of the

Democratic candidates were awarded delegates by the state with Clinton earning 42 and Sanders gaining 33.

Sources

Barone, Michael, and Chuck McCutcheon. 2014. *Almanac of American Politics.* Washington, DC: National Journal.
Campaign 2004. 2004.
USA Today, January 29. https://usatoday30.usatoday.com/news/politicselections /nation/2004-01-29-arizona-usat_x.htm.

Arizona Primary Results 2000–2016

2000

Democratic primary (3/11)		Republican primary (2/22)	
Gore	77.9	McCain	60.0
Bradley	18.9	Bush	35.7
Harder	1.6	Keyes	3.6

2004

Democratic primary (2/3)		Republican primary (2/3)	
Kerry	42.6	No Republican primary	
Clark	26.5	National convention delegates	
Dean	14.0	Uncommitted	100.0
Edwards	7.0		
Lieberman	6.7		
Kucinich	1.6		

2008

Democratic primary (2/5)		Republican primary (2/5)	
Clinton	50.4	McCain	47.2
Obama	42.4	Romney	34.5
Edwards	5.2	Huckabee	9.0
		Paul	4.2
		Giuliani	2.5
		Thompson	1.8

2012

Democratic caucuses (2/28)		Republican primary (2/28)	
Obama	100.0	Romney	46.9
		Santorum	27.1
		Gingrich	16.0
		Paul	8.6

2016

Democratic primary (3/22)		Republican primary (3/22)	
Clinton	56.3	Trump	46.0
Sanders	41.4	Cruz	27.6
		Rubio	11.6
		Kasich	10.6
		Carson	2.4

Sources: Federal Election Commission: https://transition.fec.gov/pubrec/fe2000/2000presprim.htm;
https://transition.fec.gov/pubrec/fe2004/federalelections2004.pdf;
https://transition.fec.gov/pubrec/fe2008/federalelections2008.pdf;
https://transition.fec.gov/pubrec/fe2012/federalelections2012.pdf;
https://transition.fec.gov/pubrec/fe2016/federalelections2016.pdf.

2020 Delegate Selection

Democratic

Number of delegates: 78 total delegate votes—44 district, 14 at-large, 9 pledged PLEOs, 11 unpledged PLEOs

Date of 2020 contest: March 17

What week of the delegate selection season: 7

Type of delegate selection event: Closed primary

Mode of awarding delegates: Proportional representation with 15 percent threshold

How delegates are chosen: In accordance with primary results, district delegates are selected in district caucuses; at-large and pledged PLEOs are selected at the state convention and state committee meeting

Bound for how many national conventions ballots: One

Source: https://www.thegreenpapers.com/P20/AZ-D.

Republican

Number of delegates: 57 total delegates—29 at-large (10 base, 3 party, 17 bonus), 27 in 9 congressional districts

Date of 2020 contest: TBD

What week of the delegate selection season: TBD

Type of delegate selection event: TBD. Primary was canceled

Mode of awarding delegates: TBD

How delegates are chosen: TBD

Bound for how many national conventions ballots: One

Source: https://www.thegreenpapers.com/P20/AZ-R.

—*Andrew E. Busch and Jacob S. Leischner*

Arkansas

Arkansas was part of the Democratic "Solid South" from the end of Reconstruction until well into the 20th century, and served as the political base of Bill Clinton. The state shifted decisively toward Republicans starting in the 2000 election, when Clinton's vice president, Al Gore, surprisingly lost the state. Heavily rural, lower-income, and culturally conservative, Arkansas also produced in recent years Republican governor Mike Huckabee, who ran a credible campaign for president in 2008 and made a second, less successful, effort in 2016. Republicans won every presidential election in Arkansas from 2000 to 2016, with Donald Trump outpacing former Arkansas first lady Hillary Clinton 61 to 34 percent.

For most of the 20th century, Arkansas used caucus-convention procedures to select delegates. In key convention battles, Arkansas Democrats gave their support to Al Smith in 1928, Franklin Roosevelt in 1932, Richard Russell of Georgia in 1948, Hubert Humphrey in 1968, and their favorite son, the legendary House Ways and Means Committee chair Wilbur Mills, in 1972. Arkansas held its first presidential primary in 1976, when Jimmy Carter and Ronald Reagan each won their respective party's primaries with 63 percent of the vote. There was, however, no Republican primary in 1980 and neither Republican nor Democratic primaries in 1984.

When both parties resumed their primaries in 1988, it was to participate in the first great Super Tuesday combining 16 primaries on a single day in early March. George H. W. Bush defeated Bob Dole 47–26 percent to contribute to his Super Tuesday sweep, which effectively ended Dole's viability. On the Democratic side, Al Gore beat Michael Dukakis by 37–19 percent, with Jesse Jackson obtaining 17 percent of the vote. Arkansas was one of five states Gore won that day.

From 1992 through 2004, Arkansas primaries were held in late May, rendering them largely irrelevant to the outcome of the nomination races. The sole exception was in 2008, when Hillary Clinton's crushing victory over Barack Obama in the Democratic primary came while the race was still undetermined—though even then the primary result was somewhat discounted due to Clinton's longstanding affiliation with Arkansas. In 2016, the primary was moved back to March 1. Clinton again won big— this time against Bernie Sanders—but the Republican primary was closer. Donald Trump edged out Ted Cruz by a 33–31 percent margin, while Marco Rubio came in a respectable third with 25 percent. Arkansas was emblematic of Cruz's frustration throughout the primary season, when he was frequently highly competitive with Trump in the South but was unable to consolidate the conservative vote (Ceaser, Busch, and Pitney 2017).

Source

Ceaser, James W., Andrew E. Busch, and John J. Pitney Jr. 2017. *Defying the Odds: The 2016 Elections and American Politics.* Lanham, MD: Rowman & Littlefield.

Arkansas Primary Results 2000–2016

2000

Democratic primary (5/23)		Republican primary (5/23)	
Gore	78.5	Bush	80.2
LaRouche	21.5	Keyes	19.8

2004

Democratic primary (5/18)		Republican primary (5/18)	
Kerry	66.6	Bush	97.1
Uncommitted	23.2	Uncommitted	2.9
Kucinich	5.2		
LaRouche	5.1		

2008

Democratic primary (2/5)		Republican primary (2/5)	
Clinton	70.1	Huckabee	60.5
Obama	26.3	McCain	20.2
Edwards	1.9	Romney	13.5
Uncommitted	1.1	Paul	4.8

2012

Democratic primary (5/22)		Republican primary (5/22)	
Obama	58.4	Romney	68.4
Wolfe	41.6	Paul	13.4
		Santorum	13.3
		Gingrich	4.9

2016

Democratic primary (3/1)		Republican primary (3/1)	
Clinton	66.1	Trump	32.8
Sanders	30.0	Cruz	30.5
O'Malley	1.3	Rubio	24.8
Wolfe	1.2	Carson	5.7
		Kasich	3.7
		Huckabee	1.2

Sources: Federal Election Commission:
https://transition.fec.gov/pubrec/fe2000/2000presprim.htm#AR;
https://transition.fec.gov/pubrec/fe2004/federalelections2004.pdf;
https://transition.fec.gov/pubrec/fe2008/federalelections2008.pdf;
https://transition.fec.gov/pubrec/fe2012/federalelections2012.pdf;
https://transition.fec.gov/pubrec/fe2016/federalelections2016.pdf.

2020 Delegate Selection

Democratic

Number of delegates: 36 total delegate votes—20 district, 7 at-large, 4 pledged
   PLEOs, 5 unpledged PLEOs

Date of 2020 contest: March 3

What week of the delegate selection season: 5

Type of delegate selection event: Open primary

Mode of awarding delegates: Proportional representation with a 15 percent threshold

How delegates are chosen: Delegates to the national convention are elected at the congressional district conventions or the state convention according to the primary results

Bound for how many national conventions ballots: One

Source: http://www.thegreenpapers.com/P20/AR-D

Republican

Number of delegates: 40 total delegates—28 at-large (10 base, 3 party, 15 bonus), 12 in 4 congressional districts

Date of 2020 contest: March 3

What week of the delegate selection season: 5

Type of delegate selection event: Open primary

Mode of awarding delegates: Winner-take-most—District: If a candidate wins a majority of the vote in the district, he or she receives all delegates from the district; if there is no majority, the plurality winner receives two delegates and the second-place finisher receives one

At-large: Every candidate who wins at least 15 percent of the statewide vote receives one delegate. If any candidate wins a majority of the statewide vote, he or she receives the remainder of at-large delegates. If not, the remainder is allocated proportionally among all candidates who win at least 15 percent of the vote

How delegates are chosen: In accordance with primary results, district delegates are selected at congressional district conventions; at-large delegates are selected at the state committee meeting

Bound for how many national conventions ballots: One

Source: http://www.thegreenpapers.com/P20/AR-R

—*Andrew E. Busch*

California

The "Golden State" is by far the most populous state in the Union, with 11 million more residents than second-place Texas. It also boasts an economy that would be the fifth largest in the world if California were a country. The state, where whites are now only a plurality of the population, is the epicenter of both the tech industry (Silicon Valley) and film (Hollywood), but also has one of the highest poverty rates in the country. After voting for

Republicans in every presidential election from 1968 through 1988, the state has taken a hard turn to the left and has become nearly a one-party Democratic state. Hillary Clinton defeated Donald Trump 61 percent to 31 percent in 2016, obtaining a 4.3 million vote margin that accounted for her entire national popular vote plurality and then some. This duplicated Al Gore's feat in 2000, when his 1.3 million vote California lead was two-and-a-half times greater than his national popular vote lead.

California has held a presidential primary in every election year since presidential preference primaries first started in 1912. Through 1944, the California primary was held in early May; starting in 1948, it has usually been held in early June, with exceptions in 1996–2008. The move forward was justified by California lawmakers frustrated that the giant state had little influence on nomination outcomes because the June primary was held after nominees had already been decided for all practical purposes. In 2012 and 2016, California returned to its traditional early June primary date, though the 2020 primary is scheduled for March 3.

For the first five decades of the California presidential primary, it had little impact on nominating races, though both parties gave all delegates to the primary winner. State governors such as Earl Warren sometimes ran as "favorite son" candidates, locking up their party's California delegation until the national convention. Given the number of delegates involved, California is important in any race that has not already been determined. However, neither party awards all of its California delegates to the statewide plurality winner any longer.

The 1964 Republican primary was the first California primary to make a significant difference in the race. New York governor Nelson Rockefeller, representing the party's Northeastern, liberal wing, battled U.S. senator Barry M. Goldwater of Arizona, the (somewhat reluctant) standard-bearer of the conservative movement. Mobilizing an estimated 50,000 volunteers in California, Goldwater won 51.6 to 48.4 percent. Goldwater's win sealed his nomination (White 1965).

Other notable California primaries have included:

1968: In a contest between antiwar Democrats in 1968, Robert F. Kennedy defeated Eugene McCarthy 46–42 percent on the next-to-last week of primaries, a victory that would have given him some momentum going into the Democratic national convention. (It is far from certain that he would have been nominated, as Vice President Hubert H. Humphrey already had a large lead in delegates won in nonprimary states.) However, minutes after delivering his victory speech in Los Angeles, Kennedy was assassinated by Palestinian sympathizer Sirhan Sirhan (Nelson 2014).

1972: Four years later, liberal favorite George McGovern defeated labor favorite and former vice president Hubert H. Humphrey 44–39 percent, winning all of California's delegates. When the Humphrey forces lost a vote at the national convention that would have split California's delegates proportionately, Humphrey's bid was doomed. During his losing primary campaign, Humphrey went on the attack against McGovern's plans to cut defense spending, a message that Richard Nixon picked up to great effect in the general election.

1984: In a dramatic win, underdog Democrat Gary Hart beat Walter Mondale by a 39–35 percent margin at the end of the primary season but was still unable to pull ahead in the race.

2000: In the Republican primary, held in early March, Texas governor George W. Bush solidly defeated U.S. senator John McCain of Arizona, 52 to 43 percent, after getting his campaign back on track in South Carolina. Overall, Bush won seven of the 11 primaries held that day.

2008: In the Democratic primary in early February, Hillary Clinton beat Barack Obama comfortably, confirming that the contest would be a see-saw affair all the way to the last week of primaries four months later. On the Republican side, John McCain held off Mitt Romney, his strongest rival, thus protecting the front-running status he had won in New Hampshire and South Carolina.

2016: Hillary Clinton's win punctuated her Democratic nomination victory against Senator Bernie Sanders. Controversially, media outlets had declared the day before the California primary that Clinton had passed the magic number of delegates needed to nominate, even though her delegate total included superdelegates who were free to change their votes prior to the convention (Cassidy 2016).

Sources

Cassidy, John. 2016. "The Media Called the Democratic Race a Day Early." *The New Yorker*, June 7. https://www.newyorker.com/news/john-cassidy/the-media-called-the-democratic-race-a-day-early.

Nelson, Michael. 2014. *Resilient America: Electing Nixon in 1968, Channeling Dissent, and Dividing Government.* Lawrence: University Press of Kansas.

White, Theodore H. 1965. *The Making of the President 1964.* New York: Atheneum.

California Primary Results 2000–2016

2000

Democratic primary (3/7)		Republican primary (3/7)	
Gore	81.2	Bush	60.6
Bradley	18.2	McCain	34.7
		Keyes	4.0

2004

Democratic primary (3/2)		Republican primary (3/2)	
Kerry	64.4	Bush	100.0
Edwards	19.8		
Kucinich	4.7		
Dean	4.2		
Sharpton	1.9		
Lieberman	1.7		
Clark	1.0		

2008

Democratic primary (2/5)		Republican primary (2/5)	
Clinton	51.5	McCain	42.2
Obama	43.2	Romney	34.6
Edwards	3.8	Huckabee	11.6
		Giuliani	4.4
		Paul	4.3
		Thompson	1.7

2012

Democratic primary (6/5)		Republican primary (6/5)	
Obama	100.0	Romney	79.5
		Paul	10.4
		Santorum	5.3
		Gingrich	3.7

2016

Democratic primary (6/7)		Republican primary (6/7)	
Clinton	53.1	Trump	74.8
Sanders	46.0	Kasich	11.3
		Cruz	9.5
		Carson	3.7

Sources: Guide to U.S. Elections, 7th ed., Vol. I. New York:
CQ Press/Sage; *Atlas of U.S. Presidential Elections*,
https://uselectionatlas.org/.

2020 Delegate Selection

Democratic

Number of delegates: 495 total delegate votes—272 district, 90 at-large, 54 pledged PLEOs, 79 unpledged PLEOs (superdelegates)

Date of 2020 contest: March 3

What week of the delegate selection season: 5

Type of delegate selection event: Partially open primary (D and I)

Mode of awarding delegates: Proportional representation with a 15 percent threshold

How delegates are chosen: Districted delegates are slated at preprimary caucuses and are elected in the primary; at-large and pledged PLEOs are elected by the district delegates in accordance with primary results

Bound for how many national convention ballots: One

Source: https://www.thegreenpapers.com/P20/CA-D.

Republican

Number of delegates: 172 total delegates—13 at-large (10 base, 3 party), 159 in 53 congressional districts

Date of 2020 contest: March 3

What week of the delegate selection season: 5

Type of delegate selection event: Closed primary

Mode of awarding delegates: Winner-Take-Most: District—if a presidential candidate wins a majority of the votes in a district, he or she receives all delegates from the district; if not, delegates are allocated by proportional representation with a 20 percent threshold

At-large—If a candidate wins a majority of the statewide vote, he or she receives all at-large delegates; if not, delegates are allocated by proportional representation with a 20 percent threshold

How delegates are chosen: Delegates are selected by the presidential candidates

Bound for how many national convention ballots: Two

Source: https://www.thegreenpapers.com/P20/CA-R.

—*Andrew E. Busch*

Colorado

Shaped by Western individualism, for decades Colorado was a solid part of the Republican presidential coalition. Since the 1990s, it has been transformed into a Democratic-leaning swing state, voting for Bill Clinton in 1992, Bob Dole in 1996, George W. Bush in 2000 and 2004, Barack Obama in 2008 and 2012, and Hillary Clinton by a 5 percentage point margin in 2016. Fueling the shift has been a growing Hispanic population and increasingly liberal, affluent, college-educated suburbanites.

Colorado held presidential primaries in the first week of March from 1992 to 2000, but before and after that period utilized a caucus-convention system for delegate selection. Although the 2000 primary came after both parties' races were all but wrapped up, primaries in 1992 and 1996 had a significant impact on the nomination races. In 1992, Colorado held one of the earliest primaries in the schedule on the same day as Georgia and Maryland. Former California governor Edmund G. "Jerry" Brown won a close three-way contest, defeating Bill Clinton and Paul Tsongas by a margin of 28 to 27 to 26 percent. That same day, Tsongas won Maryland and Clinton won Georgia. The three-way split meant that no one had established a clear lead in the race, which would go on for months (Ceaser and Busch, 1993). At the same time, George H. W. Bush swamped challenger Pat Buchanan by more than a two-to-one margin. In 1996, Colorado again provided an opportunity for the GOP front-runner—this time Bob Dole—to double up Buchanan's vote, helping to solidify Dole's position in the race.

During its long periods of caucus-convention processes, Colorado Democrats backed FDR in 1932, JFK in 1960, Hubert H. Humphrey in 1968, George McGovern in 1972, Jimmy Carter in 1976 and 1980, home state senator Gary Hart in 1984, and Michael Dukakis by a 2–1 margin over Jesse Jackson in 1988. Republican delegates to the national convention supported Eisenhower over Taft in 1952, but conservatives Goldwater in 1964 and Reagan over Ford in 1976. Democratic caucus results since 2004 showed John Kerry winning handily in 2004, and both Barack Obama in 2008 and Bernie Sanders in 2016 defeating Hillary Clinton decisively. In Republican caucuses in 2008 Mitt Romney beat John McCain easily, but then Rick Santorum outpaced Romney in 2012. In 2016, the Republican caucus process was a delegate selection process not formally connected to a presidential preference component for the at-large delegates. The process was tailor-made for a well-organized movement, and it produced a decisive victory for Texas senator Ted Cruz. Cruz won 17 of 21 national convention delegates chosen at congressional district conventions and all 13 at-large delegates chosen at the state convention (Bunch and Frank 2016). The Colorado delegation would become the center of the abortive "Stop Trump" movement in Cleveland.

After controversies surrounding the 2016 caucuses, Colorado voters approved a ballot initiative restoring the presidential primary. In 2020, Democrats will hold a binding primary while Republicans will hold an advisory primary with allocation of delegates determined through a caucus/convention process.

Sources

Bunch, Joey, and John Frank. 2016. "Ted Cruz Dominates Colorado GOP Convention Winning All 34 Delegates." *Denver Post*, updated April 21. https://www.denverpost.com/2016/04/09/ted-cruz-dominates-colorado-gop-convention-winning-all-34-delegates/.

Ceaser, James W., and Andrew E. Busch. 1993. *Upside Down and Inside Out: The 1992 Elections and American Politics.* Lanham, MD: Rowman & Littlefield.

Colorado Primary and Caucus Results 2000–2016

2000

Democratic primary (3/10)		Republican primary (3/10)	
Gore	71.4	Bush	64.7
Bradley	23.3	McCain	27.1
		Keyes	6.6

2004

Democratic caucuses (4/13)		Republican caucuses (4/13)	
Kerry	63.7	Bush	100.0
Uncommitted	19.6		
Kucinich	13.0		
Dean	2.5		

2008

Democratic caucuses (2/5)		Republican caucuses (2/5)	
Obama	66.5	Romney	60.1
Clinton	32.3	McCain	18.4
Uncommitted	1.0	Huckabee	12.8
		Paul	8.4

2012

Democratic caucuses (2/7)		Republican caucuses (2/7)	
Obama	100.0	Santorum	40.3
		Romney	34.9
		Gingrich	12.8
		Paul	11.8

2016

Democratic caucuses (3/1)		Republican caucuses (3/1)	
		National convention delegates elected	
Sanders	59.0	Cruz	91.9
Clinton	40.3	Uncommitted	8.1

Sources: Guide to U.S. Elections, 7th ed., Vol. I, 2000. New York: CQ / Sage; caucuses—*Atlas of U.S. Presidential Elections*. https://uselectionatlas.org/; https://www.thegreenpapers.com/P16/CO-R; Bunch, Joey, and John Frank 2016. "Ted Cruz Dominates Colorado GOP Convention Winning All 34 Delegates," *Denver Post*, updated April 21. https://www.denverpost.com /2016/04/09/ted-cruz-dominates-colorado-gop-convention-winning-all -34-delegates/.

2020 Delegate Selection

Democratic

Number of delegates: 80 total delegate votes—44 district, 14 at-large, 9 pledged PLEOs, 13 unpledged PLEOs

Date of 2020 contest: March 3

What week of the delegate selection season: 5

Type of delegate selection event: Semiopen primary (D and I)

Mode of awarding delegates: Proportional representation with a 15 percent threshold

How delegates are chosen: Delegates are selected through a caucus/convention procedure according to the primary results

Bound for how many national convention ballots: One

Source: https://www.thegreenpapers.com/P20/CO-D.

Republican

Number of delegates: 37 total delegates—16 at-large (10 base, 3 party, 3 bonus), 21 in 7 congressional districts

Date of 2020 contest: March 3

What week of the delegate selection season: 5

Type of delegate selection event: Semiopen advisory (nonbinding) primary (R and I only) combined with closed caucus/convention procedure

Mode of awarding delegates: Primary is not connected to delegate selection

How delegates are chosen: Delegates are selected at congressional district or state convention. They may run as openly pledged to a presidential candidate or as unpledged

Bound for how many national convention ballots: Two

Source: https://www.thegreenpapers.com/P20/CO-R.

—*Andrew E. Busch*

Connecticut

Connecticut, both a piece of New England and a suburb of New York City, was once reliably Republican, then home to independent-minded centrists such as Lowell Weicker and Joseph Lieberman. It is now reliably Democratic in presidential politics and voted 55 to 41 percent for Hillary Clinton in 2016, as many formerly Republican affluent suburbs and formerly Democratic working-class towns flipped allegiance (Cohen 2018).

Prior to its first presidential primary in 1980, Connecticut's major political parties selected delegates to the national convention by caucus and convention. Connecticut's Republicans consistently backed the more liberal, establishment-supported candidate, including Eisenhower against Taft in 1952, Scranton against Goldwater in 1964 (on the initial first-ballot vote), and Ford against Reagan in 1976. Democratic delegates to the national convention supported Smith in 1932, Kennedy in 1960, and Humphrey in 1968. In 1972, the Connecticut delegation split by a 3–2 ratio for George McGovern over Washington senator Henry Jackson.

The first Connecticut primary on March 25, 1980 saw George H. W. Bush defeating Ronald Reagan and Ted Kennedy beating Jimmy Carter, both by the solid but unexceptional margin of five percentage points; Bush's father Prescott had served as a U.S. senator from Connecticut. After four late March primaries in a row, Connecticut moved its primary date up to the first week of March in 1996. In 2008, as part of the national trend of "front-loading," the Connecticut primary jumped an additional month to early February. Connecticut's voice was lost amid the 15 other states holding primaries on that day, and in 2012 and 2016 the primary was moved back to the last week of April.

Some key Connecticut primaries have included:

1984: Democrat Gary Hart proved he would be a force to be reckoned with among liberal suburbanites, winning 53–29 percent against Walter Mondale.

1992: Jerry Brown edged out Bill Clinton in the Democratic primary by a 37–36 percent margin, with Paul Tsongas trailing at 20 percent. Tsongas was hurt by his inability to win another New England state neighboring his Massachusetts home, while Brown proved that he remained a factor in the Democratic race after having been written off by some pundits.

1996: Bob Dole inflicted a 54–20 percent defeat on conservative publisher and supply-side idea man Steve Forbes, who needed a win in Connecticut to right his flailing campaign.

2000: Republican John McCain scored a narrow but important 49–46 percent victory over George W. Bush, helped along by McCain's kinship with Democratic senator Joseph Lieberman and his apparent fit with Connecticut's moderate Republican voters. McCain's win helped keep him in the nomination hunt for a while longer.

2008: Back for another try for the GOP nomination, John McCain added to his wins on February 5 by again prevailing in Connecticut, this time beating Mitt Romney by nearly 20 percentage points. At the same time, in the Democratic primary, Barack Obama upset Hillary Clinton by a 51–47 percent margin in her backyard.

2016: Eight years later, Clinton reversed her misfortune, winning a tough primary against Bernie Sanders by a 52–46 percent gap. In the Republican primary, Donald Trump—like Clinton, also hailing from neighboring New York—thumped John Kasich by 30 percentage points, with Ted Cruz trailing another 10 points back. Trump's domination of the April 26 northeastern primaries in Connecticut and other states put Cruz's campaign on the ropes.

Source

Cohen, Richard with James Barnes. 2018. *Almanac of American Politics*. Washington, DC: National Journal.

Connecticut Primary Results 2000–2016

2000

Democratic primary (3/7)		Republican primary (3/7)	
Gore	55.5	McCain	48.7
Bradley	41.5	Bush	46.3
Uncommitted	3.0	Keyes	3.3

2004

Democratic primary (3/2)		Republican primary	
Kerry	58.3	No Republican primary	
Edwards	23.7	National convention delegates	
Lieberman	5.2	Bush	100.0
Dean	4.0		
Kucinich	3.2		
Clark	1.2		
LaRouche	1.1		

2008

Democratic primary (2/5)		Republican primary (2/5)	
Obama	50.7	McCain	52.0
Clinton	46.7	Romney	32.9
		Huckabee	7.0
		Paul	4.2
		Giuliani	1.6
		Uncommitted	1.6

2012

Democratic primary (4/24)		Republican primary (4/24)	
Obama	100.0	Romney	67.4
		Paul	13.5
		Gingrich	10.3
		Santorum	6.8
		Uncommitted	2.0

2016

Democratic primary (4/26)		Republican primary (4/26)	
Clinton	51.8	Trump	57.9
Sanders	46.4	Kasich	28.4
Uncommitted	1.5	Cruz	11.7
		Uncommitted	1.3

Sources: Federal Election Commission:
https://transition.fec.gov/pubrec/fe2000/2000presprim.htm#CT;
https://transition.fec.gov/pubrec/fe2004/federalelections2004.pdf;
https://transition.fec.gov/pubrec/fe2008/federalelections2008.pdf;
https://transition.fec.gov/pubrec/fe2012/federalelections2012.pdf;
https://transition.fec.gov/pubrec/fe2016/federalelections2016.pdf.

2020 Delegate Selection

Democratic

Number of delegates: 64 total delegate votes—32 district, 11 at-large, 6 pledged
    PLEOs, 15 unpledged PLEOs

Date of 2020 contest: April 28

What week of the delegate selection season: 13

Type of delegate selection event: Closed primary

Mode of awarding delegates: Proportional representation with a 15 percent threshold

How delegates are chosen: District delegates are elected by caucuses and at-large delegates and pledged PLEOs are elected by the state committee in accordance with primary results

Bound for how many national conventions ballots: One

Source: http://www.thegreenpapers.com/P20/CT-D.

Republican

Number of delegates: 28 total delegates—13 at-large (10 base, 3 party), 15 in 5 congressional districts

Date of 2020 contest: April 28

What week of the delegate selection season: 13

Type of delegate selection event: Closed primary

Mode of awarding delegates: Winner-take-most: Districts—The candidate receiving the most votes in the district receives all of the district's national convention delegates

At-large—If a candidate wins a majority of the statewide vote, he or she receives all of the at-large delegates; if no one wins a majority, delegates are allocated proportionally with a 20 percent threshold

How delegates are chosen: Candidates for president present delegate slates to the state committee in accordance with primary results. The state committee must approve the slates

Bound for how many national conventions ballots: All

Source: http://www.thegreenpapers.com/P20/CT-R.

—Andrew E. Busch

Delaware

A small mid-Atlantic state wedged between Maryland and the ocean, Delaware has rarely had much effect on presidential selection since 1800, when its sole congressman, Federalist James Bayard, was persuaded by Alexander Hamilton to vote for Thomas Jefferson in the House contingency election, thus delivering the presidency to Hamilton's arch-rival. Lightly populated and relatively affluent, Delaware has moved from politically competitive to a solid part of the Democratic presidential coalition. The state has voted for the Democratic nominee for president in every election since 1992. In 2016, Hillary Clinton defeated Donald Trump 53 percent to 42 percent.

Delaware held its first presidential primary in 1996, four days after New Hampshire. Indeed, its first four primaries were held in February in hopes that a very early primary date would compensate for the small number of delegates at stake. In 2012 and 2016, the Delaware primary was rescheduled for the fourth Tuesday of April.

Before the establishment of the Delaware presidential primary, Democratic delegations from Delaware to the national convention supported Franklin Roosevelt in 1932, Lyndon Johnson in 1960, Hubert Humphrey in 1968, Jimmy Carter in 1980, and Walter Mondale in 1984. They were closely split between Henry Jackson and George McGovern in 1972 and between Michael Dukakis and Jesse Jackson in 1988. Republicans were closely divided between Dwight D. Eisenhower and Robert Taft in 1952 and between Barry Goldwater and William Scranton in 1964, though Gerald Ford easily outpolled Ronald Reagan among Delaware Republican delegates in 1976.

Significant Delaware primaries have included:

1996: In the first Delaware primary, Republican voters shook up the race by giving Steve Forbes a solid win over the consensus front-runner, Kansas senator Bob Dole (33–27 percent), just four days after Dole had been upset by Pat Buchanan in the New Hampshire primary. For a brief time, Dole appeared to be in serious trouble.

2000: One week after his loss in New Hampshire to John McCain, Republican George W. Bush began to right his ship by beating McCain 2–1 in Delaware. For his part, Democrat Al Gore built on his narrow New Hampshire win by beating Bill Bradley again, this time by the impressive margin of 57–40 percent.

2004: Democrat John Kerry followed up on his New Hampshire win by beating John Edwards 51–25 percent in Delaware, with Howard Dean far behind.

2008: In the hard-fought Democratic primary on February 5, held three weeks after New Hampshire, Barack Obama beat Hillary Clinton 53 to 42 percent, helping to regain his footing as the race settled in for the long haul. On the Republican side, John McCain came back from his 2000 shortfall to beat Mitt Romney 45–33 percent. However, 15 other states held primaries on this day, significantly diminishing the impact of small Delaware's vote.

2016: Still locked in a serious fight with Bernie Sanders in late April, Hillary Clinton won the Democratic primary with 60 percent of the vote to Sanders's 39 percent. As part of his April 26 northeastern romp, Donald Trump won the Republican primary with 61 percent to John Kasich's 20 percent and Ted Cruz's 16 percent. Primary wins in Delaware, Connecticut, Maryland, Pennsylvania, and Rhode Island drew Trump to within one step of securing the nomination.

Delaware Primary Results 2000–2016

2000

Democratic primary (2/5)		Republican primary (2/8)	
Gore	57.2	Bush	50.7
Bradley	40.2	McCain	25.4
LaRouche	2.6	Forbes	19.6
		Keyes	3.8

2004

Democratic primary (2/3)		Republican primary	
Kerry	50.4	No Republican primary	
Lieberman	11.1	National convention delegates	
Edwards	11.0	Uncommitted	100.0
Dean	10.4		
Clark	9.5		
Sharpton	5.7		
Kucinich	1.0		

2008

Democratic primary (2/5)		Republican primary (2/5)	
Obama	53.1	McCain	45.0
Clinton	42.3	Romney	32.5
Biden	3.0	Huckabee	15.3
Edwards	1.3	Paul	4.2
		Giuliani	2.5

2012

Democratic primary		Republican primary (4/24)	
No Democratic primary		Romney	56.5
National convention delegates		Gingrich	27.1
Obama	69.7	Paul	10.6
	30.3	Santorum	5.9

2016

Democratic primary (4/26)		Republican primary (4/26)	
Clinton	59.8	Trump	60.8
Sanders	39.2	Kasich	20.4
De La Fuente	1.1	Cruz	15.9
		Carson	1.3

Sources: Federal Election Commission:
https://transition.fec.gov/pubrec/fe2000/2000presprim.htm#DE;
https://uselectionatlas.org/RESULTS/index.html;
https://transition.fec.gov/pubrec/fe2004/federalelections2004.pdf;
https://transition.fec.gov/pubrec/fe2008/federalelections2008.pdf;
https://transition.fec.gov/pubrec/fe2012/federalelections2012.pdf;
https://transition.fec.gov/pubrec/fe2016/federalelections2016.pdf.

2020 Delegate Selection

Democratic

Number of delegates: 28 total delegate votes—11 district, 4 at-large, 2 pledged PLEOs, 11 unpledged PLEOs

Date of 2020 contest: April 28

What week of the delegate selection season: 13

Type of delegate selection event: Closed primary

Mode of awarding delegates: Proportional representation with a 15 percent threshold

How are delegates chosen: District delegates are chosen at the state convention from four "subdivisions" of the state according to the primary results in each subdivision; at-large and pledged PLEOs are elected by the national convention delegates selected from the "subdivisions" according to statewide primary results

Bound for how many national conventions ballots: One

Source: http://www.thegreenpapers.com/P20/CT-D.

Republican

Number of delegates: 16 total delegates—13 at-large (10 base, 3 party), 3 in 1 congressional district

Date of 2020 contest: April 28

What week of the delegate selection season: 13

Type of delegate selection event: Closed primary

Mode of awarding delegates: Statewide winner-take-all

How are delegates chosen: Delegates to the national convention are elected by the state convention according to the primary results

Bound for how many national conventions ballots: One
Source: http://www.thegreenpapers.com/P20/CT-R.

—*Andrew E. Busch*

District of Columbia

The District of Columbia is overwhelmingly Democratic, with a population that combines large concentrations of federal employees and African Americans, perhaps the two most Democratic groups in the United States. In presidential politics, its electoral votes are the only set to have gone to both George McGovern in 1972 and Walter Mondale in 1984. Indeed, since being granted electoral votes by the Twenty-Third Amendment in 1961, the District has never voted for the Republican candidate for president. In 2016, Hillary Clinton demolished Donald Trump in DC by a margin of 81 percent to 4 percent, the largest margin enjoyed by either candidate anywhere in the country.

Though the District of Columbia is not a state, Republicans granted delegates to the District in their first presidential nominating convention in 1856 and in every subsequent convention save 1864. Democrats followed suit in 1884. DC began holding presidential primaries in 1952, when 75 percent of Democrats preferred Averill Harriman. DC Republicans held their first primary in 1956, but did not hold primaries in 1964, 1972, 1976, 2004, or 2016. In those years they reverted to caucus-convention procedures.

For most of its history the DC primary was scheduled in May, rather late in the primary season (the 1952 Democratic primary was held June 17 and was the very last primary to be held that year). In 2004, it was moved to mid-January and was the first primary of the year. It was subsequently scheduled on February 12 (2008) and April 3 (2012). In 2016, Democrats returned the DC primary to its traditional late date, voting on June 14—again, as in 1952, the last primary of the season. In lieu of a primary, Republicans held caucuses on March 12.

Notable District of Columbia primaries and caucuses include:

1968: Robert F. Kennedy, a latecomer to the Democratic nomination race, won with 63 percent of the vote. Hubert Humphrey, who refused to campaign, won 37 percent. RFK's win in the District was coupled with an important win in Indiana the same day (Nelson 2014).

1976: Jimmy Carter narrowly defeated DC nonvoting congressional representative Walter Fauntroy in the Democratic primary. Carter won 32 percent to Fauntroy's 31 percent.

1984 and 1988: Fueled by a large African American vote, Jesse Jackson won, first with 67 percent and four years later with 80 percent.

2004: In the first Democratic presidential preference primary of the year, Vermont governor Howard Dean won with 43 percent of the vote against two African American candidates, Al Sharpton (34 percent) and Illinois senator

Carol Moseley-Braun (12 percent). However, in order to not run afoul of Democratic delegate selection windows, the primary was purely a "beauty contest" primary, with delegates selected later by caucus.

2016: In March, Marco Rubio narrowly won the Republican convention over John Kasich, with Donald Trump and Ted Cruz far behind. The DC convention represented one of Rubio's few wins of the nomination contest. In June, when Democrats voted, Hillary Clinton crushed Bernie Sanders by a 79–21 percent margin, the race having been effectively declared over two weeks before.

Source

Nelson, Michael. 2014. *Resilient America: Electing Nixon in 1968, Channeling Dissent, and Dividing Government.* Lawrence: University Press of Kansas.

District of Columbia Primary and Caucus Results 2000–2016

2000

Democratic primary (5/2)		Republican primary (5/2)	
Gore	95.9	Bush	72.8
LaRouche	4.1	McCain	24.4

2004

Democratic primary (1/13)		Republican caucuses (2/10)	
		National convention delegates selected	
Dean	47.6	Bush	84.2
Sharpton	34.4	Uncommitted	15.8
Moseley-Braun	11.6		
Kucinich	8.1		
LaRouche	1.2		

2008

Democratic primary (2/12)		Republican primary (2/12)	
Obama	75.3	McCain	67.6
Clinton	23.8	Huckabee	16.4
		Paul	8.0
		Romney	6.4
		Giuliani	1.6

2012

Democratic primary (4/3)		Republican primary (4/3)	
Obama	97.4	Romney	70.1
Uncommitted	1.9	Paul	12.2
		Gingrich	10.9
		Huntsman	6.8

2016

Democratic primary (6/14)		Republican convention (3/12)	
Clinton	78.5	Rubio	37.3
Sanders	20.8	Kasich	35.5
		Trump	13.8
		Cruz	12.4

Sources: Guide to U.S. Elections, 7th ed., Vol. I. New York: CQ/Sage; https://www.thegreenpapers.com/P04/DC-R.phtml; *Atlas of U.S. Presidential Elections*, https://uselectionatlas.org/.

2020 Delegate Selection

Democratic

Number of delegates: 43 total delegate votes—11 district, 4 at-large, 2 pledged PLEOs, 26 unpledged PLEOs

Date of 2020 contest: June 2

What week of the delegate selection season: 18

Type of delegate selection event: Closed primary

Mode of awarding delegates: Proportional representation with a 15 percent threshold

How are delegates chosen: District delegates are slated in preprimary caucuses held in two districts formed out of combinations of the District of Columbia's municipal wards. Delegates are selected from these slates by the party committee in accordance with the primary results. At-large and pledged PLEOs are elected by the party committee in accordance with the primary

Bound for how many national conventions ballots: One

Source: http://www.thegreenpapers.com/P20/DC-D.

Republican

Number of delegates: 19 total delegates—19 at-large (16 base, 3 party)

Date of 2020 contest: March 14

What week of the delegate selection season: 6

Type of delegate selection event: Closed caucus/convention

Mode of awarding delegates: Winner-take-most: If a candidate for president wins a majority of convention votes, he or she receives all 19 national convention delegates; if not, delegates are allocated proportionally with a 15 percent threshold

How are delegates chosen: Delegates to the national convention are elected in the party convention

Bound for how many national convention ballots: One

Source: http://www.thegreenpapers.com/P20/DC-R.

—Andrew E. Busch

Florida

Florida has seen rapid economic development and industrialization, transforming from a rural marsh to the third largest state by population and an economy that would rank 17th in the world (Zimmerman 2018). Though demographically Florida has a reputation as a state filled with retirees, only 17 percent of residents are over 65, just 4 percent above the national average. The Hispanic population, which made up 23 percent of the population in 2010, has only continued to rise as U.S. citizens relocate from Puerto Rico in the wake of natural disasters like Hurricane Maria in 2017 (Schneider 2018). Politically, in recent years the state has leaned ever so slightly to the right. As of 2019, Republicans hold the governor's mansion, both of the state's Senate seats, and 14 out of the 27 members of the House delegation. However, at the presidential level, Florida has been a classic swing state since the 1990s, voting for George H. W. Bush in 1992, Bill Clinton in 1996, George W. Bush in 2000 and 2004, Barack Obama in 2008 and 2012, and Donald Trump (by a 48.6 percent to 47.4 percent margin) in 2016.

Florida instituted the very first presidential primary law in 1901, which allowed party officials to choose to opt into a party primary to select candidates for office. The state has held a true presidential primary every election year since 1932, when the state's Democrats overwhelmingly voted for Franklin Roosevelt. The primary was held the first week in June in 1932 and 1936, but no presidential primary was held in 1940. From 1944 to 1968, the primary was scheduled in May, but it was rescheduled to March in 1972 and has remained in that month ever since (with two exceptions of 2008 and 2012, when the primary was moved up to January). Although it is no longer positioned at the front of the primary calendar, Florida was historically one of the earlier primaries. The state's large population ensures a delegate-rich reward for the victor, particularly on the Republican side, where the state is winner-take-all.

Notable Florida primary contests include:

1972: Democratic candidate George Wallace won every county in the Florida primary and took 93 percent of the state's delegate haul. In that same contest, Senator Henry "Scoop" Jackson had his best showing in any contest of the primary season—finishing third with 13 percent to Wallace's 41 percent and Hubert Humphrey's 18 percent. Eventual nominee George McGovern finished a distant sixth with 6 percent.

1976: Four years later, Jimmy Carter edged out Wallace in a tight primary, 34 percent to 30 percent, with Scoop Jackson again coming in third, this time with a more substantial 24 percent. Carter's Florida win was a key milestone on the road to his nomination, proof that his "New South" approach could beat Wallace's "Old South" approach even on turf Wallace had commanded in 1972 (Stroud 1977). At the same time, President Gerald Ford comfortably defeated Ronald Reagan 53 to 47 percent in a crucial Southern test, part of a see-saw contest for the Republican nomination that would ultimately go all the way to the convention.

1988: Michael Dukakis won convincingly with 41 percent to runner-up Jesse Jackson's 20 percent and Dick Gephardt's 13 percent. The same day, Dukakis won in Texas, giving him victories in the two Super Tuesday states with the biggest populations and the biggest delegate hauls. It was a much-noted irony that a Massachusetts liberal like Dukakis was arguably the biggest winner on Super Tuesday, a Southern mega-primary intended by its promoters to give a moderate Democrat a leg up in the nomination race (Norrander 1992).

2008: John McCain's close victory over Mitt Romney helped further establish the candidate as the front-runner, and improved the delegate advantage that eventually pushed Romney from the race. For his part, Rudy Giuliani staked his entire campaign on Florida and left the race immediately after finishing a distant third (McAskill 2008). Hillary Clinton won the contest on the Democratic side, but did not win any delegates at the time because the Democratic National Committee stripped the contest of its rewards as a penalty for the state moving its primary outside of the primary window established by party rules. (Florida's delegates were later restored after Obama had secured the nomination.)

2012: After losing to John McCain four years before, Mitt Romney won a crucial Republican primary, defeating Newt Gingrich 46 to 32 percent.

2016: Florida senator Marco Rubio's devastating loss to Donald Trump, 27–45 percent, disproved conventional notions of his "favorite son" advantage in his home state and pushed him to drop out of the race. (The senator did win reelection to the Senate in the fall of 2016, however.) In the Democratic primary, Hillary Clinton outpolled Bernie Sanders by a 2–1 margin.

Sources

McAskill, Ewen. 2008. "Giuliani's Disastrous Strategy." *The Guardian*, January 30. https://www.theguardian.com/world/2008/jan/30/usa.rudygiuliani.

Norrander, Barbara. 1992. *Super Tuesday: Regional Politics and Presidential Primaries*. Lexington: University Press of Kentucky.

Schneider, Mike. 2018. "Census Shows Greatest Hispanic Growth Rate in North Florida." Associated Press, June 21. https://www.apnews.com/f25db7be2 a62414bab8d5f6ffaa66ce8.

Stroud, Kandy. 1977. *How Jimmy Won: The Victory Campaign from Plains to the White House*. New York: Morrow.

Zimmerman, Bill. 2018. "Florida's GDP Hits $1 Trillion Mark: As a Country, It'd Rank 17th in World." *Orlando Sentinel*, July 13. https://www.orlandosentinel .com/business/consumer/os-bz-florida-gdp-1-trillion-20180713-story.html.

Florida Primary Results 2000–2016

2000

Democratic primary (3/14)		Republican primary (3/14)	
Gore	81.8	Bush	73.8
Bradley	18.2	McCain	19.9
		Keyes	4.6

2004

Democratic primary (3/9)		Republican primary	
Kerry	77.2	No Republican primary	
Edwards	10.0	National Convention delegates	
Sharpton	2.8	Bush	97.3
Dean	2.8	Uncommitted	3.7
Kucinich	2.3		
Clark	1.4		
Lieberman	1.9		

2008

Democratic primary (1/29)		Republican primary (1/29)	
Clinton	49.8	McCain	36.0
Obama	32.9	Romney	31.0
Edwards	4.4	Giuliani	14.7
		Huckabee	13.5
		Paul	3.2
		Thompson	1.2

2012

Democratic primary (1/31)	Republican primary (1/31)	
Barack Obama (Unopposed)	Romney	46.4
	Gingrich	31.9
	Santorum	13.4
	Paul	7.0

2016

Democratic primary (3/15)		Republican primary (3/15)	
Clinton	64.4	Trump	45.7
Sanders	33.3	Rubio	27.0
O'Malley	2.3	Cruz	17.1
		Kasich	6.8
		Bush	1.8

Sources: Federal Election Commission:
https://transition.fec.gov/pubrec/fe2000/2000presprim.htm;
https://transition.fec.gov/pubrec/fe2004/federalelections2004.pdf;
https://transition.fec.gov/pubrec/fe2008/federalelections2008.pdf;
https://transition.fec.gov/pubrec/fe2012/2012pres.pdf;
https://transition.fec.gov/pubrec/fe2016/federalelections2016.pdf.

2020 Delegate Selection

Democratic

Number of delegates: 249 total delegate votes—143 district, 47 at-large, 29
    pledged PLEOs, 29 unpledged PLEOs

Date of 2020 contest: March 17

What week of the delegate selection season: 7

Type of delegate selection event: Closed primary

Mode of awarding delegates: Proportional representation with a 15 percent threshold

How delegates are chosen: District delegates are selected by congressional district caucuses according to the primary results; at-large delegates and pledged PLEOs are then selected by the district national convention delegates

Bound for how many national conventions ballots: One

Source: http://www.thegreenpapers.com/P20/FL-D.

Republican

Number of delegates: 122 total delegates—41 at-large (10 base, 3 party, 28 bonus), 81 in 27 congressional districts

Date of 2020 contest: March 17

What week of the delegate selection season: 7

Type of delegate selection event: Closed primary

Mode of awarding delegates: Statewide Winner-Take-All

How delegates are chosen: Congressional district caucuses elect district delegates; at-large delegates are elected by the state executive board

Bound for how many national conventions ballots: Three

Source: http://www.thegreenpapers.com/P20/FL-R.

—Andrew E. Busch and Richard C. Wiltshire-Gordon

Georgia

Demographically, Georgia features the third highest share of African Americans in the country, with 30 percent (trailing only Mississippi and Louisiana). The state's population rose 18 percent from 2000 to 2008, with high rates of inflow migration and few residents wishing to leave. While Georgia was politically Democratic for generations as part of the post–Civil War "Solid South," it cast its votes for Republican Barry Goldwater in 1964 and third-party presidential candidate George Wallace in 1968. Georgia voted for homegrown moderate Democrat Jimmy Carter in both 1976 and 1980, with Democratic voters rejecting Wallace in the 1976 state presidential primary—which Carter won, 84 percent to 12 percent. Bill Clinton won the state by one percentage point in the general election of 1992, but the state has voted Republican in every presidential race since 1996, with Donald Trump winning there in 2016 by five points.

Georgia held its first presidential primary on March 23, 1932, won overwhelmingly by Franklin Roosevelt. The state would not host another primary contest until 1976, however. During the long nonprimary period, Georgia delegations to the Democratic national convention supported favorite son Senator Richard Russell in 1948, Senator Lyndon Johnson in 1960, and Vice President Hubert Humphrey in 1968, though delegate support was closely split between Humphrey and Eugene McCarthy. In 1972, operating under the McGovern-Fraser reforms, the delegation was split evenly between George McGovern and Senator Henry Jackson, with George Wallace and Shirley Chisholm, the African American congresswoman from Texas, not far behind. Since the reintroduction of the presidential primary in May 1976, Georgia has scheduled its votes in early March with only one exception; in 2008, when it seemed every state had caught the front-loading fever, Georgia moved its primary ahead by one month into early February. Georgia has usually combined with one or more other southern states on the same date, and on a few occasions the state has joined Super Tuesday agglomerations.

The more significant primary races in recent years have included:

1976: On the same day Jimmy Carter demolished George Wallace, challenger Ronald Reagan defeated President Gerald Ford by a 2–1 margin. Reagan also won a crucial Midwestern showdown in Indiana, demonstrating broad appeal and taking the momentum back from Ford, who had won a big primary in Pennsylvania a week before.

1980: In a repeat of his 1976 success, Ronald Reagan won with 73 percent of the vote. His Georgia win was one of three in the South that day, giving him a strong push into the critical Illinois primary a week later.

1984: In the Democratic primary, Walter Mondale bounced back with a critical win on Super Tuesday (March 13) over Gary Hart and Jesse Jackson. Hart had piled up a string of impressive victories in the weeks before in New Hampshire, Maine, and Vermont, but Mondale regained his footing with his wins in Georgia and Alabama. Jackson had a relatively strong showing in southern primary contests throughout the primary season, winning a majority share of African American voters, but Mondale did well, too—the eventual nominee won about 25 percent of black voters in Georgia (Peterson and Coleman 1984).

1992: Democratic governor Zell Miller moved his state's primary to a week before Super Tuesday to assist candidate Bill Clinton with a tough map. Clinton won the state's contest and was able to use the victory to offset losses in Colorado and Maryland that occurred that same day (Barone and McCutcheon 2014).

2004: Democrat John Edwards visited Georgia five times in the period between the Iowa caucuses and the southern state's primary, while his opponent John Kerry visited only a single time. Despite Edwards's effort, Kerry won the primary by six points, 47 percent to 41 percent, damaging Edwards's case for the nomination so severely that the candidate withdrew from the race after his loss (Barone 2014, 415).

2008: Democratic senator Barack Obama solidified his pathway to the nomination with a convincing win over Hillary Clinton, beating her by more than a 2–1 margin. Obama was helped when civil rights legend Representative John Lewis switched his endorsement from Clinton to Obama in February 2008 (Broder and O'Connor 2008). On the Republican side, Senator John McCain narrowly lost to Governor Mike Huckabee, 34 percent to 32 percent, with Governor Mitt Romney not far behind at 30 percent. Huckabee, who performed extremely well in Southern contests throughout the 2008 presidential primary, still trailed McCain significantly in the delegate count even after his strong Super Tuesday performance, and dropped out of the race a few weeks later ("Election 2008").

2016: Hillary Clinton swamped Bernie Sanders by a 71–28 percent margin, while Donald Trump won a solid victory in the Republican primary. Marco Rubio and Ted Cruz battled for second place, with Rubio edging out Cruz. The two men had enough votes together to defeat Trump, but traded second-place finishes throughout the South.

Sources

Barone, Michael and Chuck McCutcheon. 2014. *Almanac of American Politics.* Washington, DC: National Journal.

Broder, John, and Anahad O'Connor. 2008. "Obama Wins Georgia in Night's First Prize." *New York Times*, February 5. https://www.nytimes.com/2008/02/05/us/politics/05cnd-primary.html.

"Election 2008." 2008. *New York Times*, September 16. https://web.archive.org/web/20080916170904/http://politics.nytimes.com/election-guide/2008/results/gopdelegates/index.html.

Peterson, Bill, and Milton Coleman. 1984. "Black Voters Back Jackson, Aid Mondale." *Washington Post*, March 14. https://www.washingtonpost.com/archive/politics/1984/03/14/black-voters-back-jackson-aid-mondale/0fa355a5-0288-44e2-ba77-155e253e64e0/.

Georgia Primary Results 2000–2016

2000

Democratic primary (3/7)		Republicans primary (3/7)	
Gore	83.8	Bush	67.0
Bradley	16.2	McCain	27.8
		Keyes	4.6

2004

Democratic primary (3/2)		Republican primary (3/2)	
Kerry	46.8	Bush	100.0
Edwards	41.4		
Sharpton	6.2		
Dean	1.8		
Kucinich	1.2		

2008

Democratic primary (2/5)		Republican primary (2/5)	
Obama	66.4	Huckabee	33.9
Clinton	31.1	McCain	31.6
Edwards	1.7	Romney	30.2
		Paul	2.9

2012

Democratic primary (3/6)		Republican primary (3/6)	
Obama	100.0	Gingrich	47.2
		Romney	25.9
		Santorum	20.0
		Paul	6.6

2016

Democratic primary (3/15)		Republican primary (3/15)	
Clinton	71.3	Trump	38.8
Sanders	28.2	Rubio	24.5
		Cruz	23.6
		Carson	6.2
		Kasich	5.6

Sources: Federal Election Commission:
https://transition.fec.gov/pubrec/fe2000/2000presprim.htm#top;
https://transition.fec.gov/pubrec/fe2004/federalelections2004.pdf;
https://transition.fec.gov/pubrec/fe2008/federalelections2008.pdf;
https://transition.fec.gov/pubrec/fe2012/2012pres.pdf;
https://transition.fec.gov/pubrec/fe2016/federalelections2016.pdf.

2020 Delegate Selection

Democratic

Number of delegates: 120 total delegate votes—68 district, 23 at-large, 14 pledged PLEOs, 15 unpledged PLEOs

Date of 2020 contest: March 24

What week of the delegate selection season: 8

Type of delegate selection event: Open primary

Mode of awarding delegates: Proportional representation with a 15 percent threshold.

How delegates are chosen: In accordance with the primary results, district delegates to the national convention are chosen by district caucuses; pledged PLEOs are elected by district delegates; at-large delegates are elected by the state committee

Bound for how many national conventions ballots: One

Source: https://www.thegreenpapers.com/P20/GA-D.

Republican

Number of delegates: 76 total delegates—34 at-large (10 base, 3 party, 21 bonus), 42 in 14 congressional districts

Date of 2020 contest: March 24

What week of the delegate selection season: 8

Type of delegate selection event: Semi-open primary (R & I)

Mode of awarding delegates: Winner-Take-Most: District—if a presidential candidate wins a majority of the votes in a district, he or she receives all delegates from the district; if not, the plurality winner receives two and the runner-up receives one

At-large—If a candidate wins a majority of the statewide vote, he or she receives all at-large delegates; if not, delegates are allocated by proportional representation with a 20 percent threshold; but the three party slots are allocated winner-take-all to the statewide vote leader

How delegates are chosen: District delegates are elected by congressional district conventions; at-large delegates are elected by the state convention

Bound for how many national conventions ballots: Two

Source: http://www.thegreenpapers.com/P20/GA-R.

—*Andrew E. Busch and Richard C. Wiltshire-Gordon*

Hawaii

Both vacation paradise and America's strategic outpost in the Pacific, Hawaii is characterized by a laid-back culture, a tropical climate, and liberal politics.

The island state represents a melting pot of Polynesian, Asian, and mainland influences; since the overthrow of the queen and the annexation of Hawaii by the United States in the 1890s, tensions have subsisted between native Hawaiians and outsiders. The *Almanac of American Politics* notes that Democrats have controlled the state House since statehood. Hawaii has not voted for a Republican presidential candidate since Ronald Reagan's 1984 landslide, and it gave Hillary Clinton a 32 percentage point margin against Donald Trump in 2016.

Both Democrats and Republicans began awarding national convention delegates to Hawaii in 1900, shortly after annexation by the United States, though it did not become a state until six decades later. Hawaii has always used a caucus-convention method to select its delegates. In recent years, Hawaii's caucuses have been held relatively early in the nomination calendar—in February or early March. In 2020, Hawaii Democrats will use a primary for the first time to establish presidential preference and allocate delegates, though they will continue using the caucus/convention system to select some delegates. Republicans will continue with the traditional caucus/convention system for presidential preference as well as delegate selection.

Since statehood in 1960, Democratic delegates from Hawaii threw their support to John F. Kennedy in 1960, Hubert Humphrey in 1968, Senator Henry Jackson (by a small margin) over George McGovern in 1972, Jimmy Carter in 1976 and 1980, Carter's vice president Walter Mondale in 1984, Michael Dukakis in 1988, and Bill Clinton in 1992. Republican delegates backed Richard Nixon in 1960 and 1968 and Gerald Ford against Ronald Reagan in 1976.

Significant Hawaii caucus results have included:

1988: Pat Robertson advocates dominated the Republican caucuses, obtaining the support of 81 percent of the delegates elected to the state convention. Supporters of Senator Bob Dole, who controlled the state party apparatus, tried but failed to slow the Robertson steamroller. Coming in the first week of February, the Hawaii caucuses were another early indication of the potential of Robertson and the Christian Right to shake up the Republican race, especially in settings where organization and ideological intensity were at a premium (Hawaii's Straws 1988).

2000: Republican caucuses produced an uncommitted national convention delegation that voted unanimously for George W. Bush on the floor of the national convention.

2004: In the Democratic caucuses, John Kerry beat Dennis Kucinich by 47 percent to 31 percent.

2008: Barack Obama, who grew up in Hawaii and was treated like a favorite son, defeated Hillary Clinton 76 percent to 24 percent. Meanwhile, Republican caucuses were again putting together an uncommitted delegation. At the convention, Republicans voted for eventual nominee John McCain.

2012: Mitt Romney defeated Rick Santorum 45 percent to 25 percent in the Republican caucuses.

2016: In Democratic caucuses, Bernie Sanders handily defeated Hillary Clinton with 70 percent of the vote. Republican caucuses gave Donald Trump a solid 43 to 32 percent advantage over Ted Cruz, despite Trump's complete lack of support in the state's Republican establishment. Republican caucus turnout was up significantly, and Hawaii was one of the rare caucus states where Trump bested Cruz in 2016 (Dayton 2016).

Sources

Dayton, Kevin. 2016. "Trump Wins Hawaii GOP Caucus to Cap Huge Night." *Honolulu Star-Advertiser*, May 4. https://www.staradvertiser.com/2016/03/08/breaking-news/hawaii-republican-caucus-hard-to-predict/.

"Hawaii's Straws." 1988. *Washington Post*, February 6. https://www.washingtonpost.com/archive/opinions/1988/02/06/hawaiis-straws/4340d16a-b2b3-4576-b72f-f9c958155838/.

Hawaii Caucus Results 2000–2016

2000

Democratic caucuses (3/7)		Republican caucuses (2/7-2/13)	
Delegates to state convention		Delegates to national convention	
Gore	82.1	Uncommitted	100.0
Bradley	17.9		

2004

Democratic caucuses (2/24)		Republican caucuses (1/25–2/7)	
Kerry	47.1	**Delegates to national convention**	
Kucinich	31.2	Bush	100.0
Edwards	12.6		
Dean	7.3		
Uncommitted	1.1		

2008

Democratic caucuses (2/19)		Republican caucuses (1/25–2/7)	
Obama	75.8	**Delegates to national convention**	
Clinton	23.6	Uncommitted	100.0

2012

Democratic caucuses (3/26)		Republican caucuses (3/13)	
Delegates to state convention		Romney	44.5
Obama	96.3	Santorum	25.3
Uncommitted	3.1	Paul	19.3
		Gingrich	10.9

2016

Democratic caucuses (3/26)		Republican caucuses (3/8)	
Sanders	69.8	Trump	43.3
Clinton	30.0	Cruz	32.3
		Rubio	13.2
		Kasich	10.0

Sources: Atlas of U.S. Presidential Elections, www.uselectionatlas.org;
https://www.thegreenpapers.com/PCC/T Obama.html;
https://www.thegreenpapers.com/P04/HI-R.phtml;
https://www.thegreenpapers.com/P08/HI-R.phtml.

2020 Delegate Selection

Democratic

Number of delegates: 31 total delegate votes—14 district, 5 at-large, 3 pledged PLEOs, 9 unpledged PLEOs

Date of 2020 contest: April 4

What week of the delegate selection season: 9

Type of delegate selection event: Closed primary

Mode of awarding delegates: Proportional representation with a 15 percent threshold; ranked-choice voting

How delegates are chosen: District delegates are elected by the state convention; at-large delegates and pledged PLEOs are elected by the state central committee

Bound for how many national conventions ballots: One

Source: http://www.thegreenpapers.com/P20/HI-D.

Republican

Number of delegates: 19 total delegates—13 at-large (10 base, 3 party), 6 in 2 congressional districts

Date of 2020 contest: March 10

What week of the delegate selection season: 6

Type of delegate selection event: Closed caucus/convention

Mode of awarding delegates: Proportional representation

How delegates are chosen: Each candidate for president or uncommitted slate submits a slate of delegates prior to the caucuses. When voters vote for a candidate, they are automatically voting for the slate

Bound for how many national conventions ballots: One

Source: http://www.thegreenpapers.com/P20/HI-R.

—*Andrew E. Busch*

Idaho

Just as the potato is the singular image of Idaho in pop culture, Republicans tend to be the state's singular political representation. In terms of presidential elections, Idaho is one of the most Republican states in the union, a manifestation of the party's "Leave Me Alone" coalition described by Grover Norquist (Norquist 2009). The state is so Republican that Bill Clinton only came in second place ahead of Ross Perot by 1 percent in 1992. More recently, Hillary Clinton garnered only 27 percent of the statewide vote, winning only two counties, with Trump taking nearly 60 percent of the vote share.

With this in mind, it follows that Idaho's primary elections rarely change the playing field for Democratic presidential candidates. Moreover, neither party offers much of a delegate bonanza. The state's influence in presidential nominations has not been bolstered by the scheduling of its contests, which have more often than not been late in the season, often when the nominees have already been essentially determined.

Idaho was a caucus-convention state until 1976, when it held its first presidential primary. The state's preprimary Democratic national convention delegations supported FDR in 1932, Harry Truman in 1948, JFK and LBJ in 1960, Hubert Humphrey in 1968, and in 1972 split nearly evenly between George McGovern and Senator Henry Jackson of neighboring Washington; Republicans backed Robert Taft in 1952 and Barry Goldwater in 1964. In 1976, Ronald Reagan beat Gerald Ford 74–25 percent, while Idaho's own Democratic senator Frank Church defeated Jimmy Carter 79–12 percent. Neither Reagan nor Church were saved by their outsized Idaho victories, however, and Ford and Carter went on to win their respective nominations. In 2004 and 2008, Democrats held a nonbinding preference primary coupled with caucuses for delegate selection; in 2012 and 2016, they utilized only caucuses.

For years, Idaho used an open primary, but eventually this was challenged by state Republicans. In 2011, an Idaho law went into effect implementing a closed primary as a direct result of the federal District Court's decision in *Idaho Republican Party v. Ysursa* accepting the Idaho GOP's argument that the use of an open primary violates the organization's First Amendment rights (Closed Primary Order 2011). From 1976 to 2008, the Idaho primary was scheduled in the final week of May, rendering it frequently inconsequential in the front-loaded era. In 2012 and 2016 Idaho Republicans voted in early March, though the Democratic caucuses were held later. Both Republicans and Democrats will hold binding presidential primaries in early March 2020.

Notable contests in Idaho have included:

1980: Democratic president Jimmy Carter nearly tripled challenger Edward Kennedy's primary vote, giving Carter an added boost in the home stretch of his tough renomination fight.

1984: Colorado senator Gary Hart defeated eventual Democratic nominee Walter Mondale 58 percent to 30 percent, extending his successes in the western states.

2004: Massachusetts senator John Kerry won the February Democratic caucuses, electing 55 percent of the state convention delegates to 23 percent for North Carolina's John Edwards. By May, when the nonbinding preference primary was held, Kerry had wrapped up the nomination and won 82 percent of the vote.

2008: The Idaho Democratic Party held a Super Tuesday caucus in 2008. Barack Obama won nearly 80 percent of the vote and 15 delegates to the national convention. Hillary Clinton only received 17 percent of the vote and 3 delegates. This result can be contrasted with the nonbinding preference primary held in May, when Obama only garnered 56 percent of the vote to Clinton's 37 percent.

2012: The Republican primary was held in March for the first time and was won decisively by Mitt Romney with 62 percent to Rick Santorum and Ron Paul at 18 percent. Romney dominated the southeastern corner of the state, home to a large concentration of Mormons.

2016: Both parties held March caucuses. Bernie Sanders won the Democratic caucuses with 78 percent of the vote against Hillary Clinton's 21 percent, a defeat for Clinton nearly identical to the one she suffered in 2008. On the Republican side, Ted Cruz won a clear victory against Donald Trump, one of several instances in 2016 when Cruz bested Trump in the caucus setting. Indeed, throughout the nomination season, both Sanders and Cruz excelled in caucuses, which are generally better suited than primaries for movement politics characterized by ideological intensity and strong organization.

Sources

Closed Primary Order. 2011. https://sos.idaho.gov/ELECT/ClosedPrimaryOrder .pdf.

Norquist, Grover. 2009. *Leave Us Alone: Getting the Government's Hands Off Our Money, Our Guns, Our Lives.* New York: HarperCollins.

Idaho Primary and Caucus Results 2000–2016

2000

Democratic primary (5/23)		Republican primary (5/23)	
Gore	75.7	Bush	73.5
LaRouche	8.2	Keyes	19.1

2004

Democratic caucuses (2/24)	
State convention delegates	
Kerry	55.4
Edwards	23.0
Dean	11.1
Uncommitted	6.9
Kucinich	3.7

Democratic primary (5/25)		Republican primary (5/25)	
Kerry	82.3	Bush	89.5
Kucinich	5.0		
Sharpton	2.9		

2008

Democratic caucuses (2/5)	
Obama	79.5
Clinton	17.2
Uncommitted	2.6

Democratic primary (5/27)		Republican primary (5/27)	
Obama	56.0	McCain	69.7
Clinton	37.7	Paul	23.7
Judd	1.7		

2012

Democratic caucuses (4/14)		Republican caucuses (3/6)	
State convention delegates		Romney	61.6
Obama	100.0	Santorum	18.2
		Paul	18.1
		Gingrich	2.1

2016

Democratic caucuses (3/22)		Republican primary (3/8)	
Sanders	78.0	Cruz	45.4
Clinton	21.2	Trump	28.1
		Rubio	15.9
		Kasich	7.4
		Carson	1.7

Sources: https://transition.fec.gov/pubrec/fe2000/2000presprim.htm#ID;
https://transition.fec.gov/pubrec/fe2004/federalelections2004.pdf;
https://www.thegreenpapers.com/P04/ID-D.phtml;
http://www.thegreenpapers.com/P12/ID-R;
https://transition.fec.gov/pubrec/fe2016/federalelections2016.pdf;
Atlas of U.S. Presidential Elections,
www.uselectionatlas.com.

2020 Delegate Selection

Democratic

Number of delegates: 25 total delegate votes—13 district, 4 at-large, 3 pledged PLEOs, 5 unpledged PLEOs

Date of 2020 contest: March 10

What week of the delegate selection season: 6

Type of delegate selection event: Closed primary

Mode of awarding delegates: Proportional representation with a 15 percent threshold

How delegates are chosen: Delegates to the national convention are elected by the state convention in accordance with the primary results

Bound for how many national conventions ballots: One

Source: http://www.thegreenpapers.com/P20/ID-D.

Republican

Number of delegates: 32 total delegates—26 at-large (10 base, 3 party, 13 bonus), 6 in 2 congressional districts

Date of 2020 contest: March 10

What week of the delegate selection season: 6

Type of delegate selection event: Closed primary

Mode of awarding delegates: Statewide winner-take-most: If a presidential candidate wins a majority of the statewide vote, he or she receives all national convention delegates; if not, and at least one candidate has won 20 percent or more of the vote, delegates are allocated proportionally with a 20 percent threshold; if no candidate has won at least 20 percent of the vote, delegates are simply allocated proportionally

How delegates are chosen: Each presidential candidate submits a list of proposed delegates to the national convention; delegates are elected by the state convention in accordance with the primary results

Bound for how many national conventions ballots: One

Source: http://www.thegreenpapers.com/P20/ID-R.

—Andrew E. Busch and Jacob S. Leischner

Illinois

The "Land of Lincoln" has long been divided between Chicago, now the third-largest city in America, and rural, small-town "downstate." The adult home of Barack Obama and the childhood home of Hillary Clinton, Illinois is also suffering from a big-city murder wave and a rolling state fiscal crisis rooted in extravagant public sector pensions. For decades after the Civil War the Midwestern heart of the Republican Party, Illinois turned into a coveted 20th-century swing state and, since 1992, an increasingly solid part of the Democratic base. The last Republican presidential candidate to win Illinois was George H. W. Bush in 1988, and Illinois was not even close to following the lead of other Great Lakes states Pennsylvania, Ohio, Michigan, and Wisconsin in returning to the Republican fold in 2016. Hillary Clinton defeated Donald Trump in Illinois by nearly a million votes, 55 to 38 percent.

Illinois has held a presidential primary every four years since 1912, when Theodore Roosevelt garnered 61 percent of the vote in the Republican primary and Champ Clark of neighboring Missouri won 74 percent in the Democratic vote. From its beginnings through 1964, the Illinois primary was held in early April. In 1968, the primary was scheduled in early June, then shifted to mid-March, where it has remained almost every year since 1972.

(In 2008, front-loading temporarily pushed Illinois to March 5.) Due to the large number of delegates at stake and the importance of Illinois to both parties for most of the time since 1912, the Illinois primary has frequently played a key role in nomination struggles.

Notable Illinois primaries have included:

1952: In the legendary Republican nomination battle between Dwight Eisenhower and Robert Taft, Taft won the Illinois primary with 74 percent, supported by Illinois kingmaker *Chicago Tribune*.

1960: As an indication of his electoral appeal, John F. Kennedy won the Democratic primary with nearly two-thirds of the vote as a write-in against favorite son (and two-time Democratic nominee) Adlai Stevenson and Senator Stuart Symington from Missouri.

1964: Barry Goldwater won the Republican primary, garnering 62 percent against noncandidate Margaret Chase Smith of Maine with 25 percent.

1968: The primary was held a week after the assassination of Robert Kennedy, and Illinois Democrats responded by giving 34 percent of their votes to RFK's brother Edward, who was not a candidate. The primary was won by Eugene McCarthy with 39 percent. Vice President Hubert Humphrey, carrying the torch for the pro-administration "regular" Democrats, did not compete and came in third with 17 percent of the vote. However, delegates were not bound by the primary and, under the influence of Mayor Richard Daley, 112 of 118 voted for Humphrey at the national convention.

1976: Incumbent president Gerald Ford defeated Ronald Reagan by nearly 20 percentage points, gaining a big win in his tough and ultimately successful fight for the GOP nomination. On the Democratic side, Jimmy Carter won his own big victory, obtaining 48 percent of the vote against George Wallace's 28 percent and Sargent Shriver's 16 percent.

1980: The Republican primary featured a showdown between two candidates with Illinois roots. Ronald Reagan, the favorite for the nomination, beat Congressman John Anderson, who later ran an independent campaign in the general election, by a solid 48 to 37 percent margin. George H. W. Bush finished a distant third with 11 percent. Reagan's win put an end to Anderson's best shot at gaining in the race. In the Democratic primary, Jimmy Carter won Illinois again, demolishing Edward Kennedy 65 to 30 percent. Kennedy seemed finished, but soon came back in New York and Connecticut to revive his campaign (Busch 2005).

1984: In an important test of strength, former vice president Walter Mondale defeated Colorado senator Gary Hart 40 to 35 percent; Jesse Jackson, who called Chicago home, ended with 21 percent. Mondale appeared to be trailing in Illinois, but came back in a debate with Hart nine days before the Illinois primary when he successfully used a Wendy's hamburgers advertising line—"Where's the beef?"—to puncture Hart's vague promises of "new ideas" (Spears 2018).

1988: One week after his sweep of Super Tuesday, George H. W. Bush beat Bob Dole 55–36 percent to further strengthen his hold on the Republican nomination.

1992: Bill Clinton followed up his own Super Tuesday success with a win in Illinois, outpolling his closest competitor (Paul Tsongas) by a 2–1 margin.

2008: In the Democratic primary between Illinois senator Barack Obama and Illinois native Hillary Clinton, Obama gained the upper hand, winning in a 65–33 percent blowout. Obama carried Chicago, while Clinton did best downstate. The competitive Republican primary was won by John McCain on his way to the nomination. McCain collected 48 percent of the vote to Mitt Romney's 29 percent and Mike Huckabee's 17 percent.

2012: On his return visit four years later, Mitt Romney had better success, winning the Republican primary by 12 percentage points over Rick Santorum.

2016: Donald Trump continued his march through the Republican primaries over his divided opponents. Trump garnered 39 percent of the vote, Ted Cruz won 30 percent, John Kasich 20 percent, and Marco Rubio 9 percent. Hillary Clinton greatly improved on her 2008 Illinois showing, but barely held on to a 51 to 49 percent win over insurgent Bernie Sanders.

Sources

Busch, Andrew E. 2005. *Reagan's Victory: The Presidential Election of 1980 and the Rise of the Right.* Lawrence: University Press of Kansas.

Spears, Steve. 2018. "On This Date, Wendy's First Asked: Where's the Beef?" *Tampa Bay Times,* January 10. https://www.tampabay.com/blogs/80s/2018/01/10/on-this-date-wendys-first-asked-wheres-the-beef/.

Illinois Primary Results 2000–2016

2000

Democratic primary (3/21)		Republican primary (3/21)	
Gore	84.4	Bush	67.4
Bradley	14.2	McCain	21.5
LaRouche	1.4	Keyes	9.0
		Forbes	1.4

2004

Democratic primary (3/16)		Republican primary (3/16)	
Kerry	71.7	Bush	100.0
Edwards	10.8		
Braun	4.4		
Dean	3.9		
Sharpton	3.0		
Kucinich	2.3		
Lieberman	2.0		
Clark	1.6		

2008

Democratic primary (2/5)		Republican primary (2/5)	
Obama	64.7	McCain	47.5
Clinton	32.8	Romney	28.6
Edwards	2.0	Huckabee	16.5
		Paul	5.0
		Giuliani	1.3

2012

Democratic primary (3/20)		Republican primary (3/20)	
Obama	100.0	Romney	46.7
		Santorum	35.0
		Paul	9.3
		Gingrich	8.0

2016

Democratic primary (3/15)		Republican primary (3/15)	
Clinton	50.6	Trump	38.8
Sanders	48.6	Cruz	30.2
		Kasich	19.7
		Rubio	8.7

Sources: Federal Election Commission:
https://transition.fec.gov/pubrec/fe2000/2000presprim.htm#IL;

https://transition.fec.gov/pubrec/fe2004/federalelections2004.pdf;
https://transition.fec.gov/pubrec/fe2008/federalelections2008.pdf;
https://transition.fec.gov/pubrec/fe2012/federalelections2012.pdf;
https://transition.fec.gov/pubrec/fe2016/federalelections2016.pdf.

2020 Delegate Selection

Democratic

Number of delegates: 184 total delegate votes—101 district, 34 at-large, 20 pledged PLEOs, 29 unpledged PLEOs

Date of 2020 contest: March 17

What week of the delegate selection season: 7

Type of delegate selection event: Open primary

Mode of awarding delegates: Proportional representation with 15 percent threshold

How delegates are chosen: Candidates for district delegates to the national convention must file nominating petitions, a statement of candidacy, and a declaration of presidential preference, and are elected in the district-level primary; at-large delegates and pledged PLEOs are elected at state headquarters by the district-level delegates according to the statewide results of the primary

Bound for how many national conventions ballots: One

Source: http://www.thegreenpapers.com/P20/IL-D.

Republican

Number of delegates: 67 total delegates—13 at-large (10 base, 3 party), 54 in 18 congressional districts

Date of 2020 contest: March 17

What week of the delegate selection season: 7

Type of delegate selection event: Open primary

Mode of awarding delegates: At-large: Winner-take-all based on statewide primary vote. District: Delegate selection primary accompanied by nonbinding (advisory) presidential preference vote

How delegates are chosen: At-large delegates to the national convention are elected at the state convention; district delegates are listed individually on the ballot and are elected directly in the district primary. Candidates for district delegate must declare a presidential preference (or their uncommitted status)

Bound for how many national conventions ballots: One

Source: http://www.thegreenpapers.com/P20/IL-R.

—Andrew E. Busch

Indiana

Indiana has long combined a strong industrial base and a bountiful agricultural sector. The people of Indiana are descendants of its original settlers with most Yankees historically being Republican and most Butternuts, having migrated from Kentucky and the South, leaning Democratic. At the presidential level, Indiana's cultural conservatism and traditions have kept it right-leaning and Republican for several generations (Cohen and Barnes 2016). In 1964, the state voted for Democrat Lyndon Johnson, but since then, it has voted Republican with the exception of Barack Obama's bare .03 percent win over John McCain in 2008. In 2016, Donald Trump defeated Hillary Clinton by 56 percent to 37 percent.

Presidential primaries began in Indiana in 1920 for the Republicans and in 1928 for the Democrats. No primary was held in either party from 1932 to 1952. Presidential primaries were reinstated in Indiana in 1956 and have continued since then. In scheduling its primary, no state has been more consistent than Indiana. Every Indiana presidential primary ever held has taken place in the first eight days of May. Scheduled in the thick of the back-loaded nomination fight, Indiana primaries in earlier years were frequently important. As the bulk of the primary calendar moved forward, the state increasingly voted after nominations were effectively decided. Exceptions in recent years included the Democratic primary in 2008 and both Republican and Democratic primaries in 2016.

Significant Indiana primaries have included:

1964: The Democratic primary was fought between Alabama governor George Wallace and Indiana's governor Matthew Welsh standing in for Lyndon Johnson. Welsh ran on the slogan, "Clear the way for LBJ, vote for Welsh on the fifth of May" (Rovere 1964). Wallace attracted more than 30 percent of the votes, making Indiana the second of three states where Wallace shocked the political establishment in 1964 (Indiana was preceded by Wisconsin and followed by Maryland).

1968: Senator Robert Kennedy won the Democratic primary with 42 percent of the vote, defeating Indiana governor Roger D. Branigin (31 percent) and Senator Eugene McCarthy (27 percent). Indiana was Kennedy's first win in his confrontation with McCarthy. For his part, Branigin had been lured onto the ballot to serve as a surrogate for Lyndon Johnson as Matthew Welsh had done in 1964. Once LBJ left the race, Branigin hoped a good showing could lead to an offer of the vice presidency (Nelson 2014, 96–97).

1972: Hubert Humphrey won the Democratic primary over George Wallace, 47 to 41 percent. Coupled with his win in Ohio the same day, Humphrey's victory put him in a strong position to contend for the nomination, though it was ultimately won by George McGovern.

1976: In a major showdown in the Republican race, Ronald Reagan edged out incumbent president Gerald Ford 51–49 percent. The win was particularly important to Reagan as it was his first primary victory in a non-Southern state (Shirley 2005).

1980: Locked in contested races, both parties' front-runners cruised to big wins as Republican Ronald Reagan garnered 74 percent of the vote and Democrat Jimmy Carter won 68 percent against Edward Kennedy.

1984: Colorado senator Gary Hart eked out a 42–41 percent win against Walter Mondale, beating Mondale in a Rust Belt state that seemed like a fit for the Minnesotan. Despite his loss in Indiana, Mondale ultimately won the Democratic nomination.

2008: Hillary Clinton was still battling Barack Obama after victories in Ohio and Pennsylvania. The political circumstances and demographics of the state favored Clinton and she held onto a 51–49 percent win.

2016: Indiana had one of the latest Republican primaries on May 3, and it was widely seen as the last chance for the "Stop Trump" movement. After his big win in Wisconsin in early April, Ted Cruz had suffered a series of setbacks in northeastern states, and he had to win Indiana to remain viable. Days before the vote, Cruz took the unusual step of preemptively announcing his vice presidential choice, former rival Carly Fiorina of California. Donald Trump countered by implying, based on a photo in the *National Enquirer*, that Cruz's father had something to do with the assassination of John F. Kennedy. Despite a (somewhat tepid) endorsement of Cruz by Governor Mike Pence, Donald Trump defeated Cruz handily and clearly emerged as the Republican nominee. Cruz and John Kasich, who finished a distant third in Indiana, suspended their presidential campaigns. On the Democratic side, Bernie Sanders kept up his fight against Hillary Clinton, beating Clinton 53–47 percent (Ceaser, Busch, and Pitney 2017).

Sources

Ceaser, James W., Andrew E. Busch, and John J. Pitney Jr. 2017. *Defying the Odds: The Elections of 2016 and American Politics.* Lanham, MD: Rowman & Littlefield.

Cohen, Richard E., and James A. Barnes. 2016. *The Almanac of American Politics.* Washington, DC: National Journal.

Nelson, Michael. 2014. *Resilient America: Electing Nixon in 1968, Channeling Dissent, and Dividing Government.* Lawrence: University Press of Kansas.

Rovere, Richard. 1964. "Letter from Washington." *The New Yorker*, May 9. https://www.newyorker.com/magazine/1964/05/16/letter-from-washington-george-wallace.

Shirley, Craig. 2005. *Reagan's Revolution: The Untold Story of the Campaign That Started It All.* Nashville, TN: Thomas Nelson, 2005.

Indiana Primary Results 2000–2016

2000

Democratic primary (5/2)		Republican primary (5/2)	
Gore	74.9	Bush	81.2
Bradley	21.9	McCain	18.8
LaRouche	3.2		

2004

Democratic primary (5/4)		Republican primary (5/4)	
Kerry	72.8	Bush	100.0
Edwards	11.2		
Dean	6.8		
Kucinich	2.2		
LaRouche	1.5		

2008

Democratic primary (5/6)		Republican primary (5/6)	
Clinton	50.6	McCain	77.6
Obama	49.4	Huckabee	9.9
		Paul	7.7
		Romney	4.7

2012

Democratic primary (5/8)		Republican primary (5/8)	
Obama	100.0	Romney	61.6
		Paul	15.5
		Santorum	13.4
		Gingrich	6.5

2016

Democratic primary (5/3)		Republican primary (5/3)	
Sanders	52.5	Trump	53.3
Clinton	47.5	Cruz	36.6
		Kasich	7.6

Sources: Federal Election Commission:

https://transition.fec.gov/pubrec/fe2000/2000presprim.htm;
https://transition.fec.gov/pubrec/fe2004/federalelections2004.pdf;
https://transition.fec.gov/pubrec/fe2008/federalelections2008.pdf;
https://transition.fec.gov/pubrec/fe2012/2012pres.pdf;
https://transition.fec.gov/pubrec/fe2016/federalelections2016.pdf.

2020 Delegate Selection

Democratic

Number of delegates: 77 total delegate votes—46 district, 15 at-large, 9 pledged PLEOs, 7 unpledged PLEOs

Date of 2020 contest: May 5

What week of the delegate selection season: 14

Type of delegate selection event: Open primary

Mode of awarding delegates: Proportional representation with a 15 percent threshold

How delegates are chosen: Delegates to the national convention are elected by the state convention in accordance with primary results

Bound for how many national conventions ballots: One

Source: http://www.thegreenpapers.com/P20/IN-D.

Republican

Number of delegates: 58 total delegates—31 at-large (10 base, 3 party, 18 bonus), 27 in 9 congressional districts

Date of 2020 contest: May 5

What week of the delegate selection season: 14

Type of delegate selection event: Open primary

Mode of awarding delegates: At-large: Winner-take-all based on statewide vote. District: Winner-take-all based on district vote

How delegates are chosen: At-large delegates are slated prior to the primary by the state committee; district delegates are slated prior to the primary by congressional district caucuses

Bound for how many national conventions ballots: One

Source: http://www.thegreenpapers.com/P20/IN-R.

—Andrew E. Busch and Nandeeni K. Patel

Iowa

An agricultural state with some manufacturing outposts, Iowa is older and less racially diverse than the average American state. Iowa is a swing state in presidential politics. It voted for Al Gore in 2000, George W. Bush in 2004, Barack Obama in 2008 and 2012, and Donald Trump in 2016, by a surprisingly large 51 to 42 percent margin. The state possesses a bit of an isolationist streak in foreign policy, its Democrats lean to the left, and its Republicans include a larger-than-average proportion of Evangelical Protestants, often pushing Republican races toward more socially conservative candidates.

Iowa is, as almost all close followers of American politics know, a caucus state. Prior to the McGovern-Fraser Commission report, the Iowa caucuses were held relatively late in the nominating season. In order to comply with the new rules and meet required deadlines, Iowa Democrats moved the caucus up to January in 1972. Republicans followed in 1976. Though George McGovern's supporters dominated the 1972 caucuses, the change in schedule went largely unnoticed until Jimmy Carter's campaign in 1976 concluded that Iowa, then the first contest in the country, presented an ideal opportunity to pitch the unknown Carter in a small, retail setting. If he succeeded, he would reap massive early publicity that could make him a household name and launch his foray into subsequent states. Carter did "win," outpolling the other candidates (though not the "uncommitted"), and succeeded in gaining momentum that swept him into a first-place finish in the New Hampshire primary five weeks later and ultimately the Democratic nomination (Busch 2008, 56).

In recent decades, Iowa caucuses have typically been held eight days before the New Hampshire primary. At the height of the front-loading trend, in 2008, Iowa voted as early as January 3, and some observers wondered if the event might slide into late December of the preceding year. In 2016, the national parties moved the starting date for the nominating process back to February 1. Iowa caucuses were held that day.

Ever since Carter's iconic Iowa campaign, lesser-known candidates have looked to the Iowa caucuses as their chance for a big breakthrough. Iowa now receives media coverage and campaign attention comparable to New Hampshire. Together, Iowa and New Hampshire have become key gatekeepers of the presidential nominating system. A candidate does not have to win Iowa to win his or her party's nomination, but since 1976 only one nominee (Bill Clinton in 1992) has failed to win either Iowa or New Hampshire and only one nominee (John McCain in 2008) failed to finish in the top three in both.

Prior to 1980, Iowa delegations were frequently closely divided in both parties. Republicans gave both Dwight Eisenhower in 1952 and Barry Goldwater in 1964 a modest edge over their opponents; Democrats essentially split between Eugene McCarthy and Hubert Humphrey in 1968, and Republicans did the same between Gerald Ford and Ronald Reagan in 1976. In a number of races since 1976, Iowa has been discounted because of the presence of a favorite-son or virtual favorite-son candidate. These have included Representative Richard Gephardt of Missouri in 1988, Senator Bob Dole of Kansas (sometimes called "Iowa's third senator") in 1988 and 1996, and Senator Tom Harkin of Iowa in 1992.

While Republicans take a vote of presidential preference that is collected and reported, Democrats report only the number of delegates to the state convention elected in the caucuses for each candidate. Democrats sought to introduce two major innovations in their 2020 caucuses: the addition of a "virtual caucus" allowing online voting for six days prior to the in-person caucuses on February 3, which would use "ranked voting," in which the second- or third-place choices of voters can be redistributed to those candidates if the first-choice candidate does not receive votes that meet the 15 percent threshold. However, the Democratic National Committee disallowed the virtual caucus.

Key Iowa caucus results after 1976 have included:

1980: Jimmy Carter started his fight for renomination against Edward Kennedy on a strong footing, winning a 59–31 percent victory over Kennedy, who had hoped to hold Carter below 50 percent. On the Republican side, George H. W. Bush won a narrow 31.5 percent to 29.4 percent upset victory over Ronald Reagan, whose strategists had thought Iowa secure. Bush briefly gained the upper hand in the nomination race, declaring that he had the "Big Mo" (momentum), until Reagan won the New Hampshire primary five weeks later (Busch 2005, 62–66).

1984: Walter Mondale won the Democratic caucuses, as expected, but insurgent Gary Hart of Colorado finished second, beating expectations and putting himself in a position to win New Hampshire.

1988: Bob Dole's Republican caucus victory was not unexpected, but televangelist Pat Robertson's second-place showing shocked the political world and confirmed the new power of the Christian Right hinted at in the earlier Michigan and Hawaii caucuses.

2000: Vice President Al Gore defeated Bill Bradley handily, setting up a showdown in New Hampshire that would define the remainder of the race. George W. Bush also won, defeating publisher Steve Forbes, allowing Bush to begin consolidating the conservative vote.

2004: In the Democratic caucuses, John Kerry defeated John Edwards and Howard Dean, as well as Iowa's neighbor Richard Gephardt, winner of the 1988 caucuses. Kerry's victory capped a month-long comeback from the edge of presidential oblivion and propelled him to a come-from-behind win against Vermont governor Howard Dean in the New Hampshire primary. Gephardt's chief of staff remarked, "In my experience, John Kerry winning Iowa was the single most important victory anyone has ever had" (Simon 2004, 34). In his concession speech, Dean let out a scream that was soon the subject of widespread ridicule and parody, further damaging his campaign.

2008: Barack Obama won a stunning victory in the Democratic caucuses, beating John Edwards and Hillary Clinton, the favorite, who finished third. The results put Clinton on the defensive and made New Hampshire seem like a must-win for her. They also established Obama as a real force to be reckoned with. On the Republican side, front-runner John McCain more or less conceded Iowa, choosing to focus on New Hampshire. He finished fourth in Iowa. Arkansas governor Mike Huckabee, a favorite of social conservatives, came in first, followed by Mitt Romney. The Republican race would soon turn into a contest between McCain, Huckabee, and Romney.

2012: Another favorite of social conservatives, former Pennsylvania senator Rick Santorum, edged out Mitt Romney by a handful of votes (24.56 percent to 24.53 percent). However, the final votes pushing Santorum over the top were not tabulated until days later, leaving the initial impression that Romney was the narrow victor (Zeleny 2012).

2016: In the Democratic caucuses, Hillary Clinton won 49.8 percent of the delegates elected to the state convention, while Bernie Sanders won 49.6 percent. Because no overall popular vote was tabulated, Sanders supporters complained that their man might actually have had more votes statewide than Clinton ("Bernie Sanders" 2016). In a crowded Republican field, Senator Ted Cruz of Texas beat Donald Trump 27 percent to 24 percent, raising the question of whether Trump's apparent strength was illusory. Cruz won with substantial support from Iowa's evangelicals, and in spite of touching the "third rail" of Iowa politics by criticizing ethanol subsidies. Senator Marco Rubio of Florida finished a close third with 23 percent and seemed poised to challenge in New Hampshire. Jeb Bush, brother of George W. Bush and son of George H. W. Bush, finished in sixth place with less than 2 percent of the vote, despite having more spent on his behalf than any other Republican candidate.

Sources

"Bernie Sanders Wants Raw Vote Count Released after Tight Finish in Iowa Caucuses." 2016. *The Guardian*, February 2. https://www.theguardian.com /us-news/2016/feb/02/bernie-sanders-requests-vote-count-tight-finish -iowa-caucus-clinton.

Busch, Andrew E. 2005. *Reagan's Victory: The Presidential Election of 1980 and the Rise of the Right*. Lawrence: University Press of Kansas.

Busch, Andrew E. 2008. "The Reemergence of the Iowa Caucuses: A New Trend, an Aberration, or a Useful Reminder?" In William G. Mayer, ed., *The Making of the Presidential Candidates 2008*. Lanham, MD: Rowman & Littlefield.

Simon, Roger. 2004. "Turning Point." *U.S. News & World Report*, July 19–26.

Zeleny, Jeff. 2012. "Romney Wins Iowa by 8 Votes." *New York Times*, January 3. https://www.nytimes.com/2012/01/04/us/politics/santorum-and-romney -fight-to-a-draw.html.

Iowa Caucus Results 2000–2016

2000

Democratic caucus (1/24)		Republican (1/24)	
Gore	63.4	Bush	41.0
Bradley	34.9	Forbes	30.5
Uncommitted	1.7	Keyes	14.3
		Bauer	8.5
		McCain	4.7
		Hatch	1.0

2004

Democratic caucus (1/19)		Republican caucus (1/19)	
Kerry	37.1	**Delegates to national convention**	
Edwards	32.6	Uncommitted	100.0
Dean	17.4		
Gephardt	11.2		
Kucinich	1.0		

2008

Democratic caucus (1/3)		Republican caucus (1/3)	
Obama	37.6	Huckabee	34.4
Edwards	29.8	Romney	25.2
Clinton	29.5	Thompson	13.4
Richardson	2.1	McCain	13.1
		Paul	10.0
		Giuliani	3.5

2012

Democratic caucus (1/3)		Republican caucus (1/3)	
Obama	94.0	Santorum	24.5
Not announced	5.0	Romney	24.5
		Paul	21.4
		Gingrich	13.3
		Perry	10.3
		Bachmann	5.0

2016

Democratic caucus (2/1)		Republican caucus (2/1)	
Clinton	49.8	Cruz	27.6
Sanders	49.6	Trump	24.3
		Rubio	23.1
		Carson	9.3
		Paul	4.5
		Bush	2.8
		Fiorina	1.9
		Kasich	1.9
		Huckabee	1.8
		Christie	1.8

Sources: Iowa Caucuses, Caucus History, *Des Moines Register.*
http://data.desmoinesregister.com/iowa-caucus/history/index.php#2016/dem;
https://www.thegreenpapers.com/P04/IA-R.phtml;
https://www.thegreenpapers.com/P12/IA-D.

2020 Delegate Selection

Democratic

Number of delegates: 49 total delegate votes—27 district, 9 at-large, 5 pledged
   PLEOs, 8 unpledged PLEOs

Date of 2020 contest: February 3

What week of the delegate selection season: 1

Type of delegate selection event: Closed caucus

Mode of awarding delegates: Proportional representation with 15 percent threshold based on state delegate equivalency results of the precinct and virtual
   caucuses

How delegates are chosen: District national convention delegates are elected by
   congressional district conventions and at-large delegates are elected by state
   convention in accordance with caucus results

Bound for how many national conventions ballots: One

Source: http://www.thegreenpapers.com/P20/IA-D.

Republican

Number of delegates: 40 total delegates—28 at-large (10 base, 3 party, 15 bonus),
   12 in 4 congressional districts

Date of 2020 contest: February 3

What week of the delegate selection season: 1

Type of delegate selection event: Closed caucus

Mode of awarding delegates: Proportional representation based on statewide vote

How delegates are chosen: In accordance with statewide caucus results, district national convention delegates are elected by congressional district conventions and at-large delegates are elected by the state convention

Bound for how many national conventions ballots: One

Source: http://www.thegreenpapers.com/P20/IA-R.

Andrew E. Busch

Kansas

Like its prairie sisters in the Dakotas and Nebraska, Kansas combines a stolid conservatism and a streak of agrarian populism. One of the most consistently Republican states in the country, Kansas has not voted for a Democratic candidate for president since Lyndon Johnson in 1964. In 2016, Donald Trump won the state by a margin of 56 percent to 36 percent. However, Kansas Republicans are often bitterly divided between a moderate "country club Republican" faction and harder-edged conservatives, frequently social conservatives.

Kansas has never used a presidential primary, utilizing only caucus-convention processes for delegate selection. In 1952, the Republican delegation backed home state hero Dwight Eisenhower; in 1964, they threw their votes to Barry Goldwater; in 1976, Gerald Ford prevailed over Ronald Reagan. On the Democratic side, Kansas delegates supported John F. Kennedy in 1960, Hubert Humphrey in 1968, George McGovern in 1972, Jimmy Carter in 1980, Walter Mondale in 1984, Michael Dukakis in 1988, and Bill Clinton in 1992.

Since 2000, the Kansas caucuses have been scheduled in February or early March. In 2000 and 2004, they came after key rivals to the front-runners had already dropped out of the race or been rendered ineffective. However, caucuses in 2008–2016 were held while nomination races were still unfolding, giving Kansas some influence over the outcome. Kansas Democrats will be using a binding presidential primary for the first time in 2020, while the GOP dropped its caucuses.

Notable Kansas caucuses in recent years have included:

2008: Barack Obama defeated Hillary Clinton by a 3–1 margin, adding to Obama wins in seven state primaries that day. On the Republican side, Mike Huckabee won three in five votes, more than doubling John McCain's vote total.

2012: As happened four years before, the social conservative wing of the Kansas Republicans prevailed as Republican caucuses gave the advantage to Rick Santorum over Mitt Romney, 51 percent to 21 percent.

2016: Democratic caucus-goers chose Bernie Sanders over Hillary Clinton by a 2–1 margin. In the Republican caucuses, Ted Cruz beat Donald Trump by a similar ratio. Both Cruz and Sanders swept all of the state's congressional districts and did particularly well in and around Wichita (Kansas Caucus

Results 2016). In both cases, the more ideologically intense candidate took advantage of the caucus format, which emphasizes organization and commitment. Cruz's victory came a few days after polls showed him trailing Trump by six percentage points statewide (Ballotpedia).

Sources

Ballotpedia. "Presidential Election in Kansas, 2016." https://ballotpedia.org /Presidential_election_in_Kansas,_2016.
"Kansas Caucus Results." 2016. *New York Times*, March 5. https://www.nytimes .com/elections/2016/results/primaries/kansas.

Kansas Caucus Results 2000–2016

2000

Democratic caucuses (state conv. 5/6)		Republican caucuses (state conv. 5/25)	
Delegates to national convention		Delegates to national convention	
Gore	86.0	Bush	100.0
Uncommitted	14.0		

2004

Democratic caucuses (3/13)		Republican caucuses (3/1)	
Regional caucus delegates elected		Delegates to national convention	
Kerry	71.9	Bush	100.00
Kucinich	10.2		
Edwards	8.7		
Dean	6.7		
Uncommitted	1.7		

2008

Democratic caucuses (2/5)		Republican caucuses (2/9)	
Obama	74.0	Huckabee	59.6
Clinton	25.8	McCain	23.5
		Paul	11.2
		Romney	3.4
		Keyes	1.5

2012

Democratic local conventions (4/14)		Republican caucuses (3/10)	
Obama	100.0	Santorum	51.2
		Romney	20.9
		Gingrich	14.4
		Paul	12.6

2016

Democratic caucuses (3/5)		Republican caucuses (3/5)	
Sanders	67.7	Cruz	47.5
Clinton	32.3	Trump	23.4
		Rubio	16.8
		Kasich	11.1

Sources: Atlas of U.S. Presidential Elections, www.uselectionatlas.org;
https://www.thegreenpapers.com/PCC/Tabul.html;
https://www.thegreenpapers.com/P04/KS-D.phtml;
https://www.thegreenpapers.com/P04/KS-R.phtml.

2020 Delegate Selection

Democratic

Number of delegates: 39 total delegate votes—22 district, 7 at-large, 4 pledged PLEOs, 6 unpledged PLEOs

Date of 2020 contest: May 2

What week of the delegate selection season: 13

Type of delegate selection event: Closed primary

Mode of awarding delegates: Proportional representation with a 15 percent threshold; ranked choice voting

How delegates are chosen: In accordance with primary results, district delegates to the national convention are elected by congressional district conventions; at-large delegates and pledged PLEOs are elected by the state committee

Bound for how many national conventions ballots: One

Source: http://www.thegreenpapers.com/P20/KS-D.

Republican

Number of delegates: 39 total delegates—27 at-large (10 base, 3 party, 14 bonus), 12 in 4 congressional districts

Date of 2020 contest: May 9

What week of the delegate selection season: 5

Type of delegate selection event: State convention (presumed); caucuses were
cancelled

Mode of awarding delegates: Vote by state convention

Bound for how many national conventions ballots: All

Source: http://www.thegreenpapers.com/P20/KS-R.

—*Andrew E. Busch*

Kentucky

Kentucky is a border state with a Southern culture but Union loyalties, mix-
ing horse racing and bourbon with coal mining and Appalachian poverty.
Kentucky was long something of a swing state that produced notable legislative leaders on both sides of the aisle, including Senator and then Vice President Alben Barkley and Senator Mitch McConnell, first elected in 1984 and
still serving. (This is not to mention the inestimable Henry Clay in the early
19th century.) The state has recently trended Republican, voting narrowly for
Bill Clinton in the 1990s, giving George W. Bush 57 percent in 2000, and
voting 63 percent for Donald Trump in 2016.

Kentucky held its first presidential primary in 1976. In both Republican
and Democratic parties, national convention delegations in the caucus era
were typically found in the more conservative wing of their party, though
Democrats also eschewed segregationist disruptors. Republican delegations
from Kentucky favored Robert Taft in 1952 and Barry Goldwater in 1964;
Democrats preferred Lyndon Johnson in 1960, Hubert Humphrey in 1968,
and Washington senator Henry Jackson in 1972. They stuck with Harry
Truman in 1948 against the anti–civil rights walkout by some Southern
delegates.

With only two exceptions, Kentucky's primaries have been held in May,
usually in the second half of the month. In 1988, Kentucky chose to join
the 16-state Super Tuesday on March 8. In 1984, neither party held a primary, as both reverted to caucuses; in 2016, Democrats held a primary in
May but Republicans held caucuses in early March. With a late May primary, Kentucky has struggled to make a significant impact in the front-
loaded era. However, there have been some notable Kentucky primaries,
including:

1976: In the first Kentucky primary, Gerald Ford won an important victory over Ronald Reagan, 51 to 47 percent, part of the long back-and-forth
between the two. At the same time, Jimmy Carter defeated George Wallace
59 to 17 percent, another in a string of defeats inflicted by "New South"
Carter over "Old South" Wallace.

1988: On Super Tuesday, George H. W. Bush crushed Bob Dole in the
Republican primary, extending the nationwide victory that effectively ended

Dole's chances. In the Democratic primary, Al Gore won 46 percent to Michael Dukakis's 19 percent. Kentucky was one of the five states Gore won that day.

2008: With the Democratic race still undecided in late May, Hillary Clinton beat Barack Obama by 66 percent to 30 percent.

2012: A little-noticed sign of Kentucky's dissatisfaction with the national Democratic Party came in the Democratic primary when unopposed incumbent President Barack Obama received only 58 percent of the vote, while 42 percent voted for uncommitted delegates.

2016: In the Republican caucuses held in early March, Donald Trump narrowly defeated Ted Cruz 36 percent to 32 percent. Marco Rubio finished third with 16 percent and John Kasich fourth with 12 percent. Kentucky was another one of several early states where Cruz came close to Trump, but not close enough. In the May 17 Democratic primary, Hillary Clinton held off Bernie Sanders by a margin of 46.8 to 46.3 percent, a surprisingly strong finish for the Vermont socialist in a state Clinton had won by 36 percentage points against Obama eight years before.

Kentucky Primary and Caucus Results 2000–2016

2000

Democratic primary (5/23)		Republican primary (5/23)	
Gore	71.3	Bush	83.0
Bradley	14.7	McCain	6.3
Uncommitted	11.8	Keyes	4.8
LaRouche	2.2	Bauer	2.6
		Uncommitted	2.0
		Forbes	1.3

2004

Democratic primary (5/18)		Republican primary (5/18)	
Kerry	60.1	Bush	92.5
Edwards	14.5	Uncommitted	7.5
Uncommitted	9.2		
Lieberman	4.8		
Dean	3.6		
Clark	2.8		
Sharpton	2.2		
Kucinich	2.0		

2008

Democratic primary (5/20)		Republican primary (5/20)	
Clinton	65.5	McCain	72.3
Obama	30.0	Huckabee	8.3
Uncommitted	2.6	Paul	6.8
Edwards	2.0	Uncommitted	5.4
		Romney	4.7
		Giuliani	1.5
		Keyes	1.0

2012

Democratic primary (5/22)		Republican primary (5/22)	
Obama	57.9	Romney	66.8
Uncsommitted	42.2	Paul	12.5
		Santorum	8.9
		Gingrich	6.0
		Uncommitted	5.9

2016

Democratic primary (5/17)		Republican caucuses (3/5)	
Clinton	46.8	Trump	35.9
Sanders	46.3	Cruz	31.6
Uncommitted	5.3	Rubio	16.4
O'Malley	1.3	Kasich	14.4

Sources: Federal Election Commission:
https://transition.fec.gov/pubrec/fe2000/2000presprim.htm#KY;
https://transition.fec.gov/pubrec/fe2004/federalelections2004.pdf;
https://transition.fec.gov/pubrec/fe2008/federalelections2008.pdf;
https://transition.fec.gov/pubrec/fe2012/federalelections2012.pdf;
https://transition.fec.gov/pubrec/fe2016/federalelections2016.pdf; also
https://www.nytimes.com/elections/2016/results/primaries/Kentucky.

2020 Delegate Selection

Democratic

Number of delegates: 52 total delegate votes—30 district, 10 at-large, 6 pledged
PLEOs, 6 unpledged PLEOs

Date of 2020 contest: May 19

What week of the delegate selection season: 16

Type of delegate selection event: Closed primary

Mode of awarding delegates: Proportional representation with a 15 percent threshold

How delegates are chosen: According to the primary results, district delegates to the national convention are elected by congressional district conventions and at-large delegates and pledged PLEOs are elected by the state convention

Bound for how many national conventions ballots: One

Source: http://www.thegreenpapers.com/P20/KY-D.

Republican

Number of delegates: 46 total delegates—28 at-large (10 base, 3 party, 15 bonus), 18 in 6 congressional districts

Date of 2020 contest: March 21

What week of the delegate selection season: 8

Type of delegate selection event: Closed caucus/convention

Mode of awarding delegates: Statewide winner-take-all

How delegates are chosen: According to the caucus results, district delegates to the national convention are elected by congressional district conventions and at-large delegates are elected by the state convention

Bound for how many national conventions ballots: One

Source: http://www.thegreenpapers.com/P20/KY-R.

—*Andrew E. Busch*

Louisiana

With a strong French influence in New Orleans, Louisiana is a unique Southern state, divided between a heavily Catholic south and an evangelical Protestant north. One-third of Louisiana's population is also African American, the second-highest rate in the nation. Oil and gas exports are critical to Louisiana's economy and to its politics. Though a part of the Democratic "Solid South," Louisiana was not as "solid" as other Deep South states, voting for Dixiecrat Strom Thurmond in 1948 and Republican president Dwight Eisenhower in 1956. As other Southern states transitioned to solid Republican presidential support, Louisiana voted for Democrat Bill Clinton in 1992 and 1996. Since 2000, the state has only supported Republican presidential candidates, while still sometimes electing Democratic senators such as John Breaux and Mary Landrieu. In 2016, Donald Trump won the state over Hillary Clinton by a 58 percent to 38 percent margin.

Prior to 1980, Democratic convention delegations backed Franklin Roosevelt in 1932, Richard Russell in 1948, Lyndon Johnson in 1960, Hubert Humphrey in 1968, and Shirley Chisholm in 1972, before splitting evenly between Jimmy Carter and Edmund "Jerry" Brown in 1976. The seating of a pro-Eisenhower delegation in a Republican credentials dispute contributed to Ike's victory in 1952. Louisiana Republicans subsequently spearheaded Barry Goldwater's success, not only giving him all their votes in 1964 but being one of two delegations that gave him votes in 1960, prompting the first serious "Goldwater for President" rumblings. In 1976, the Louisiana delegation backed Ronald Reagan.

Louisiana held its first presidential primary on April 5, 1980. The state moved the primary date back to early May in 1984, then up to March in 1988, where it has remained for the most part since then (with the exception of 2008's February contest). However, in 1996, Louisiana Republicans tried to lead the process by holding caucuses a week before Iowa. Significant races in recent years include:

1984: Jesse Jackson Jr. won the Democratic primary, defeating runner-up Gary Hart by nearly 20 points, 43 percent to 25 percent. The state legislature attempted to cancel the primary in 1983, but Jackson's supporters mounted a legal challenge and the courts ordered the election to go on. Louisiana marked the first state Jackson won (though he had won the primary in the District of Columbia a week earlier). Eventual Democratic nominee Walter Mondale finished third with 22 percent, but had not actively campaigned, focusing his campaign's efforts instead on the Texas contest held the same day (Gailey 1984).

1996: Patrick J. Buchanan won the February 6 Republican caucuses, upsetting Senator Phil Gramm of neighboring Texas. Gramm was favored in the caucuses, which were scheduled before the Iowa caucuses by Gramm supporters in hopes of boosting his candidacy, but Buchanan seized conservative religious voters by a 2–1 margin. Other GOP candidates, including eventual nominee Senator Bob Dole of Kansas, did not even compete in the state—Lamar Alexander called the contest "a media sideshow arranged to help the campaigns of two sagging candidates" (Berke 1996). In mid-March, Louisiana Republicans also held an advisory primary, which Dole won handily.

2008: Republican Mike Huckabee narrowly edged out John McCain, while in the Democratic contest, Barack Obama beat Hillary Clinton by 20 percentage points.

2012: Social conservative hero Rick Santorum beat Mitt Romney by more than 20 percentage points, slowing Romney's progress toward the Republican nomination.

2016: Donald Trump edged out Senator Ted Cruz, 41.5 percent to 37.8 percent, to win the Republican primary contest. On the Democratic side, Hillary Clinton routed Bernie Sanders, 71 percent to 23 percent. Sanders won just two of the state's 64 parishes.

Sources

Berke, Richard. 1996. "Buchanan Wins in Louisiana in Blow to Gramm Campaign." *The New York Times*, February 7. https://www.nytimes.com/1996/02/07/us/politics-the-caucuses-buchanan-wins-in-louisiana-in-blow-to-gramm-campaign.html.

Gailey, Phil. 1984. "Jackson Takes Louisiana Vote in Low Turnout." *The New York Times*, May 6. https://www.nytimes.com/1984/05/06/us/jackson-takes-louisiana-vote-in-low-turnout.html.

Louisiana Primary Results 2000–2016

2000

Democratic primary (3/14)		Republican primary (3/14)	
Gore	73.0	Bush	83.6
Bradley	19.9	McCain	8.9
LaRouche	3.9	Keyes	5.7
Crow	3.2	Forbes	1.0

2004

Democratic primary (3/9)		Republican primary (3/9)	
Kerry	69.7	Bush	96.1
Edwards	16.1	Wyatt	3.9
Dean	4.9		
Clark	4.4		
McGaughey	2		
Kucinich	1.5		
LaRouche	1.4		

2008

Democratic primary (2/9)		Republican primary (2/9)	
Obama	57.4	Huckabee	43.2
Clinton	35.6	McCain	41.9
Edwards	3.4	Romney	6.3
Biden	1.6	Paul	5.3
Richardson	1.1		

2012

Democratic primary (3/24)		Republican primary (3/24)	
Obama	76.5	Santorum	49.0
Wolfe	11.8	Romney	26.7
Ely	6.6	Gingrich	15.9
Richardson	5.2	Paul	6.2
		Roemer	1.2

2016

Democratic primary (3/5)		Republican primary (3/5)	
Clinton	71.1	Trump	41.5
Sanders	23.2	Cruz	37.8
Burke	1.5	Rubio	11.2
Wolfe	1.5	Kasich	6.4
		Carson	1.5

Sources: Federal Election Commission:
https://transition.fec.gov/pubrec/fe2000/2000presprim.htm#top;
https://transition.fec.gov/pubrec/fe2004/federalelections2004.pdf;
https://transition.fec.gov/pubrec/fe2008/federalelections2008.pdf;
https://transition.fec.gov/pubrec/fe2012/2012pres.pdf;
https://transition.fec.gov/pubrec/fe2016/federalelections2016.pdf.

2020 Delegate Selection

Democratic

Number of delegates: 57 total delegate votes—32 district, 11 at-large, 7 pledged PLEOs, 7 unpledged PLEOs.

Date of 2020 contest: April 4

What week of the delegate selection season: 9

Type of delegate selection event: Closed primary 0

Mode of awarding delegates: Proportional representation with a 15 percent threshold

How delegates are chosen: District delegates to the national convention are elected according to the primary results by mail-in congressional district caucuses; at-large delegates and pledged PLEOs are elected by the state central committee

Bound for how many national conventions ballots: One

Source: https://www.thegreenpapers.com/P20/LA-D.

Republican

Number of delegates: 46 total delegates—28 at-large (10 base, 3 party, 15 bonus), 18 in 6 congressional districts

Date of 2020 contest: April 4

What week of the delegate selection season: 9

Type of delegate selection event: Closed primary

Mode of awarding delegates: District delegates are allocated by proportional representation based on the district primary results; at-large delegates are allocated by proportional representation with a 20 percent threshold based on the statewide primary results

How delegates are chosen: Candidates for district delegates to the national convention are nominated by preprimary district caucuses and elected by congressional district meetings at the state convention according to district primary results; at-large delegates are elected by the whole state convention according to state primary results

Bound for how many national conventions ballots: One

Source: https://www.thegreenpapers.com/P20/LA-R.

—*Andrew E. Busch and Richard C. Wiltshire-Gordon*

Maine

A largely rural Yankee state that started as a noncontiguous part of Massachusetts, Maine has shifted toward Democrats at the presidential level along with other New England states. However, the more rural and working-class inland half of the state is competitive. In the 2016 election, Hillary Clinton won Maine's coastal congressional district handily while Donald Trump narrowly won the inland district, and with it one of Maine's electoral votes. Maine's independent streak shows itself in other ways, starting with long-serving senator Susan Collins, one of the few remaining liberal Republicans in the Senate. Maine was the only state where independent Ross Perot exceeded 30 percent of the vote in 1992, and the only one where Perot finished second, ahead of George H. W. Bush.

Maine has typically used a caucus-convention system for delegate selection, though both Democrats and Republicans used a primary in 1996 and 2000. State law has again been changed to return to a primary election in 2020. Prior to 1996, both parties frequently sent national convention delegations that were divided. Republicans sent a delegation that was split 11–5 for Eisenhower over Taft in 1952 and 15–5 for Gerald Ford over Ronald Reagan in 1976; in the contentious 1964 race, Maine punted and cast its votes for favorite-daughter Margaret Chase Smith. Similarly, Democrats in 1972 gave their convention votes to home senator Edmund Muskie, who had been favored to win it all at the beginning of the nomination season. Democrats also supported JFK in 1960 and Hubert Humphrey in 1968, but split 11–11 over Carter versus Kennedy in 1980, 13–13 over Mondale versus Hart in 1984, 17–12 in favor of Dukakis over Jackson in 1988, and 14–13 in favor of Clinton against Brown in 1992.

In the 1996 primary, Republican Bob Dole easily defeated Pat Buchanan (46–25 percent). Four years later, Al Gore beat Bill Bradley 54 percent to 41 percent in the Democratic primary as George W. Bush, with his family's Maine connection, beat John McCain 51 to 44 percent.

When Maine returned to caucuses, key results included:

2004: In a battle of New Englanders, John Kerry outpaced Howard Dean in state convention delegates by 47 to 27 percent.

2008: In the midst of an impressive caucus winning record, Barack Obama defeated Hillary Clinton by winning 59 percent of state convention delegates to Hillary Clinton's 40 percent. On the Republican side, Mitt Romney gained 51 percent of the state delegates to John McCain's 21 percent and Ron Paul's 18 percent.

2012: Mitt Romney again prevailed narrowly in the Republican caucuses, with 38 percent of the state convention delegates to Ron Paul's 36 percent.

2016: Bernie Sanders defeated Hillary Clinton by collecting 64 percent of the state convention delegates to Clinton's 35 percent, extending his dominance in caucus settings. Also consistent with results in other states, Ted Cruz won the Republican caucus vote, defeating Donald Trump by 46 to 32 percent.

Maine Primary and Caucus Results 2000–2016

2000

Democratic primary (3/7)		Republican primary (3/7)	
Gore	54.0	Bush	51.0
Bradley	41.3	McCain	44.0
Uncommitted	4.1	Keyes	3.1
		Uncommitted	1.1

2004

Democratic caucuses (2/8)		Republican caucuses (1/2)	
State convention delegates		**Delegates to national convention**	
Kerry	47.1	Uncommitted	100.0
Dean	27.1		
Kucinich	13.8		
Edwards	7.0		
Clark	3.6		
Uncommitted	1.2		

2008

Democratic caucuses (2/10)		Republican caucuses (2/1–2/3)	
State convention delegates		**State convention delegates**	
Obama	59.4	Romney	52.0
Clinton	39.9	McCain	21.1
		Paul	18.4
		Huckabee	5.7
		Uncommitted	2.4

2012

Democratic caucuses (2/26)		Republican caucuses (1/29–3/3)	
Delegates to national convention		**State convention delegates**	
Obama	83.8	Romney	38.0
Uncommitted	16.2	Paul	36.1
		Santorum	18.2
		Gingrich	6.5

2016

Democratic caucuses (3/6)		Republican caucuses (3/5)	
State convention delegates		Cruz	45.9
Sanders	64.3	Trump	32.6
Clinton	35.5	Kasich	12.2
		Rubio	8.0

Sources: *Atlas of U.S. Presidential Elections*,
https://uselectionatlas.org/RESULTS/;
https://www.thegreenpapers.com/P04/ME-R.phtml;
https://www.thegreenpapers.com/P08/ME-D.phtml;
https://www.thegreenpapers.com/P08/ME-R.phtml;
http://www.thegreenpapers.com/P12/ME-D;
https://www.thegreenpapers.com/P12/ME-R.

2020 Delegate Selection

Democratic

Number of delegates: 32 total delegate votes—16 district, 5 at-large, 3 pledged PLEOs, 8 unpledged PLEOs

Date of 2020 contest: March 3

What week of the delegate selection season: 5

Type of delegate selection event: Closed primary

Mode of awarding delegates: Proportional representation with a 15 percent threshold; ranked choice voting

How delegates are chosen: National convention delegates are elected at the state convention in accordance with the caucus results

Bound for how many national conventions ballots: One

Source: https://www.thegreenpapers.com/P20/ME-D.

Republican

Number of delegates: 22 total delegates—16 at-large (10 base, 3 party, 3 bonus), 6 in 2 congressional districts

Date of 2020 contest: March 3

What week of the delegate selection season: 5

Type of delegate selection event: Closed primary. However, the primary depends on the party certifying that there is a contest between candidates. Otherwise, procedure will revert to a caucus held on March 7

Mode of awarding delegates: Winner-take-most: If a candidate for president wins more than half of Maine's statewide caucus vote, he or she will receive all of Maine's delegates to the national convention. If no candidate wins a majority of votes, delegates will be allocated proportionally with a 10 percent threshold

How delegates are chosen: District delegates to the national convention will be elected by district caucuses held at the time of the state convention; at-large delegates will be elected by the state convention as a whole

Bound for how many national conventions ballots: All

Source: https://www.thegreenpapers.com/P20/ME-R.

—Andrew E. Busch

Maryland

Initially an English colony that served as a refuge for Roman Catholics, Maryland was one of the "border states" that had considerable Confederate sympathies but remained in the Union (under duress). Today, bolstered by a substantial African American population and a large contingent of federal employees living in the Washington suburbs, Maryland is strongly Democratic at the presidential level. It has elected Republican governors several times in recent years, but no Republican presidential candidate has won Maryland since 1988. In 2016, Hillary Clinton beat Donald Trump 60 percent to 34 percent, though Trump prevailed in Maryland's less populated Eastern Shore and western wedge.

Maryland started holding presidential primaries in 1912 and has held one every presidential year but 1916, 1948, and 1968. In 1936, 1952, and 1960 only Democrats held a primary; in 1940 and 1944 only Republicans did. In 1920 through 1932, Democrats held a primary but no candidate names were entered. For the first 72 years, Maryland scheduled its primaries in May. In 1988, the state shifted its primary date to early March to join the 15 other states holding primaries on the first big Super Tuesday. In 2008, Maryland moved up by a month as part of the national front-loading stampede, but then moved back to April in 2012 and 2016.

Notable Maryland primaries have included:

1912: In Maryland's first primary, Republicans gave Theodore Roosevelt a 53–47 percent victory over incumbent president William Howard Taft. Champ Clark of Missouri won handily over Woodrow Wilson, 54 to 34 percent.

1964: Alabama governor George C. Wallace won more than 4 of every 10 votes against Lyndon Johnson's stand-in, Governor Daniel B. Brewster. Wallace's 43 percent showing according to official tabulations was alleged by some to have been artificially deflated by the state's Democratic machine (Crass 1976, 71). In combination with Wallace's stronger than expected showings in Indiana and Wisconsin earlier, Maryland revealed the possibility of a white working-class backlash against civil rights and helped launch him toward his independent run for the presidency in 1968.

1972: Returning to the scene of his 1964 surprise, George Wallace won the Democratic primary with 39 percent of the vote to Hubert Humphrey's 27 percent and George McGovern's 22 percent. What might have been an important victory for Wallace late in the primary season was marred by an assassination attempt at a campaign event at a Maryland mall days before the vote that left Wallace paralyzed from the waist down.

1976: While President Gerald Ford was beating Ronald Reagan 58 to 42 percent in the Republican primary, California governor Edmund G. "Jerry" Brown was breathing life into his late-starting campaign by defeating Jimmy Carter 48–37 percent in the Democratic primary.

1988: Voting on Super Tuesday, Maryland Republicans backed George H. W. Bush over Bob Dole by 20 points while Democrats gave Michael Dukakis a 46–29 victory over Jesse Jackson. Four years earlier, the Democratic establishment favorite Walter Mondale had dispatched Jackson by the nearly identical score of 43 to 26 percent.

1992: In the Democratic primary, Paul Tsongas of Massachusetts defeated Bill Clinton 41 to 34 percent. Jerry Brown, hoping for a reprise of his critical Maryland win in 1976, won only 8 percent of the vote. Colorado and Georgia also voted on March 3, and each major Democratic contender won one of the three.

2000: George W. Bush defeated John McCain in the Republican primary. Maryland joined other states to give Bush wins in seven of the 11 Republican primaries held that day. McCain never recovered.

2004: John Kerry crushed John Edwards in the Democratic primary, 60 percent to 25 percent. Kerry's Super Tuesday sweep essentially assured his nomination.

2008: John McCain reversed his 2000 loss, beating nearest competitor Mike Huckabee by nearly a 2–1 margin in the GOP contest. On the Democratic side, Barack Obama similarly smothered Hillary Clinton 61–36 percent.

2016: Along with several northeastern states, Maryland gave Donald Trump a big win over John Kasich and a bigger win over Ted Cruz. Cruz was severely deflated just in time for the critical Indiana primary a week later. For her part, Hillary Clinton flipped the 2008 script, beating Bernie Sanders by 30 percentage points in a race that was still undecided.

Source

Crass, Philip. 1976. *The Wallace Factor.* New York: Mason Charter.

Maryland Primary Results 2000–2016

2000

Democratic primary (3/7)		Republican primary (3/7)	
Gore	67.3	Bush	56.2
Bradley	28.5	McCain	36.2
Uncommitted	3.3	Keyes	6.7

2004

Democratic primary (3/2)		Republican primary (3/2)	
Kerry	59.6	Bush	100.0
Edwards	25.6		
Sharpton	4.5		
Dean	2.6		
Kucinich	1.8		
Uncommitted	1.8		
Lieberman	1.1		

2008

Democratic primary (2/12)		Republican primary (2/12)	
Obama	60.7	McCain	54.8
Clinton	35.8	Huckabee	28.5
Uncommitted	1.3	Romney	7.0
Edwards	1.2	Paul	6.0
		Giuliani	1.4
		Keyes	1.1

2012

Democratic primary (4/3)		Republican primary (4/3)	
Obama	88.5	Romney	49.3
Uncommitted	11.6	Santorum	28.7
		Gingrich	11.0
		Paul	9.5

2016

Democratic primary (4/26)		Republican primary (4/26)	
Clinton	62.5	Trump	54.1
Sanders	33.8	Kasich	23.2
Uncommitted	3.3	Cruz	19.0
		Carson	1.3

Sources: Federal Election Commission:
https://transition.fec.gov/pubrec/fe2000/2000presprim.htm#MD;

https://transition.fec.gov/pubrec/fe2004/federalelections2004.pdf;
https://transition.fec.gov/pubrec/fe2008/federalelections2008.pdf;
https://transition.fec.gov/pubrec/fe2012/federalelections2012.pdf;
https://transition.fec.gov/pubrec/fe2016/federalelections2016.pdf.

2020 Delegate Selection

Democratic

Number of delegates: 102 total delegate votes—52 district, 17 at-large, 10 pledged PLEOs, 23 unpledged PLEOs

Date of 2020 contest: April 28

What week of the delegate selection season: 13

Type of delegate selection event: Closed primary

Mode of awarding delegates: Proportional representation with a 15 percent threshold

How delegates are chosen: District delegates are elected in the congressional district primary in accordance with the allocation determined by the primary results; at-large delegates and pledged PLEOs are elected by the state central committee in accordance with statewide primary results

Bound for how many national conventions ballots: One

Source: http://www.thegreenpapers.com/P20/MD-D.

Republican

Number of Delegates: 38 total delegates—14 at-large (10 base, 3 party, 1 bonus), 24 in 8 congressional districts

Date of 2020 contest: April 28

What week of the delegate selection season: 13

Type of delegate selection event: Closed primary

Mode of awarding delegates: Winner-take-all (statewide and district)—The presidential candidate winning the most votes in each congressional district primary will receive all of that district's delegates to the national convention; the candidate winning the most votes statewide will receive all at-large delegates

How are delegates chosen: District delegates are elected directly in the congressional district primary; at-large delegates are elected by the state convention in accordance with statewide primary results

Bound for how many national conventions ballots: Two

Source: http://www.thegreenpapers.com/P20/MD-R.

—Andrew E. Busch

Massachusetts

The most populous state in New England and the flashpoint of the American Revolution, Massachusetts has become a center for higher education and high technology. Massachusetts has also developed into nearly a one-party Democratic state, though Republicans frequently persuade voters to elect governors and Scott Brown won the special U.S. Senate vacancy election in 2010 following Edward Kennedy's death. No Republican has won a presidential election in Massachusetts since Ronald Reagan in 1984, and the Bay State famously provided George McGovern with his only state victory in 1972.

Massachusetts has been holding presidential primaries since they made their debut in 1912, when William Howard Taft edged out Theodore Roosevelt by a 50–48 percent margin—one of Taft's few primary wins against the Rough Rider. Until 1976, the Massachusetts primary was scheduled in the last week of April. It shifted to early March, where it stayed through 2016 with the exception of a February 5 primary in 2008 that coincided with 15 other primaries.

Pivotal presidential primaries in Massachusetts have included:

1932: Trading on his popularity in heavily Catholic Massachusetts, 1928 Democratic nominee Al Smith fought for a rematch against President Herbert Hoover. Smith defeated Franklin Roosevelt handily (73–27 percent) in a battle of New York governors.

1952: Dwight D. Eisenhower blew out Sen. Robert Taft 70 percent to 30 percent in the Republican primary. At the same time, portending his broad-based victory in November, Eisenhower also finished second in the Democratic primary with over 30 percent of the vote.

1968: In a battle between anti–Vietnam War insurgents, Eugene McCarthy won the Democratic primary by a runaway margin, beating write-in candidate Robert F. Kennedy 49 to 27 percent. Hubert Humphrey finished a distant third at 18 percent.

1972: Three weeks after his breakthrough win in Wisconsin, George McGovern crushed Edmund Muskie of Maine on his own New England turf, with 53 percent to Muskie's 21 percent.

1976: Gerald Ford barely held on to defeat Ronald Reagan 49–48 percent. At the same time, Senator Henry Jackson of Washington, known for his tough anti-Soviet stance, won the primary with 22 percent in a split field. Jimmy Carter, who had won in New Hampshire one week before, finished fourth with 14 percent. Jackson was, for a moment, a hot commodity, while Carter's New Hampshire momentum was dimmed. Jackson's win and Reagan's near-win in liberal Massachusetts seemed to indicate that the country was shifting to the right.

1980: Reagan again came close, though Yankee George H. W. Bush outpolled John Anderson and Reagan 31 to 30.7 to 28.8 percent in the Republican primary. The conservative former governor of California and eventual nominee narrowly won the Vermont primary the same day, proving he was competitive across New England.

1984: Gary Hart won the Democratic primary against Walter Mondale by 39 to 26 percent. In a moment of nostalgia, 21 percent voted for George McGovern, who had quixotically entered the 1984 Democratic nomination race.

2000: Republican John McCain doubled George W. Bush's vote, winning by 65–32 percent on a day when 10 other states held primaries. Bush won most of the others.

2008: On a Super Tuesday in early February crowded with 15 other primaries, Hillary Clinton beat Barack Obama 51 to 41 percent in the Democratic contest.

2016: Eight years later, Clinton more narrowly defeated Bernie Sanders in a state seemingly tailor-made for Sanders: Clinton 50.1, Sanders 48.7. On the Republican side, Donald Trump handily defeated his rivals, beating the closest one (John Kasich) by 49 to 18 percent. On March 1, Massachusetts gave Trump the highest primary vote total he would enjoy until late April.

Massachusetts Primary Results 2000–2016

2000

Democratic primary (3/7)		Republican primary (3/7)	
Gore	59.8	McCain	64.7
Bradley	37.2	Bush	31.8
No preference	2.0	Keyes	2.5

2004

Democratic primary (3/2)		Republican primary (3/2)	
Kerry	71.7	Bush	88.9
Edwards	17.6	No preference	8.6
Kucinich	4.1		
Dean	2.8		
Sharpton	1.0		

2008

Democratic primary (2/5)		Republican primary (2/5)	
Clinton	56.0	Romney	51.1
Obama	40.6	McCain	40.9
Edwards	1.6	Huckabee	3.8
		Paul	2.7

2012

Democratic primary (3/6)		Republican primary (3/6)	
Obama	86.5	Romney	72.1
No preference	10.9	Santorum	12.1
		Paul	9.5
		Gingrich	4.6

2016

Democratic primary (3/1)		Republican primary (3/1)	
Clinton	49.9	Trump	49.1
Sanders	48.5	Kasich	18.0
		Rubio	17.8
		Cruz	9.5
		Carson	2.6
		Bush	1.0

Sources: Federal Election Commission:
https://transition.fec.gov/pubrec/fe2000/2000presprim.htm#MA;
https://transition.fec.gov/pubrec/fe2004/federalelections2004.pdf;
https://transition.fec.gov/pubrec/fe2008/federalelections2008.pdf;
https://transition.fec.gov/pubrec/fe2012/federalelections2012.pdf;
https://transition.fec.gov/pubrec/fe2016/federalelections2016.pdf.

2020 Delegate Selection

Democratic

Number of delegates: 114 total delegate votes—59 district, 20 at-large, 12 pledged PLEOs, 23 unpledged PLEOs

Date of 2020 contest: March 3

What week of the delegate selection season: 5

Type of delegate selection event: Semiopen primary (D & I)

Mode of awarding delegates: Proportional representation with a 15 percent threshold

How delegates are elected: District delegates to the national convention are elected by congressional district caucuses in accordance with district primary results; at-large delegates and pledged PLEOs are elected by the state committee in accordance with statewide primary results

Bound for how many national conventions ballots: One

Source: http://www.thegreenpapers.com/P20/MA-D.

Republican

Number of delegates: 41 total delegates—14 at-large (10 base, 3 party, 1 bonus), 27 in 9 congressional districts

Date of 2020 contest: March 3

What week of the delegate selection season: 5

Type of delegate selection event: Semiopen primary (R & I)

Mode of awarding delegates: Statewide winner-take-most: If a candidate for president wins more than 50 percent of the statewide vote, he or she receives all delegates; if not, delegates are shared proportionally around a 20 percent cutoff

How are delegates chosen: District delegates to the national convention are elected by congressional district conventions and at-large delegates are elected by the state committee in accordance with the statewide primary results

Bound for how many national conventions ballots: All

Source: http://www.thegreenpapers.com/P20/MA-R.

—*Andrew E. Busch*

Michigan

In the beginning of its formation as an American state, Michigan was primarily composed of Yankee reformers and abolitionists. Michigan was one of the birthplaces of the Grand Old Party and one of the most Republican states in the nation. During the Great Depression, the political identity of the state shifted left as autoworkers became a heavily Democratic voting bloc. After an early-century boom, Michigan lost representation in Congress and electoral votes from 1970 to 2010 along with other "Rust Belt" states (Barone and McCutcheon 2014). Michigan voted Republican for five presidential elections in a row from 1972 to 1988, then voted Democratic in the six presidential elections from 1992 through 2012. In the 2016 presidential election, Michigan went Republican when Donald Trump won the state by roughly 0.23 percent of the vote against Hillary Clinton.

Michigan has had a long history of moving back and forth between primaries and caucuses for presidential delegate selection. Its first presidential primary was held in 1916. In 1931, the legislature repealed the presidential primary, and it was not reinstated until 1972. In the years between 1932 and 1972, Michigan's Democratic delegations to the national convention backed FDR in 1932, JFK in 1960, and Hubert Humphrey in 1968. Their GOP counterparts supported Eisenhower in 1952 and Michigan governor George Romney in 1964.

Primaries were held in mid-May in 1972, 1976, and 1980, before the state reverted to caucuses in 1984–1992. Primaries were again used by both parties in 1996 (March 19) and by Republicans in 2000 (February 22); caucuses were held by Democrats in 2000 and by both parties in 2004; and primaries by both parties in 2008–2016. More than once, Michigan's open primary helped deliver victory to a maverick candidate.

Notable Michigan contests have included:

1916: In Michigan's first presidential primary election, auto magnate Henry Ford won the Republican primary with 47 percent of the vote.

1972: Days after Democratic candidate George Wallace was paralyzed due to an assassination attempt, he won the Democratic primaries in Michigan and Maryland. Wallace won Michigan with 51 percent of the vote to George McGovern's 27 percent and Hubert Humphrey's 16 percent. Some Democrats complained that Republican voters had voted for Wallace in the open primary to embarrass the Democratic Party (Rosenthal 1972).

1976: While home-state Republican president Gerald Ford was trouncing Ronald Reagan by a 2–1 margin, Jimmy Carter was winning the Democratic primary by the razor-thin margin of 43.4 percent to 43.1 percent over Morris Udall. Michigan was one of a series of narrow defeats for Udall, who was only a few thousand votes in a few states away from becoming a much more serious contender.

1980: George H. W. Bush defeated Ronald Reagan by 25 percentage points, but Bush's victory came too late to save his tottering campaign. Reagan's lead in delegates was insurmountable, and Bush dropped out of the race not long after.

1988: The first round of the Republican caucuses were held in August 1986, and observers were surprised when the caucuses were dominated by an alliance of supporters of New York congressman Jack Kemp (of Kemp-Roth tax-cutting fame) and televangelist Pat Robertson. However, at later stages of the process, the Kemp-Robertson alliance fell apart. Ultimately, Vice President George H. W. Bush came out on top in delegates to the national convention. Democratic caucuses were won by Jesse Jackson in one of Jackson's early wins (Cook 1988).

1992: On his way to the Democratic nomination, Democratic candidate Bill Clinton won the Michigan Democratic primary with 51 percent of the vote, nearly doubling Jerry Brown's total.

2000: Arizona senator John McCain defeated eventual Republican nominee George W. Bush by 51 to 43 percent. McCain benefited from many Democrats crossing over to vote for him in the open primary (Barabak 2000). McCain's win revived his campaign after a tough loss to Bush in South Carolina.

2008: In a dramatic reversal of fortune for John McCain, Mitt Romney defeated McCain, who would go on to win the GOP nod, by roughly 10 percent of the vote. Romney's father, George Romney, had served as the 43rd governor of Michigan, making Michigan one of the candidate's multiple "home states." Romney's win was essential to his strategy and gave his campaign a new (though short-lived) lease on life. On the Democratic side, Hillary Clinton won with 55 percent of the vote. However, both major parties had announced that no state could hold presidential primaries before February 5; Michigan's primary was set for January 15. The national Democratic Party declared that Michigan would forfeit its delegates at the national convention, while the national Republican Party indicated it would only seat half of Michigan's delegates. Due to the political controversy, four Democratic candidates, including Barack Obama, withdrew from the party's primary ballot. Ultimately, Democrats relented and seated all of Michigan's delegates but Republicans acted upon their declaration (Ceaser, Busch, and Pitney 2009).

2012: Romney narrowly won the Republican primary against Rick Santorum, avoiding the potential disaster for his campaign that would have ensued had he lost one of his "home states."

2016: Despite speculation that the Michigan primary might offer an opportunity for Ohio governor John Kasich, Donald Trump won the Republican primary with 37 percent of the vote. Texas senator Ted Cruz nosed out Kasich for second place, with 24.7 percent of the vote to Kasich's 24.3 percent. In the Democratic primary, Bernie Sanders's one-point win took Hillary Clinton's campaign by surprise. Some believed that voters supported Sanders in part due to the 2008 Democratic fiasco in which Clinton was the only major candidate on the ballot (Lee, Zeleny, Bash, and Merica 2016). However, Clinton quickly recovered to win the next five states.

Sources

Barabak, Mark Z. 2000. "McCain Rebounds, Wins Primaries in Michigan, Arizona." *Los Angeles Times*, February 23. https://www.latimes.com/archives/la-xpm-2000-feb-23-mn-1707-story.html.

Barone, Michael, and Chuck McCutcheon. 2014. *The Almanac of American Politics 2014*. Washington, DC: National Journal.

Ceaser, James W., Andrew E. Busch, and John J. Pitney Jr. 2009. *Epic Journey: The 2008 Elections and American Politics*. Lanham, MD: Rowman & Littlefield.

Cook, Rhodes. 1988. "GOP's View of Delegate Rules Invites Procedural Shenanigans." *CQ Weekly Report*, February 6.

Lee, M. J., Jeff Zeleny, Dana Bash, and Dan Merica. 2016. "What Went Wrong for Hillary Clinton in Michigan?" CNN, March 9. https://www.cnn.com/2016/03/09/politics/hillary-clinton-michigan-loss/index.html

Rosenthal, Jack. 1972. "Survey Ties Issues, Not Shooting, to Wallace Victory." *New York Times*, May 17.

Michigan Primary Results 2000–2016

2000

Democratic primary (2/22)		Republican primary (2/22)	
Uncommitted	70.6	Bush	51.0
LaRouche	29.4	McCain	43.1
		Keyes	4.6

2004

Democratic caucuses (2/7)		Republican caucuses (2/7)	
Kerry	51.8	**Delegates to national convention**	
Dean	16.5	Bush	100.0
Edwards	13.4		
Sharpton	7.0		
Clark	6.7		
Kucinich	3.2		

2008

Democratic primary (1/15)		Republican primary (1/15)	
Clinton	55.2	Romney	38.9
Uncommitted	40.17	McCain	29.7
Kucinich	3.7	Huckabee	16.1
		Paul	6.3
		Thompson	3.7

2012

Democratic primary (2/28)		Republican primary (2/28)	
Obama	89.3	Romney	41.4
Uncommitted	10.7	Santorum	37.9
		Paul	11.6
		Gingrich	6.5

2016 (March 8)

Democratic primary (3/8)		Republican primary (3/8)	
Sanders	49.7	Trump	36.6
Clinton	48.3	Cruz	24.7
Uncommitted	1.8	Kasich	24.3
		Rubio	9.3
		Uncommitted	1.7

Sources: https://www.thegreenpapers.com/P04/MI-R.phtml;
https://www.thegreenpapers.com/P04/MI-D.phtml;
Federal Election Commission:
https://transition.fec.gov/pubrec/fe2000/2000presprim.htm#MI;
https://transition.fec.gov/pubrec/fe2008/federalelections2008.pdf;
https://transition.fec.gov/pubrec/fe2012/2012pres.pdf;
https://transition.fec.gov/pubrec/fe2016/federalelections2016.pdf.

2020 Delegate Selection

Democratic

Number of delegates: 147 total delegate votes—82 district, 27 at-large, 16 pledged PLEOs, 22 unpledged PLEOs

Date of 2020 contest: March 10

What week of the delegate selection season: 6

Type of delegate selection event: Open primary

Mode of awarding delegates: Proportional representation with a 15 percent threshold

How delegates are chosen: District delegates to the national convention are elected by congressional district conventions in accordance with the district's primary results; at-large delegates and pledged PLEOs are elected by the state central committee in accordance with statewide primary results

Bound for how many national conventions ballots: One

Source: http://www.thegreenpapers.com/P20/MI-D.

Republican

Number of delegates: 73 total delegates—31 at-large (10 base, 3 party, 18 bonus), 42 in 14 congressional districts

Date of 2020 contest: March 10

What week of the delegate selection season: 6

Type of delegate selection event: Open primary

Mode of awarding delegates: Statewide Winner-Take-Most: A candidate for president who wins a statewide majority of the primary vote wins all delegates; if no candidate has a majority, delegates are distributed proportionally with a 20 percent threshold. If no candidate has 20 percent, the threshold is the vote percentage of the leading candidate minus 5 percentage points

How delegates are chosen: In accordance with the statewide primary results, district delegates to the national convention are elected by district meetings held at the state convention, and a slate of at-large delegates is proposed by the state convention credentials committee and is elected by the whole state convention

Bound for how many national conventions ballots: One

Source: http://www.thegreenpapers.com/P20/MI-R.

—*Andrew E. Busch and Nandeeni K. Patel*

Minnesota

Settled by Scandinavians and Germans, Minnesota has a political culture largely defined by socially conservative Republicans and progressive labor Democrats. The state has been home to past liberal leaders such as Senators Hubert Humphrey, Eugene McCarthy, and Walter Mondale, all of whom ran for president. Minnesota has not voted for a Republican candidate for president since Richard Nixon in 1972, though Ronald Reagan and Donald Trump both came close to winning the state. In 2016, Trump was edged by Hillary Clinton, 46.4 percent to 44.9 percent.

Minnesota has usually used caucus-convention procedures to pick delegates to the national conventions, but it has held presidential primaries in four years. Democrats and Republicans have announced that they will be using presidential primaries again in 2020. The four primaries held by Minnesota prior to 2020 included:

1916: Voters in the Republican primary supported Albert Cummins of neighboring Iowa while Democratic primary voters backed incumbent president Woodrow Wilson.

1952: Hometown favorite Harold Stassen won in the GOP primary against Dwight Eisenhower, 44 to 37 percent. It was Stassen's third presidential campaign; a serious contender the first few times, he would later become a quadrennial name on the Republican primary ballot, receiving his last primary votes in 1988. Hubert Humphrey, another favorite son, won 80 percent in the Democratic primary.

1956: As an incumbent president, Dwight Eisenhower got 98 percent of the Republican primary vote, while Democrat Estes Kefauver beat Adlai Stevenson 56–43 percent.

1992: In the April 7 Republican primary, President George H. W. Bush beat challenger Pat Buchanan by 64 to 24 percent. In the Democratic primary, Bill Clinton edged Edmund G. Brown by a margin of 31.1 percent to 30.6 percent. Minnesota completed Clinton's sweep of Kansas, Wisconsin, and New York the same day.

Outside of the four primaries, Minnesota Democratic national convention delegations supported FDR in 1932. In 1980, Minnesota's delegates supported Jimmy Carter, but in 1988 a majority backed Jesse Jackson over Michael Dukakis. Republican delegations from Minnesota supported favorite son Congressman Walter Judd in 1964, and backed President Gerald Ford against Ronald Reagan in 1976.

Notable caucuses have included:

1968: Supporters of antiwar insurgent Eugene McCarthy and Vice President Hubert Humphrey—both Minnesotans—battled in Democratic caucuses across Minnesota. Though outmatched, where McCarthy organized he was able to scratch out a dozen delegates to the national convention.

1972: The antiwar energy on the left that had propelled McCarthy in 1968 was just as mobilized, and much better organized, than in 1968. This time, it was supporters of George McGovern who tried to flood the Democratic caucuses. Nevertheless, Hubert Humphrey's home field advantage won the day again, and Humphrey ended with 46 national convention delegates to McGovern's 11.

2004: Democratic caucuses gave a victory to Massachusetts senator John Kerry, who obtained 51 percent of the vote to John Edwards's 27 percent and Dennis Kucinich's 17 percent. Kerry also swept eight of the nine primaries held that day, losing only to Howard Dean in his home state of Vermont.

2008: Republican Mitt Romney defeated eventual nominee John McCain by nearly 20 percentage points. However, the bigger story was in the Democratic caucuses, where Barack Obama trounced Hillary Clinton by a 3–1 margin—and drove a massive caucus turnout for Democrats. The turnout of 213,000 shattered the previous record of around 80,000 set in 1968 or 1972 (Stassen-Berger 2008; "Democratic-Farmer-Labor Party Results").

2012: Former Pennsylvania senator Rick Santorum won the GOP caucuses with 45 percent to Ron Paul's 27 percent. Eventual nominee Mitt Romney finished third, a disappointment for Romney considering his Minnesota win four years before. Santorum's win in the Missouri primary the same day helped establish him as the chief competition to Romney.

2016: Democrat Bernie Sanders crushed Hillary Clinton 62 to 38 percent, once again demonstrating Sanders's strength in caucus states. At the same time, Marco Rubio momentarily breathed life into his struggling campaign by coming in first in the Republican caucuses with 37 percent of the vote to Ted Cruz's 29 percent and Donald Trump's 21 percent.

Sources

"Democratic-Farmer-Labor Party Results." https://web.archive.org/web/200802
13200436/http://caucusresults.sos.state.mn.us/ResultsPreferentialBallot
.aspx.
Stassen-Berger, Rachel E. 2008. "Nearly 200,000 Turn Out in Obama Victory."
St. Paul Pioneer Press, February 6. https://www.twincities.com/2008/02/05
/nearly-200000-turn-out-in-obama-victory/.

Minnesota Caucus Results 2000–2016

2000

Democratic caucuses (3/11)		Republican caucuses (3/7)	
Approximate results		Bush	62.7
Gore	74.0	Keyes	17.9
Bradley	12.0	McCain	17.4
Uncommitted	11.0		
Harder	3.0		

2004

Democratic caucuses (3/2)		Republican caucuses (3/2)	
Kerry	50.7	**Delegates to national convention**	
Edwards	27.0	Uncommitted	100.0
Kucinich	17.0		
Uncommitted	2.2		
Dean	2.0		

2008

Democratic caucuses (2/5)		Republican caucuses (2/5)	
Obama	66.4	Romney	41.4
Clinton	32.2	McCain	22.0
		Huckabee	19.9
		Paul	15.7

2012

Democratic caucuses (2/7)		Republican caucuses (2/7)	
Obama	96.3	Santorum	45.0
Uncommitted	3.7	Paul	27.1
		Romney	16.9
		Gingrich	10.8

2016

Democratic caucuses (3/1)		Republican caucuses (3/1)	
Sanders	61.2	Rubio	36.2
Clinton	38.1	Cruz	29.0
		Trump	21.4
		Carson	7.4
		Kasich	5.8

Sources: https://www.thegreenpapers.com/PCC/Tabul.html;
https://www.thegreenpapers.com/P04/MN-R.phtml;
https://www.thegreenpapers.com/P04/MN-D.phtml;
https://www.thegreenpapers.com/P08/MN-D.phtml;
https://www.thegreenpapers.com/P08/MN-R.phtml;
http://www.thegreenpapers.com/P12/MN-D;
http://www.thegreenpapers.com/P12/MN-R;
https://www.thegreenpapers.com/P16/MN-D;
https://www.thegreenpapers.com/P16/MN-R.

2020 Delegate Selection

Democratic

Number of delegates: 92 total delegate votes—49 district, 16 at-large, 10 pledged PLEOs, 17 unpledged PLEOs

Date of 2020 contest: March 3

What week of the delegate selection season: 5

Type of delegate selection event: Closed primary

Mode of awarding delegates: Proportional representation with a 15 percent threshold

How delegates are chosen: In accordance with district primary results, district delegates to the national convention are elected by congressional district conventions; in accordance with state primary results, at-large delegates and pledged PLEOs are elected by the state convention

Bound for how many national conventions ballots: One

Source: https://www.thegreenpapers.com/P20/MN-D.

Republican

Number of delegates: 39 total delegates—15 at-large (10 base, 3 party, 2 bonus), 24 in 8 congressional districts

Date of 2020 contest: March 3

What week of the delegate selection season: 5

Type of delegate selection event: Closed primary

Mode of awarding delegates: Winner-take-most: If a candidate for president wins 85 percent or more of the statewide vote, he or she receives all delegates to the national convention. If not, district delegates are allocated proportionally based on the district vote with a 10 percent threshold and at-large delegates are allocated proportionally based on the statewide vote with a 10 percent threshold

How delegates are chosen: District delegates to the national convention are elected by congressional district conventions according to district primary results; at-large delegates are elected by the state convention according to state primary results

Bound for how many national conventions ballots: One

Source: https://www.thegreenpapers.com/P20/MN-R.

—Andrew E. Busch

Mississippi

Though Mississippi made up a key part of the Democratic "Solid South" for decades after the Civil War, it voted for Dixiecrat Strom Thurmond in 1948, Republican senator Barry Goldwater in 1964, and segregationist independent candidate George Wallace in 1968. Since Ronald Reagan defeated Jimmy Carter 49.4 percent to 48.1 percent in 1980, the state has voted Republican in every presidential election. In 2016, Donald Trump prevailed by nearly 18 percentage points, up from Mitt Romney's 11-point margin of victory over President Barack Obama in 2012. Mississippi has the highest proportion of African Americans of any state (around 36 percent), and has long struggled with both white and black poverty.

Mississippi held its first presidential primary on the Republican side on June 3, 1980, after Ronald Reagan had already secured the nomination. Democrats held their first primary in 1988, when Mississippi moved its date from early June up to Super Tuesday, March 8. It still holds the contest in the middle of that month (though Republicans did not hold a primary in 2004, when incumbent President George W. Bush was running for renomination unopposed).

In the era before primaries, Mississippi's Democratic delegates walked out of the 1948 convention to protest the party's liberal civil rights plank, then gave their convention votes in 1960 to segregationist governor Ross Barnett. After implementation of the Voting Rights Act, the composition of the delegates changed dramatically, and Mississippi split its 1972 votes between George McGovern and black congresswoman Shirley Chisholm. Other significant party races in Mississippi have included:

1964: Frustrated with a lack of African American representation on the state delegation, a coalition of black and white liberal Democrats formed their own integrated party, the Mississippi Freedom Democratic Party (MFDP), at the 1964 Democratic National Convention in Atlantic City, New Jersey. President Johnson worried that publicly supporting the MFDP would hurt him with Southern white voters and the party was not recognized at the convention (Mastrovita).

1976: Locked in a tight battle for the GOP nomination with incumbent president Gerald Ford before the convention, Ronald Reagan gambled and announced his preferred running mate, Pennsylvania senator Richard Schweiker, in an effort to win support from moderate northeastern Republicans. In reaction against Reagan's announcement, the Mississippi delegation flipped to Ford at a crucial moment before the final roll call vote (Edwards). Reagan campaign manager John Sears later attested that if "Mississippi stayed with us instead of going as a bloc to Ford . . . I think we might have been nominated . . . it was that close" (NPR).

1988: As part of the first gigantic Super Tuesday, the Mississippi Republican primary gave George H. W. Bush a 66 percent to 17 percent victory over Kansas senator Bob Dole, a result repeated across the South. More surprising to the political world was the Democratic primary, won 45 percent to 34 percent by Jesse Jackson over Senator Al Gore of Tennessee. Jackson also won Super Tuesday primaries in Alabama, Georgia, Louisiana, and Virginia, and established himself as a serious contender in the Democratic nomination race.

2008: Boosted by African American turnout, Barack Obama outpolled Hillary Clinton in the Democratic primary by a 61–37 percent margin.

2016: As in many other states in the Deep South during the primaries, Hillary Clinton reversed her 2008 loss and resoundingly won the 2016 Mississippi primary based on overwhelming support from African Americans ("Mississippi Results"). The former secretary of state defeated Senator Bernie Sanders 83 percent to 17 percent. On the Republican side, Donald Trump won the state comfortably, beating Senator Ted Cruz 47–36 percent.

Sources

Edwards, Lee. "Ronald Reagan vs. Gerald Ford: The 1976 GOP Convention Battle Royal." National Interest. https://nationalinterest.org/blog/the-buzz /ronald-reagan-vs-gerald-ford-the-1976-gop-convention-battle-15818.

Mastrovita, Mandy. "The 1964 Democratic National Convention and the Mississippi Freedom Democratic Party." Digital Library of Georgia. https://blog.dlg.galileo.usg.edu/?p=3793.

"Mississippi Results." 2008. *The New York Times.* https://web.archive.org/web/20080916170904/http://politics.nytimes.com/election-guide/2008/results/gopdelegates/index.html.

NPR. "1976: The Last Time Republicans Duked It Out to the Last, Heated Minute." https://www.npr.org/2016/03/13/470271684/1976-the-last-time-republicans-duked-it-out-to-the-last-heated-minute.

Mississippi Primary Results 2000–2016

2000

Democratic primary (3/14)		Republican primary (3/14)	
Gore	89.6	Bush	87.9
Bradley	8.6	Keyes	5.6
LaRouche	1.8	McCain	5.5

2004

Democratic primary (3/9)		Republican primary	
Kerry	78.4	No Republican primary	
Edwards	7.3	National Convention delegates	
Sharpton	5.2	Bush	92.1
Dean	2.6	Uncommitted	7.9
Clark	2.5		
Uncommitted	1.8		
Kucinich	1.0		

2008

Democratic primary (3/11)		Republican primary (3/11)	
Obama	61.1	McCain	78.9
Clinton	36.7	Huckabee	12.5
		Paul	3.9
		Romney	1.5
		Thompson	1.5

2012

Democratic primary (3/13)		Republican primary (3/13)	
Obama	100.0	Santorum	32.7
		Gingrich	31.2
		Romney	30.7
		Paul	4.4

2016

Democratic primary (3/8)		Republican primary (3/8)	
Clinton	82.5	Trump	47.2
Sanders	16.6	Cruz	36.1
		Kasich	8.8
		Rubio	5.3
		Carson	1.4

Sources: Federal Election Commission:
https://transition.fec.gov/pubrec/fe2000/2000presprim.htm#top;
https://transition.fec.gov/pubrec/fe2004/federalelections2004.pdf;
https://transition.fec.gov/pubrec/fe2008/federalelections2008.pdf;
https://transition.fec.gov/pubrec/fe2012/2012pres.pdf;
https://transition.fec.gov/pubrec/fe2016/federalelections2016.pdf.

2020 Delegate Selection

Democratic

Number of delegates: 41 total delegate votes—23 district, 8 at-large, 5 pledged PLEOs, 5 unpledged PLEOs

Date of 2020 contest: March 10

What week of the delegate selection season: 6

Type of delegate selection event: Open primary

Mode of awarding delegates: Proportional representation with a 15 percent threshold

How delegates are chosen: District delegates to the national convention are elected by congressional district conventions in accordance with district primary results; at-large delegates and pledged PLEOs are elected by the state convention in accordance with state primary results

Bound for how many national conventions ballots: One

Source: https://www.thegreenpapers.com/P20/MS-D.

Republican

Number of delegates: 39 total delegates—127 at-large, 12 in 4 congressional districts

Date of 2020 contest: March 10

What week of the delegate selection season: 6

Type of delegate selection event: Open primary

Mode of awarding delegates: At-large: Proportional representation based on state primary vote with a 15 percent threshold. District: Winner-Take-Most—A presidential candidate who wins a majority of the vote in a district primary receives all three national convention delegates; if no candidate wins a majority of the vote, the plurality winner receives two delegates and the runner-up one delegate

How are delegates chosen: District and at-large delegates are chosen at the state convention

Bound for how many national conventions ballots: All

Source: https://www.thegreenpapers.com/P20/MS-R.

—*Andrew E. Busch and Richard C. Wiltshire-Gordon*

Missouri

A border state that served as a presidential bellwether for decades, Missouri combines urban centers in St. Louis and Kansas City with a socially conservative rural agricultural middle and the Ozarks in the state's southwest. In recent years, Missouri has shifted heavily toward Republicans at the presidential level, giving Mitt Romney 54 percent in 2012 and Donald Trump 56 percent in 2016. The last Democratic presidential candidate to win Missouri was Bill Clinton in 1996.

Missouri relied on caucus-convention procedures for delegate selection until 1988. In those years, Missouri delegates to the national convention backed favorite son Stuart Symington in 1960, Hubert Humphrey in 1968, Henry Jackson in 1972, Jimmy Carter in 1980, and Carter's vice president Walter Mondale in 1984. Republican delegations from Missouri overwhelmingly supported Eisenhower over Taft in 1952, Goldwater in 1964, and Reagan over Ford in 1976. Missouri's first presidential primary in 1988 was scheduled on Super Tuesday with 16 other state primaries. The Democratic contest was a foregone conclusion, as Missouri congressman Richard Gephardt ran away with the vote. The desire to boost Gephardt's campaign was a significant factor in Missouri's decision to hold a primary that year (Cain and Mullin 2002). The Republican primary was won by George H. W. Bush by the thin margin of 42 to 41 percent over Bob Dole, who hailed from neighboring Kansas. Missouri was Dole's closest shot at preventing a Bush sweep on Super Tuesday.

Missouri then took a break for two election cycles, using caucuses again before returning to primaries in 2000. In 2000 and 2016, the primary was held in the first half of March. In between, in 2004, 2008, and 2012, Missouri scheduled its primary in the first week of February.

Key primaries in that period included:

2000: In the Republican primary, held on Super Tuesday, Texas governor George W. Bush outpolled Arizona senator John McCain 58 to 35 percent. Missouri was one of seven Super Tuesday primaries won by Bush, while McCain picked up four.

2004: In the Democratic primary, John Kerry beat John Edwards by a 2–1 margin, helping solidify Kerry's front-running status a week after his come-from-behind win in New Hampshire.

2008: Republican John McCain eked out a 33–32 percent win against Mike Huckabee in a state Huckabee had targeted (and that was next door to Huckabee's own Arkansas). Missouri was one of nine primaries won by McCain that day.

2012: Riding a wave of support from social conservatives, Rick Santorum beat Mitt Romney by 30 percentage points, helping establish Santorum as the main Republican alternative to Romney. Santorum's win packed a bigger punch because Missouri was the only presidential primary held on February 7.

2016: In two nail-biters, Donald Trump won the Republican primary and Hillary Clinton won the Democratic primary. Trump's 40.8 percent to 40.6 percent win over Ted Cruz and Clinton's 49.6 percent to 49.4 percent win over Bernie Sanders were the two closest results in Missouri presidential primary history. They shaped the race on both sides, largely by narrowly depriving Cruz and Sanders of much-needed wins at a critical juncture in the races.

Source

Cain, Bruce E., and Megan Mullin. 2002. "Competing for Attention and Votes: The Role of State Parties in Setting Presidential Nomination Rules." In L. Sandy Maisel, ed., *The Parties Respond: Changes in American Parties and Campaigns*. Boulder, CO: Westview Press.

Missouri Primary Results 2000–2016

2000

Democratic primary (3/7)		Republican primary (3/7)	
Gore	64.6	Bush	57.9
Bradley	33.6	McCain	35.3
Uncommitted	1.3	Keyes	5.7

2004

Democratic primary (2/3)		Republican primary (2/3)	
Kerry	50.6	Bush	95.1
Edward	24.6	Uncommitted	3.1
Dean	8.7	Wyatt	1.0
Clark	4.4		
Lieberman	3.5		
Sharpton	3.4		
Gephardt	2.0		
Kucinich	1.2		
Uncommitted	1.0		

2008

Democratic primary (2/5)		Republican primary (2/5)	
Obama	49.3	McCain	33.0
Clinton	47.9	Huckabee	31.5
Edwards	2.0	Romney	29.3
		Paul	4.5

2012

Democratic primary (2/7)		Republican primary (2/7)	
Obama	88.4	Santorum	55.2
Uncommitted	6.3	Romney	25.3
Terry	2.7	Paul	12.2
Wolfe	1.4	Uncommitted	3.9
Richardson	1.2		

2016

Democratic primary (3/15)		Republican primary (3/15)	
Clinton	49.6	Trump	40.8
Sanders	49.4	Cruz	40.6
		Kasich	10.1
		Rubio	6.1

Sources: Federal Election Commission:
https://transition.fec.gov/pubrec/fe2000/2000presprim.htm#MO;
https://transition.fec.gov/pubrec/fe2004/federalelections2004.pdf;
https://transition.fec.gov/pubrec/fe2008/federalelections2008.pdf;
https://transition.fec.gov/pubrec/fe2012/federalelections2012.pdf;
https://transition.fec.gov/pubrec/fe2016/federalelections2016.pdf.

2020 Delegate Selection

Democratic

Number of delegates: 78 total delegate votes—44 district, 15 at-large, 9 pledged PLEOs, 10 unpledged PLEOs

Date of 2020 contest: March 10

What week of the delegate selection season: 6

Type of delegate selection event: Open primary

Mode of awarding delegates: Proportional representation with a 15 percent threshold

How delegates are chosen: In accordance with primary results, district delegates to the national convention are elected by congressional district conventions, at-large delegates are elected by the state convention, and pledged PLEOs are elected by the state committee

Bound for how many national conventions ballots: One

Source: http://www.thegreenpapers.com/P20/MO-D.

Republican

Number of delegates: 54 total delegates—30 at-large (10 base, 3 party, 17 bonus), 24 in 8 congressional districts

Date of 2020 contest: March 10

What week of the delegate selection season: 6

Type of delegate selection event: Semiopen primary (R & I)

Mode of awarding delegates: Winner-take-most: If a candidate for president wins a majority of the primary vote statewide, he or she receives all the state's delegates to the national convention; if not, the plurality winner of each congressional district receives 5 delegates and the remaining 14 delegates are allocated to the statewide plurality winner

How delegates are chosen: In accordance with the primary results, district delegates are elected by congressional district conventions and at-large delegates are elected by the state convention

Bound for how many national conventions ballots: One

Source: http://www.thegreenpapers.com/P20/MO-R.

—*Andrew E. Busch*

Montana

Montana is a monumental state, replete with an unmatched environment featuring everything from mountains to plains to plateaus. It is the fourth largest state in the Union by area, but holds only the 44th biggest statewide population. In the 1890s, Montana was a hotbed of pro-silver populism, and the state was historically the most Democratic of the Rocky Mountain states, with strong representation of labor unions and working classes (Barone and McCutcheon 2014). In recent years, Montana has embraced more traditionally Republican ideas, including resistance to federal edicts and high taxes. Montana is also hospitable to Libertarians and independents, and in 1992 Ross Perot finished with 26 percent of the general election vote, making the state among Perot's half-dozen strongest. Bill Clinton won Montana that year, but it has voted for the GOP presidential candidate every four years since then. In 2016, Donald Trump defeated Hillary Clinton by a 56–35 percent margin.

A presidential primary was held in Montana in 1916 through 1924. Then, in every presidential year from 1928 through 1972 except for one (1956), the state utilized caucus-convention procedures for delegate selection. Montana's Democratic delegations supported Franklin Roosevelt in 1932, John F. Kennedy in 1960, Hubert Humphrey in 1968, and George McGovern in 1972. GOP national convention delegates backed Robert Taft in 1952, Barry Goldwater in 1964, and Richard Nixon in 1968.

Montana's presidential primary was reinstated in 1976 and has been used every year since then. The Montana primary has been scheduled among the very latest primaries in the nation, during the first eight days of June. In 2020, Montana's small population will produce only 22 delegates for the Democratic National Nominating Convention and 27 for its Republican counterpart. These low delegate counts coupled with a late-in-the-game primary have given Montana a relatively uninfluential place in the primary pantheon, especially once front-loading became established and most nominations were decided early. Nevertheless, there have been some notable Montana primaries, including:

1976: In the year of the state's first presidential primaries, conservative Republican challenger Ronald Reagan beat President Gerald Ford by a 63–35 percent margin. In his late and ultimately unsuccessful charge, Senator Frank Church, from neighboring Idaho, outpolled Jimmy Carter 59–25 percent in the Democratic primary.

1980: Still engaged in a Democratic nomination race with an uncertain outcome, Jimmy Carter defeated Edward Kennedy 52–37 percent.

1992: Bill Clinton won with 47 percent of the vote. "No preference" was the choice of 24 percent and former California governor Edmund Brown the preference of 19 percent.

2008: In the ongoing Democratic race, Barack Obama beat Hillary Clinton by 57 to 41 percent. Together with delegates won in the South Dakota primary and superdelegate endorsements the same day, Obama was able for the first time in the race to claim enough delegates to be nominated.

2016: Both the Democratic and Republican primaries were held after the nominees were all but decided. Donald Trump, having in hand the necessary number of delegates to be nominated and with no significant primary remaining in contention, won 74 percent of the Republican vote and secured all 27 Montana delegates. On the Democratic side, Hillary Clinton became the presumptive nominee (the first woman of a major party to do so) on June 6, one day before the Montana primary. However, in a sign of residual voter resistance to Clinton that would follow her into the general election, Bernie Sanders captured 51 percent of the Montana vote to Clinton's 44 percent.

Source

Barone, Michael, and Chuck McCutcheon. 2014. *The Almanac of American Politics 2014*. Washington, DC: National Journal.

Montana Primary Results 2000–2016

2000

Democratic primary (6/6)		Republican primary (6/6)	
Gore	77.9	Bush	77.6
No preference	22.1	Keyes	18.3
		No preference	4.1

2004

Democratic primary (6/8)		Republican primary (6/8)	
Kerry	68.0	Bush	94.4
Kucinich	10.4	No preference	5.6
Edwards	9.1		
No preference	7.4		
Clark	4.4		

2008

Democratic primary (6/3)		Republican primary (6/3)	
Obama	56.6	McCain	76.0
Clinton	41.1	Paul	21.5
No preference	2.4	No preference	2.4

2012

Democratic primary (6/5)		Republican primary (6/5)	
Obama	90.1	Romney	68.4
No preference	9.4	Paul	14.4
		Santorum	8.9
		Gingrich	4.4
		No preference	3.9

2016

Democratic primary (6/7)		Republican primary (6/7)	
Sanders	51.6	Trump	73.7
Clinton	44.2	Cruz	9.4
No preference	4.3	Kasich	6.9
		No preference	4.7
		Rubio	3.3
		Bush	2.1

Sources: Federal Election Commission:
https://transition.fec.gov/pubrec/fe2000/2000presprim.htm;
https://transition.fec.gov/pubrec/fe2004/federalelections2004.pdf;
https://transition.fec.gov/pubrec/fe2008/federalelections2008.pdf;
https://transition.fec.gov/pubrec/fe2012/federalelections2012.pdf;
https://transition.fec.gov/pubrec/fe2016/federalelections2016.pdf.

2020 Delegate Selection

Democratic

Number of delegates: 22 total delegate votes—11 district, 3 at-large, 2 pledged PLEOs, 6 unpledged PLEOs

Date of 2020 contest: June 2

What week of the delegate selection season: 18

Type of delegate selection event: Open primary

Mode of awarding delegates: Proportional representation with a 15 percent threshold

How delegates are chosen: Delegates to the national convention are elected by the state convention in accordance with the primary results

Bound for how many national conventions ballots: One

Source: https://www.thegreenpapers.com/P20/MT-D.

Republican

Number of delegates: 27 total delegates—24 at-large (10 base, 3 party, 11 bonus), 3 in 1 congressional district

Date of 2020 contest: June 2

What week of the delegate selection season: 18

Type of delegate selection event: Open primary

Mode of awarding delegates: Statewide winner-take-all

How delegates are chosen: Prior to the primary, the state convention slates delegates for the national convention; delegates are elected in the primary itself, according to the results of the primary

Bound for how many national conventions ballots: One

Source: https://www.thegreenpapers.com/P20/MT-R.

—*Andrew E. Busch and Jacob S. Leischner*

Nebraska

Nebraska is a prairie state with one large metropolitan area (Omaha), a renowned college football program, and hundreds of miles of wheat fields. With a political culture combining rural conservatism and residual turn-of-the-century agrarian progressivism, Nebraska is a solidly Republican state that has the only nonpartisan and one-house state legislature in the country. It is also one of two states that allocates its electoral votes by the district method; in 2008, Barack Obama won an electoral vote by squeezing out a win in the congressional district centered in Omaha. The last Democrat to win Nebraska as a whole was Lyndon Johnson in 1964, and before that, Franklin Roosevelt in 1936. In 2016, Donald Trump defeated Hillary Clinton by 59 to 34 percent.

Nebraska was one of the earliest adopters of the presidential primary in 1912, when Theodore Roosevelt trounced William Howard Taft 59 percent to 22 percent. For the next four decades, Nebraska primaries were scheduled in April. In 1956, the primary was moved to mid-May, where it has remained since. In 2008–2016, while Republicans retained the traditional binding primary, Democrats held caucuses for delegate binding in addition to an advisory "beauty contest" primary. Democrats announced in 2018 that they will be using a binding primary in 2020, discontinuing use of caucuses.

In recent decades, the May primary has often worked to minimize Nebraska's influence, though primaries in the earlier back-loaded era were not infrequently a factor in nomination races despite Nebraska's modest population and delegate strength. Some notable Nebraska primaries have included:

1932: In a warning sign of impending electoral doom, incumbent president Herbert Hoover was thrashed 74 percent to 26 percent in the Republican primary by former U.S. senator Joseph I. France of Maryland, who had not held public office for nearly a decade.

1948: "Boy Wonder" Harold Stassen of Minnesota won the Republican primary with 44 percent to eventual nominee Thomas Dewey's 35 percent to Robert Taft's 12 percent. That year, Nebraska was only the fourth primary held, and Stassen had won two of the four, establishing him as a major contender. Four years before, Stassen had won two-thirds of the Nebraska vote in the primary to Dewey's 25 percent.

1952: In a turnaround from four years before, Robert Taft won a tough Republican primary race, defeating Dwight Eisenhower 36–30 percent. Harold Stassen failed to keep his Nebraska winning streak alive, falling to 24 percent of the vote.

1964: In the Republican primary, Barry Goldwater came in first with 49 percent. Other candidates—led by Richard Nixon at 32 percent and Henry Cabot Lodge at 16 percent—gained votes as write-ins. Nebraska was an important win for Goldwater but also showed his limits.

1968: In an important Democratic showdown, latecomer Robert F. Kennedy beat Eugene McCarthy 52 percent to 31 percent. Coming a week after Kennedy's wins in Indiana and the District of Columbia, the Nebraska results confirmed that the momentum in the competition between Kennedy and McCarthy had shifted toward RFK for the time being.

1972: In a May 9 Democratic primary, George McGovern beat Hubert Humphrey by 41 to 34 percent, the only McGovern win between Massachusetts on April 25 and Oregon on May 23.

1976: The Democratic primary featured a narrow 39–38 percent victory by Idaho senator Frank Church against Jimmy Carter, launching Church's late run for the nomination. In the hard-fought Republican race between incumbent president Gerald Ford and challenger Ronald Reagan, Reagan beat Ford 55–45 percent. Reagan's third primary win in a row helped keep the see-saw race going.

1984: Democrat Gary Hart from neighboring Colorado beat Walter Mondale by a more than 2–1 margin. Building on a surprising win in Ohio one week before, Hart's Nebraska victory was part of an extended winning streak that kept him a viable contender until the end of the primary season.

2008: Foreshadowing unexpected strength in Nebraska in the general election, Barack Obama dominated the February Democratic caucuses, outpolling Hillary Clinton 68 to 32 percent. In May, Obama edged Clinton 49–47 percent in the advisory primary as the two contenders for the Democratic nomination remained locked in a race that could go either way.

2016: In a repeat of 2008, Democratic caucuses in March saw Bernie Sanders defeat Hillary Clinton handily. Clinton again did much better in the advisory primary two months later, actually defeating Sanders by a solid 6-point margin. However, the primary did not affect delegate allocation. Donald Trump won the Republican primary, but his 61 percent share in a vote held when he was the only active candidate remaining in the GOP field was indicative of skepticism or downright hostility toward Trump by many Nebraska Republicans, including outspoken senator Ben Sasse.

Nebraska Primary Results 2000–2016

2000

Democratic primary (5/9)		Republican primary (5/9)	
Gore	70.0	Bush	78.2
Bradley	26.5	McCain	15.1
LaRouche	3.0	Keyes	6.5

2004

Democratic primary (5/11)		Republican primary (5/11)	
Kerry	73.3	Bush	100.0
Edwards	14.0		
Dean	7.5		
Kucinich	2.1		
Sharpton	1.9		
LaRouche	1.1		

2008

Democratic caucuses (2/9)		Republican primary (5/13)	
Obama	67.5	McCain	87.0
Clinton	32.2	Paul	13.0

Democratic primary (5/13)	
Obama	49.4
Clinton	46.5
Gravel	4.1

2012

Democratic caucuses (4/12)		Republican primary (5/15)	
Delegates to national convention		Romney	70.9
Available	86.6	Santorum	13.9
Uncommitted	13.4	Paul	10.0
		Gingrich	5.2

Democratic primary (5/15)	
Obama	100.0

2016

Democratic caucuses (3/5)		Republican primary (5/10)	
Sanders	57.1	Trump	61.5
Clinton	42.9	Cruz	18.4
		Kasich	11.4
		Carson	5.0
		Rubio	3.6

Democratic primary (5/10)	
Clinton	53.1
Sanders	46.9

Sources: https://www.thegreenpapers.com/P08/NE-D.phtml;
http://www.thegreenpapers.com/P12/NE-D;
https://www.thegreenpapers.com/P16/NE-D; Federal Election Commission:
https://transition.fec.gov/pubrec/fe2000/2000presprim.htm#NE;
https://transition.fec.gov/pubrec/fe2004/federalelections2004.pdf;
https://transition.fec.gov/pubrec/fe2008/federalelections2008.pdf;
https://transition.fec.gov/pubrec/fe2012/federalelections2012.pdf;
https://transition.fec.gov/pubrec/fe2016/federalelections2016.pdf.

2020 Delegate Selection

Democratic

Number of delegates: 29 total delegate votes—17 district, 5 at-large, 3 pledged
PLEOs, 4 unpledged PLEOs

Date of 2020 contest: May 12

What week of the delegate selection season: 15

Type of delegate selection event: Semiopen primary (D & I)

Mode of awarding delegates: Proportional representation with 15 percent threshold

How delegates are chosen: National convention delegates are elected by the state convention according to the primary results

Bound for how many national conventions ballots: One

Source: http://www.thegreenpapers.com/P20/NE-D.

Republican

Number of delegates: 36 total delegates—27 at-large (10 base, 3 party, 14 bonus), 9 in 3 congressional districts

Date of 2020 contest: May 12

What week of the delegate selection season: 15

Type of delegate selection event: Closed primary

Mode of awarding delegates: Statewide winner-take-all

How delegates are chosen: In keeping with primary results, district delegates to the national convention are elected by congressional district caucuses held during the state convention; at-large delegates are elected by the state convention as a whole

Bound for how many national conventions ballots: Two

Source: http://www.thegreenpapers.com/P20/NE-R.

—Andrew E. Busch

Nevada

Nevada is a state of contradictions, a "land of boom and bust" (Barone and McCutcheon 2014). In recent decades it has combined the conservatism of a Senator Paul Laxalt, one of Ronald Reagan's closest confidants, with a thriving business in gambling and legal prostitution. This is further exemplified in the success of the state's labor unions despite national decline and a more difficult legal environment (Garcia 2018). Nevada is now a swing state in presidential politics; since Bill Clinton's elevation to the presidency in 1992, the presidential candidate who has won the state of Nevada has won the presidency, with the exception of Hillary Clinton, who won the Silver State over Donald Trump 47.9 to 45.5 percent. This, coupled with Nevada's early primary date, has made it an extremely important target state for both parties' primary candidates.

Nevada first held a presidential primary in 1976 and again in 1980, both times in late May. In 1981, the state legislature ordered a change back to closed caucuses, which would be run by the parties themselves (Kennison 2016). Nevada's reconstituted caucuses were held much earlier in the season, generally ranging from January to March. Since 1984, only Republicans in 1996 have held a primary in Nevada; all other contests have been caucuses.

Nevada's earlier placement ultimately gave it a newfound status. For 2012 and 2016, both major parties agreed that Nevada would be one of only four states allowed to hold delegate selection contests prior to March 1 (the other three were Iowa, New Hampshire, and South Carolina). Nevada's early-in-the-season timing was due mainly to advocacy by then–Senate Majority Leader Harry Reid, who argued that Iowa and New Hampshire were not representative and that Nevada, with its growing minority population, guaranteed better representation of important bases of the Democratic Party—Latino voters and organized labor (Kennison 2016). On the Republican side, though, Nevada's caucuses are frequently overshadowed by South Carolina's primary, held just before Nevada. In 2020, Republicans canceled both of those contests.

Nevada delegations in past Democratic nomination battles backed Franklin Roosevelt in 1932, split closely between John F. Kennedy and Lyndon Johnson in 1960, strongly supported Hubert Humphrey in 1968 and George Wallace in 1972, split between Gary Hart and Walter Mondale in 1984, and backed Michael Dukakis in 1988. Republicans gave Robert Taft a slight edge over Ike in 1952 but backed Barry Goldwater heavily in 1964. More recent notable Nevada contests have included:

1976: Battling incumbent president Gerald Ford for the Republican nomination, Ronald Reagan destroyed Ford by a 66–29 percent margin in Nevada's first primary. At the same time, California governor Edmund "Jerry" Brown gave Jimmy Carter a 53 to 23 percent shellacking as part of Brown's late and ultimately unsuccessful drive for the Democratic nomination.

1980: Toward the end of his renomination race against Senator Edward Kennedy, President Jimmy Carter defeated Kennedy 38 to 29 percent. In one sign of trouble for Carter—there were many that year—34 percent of Democratic primary voters marked their ballots "none of the above."

2008: In the Democratic caucuses, Hillary Clinton edged Barack Obama 51 percent to 45 percent, an unusual case of Clinton outperforming Obama in a caucus setting. Within 10 days, though, her victory was upstaged by Obama's big win in the South Carolina primary. In the GOP caucuses, Mitt Romney came out on top, winning 51 percent against a scattered field. Ron Paul ended with 14 percent, John McCain with 13 percent, and Mike Huckabee with 8 percent.

2012: In a near-repeat of the Republican caucuses four years before, Mitt Romney placed first with 50 percent, followed by Newt Gingrich with 21 percent, Ron Paul with 19 percent, and Rick Santorum with 10 percent. In both 2008 and 2012, Romney had a built-in advantage in Nevada, which contains a substantial Mormon population.

2016: Repeating her success from 2008, Hillary Clinton beat Bernie Sanders 53 percent to 47 percent in the Democratic caucuses. Again Clinton did much better in Nevada's caucuses than in other caucuses nationwide, undoubtedly aided by Hispanic support and Harry Reid's hospitality machine. On the Republican side, Donald Trump beat Marco Rubio and Ted Cruz with 46 percent to Rubio's 24 percent and Cruz's 21 percent in caucuses experiencing high turnout but marred by chaos (Wofford 2016).

Sources

Barone, Michael, and Chuck McCutcheon. 2014. *The Almanac of American Politics 2014*. Washington, DC: National Journal.

Garcia, Reuben. 2018. "Nevada's Unions Show How Organized Labor Can Flourish Even After an Adverse Supreme Court Ruling." *The Conversation*, June 28. http://theconversation.com/nevadas-unions-show-how-organized -labor-can-flourish-even-after-an-adverse-supreme-court-ruling-99067.

Kennison, Heather. 2016. "First in the West: The History of Nevada's Caucus." *Elko Daily Free Press*, January 25. https://elkodaily.com/news/first-in-the -west-the-history-of-nevada-s-caucus/article_60b4bb34-78e4-5e65 -86f4-1bf0b4b9e52e.html.

Wofford, Taylor. 2016. "At Nevada GOP Caucuses, Chaos Reigns." *Newsweek*, February 24. https://www.newsweek.com/nevada-republican-caucuses -chaos-429958.

Nevada Caucus Results 2000–2016

2000

Democratic caucuses (3/12)		Republican caucuses (2/23)	
Delegates to state convention		Delegates to national convention	
Gore	97.6	Uncommitted	100.0
Bradley	2.4		

2004

Democratic caucuses (2/14)		Republican caucuses (2/10)	
Kerry	62.9	**Delegates to national convention**	
Howard	16.8	Uncommitted	100.0
Edwards	10.4		
Kucinich	6.7		
Uncommitted	2.5		

2008

Democratic caucuses (1/19)		Republican caucuses (1/19)	
County delegates		Romney	51.1
Clinton	50.8	Paul	13.7
Obama	45.1	McCain	12.8
Edwards	3.7	Huckabee	8.2
		Thompson	7.9
		Giuliani	4.3
		Hunter	2.0

2012

Democratic caucuses (2/4)		Republican caucuses (2/4)	
Delegates to national convention		Romney	50.0
Uncommitted	18.1	Gingrich	21.1
Available	81.8	Paul	18.7
		Santorum	9.9

2016

Democratic caucuses (2/20)		Republican caucuses (2/23)	
Clinton	52.6	Trump	45.8
Sanders	47.3	Rubio	23.8
		Cruz	21.3
		Carson	4.8
		Kasich	3.6

Sources: https://www.thegreenpapers.com/PCC/Tabul.html;
https://www.thegreenpapers.com/P04/NV-D.phtml;
https://www.thegreenpapers.com/P04/NV-R.phtml;
https://www.thegreenpapers.com/P08/NV-D.phtml;
https://www.thegreenpapers.com/P08/NV-R.phtml;
http://www.thegreenpapers.com/P12/NV-D;
http://www.thegreenpapers.com/P12/NV-R;
https://www.thegreenpapers.com/P16/NV-D;
https://www.thegreenpapers.com/P16/NV-R.

2020 Delegate Selection

Democratic

Number of Delegates: 48 total delegate votes—23 district, 8 at-large, 5 pledged PLEOs, 12 unpledged PLEOs

Date of 2020 contest: February 22

What week of the delegate selection season: 4

Type of delegate selection event: Closed caucus

Mode of awarding delegates: Proportional representation with a 15 percent threshold

How delegates are chosen: National convention delegates are elected by the state convention in accordance with the caucus vote

Bound for how many national conventions ballots: One

Source: https://www.thegreenpapers.com/P20/NV-D.

Republican

Number of delegates: 25 total delegates—13 at-large (10 base, 3 party), 12 in 4 congressional districts

Date of 2020 contest: TBD

What week of the delegate selection season: TBD

Type of delegate selection event: State Central Committee meeting

Mode of awarding delegates: TBD

How delegates are chosen: Elected by State Republican Central Committee

Bound for how many national conventions ballots: One

Source: https://www.thegreenpapers.com/P20/NV-R.

—*Andrew E. Busch and Jacob S. Leischner*

New Hampshire

The most storied, and almost always the first, presidential primary of the nominating season is in New Hampshire. Once a rock-ribbed Republican state dominated by a conservative newspaper, the *Manchester Union-Leader*, New Hampshire has drifted into swing state status. Democrats have won the last four presidential elections, but often by a whisker: three of the last five presidential votes in New Hampshire have been decided by less than a percent and a half. In 2016, Hillary Clinton prevailed over Donald Trump by .37 percent.

Democrats and Republicans alike have a strong tendency to give a boost to mavericks and outsiders in their primaries, a tendency undergirded by the right of independent voters to cast a ballot in the party primary of their choice. While winning New Hampshire is not a guarantee of winning the nomination, not finishing in the top handful of candidates is usually fatal. Consequently, the New Hampshire primary gets much more attention from candidates and media than most other primaries, especially when one considers the relatively small population of the state (under 1.4 million in 2018).

Critics say New Hampshire is unrepresentative of the U.S. population and wields too much influence. (The same criticism is leveled at Iowa, which holds caucuses eight days before New Hampshire's primary.) Defenders argue that it is beneficial for the primary season to be led off by small states where "retail politicking" is both possible and expected, where voters get a chance to evaluate candidates in person and not just in a television ad or televised debate (Mayer and Busch 2004, 160–165).

New Hampshire began using a primary in 1916. That year, voting on March 14, New Hampshire was the third primary (voting after Indiana and Minnesota). Four years later, New Hampshire voted first. It has been the first primary in every presidential election year since then, with the exception of 1980 (when Puerto Rico snuck in ahead of the Granite State) and 2004 (when the District of Columbia held a beauty contest vote before New Hampshire but selected delegates after). Since 1972, Iowa has held first-round caucuses prior to New Hampshire's primary, and in a few recent years, other states held first-round caucuses before Iowa. The New Hampshire legislature has even enacted a law that instructs the secretary of state to use his or her discretion to move the date of the primary earlier if necessary to remain the first primary. While New Hampshire has generally preserved its first primary in the nation status since 1920, the actual date of its primary election has shifted over time. Held in March (usually early March) through 1980, it moved up into February in 1984 and then into January in 2004. In 2016, New Hampshire moved back to February 9. To prevent constant shifting up of the primary calendar and to address concerns that early influential primaries were not representative enough, the national Democratic and Republican parties have agreed to coordinate a schedule that begins no earlier than February 1; allows Iowa, New Hampshire, Nevada, and South Carolina to vote in February; and allows other states to begin voting on March 1.

Through 1948, New Hampshire's primary almost always elected unpledged delegates without a formal presidential preference component, though delegates often informally made known their preferences. Starting in 1952, a preference primary allowed voters to indicate their presidential choices. Now, due to its reputation and its placement on the calendar, as long as there is a real contest within a party, New Hampshire always has significance in the contest.

Some notable New Hampshire primaries have included:

1952: In their first test of strength, Dwight Eisenhower defeated Robert Taft by 50 to 39 percent in the Republican primary. In the Democratic primary,

Tennessee senator Estes Kefauver beat incumbent president Harry Truman. Shortly thereafter, Truman announced he was not seeking reelection.

1964: Henry Cabot Lodge of Massachusetts, then serving as U.S. ambassador to South Vietnam, surged past New York governor Nelson Rockefeller and Arizona senator Barry Goldwater to win 36 percent as a write-in candidate. Goldwater finished with 22 percent and Rockefeller with 21 percent. Goldwater had widely been expected to win, but lost his lead after a number of improvident statements suggesting he might make Social Security voluntary or put nuclear weapons under the control of NATO battlefield commanders, statements that would come back to haunt him in the general election.

1968: Shortly after the end of the communist Tet Offensive against South Vietnam, voters in New Hampshire gave antiwar insurgent Democrat Eugene McCarthy 42 percent against incumbent Lyndon Johnson's 49 percent. Though Johnson won the vote, McCarthy's unexpected strength helped convince him, like Truman in 1952, to end his quest for another term a few weeks later.

1972: Democrat Edmund Muskie, thought to be the big front-runner in the race, managed to hold on to a 46 to 37 percent win against antiwar senator George McGovern. Muskie's subpar win and McGovern's surprisingly strong finish contributed to Muskie's ultimate collapse and established McGovern as a key alternative. Muskie was also hurt by an episode in which, while campaigning in New Hampshire, he appeared to lose emotional control while responding to a *Manchester Union-Leader* story critical of his wife and the release of a letter under his name disrespectful of Maine's "Canuck" population. The letter was later found to be a forgery arranged by the Nixon campaign.

1976: Incumbent Republican president Gerald Ford eked out a 49 to 48 percent win versus conservative challenger Ronald Reagan in a state Reagan was expected to win. Reagan was nearly knocked out of the race, but righted himself and carried on a fight with Ford that did not end until the national convention. However, New Hampshire might have cost Reagan the nomination, which he ended up losing by a whisker. On the Democratic side, Jimmy Carter capitalized on his success in Iowa to win New Hampshire with 28 percent to Morris Udall's 23 percent.

1980: As president, Jimmy Carter held on to a close 52–48 percent win against challenger Edward Kennedy. While Kennedy subsequently enjoyed a number of surges during the primary season, he never fully recovered. On the Republican side, front-runner Ronald Reagan was reeling after a surprising loss in Iowa to George H. W. Bush. Reagan then dominated two televised candidate debates, one in Manchester and one in Nashua, and went on to win New Hampshire in a 50–23 percent blowout against Bush. Like Carter, Reagan never really looked back (Busch 2005, 65–68).

1984: Touting "new ideas," Colorado senator (and former campaign manager for George McGovern) Gary Hart cut down Walter Mondale 37 percent to 28 percent. Ohio senator and former astronaut John Glenn, who entered the race with high hopes, was held to 12 percent and dropped out soon after. Only with difficulty did Mondale regain his footing and ultimately win the Democratic nomination.

1988: Having come in third in Iowa behind Kansas senator Bob Dole and televangelist Pat Robertson, Vice President George H. W. Bush gained a decisive edge over Dole in antitax New Hampshire by pummeling Dole for refusing to sign a "No New Taxes" pledge. Bush's 38 to 28 percent win put him on a strong path toward Super Tuesday, where he nearly swept Dole and cemented his nomination. On the Democratic side, Governor Michael Dukakis from neighboring Massachusetts made the most of his home-town advantage, beating Richard Gephardt and Paul Simon 36 to 20 to 17 percent. Like Bush, Dukakis would go on to win his party's nomination.

1992: Another Massachusetts figure, Senator Paul Tsongas, won with 33 percent. However, the big story of the day was Bill Clinton, who brought himself back up to a respectable second-place finish with 25 percent after a number of damaging allegations had rocked his campaign. Calling himself "The Comeback Kid," Clinton turned his second-place finish into a moral victory and used it as a springboard for future primary successes (Kamarck 2016, 41). Meanwhile, Republican president George H. W. Bush held off pugnacious challenger Pat Buchanan, but not before Buchanan made it a closer race than anyone expected. Bush would go on to win every subsequent primary, but his 53–37 percent win indicated trouble ahead for the incumbent.

1996: The New Hampshire G.O.P. primary turned into a three-way race between the top three finishers in the Iowa caucuses: Bob Dole vs. Pat Buchanan vs. Lamar Alexander, governor of Tennessee. With Alexander rising rapidly in the polls, Dole's campaign decided he posed a bigger long-range threat than Buchanan. Resources were shifted to attacking Alexander, who fell back to a close third at the finish line. Buchanan won a narrow first place, but the real winner was arguably Dole, who had blunted the more serious long-term threat from Tennessee (Ceaser and Busch 1997).

2000: With an establishment vs. maverick contest shaping up on both sides, an informal but crucial contest was the battle between Republican maverick John McCain and Democratic maverick Bill Bradley for the votes of New Hampshire's independents. McCain won that contest, and with it the Republican primary against George W. Bush. Having lost the informal contest to McCain, Bradley lost to Al Gore in the Democratic primary 50–46 percent. McCain gained a boost but could not sustain it, and Bush went on to gain the nomination. Gore was never really threatened by Bradley again (Ceaser and Busch 2001).

2004: In the Democratic primary, Vermont governor Howard Dean, representing the progressive "netroots" and anti–Iraq War movement, led the New Hampshire polls for some time until Massachusetts senator John Kerry made his move in early January. Kerry won going away, 38 to 26 percent.

2008: Returning to the scene of his 2000 victory, John McCain gained a similar victory over former Massachusetts governor Mitt Romney. This time, McCain was able to capitalize on his win and ride it to the nomination. On the Democratic side, Hillary Clinton prevented the possible collapse of her campaign by beating Barack Obama 39 to 37 percent after being upset in Iowa. Senator John Edwards's 12 percent finish put Edwards's campaign in a hole it could not escape.

2012: Hoping for better success four years later, Mitt Romney focused on New Hampshire and won, beating libertarian hero Ron Paul 39 percent to 23 percent in the Republican primary.

2016: Facing Hillary Clinton, who had narrowly won the Iowa caucuses, Vermont senator Bernie Sanders won with room to spare—60 percent to Clinton's 38 percent. Donald Trump won the Republican primary after having lost in Iowa. Trump defeated John Kasich by a 2–1 margin, with Ted Cruz, Jeb Bush, and Marco Rubio far behind. Rubio was particularly damaged, as his third-place Iowa finish had initially led to a boost in his polling in New Hampshire that put him on track to finish second or even compete for the win. A catastrophic few minutes in a televised debate the weekend before the vote stopped his momentum, and he finished in fifth place.

Sources

Busch, Andrew E. 2005. *Reagan's Victory: The Presidential Election of 1980 and the Rise of the Right.* Lawrence: University Press of Kansas.

Ceaser, James W., and Andrew E. Busch. 1997. *Losing to Win: The 1996 Elections and American Politics.* Lanham, MD: Rowman & Littlefield.

Ceaser, James W., and Andrew E. Busch. 2001. *The Perfect Tie: The True Story of the 2000 Elections.* Lanham, MD: Rowman & Littlefield.

Kamarck, Elaine C. 2016. *Primary Politics,* 2nd ed. Washington, DC: Brookings Institution.

Mayer, William G., and Andrew E. Busch. 2004. *The Front-Loading Problem in Presidential Nominations.* Washington, DC: Brookings Institution.

New Hampshire Primary Results 2000–2016

2000

Democratic primary (2/1)		Republican primary (2/1)	
Gore	49.7	McCain	48.5
Bradley	45.6	Bush	30.4
		Forbes	12.7
		Keyes	6.4

2004

Democratic primary (1/27)		Republican primary (1/27)	
Kerry	38.4	Bush	79.8
Dean	26.3	Kerry (WI)	4.2
Clark	12.4	Dean (WI)	2.7
Edwards	12.1	Clark (WI)	2.1
Lieberman	8.6	Edwards (WI)	1.6
Kucinich	1.4	Scattered (WI)	1.4
		Lieberman (WI)	1.4
		Bosa	1.2
		Buchanan	1.2
		Rigazio	1.2

2008

Democratic primary (1/8)		Republican primary (1/8)	
Clinton	39.1	McCain	37.0
Obama	36.5	Romney	31.6
Edwards	16.9	Huckabee	11.2
Richardson	4.6	Giuliani	8.5
Kucinich	1.4	Paul	7.7
		Thompson	1.2

2012

Democratic primary (1/10)		Republican primary (1/10)	
Obama	80.9	Romney	39.3
Paul (WI)	3.8	Paul	22.9
Romney (WI)	3.0	Huntsman	16.9
Huntsman (WI)	2.0	Santorum	9.4
Cowan	1.6	Gingrich	9.4
Supreme	1.4		
Scattered (WI)	1.3		

2016

Democratic primary (1/9)		Republican primary (1/9)	
Sanders	60.1	Trump	35.2
Clinton	37.7	Kasich	15.7
		Cruz	11.6
		Bush	11.0
		Rubio	10.5
		Christie	7.4
		Fiorina	4.1
		Carson	2.3

Sources: Federal Election Commission:
https://transition.fec.gov/pubrec/fe2000/2000presprim.htm#NH;
https://transition.fec.gov/pubrec/fe2004/federalelections2004.pdf;
https://transition.fec.gov/pubrec/fe2008/federalelections2008.pdf;
https://transition.fec.gov/pubrec/fe2012/federalelections2012.pdf;
https://transition.fec.gov/pubrec/fe2016/federalelections2016.pdf.

2020 Delegate Selection

Democratic

Number of delegates: 33 total delegate votes—16 district, 5 at-large, 3 pledged PLEOs, 9 unpledged PLEOs

Date of 2020 contest: February 11

What week of the delegate selection season: 2

Type of delegate selection event: Semiopen primary (D & I)

Mode of awarding delegates: Proportional representation with a 15 percent threshold

How delegates are chosen: District delegates to the national convention are slated by presidential preference in a preprimary congressional district caucus and are elected according to the primary results; at-large delegates and pledged PLEOs are elected by the district delegates

Bound for how many national conventions ballots: One

Source: http://www.thegreenpapers.com/P20/NH-D.

Republican

Number of delegates: 22 total delegates—16 at-large (10 base, 3 party, 3 bonus), 6 in 2 congressional districts

Date of 2020 contest: February 11

What week of the delegate selection season: 2

Type of delegate selection event: Semiopen primary (R & I)

Mode of awarding delegates: Proportional representation based on statewide primary vote with 10 percent threshold

How delegates are chosen: Candidates for president submit a list of delegate candidates to the secretary of state before the primary; after the primary, the secretary of state notifies candidates of how many delegates they won, and candidates have 10 days to designate who from their list will fill their delegate positions to the national convention

Bound for how many national conventions ballots: All

Source: http://www.thegreenpapers.com/P20/NH-R.

—Andrew E. Busch

New Jersey

Stereotypically notorious for mafia activity, political corruption, and rough inner city zones such as Newark, Trenton, and Camden, New Jersey is also home to rolling hills, dairy farms, miles of pine forest wilderness, picturesque towns, and affluent suburbs. It tends toward liberal Democrats and moderate Republicans. Now heavily Democratic at the presidential level, New Jersey gave 55 percent of its votes to Hillary Clinton and 41 percent to Donald Trump in 2016. Democrats have won every presidential election in New Jersey since 1992.

New Jersey has been holding presidential primaries since primaries began nationally in 1912. In that primary, held on May 28, Theodore Roosevelt trounced William Howard Taft with 56 percent of the vote. From 1916 to 1924, the New Jersey primary was scheduled in late April; from 1928 through 1944 in mid-May; from 1948 through 1964 in late April; and from 1968 to today in early June—with the exception of 2008, when New Jersey joined the front-loading bandwagon and scheduled its primary on February 5.

Notable New Jersey primaries included:

1932: Former senator Joseph I. France of Maryland beat incumbent president Herbert Hoover 93 percent to 7 percent in the Republican primary, while Al Smith and Franklin Roosevelt, both from neighboring New York, battled it out in the Democratic primary. Smith won that battle, 62 to 38 percent, though he lost the nomination to FDR.

1948: Another neighbor from New York, Republican Thomas Dewey, outpolled Harold Stassen 41 to 35 percent on his way to the GOP nomination.

1952: Dwight Eisenhower defeated Robert Taft 61 to 36 percent.

1964: Henry Cabot Lodge of Massachusetts won a solid victory from the perch of his ambassadorship in South Vietnam, beating Barry Goldwater and Richard Nixon by 48 percent for Lodge, 28 percent for Goldwater, and 22 percent for Nixon.

1968: Divided Democrats gave Eugene McCarthy 36 percent, Robert F. Kennedy 31 percent, and Hubert Humphrey (who was concentrating his efforts on nonprimary states) 20 percent. The New Jersey primary was held the same day as the California primary and was overshadowed by the assassination of Kennedy in Los Angeles that night.

1972: African American congresswoman Shirley Chisholm received two-thirds of the vote against North Carolina's Terry Sanford on the last day of the Democratic primaries. Chisholm was the first black candidate to run for president in a major party.

1980: Democratic challenger Ted Kennedy thrashed President Jimmy Carter 56 percent to 38 percent on the final major primary day of the year. Along with the Garden State, Kennedy closed out the primary season with wins in California, New Mexico, Rhode Island, and South Dakota, breathing some life into his campaign though Carter retained a strong lead in delegates.

1984: Establishment favorite Walter Mondale beat Colorado senator Gary Hart in the Democratic primary by 45–30 percent. Jesse Jackson trailed with 24 percent.

2008: Voting with 15 other primary states toward the beginning of the primary season, New Jersey voters backed Republican John McCain over Mitt Romney by 55–28 percent and Democrat Hillary Clinton over Barack Obama by 54–44 percent.

2016: Donald Trump won the Republican primary with 80 percent of the vote against token opposition. As in 2008, Hillary Clinton demolished her rival, this time Vermont senator Bernie Sanders, 63 percent to 37 percent. Both already had enough delegates to assure nomination.

New Jersey Primary Results 2000–2016

2000

Democratic primary (6/2)		Republican primary (6/2)	
Gore	94.9	Bush	83.6
LaRouche	5.1	Keyes	16.4

2004

Democratic primary (6/8)		Republican primary (6/8)	
Kerry	92.3	Bush	100.0
Kucinich	4.3		
LaRouche	2.1		
Ballard	1.3		

2008

Democratic primary (2/5)		Republican primary (2/5)	
Clinton	53.8	McCain	55.4
Obama	43.9	Romney	28.3
Edwards	1.4	Huckabee	8.2
		Paul	4.8
		Giuliani	2.7

2012

Democratic primary (6/5)		Republican primary (6/5)	
Obama	100.0	Romney	81.3
		Paul	10.4
		Santorum	5.2
		Gingrich	3.1

2016

Democratic primary (6/7)		Republican primary (6/7)	
Clinton	63.3	Trump	80.4
Sanders	36.7	Kasich	13.4
		Cruz	6.2

Sources: Federal Election Commission:
https://transition.fec.gov/pubrec/fe2000/2000presprim.htm#NJ;
https://transition.fec.gov/pubrec/fe2004/federalelections2004.pdf;
https://transition.fec.gov/pubrec/fe2008/federalelections2008.pdf;
https://transition.fec.gov/pubrec/fe2012/federalelections2012.pdf;
https://transition.fec.gov/pubrec/fe2016/federalelections2016.pdf.

2020 Delegate Selection

Democratic

Number of delegates: 128 total delegate votes—70 district, 23 at-large, 14 pledged PLEOs, 21 unpledged PLEOs

Date of 2020 contest: June 2

What week of the delegate selection season: 19

Type of delegate selection event: Semiopen primary (D & I)

Mode of awarding delegates: Proportional representation with a 15 percent threshold

How delegates are chosen: Slates of district delegates to the national convention approved by the presidential candidates appear on the primary and are elected directly in the primary according to the primary results; at-large delegates and pledged PLEOs are elected at the state convention according to the statewide primary results

Bound for how many national conventions ballots: One

Source: http://www.thegreenpapers.com/P20/NJ-D.

Republican

Number of delegates: 49 total delegates—13 at-large (10 base, 3 party), 36 in 12 congressional districts

Date of 2020 contest: June 2

What week of the delegate selection season: 19

Type of delegate selection event: Semiopen primary (R & I)

Mode of awarding delegates: Winner-take-all based on the statewide vote

How delegates are chosen: Delegate candidates appear on the primary ballot in slates committed to presidential candidates and are elected directly according to the statewide primary results

Bound for how many national conventions ballots: One

Source: http://www.thegreenpapers.com/P20/NJ-R.

—Andrew E. Busch

New Mexico

New Mexico's unique culture blends Native American, Spanish, and Anglo traditions, as well as ranching, energy research, and Santa Fe arts. With a large Hispanic population, New Mexico has leaned Democratic at the presidential level but has frequently had Republican governors such as Gary Johnson and Susana Martinez and is close enough often enough to be considered a swing state. George W. Bush came within 366 votes of Al Gore in 2000 and did win New Mexico in 2004. Democrats have won the last three times, including Hillary Clinton's 48–40 percent win over Donald Trump in 2016. Gary Johnson, running as the Libertarian Party candidate for president, garnered another 9 percent, his best showing in the country.

Democratic delegations selected by caucus-convention supported Franklin Roosevelt in 1932 and Lyndon Johnson in 1960, while giving Hubert Humphrey a slight edge over Eugene McCarthy in 1968. Republicans overwhelmingly backed Barry Goldwater in 1964 and Ronald Reagan in 1976 after having split closely between Robert Taft and Dwight Eisenhower in 1952. New Mexico held its first presidential primary in 1972. In 1976 it went back to caucuses, then returned to a primary in 1980. New Mexico has held a presidential primary since then, with the exception of 2004 and 2008, when Republicans held a primary but Democrats used caucuses. The state has traditionally held its primaries and caucuses in the first week of June when nominations have all but been decided. Nevertheless, New Mexico has had some interesting contests, including:

1972: New Mexico's first primary saw the eventual Democratic nominee George McGovern gather just over 33 percent of the vote total. Still, this was the largest share, resulting in McGovern receiving 10 of the state's delegates. Not far behind, George Wallace gained 8 delegates by earning 29 percent of the vote. Hubert Humphrey, landing in third, received no delegate despite a respectable showing of 26 percent.

1980: In the Democratic primary, challenger Edward Kennedy defeated President Jimmy Carter 46 percent to 42 percent, helping Kennedy close out the primary season with a flourish. With New Mexico, Kennedy won five of the eight primaries held that day, including California and New Jersey. Although Carter continued to hold a large lead in delegates, Kennedy was encouraged to carry the fight all the way to the Democratic national convention.

1984: Senator Gary Hart from neighboring Colorado beat Walter Mondale 47 percent to 36 percent. Like Kennedy in 1980, Hart gained some momentum by winning New Mexico, California, and South Dakota on the last day of primaries, while Mondale won West Virginia and New Jersey.

2008: New Jersey Democrats used caucuses and moved their contest date up to Super Tuesday (February 5) in a bid to aid the presidential candidacy of former governor Bill Richardson. However, Richardson withdrew from the race in January, allowing for a one-on-one contest between Hillary Clinton and Barack Obama (Skelly 2016). Clinton captured 49 percent of the vote to Obama's 48 percent.

2016: New Mexico's primary returned to its previous June date. Hillary Clinton prevailed over Bernie Sanders by a 52–48 percent margin, a surprisingly strong finish in defeat for the senator from Vermont given that Clinton had been declared the presumptive nominee by the news media the day before the primary. Clinton gained the majority of Hispanic and Native American votes, while Sanders captured the majority in Bernalillo County, the most populous county in New Mexico (New Mexico Primary Results).

Sources

New Mexico Primary Results. 2016. *New York Times*, June 7. https://www.nytimes .com/elections/2016/results/primaries/new-mexico.

Skelly, Geoffrey. 2016. "The Modern History of the Democratic Presidential Primary, 1972–2008." Center for Politics, February 4. http://www.centerfor politics.org/crystalball/articles/the-modern-history-of-the-democratic -presidential-primary-1972-2008/.

New Mexico Primary and Caucus Results 2000–2016

2000

Democratic primary (6/6)		Republican primary (6/6)	
Gore	74.6	Bush	82.6
Bradley	20.6	McCain	10.1
LaRouche	2.3	Keyes	6.5

2004

Democratic caucuses (2/3)		Republican primary (6/6)	
Kerry	42.6	Bush	100.0
Clark	20.4		
Dean	16.3		
Edwards	11.2		
Kucinich	5.5		
Lieberman	2.5		

2008

Democratic caucuses (2/5)		Republican primary (6/3)	
Clinton	48.9	McCain	86.0
Obama	47.8	Paul	14.0
Edwards	1.4		

2012

Democratic primary (6/5)		Republican primary (6/5)	
Obama	100.0	Romney	73.3
		Santorum	10.5
		Paul	10.3
		Gingrichs	5.8

2016

Democratic primary (6/7)		Republican primary (6/7)	
Clinton	51.5	Trump	70.7
Sanders	48.5	Cruz	13.3

Kasich	7.6
Carson	3.7
Bush	3.4
Fiorina	1.4

Sources: https://transition.fec.gov/pubrec/fe2000/2000presprim.htm#NM; http://www.sos.state.nm.us/uploads/files/Election%20Results /statewidePrim04.pdf; https://uselectionatlas.org/RESULTS/state .php?year=2004&fips=35&f=&off=0&elect=1&f=0; https://transition.fec.gov/pubrec/fe2008/federalelections2008.pdf; https://uselectionatlas.org/RESULTS/state.php?year=2008&fips =35&f=&off=0&elect=1&f=0; https://www.nytimes.com/elections/2012/primaries/states/new -mexico.html; https://uselectionatlas.org/RESULTS/state.php?year=2008&fips =35&f=&off=0&elect=1&f=0; https://www.nytimes.com/elections/2016/results/primaries/new-mexico.

2020 Delegate Selection

Democratic

Number of delegates: 40 total—19 district, 6 at-large, 4 pledged PLEOs, 11 unpledged PLEOs

Date of 2020 contest: June 2

What week of the delegate selection season: 18

Type of delegate selection event: Closed primary

Mode of awarding delegates: Proportional representation with a 15 percent threshold

How delegates are chosen: District delegates to the national convention are elected by congressional district conventions according to the district primary results; at-large delegates and pledged PLEOs are elected by the state convention according to statewide primary results

Bound for how many national conventions ballots: One

Source: https://www.thegreenpapers.com/P20/NM-D.

Republican

Number of delegates: 22 total delegates—13 at-large (10 base, 3 party), 9 in 3 congressional districts

Date of 2020 contest: June 2

What week of the delegate selection season: 18

Type of delegate selection event: Closed primary

Mode of awarding delegates: Proportional representation based on statewide vote with a 15 percent threshold

How delegates are elected: In accordance with the primary results, district delegates to the national convention are elected by congressional district meetings at the state convention and at-large delegates are elected by the state convention as a whole

Bound for how many national conventions ballots: One

Source: https://www.thegreenpapers.com/P20/NM-R.

—*Andrew E. Busch and Jacob S. Leischner*

New York

For a large portion of the 20th century, the Empire State was one of the most pivotal states in presidential politics. Since the 1911 Triangle Shirtwaist Fire, New York has been one of the most active states driving America toward the welfare state by passing labor, safety, and social insurance laws such as minimum wage and rent control. New York has been the home state of Democrats including Al Smith and Franklin Roosevelt and Republicans including Theodore Roosevelt, Thomas Dewey, and Nelson Rockefeller. Historically, Democrats carried the New York City Catholic vote with the Republicans winning the upstate Protestants (Barone and McCutcheon 2014). In national politics today, New York is one of the most Democratic states due to its large Jewish, black, and Hispanic populations, and the last Republican to win New York's electoral votes was George H. W. Bush in 1988. In 2016, Hillary Clinton, who became a New York resident to run for U.S. Senate in 2000, defeated fellow New Yorker Donald Trump by 59 to 37 percent.

Although New York has often been a crucial battleground in presidential nomination contests, battles were frequently hidden from easy public view. New York's first presidential primary was held in 1912 when Republicans conducted a delegate primary with no presidential preference attached. Primaries were held again, by both Republicans and Democrats, in 1916 and 1920, but were discontinued from 1924 through 1964. In 1968 through 1976, New York again held pure delegate primaries disconnected from a presidential preference vote. In keeping with national Democratic reforms, from 1980 to the present Democrats have held preference primaries (though in 1996 they suspended their primary since Bill Clinton was running for renomination unopposed). Republicans continued holding their delegate primary in 1980, then held no primary in 1984–1992 and again in 2004. Republican primaries in 1996, 2000, and 2008–2016 have been preference primaries.

On the Democratic side, some key delegate results in nonpreference primary years have included Franklin Roosevelt's narrow advantage over Al Smith on the first ballot in 1932, John F. Kennedy's overwhelming lead in

1960, Hubert Humphrey's narrow edge over Eugene McCarthy in 1968, and George McGovern's big win in 1972. McGovern's important delegate win in New York was deeply ironic, coming as it did in an unreformed delegate primary in violation of McGovern-Fraser Commission guidelines. New York's liberal GOP delegations backed Dwight Eisenhower over Robert Taft in 1952, New Yorker Nelson Rockefeller over Barry Goldwater in 1964, and President Gerald Ford over Ronald Reagan in 1976.

Key New York preference primaries have included:

1980: Democratic president Jimmy Carter was embarrassed by challenger Edward Kennedy, 59 percent to 41 percent. Kennedy's impressive win, accompanied by a win in Connecticut the same day, came just as many observers had concluded that the Massachusetts senator was finished. New York gave Kennedy a second wind and allowed him to remain in the race, tormenting Carter all the way to the convention (Busch 2005).

1984: Walter Mondale defeated Gary Hart and Jesse Jackson by 45 percent to 27 percent to 25 percent, a big win for Mondale on his road to the Democratic nomination.

1988: Democrat Michael Dukakis won a critical victory against Jesse Jackson, 51 to 37 percent. Finishing in distant third was Tennessee senator and future vice president Al Gore, who introduced an attack on Dukakis focusing on a prisoner, Willie Horton, who took advantage of a Massachusetts prison furlough program to go on a violent crime spree. George H. W. Bush's Republican campaign would later pick up on the Willie Horton issue and use it to devastating effect in the fall (Pitney 2019).

1992: In a tough contest, Bill Clinton beat Paul Tsongas 41 to 29 percent, with Edmund "Jerry" Brown coming in a close third with 26 percent. That same day (April 7) Clinton also won primaries in Minnesota, Wisconsin, and Kansas, solidifying his lead in the Democratic nomination race.

1996: In the GOP primary, Bob Dole outpolled publisher Steve Forbes by nearly 2–1, dashing Forbes's hopes of leveraging his New York ties into an important win and a large number of delegates.

2000: Republican George W. Bush beat chief rival John McCain 51–43 percent, while Democrat Al Gore crushed Bill Bradley from neighboring New Jersey by a 2–1 margin.

2004: Massachusetts senator John Kerry defeated North Carolina senator John Edwards 61 percent to 20 percent. Combined with wins in California, Ohio, and a number of smaller states that day, Kerry's New York victory essentially ended the Democratic nomination race.

2008: On Super Tuesday (February 5), Hillary Clinton defeated Barack Obama in the New York Democratic Primary by 17 percentage points. However, throughout the country, the day was nearly a split verdict: Clinton won nine primaries, Obama seven, so New York was far from a knockout. On the Republican side, John McCain came back from his 2000 loss to defeat Mitt Romney handily.

2016: As expected, Hillary Clinton won her adopted home state again, beating Bernie Sanders in the Democratic primary by 16 percentage points. In the Republican primary, Donald Trump won by a margin of 35 percentage points. Governor John Kasich came in second with 25 percent of the vote in comparison to Trump's 60 percent. Senator Ted Cruz paid a heavy price for assailing "New York values" during the campaign for Iowa. Cruz finished a distant third. Trump's big win in New York was followed one week later by a sweep of other Northeastern states, giving the billionaire decisive momentum going into the Indiana primary (Ceaser, Busch, and Pitney 2017).

Sources

Barone, Michael, and Chuck McCutcheon. 2014. *Almanac of American Politics 2014.* Washington, DC: National Journal.

Busch, Andrew E. 2005. *Reagan's Victory: The 1980 Presidential Election and the Rise of the Right.* Lawrence: University Press of Kansas.

Ceaser, James W., Andrew E. Busch, and John J. Pitney Jr. 2017. *Defying the Odds: The 2016 Elections and American Politics.* Lanham, MD: Rowman & Littlefield.

Pitney, John J., Jr. 2019. *After Reagan: Bush, Dukakis and the 1988 Election.* Lawrence: University Press of Kansas.

New York Primary Results 2000–2016

2000

Democratic primary (3/7)		Republican primary (3/7)	
Gore	65.6	Bush	51.0
Bradley	33.5	McCain	43.4
		Keyes	3.3
		Forbes	2.3

2004

Democratic primary (3/2)		Republican primary (3/2)	
Kerry	61.2	**Primary cancelled**	
Edwards	20.1	**Delegates to national convention**	
Sharpton	8.0	Bush	87.5
Kucinich	5.1	Uncommitted	12.5
Dean	2.9		
Lieberman	1.3		

2008

Democratic primary (2/5)		Republican primary (2/5)	
Clinton	57.4	McCain	51.8
Obama	40.3	Romney	27.7
Edwards	1.2	Huckabee	10.7
		Giuliani	3.6

2012

Democratic primary (4/24)		Republican primary (4/24)	
Obama	100.0	Romney	62.7
		Paul	14.6
		Gingrich	12.7
		Santorum	10.0

2016

Democratic primary (4/19)		Republican primary (4/19)	
Clinton	58.0	Trump	60.2
Sanders	42.0	Kasich	25.1
		Cruz	14.8

Sources: https://www.thegreenpapers.com/P04/NY-R.phtml;
Federal Election Commission:
https://transition.fec.gov/pubrec/fe2000/2000presprim.htm;
https://transition.fec.gov/pubrec/fe2004/federalelections2004.pdf;
https://transition.fec.gov/pubrec/fe2008/federalelections2008.pdf;
https://transition.fec.gov/pubrec/fe2012/2012pres.pdf;
https://transition.fec.gov/pubrec/fe2016/federalelections2016.pdf.

2020 Delegate Selection

Democratic

Number of delegates: 270 total delegate votes—146 district, 49 at-large, 29 pledged PLEOs, 46 unpledged PLEOs

Date of 2020 contest: April 28

What week of the delegate selection season: 13

Type of delegate selection event: Closed primary

Mode of awarding delegates: Proportional representation with a 15 percent threshold

How delegates are chosen: Candidates for district delegates to the national convention appear on the primary ballot and are elected according to the district primary results; at-large delegates and pledged PLEOs are elected by the state committee according to the statewide primary results

Bound for how many national conventions ballots: One

Source: http://www.thegreenpapers.com/P20/NY-D.

Republican

Number of delegates: 95 total delegates—14 at-large (10 base, 3 party, 1 bonus), 81 in 27 congressional districts

Date of 2020 contest: April 28

What week of the delegate selection season: 13

Type of delegate selection event: Closed primary

Mode of awarding delegates: Winner-Take-Most: At-large—If a candidate for president wins a majority of the primary vote statewide, he or she receives all at-large delegates; if there is no majority winner, delegates are allocated by proportional representation with a 20 percent threshold

District—If a candidate for president wins a majority of the district vote or is the only candidate to win 20 percent of the vote, he or she receives all delegates from that district; otherwise, the top vote-getter gets 2 delegates and the runner-up gets 1 delegate

How delegates are chosen: District delegates to the national convention are elected in congressional district meetings according to the primary results; at-large delegates are elected by the state committee according to the results of the primary

Bound for how many national conventions ballots: One

Source: http://www.thegreenpapers.com/P20/NY-R.

—Andrew E. Busch and Nandeeni K. Patel

North Carolina

Demographically, North Carolina has seen major shifts as a paragon of the "New South." The overall population of the state nearly doubled from 1970 to 2008, while the Hispanic population increased by a factor of eight from 1990 to 2007. The culture of the South has met with the high-tech culture of the Research Triangle, the PhD-heavy region between the University of North Carolina–Chapel Hill, North Carolina State University, and Duke University. Politically, the state has tended to vote Republican, although it has also exhibited ambivalence, not too long ago sending liberal senator John Edwards and conservative senator Jesse Helms to Washington to both serve the state at the same time. At the presidential level, since 2000, the state has voted for Republican presidential candidates in every election save 2008, when Barack Obama narrowly won the state over Senator John McCain. In 2016, Donald Trump won the state with a three-point margin, 49–46 percent.

North Carolina held its first presidential primary on June 5, 1920, the last primary of that election cycle. The next primary the state held was not until over 50 years later, on May 6, 1972. North Carolina has held a presidential primary every four years since then, with the exception of 2004, when the parties held caucuses for delegate selection. From 1972 through 2016, the state has scheduled its primary in early May eight times and in March three times, most recently in 2016. Notable North Carolina primaries have included:

1972: The first North Carolina primary of the modern era featured a showdown between Democrat George Wallace, representing the "Old South," and North Carolina governor Terry Sanford, representing the "New South." Other serious Democratic candidates, all more liberal than Wallace, stayed out of the state to give Sanford the best shot of beating the Alabaman. Wallace won anyway, 50–37 percent.

1976: Contested nominations in both parties made North Carolina a pivotal state. George Wallace returned to the Democratic primary, but was defeated handily (54–35 percent) by Jimmy Carter, that year's representative of the "New South." Carter's win, coming only two weeks after another win over Wallace in Florida, wrecked Wallace's campaign and established Carter as the master of the South. On the Republican side, where conservative challenger Ronald Reagan was battling President Gerald Ford, Reagan was on the ropes after five straight primary losses. Advised by some to throw in the towel, Reagan went on the offensive in North Carolina and defeated Ford 52 percent to 46 percent to gain his first primary win of 1976. His campaign rescued, Reagan clawed his way back into the race, fighting Ford all the way to the convention (Shirley 2005).

1980: Jimmy Carter and Ronald Reagan again won, more decisively than four years before. Carter beat Edward Kennedy 70–18 percent, while Reagan dispatched George H. W. Bush by a margin of 68 percent to 22 percent. North Carolina was, for both winners, one of three blowout victories that day, the other two being in Indiana and Tennessee.

1984: Eventual Democratic nominee Walter Mondale defeated Colorado senator Gary Hart 36 percent to 30 percent in the midst of a long nomination battle.

1988: In the first mega–Super Tuesday, Vice President George H. W. Bush outpolled Kansas senator Bob Dole 45–39 percent in the Republican primary, part of a Super Tuesday record that propelled Bush to the nomination. On the Democratic side, Tennessee senator Al Gore edged out a 35–33 percent win over Jesse Jackson. Of 16 primaries that day, Gore won North Carolina and four others; Jackson and Massachusetts governor Michael Dukakis won comparable numbers.

2008: Democrat Barack Obama defeated Hillary Clinton 56 to 42 percent in a May primary, winning an important victory going into the homestretch of the race. Obama's North Carolina win more than balanced out his narrow loss in Indiana the same day.

2016: Eight years later, North Carolina voted in March for the first time since 1988. Clinton reversed the 2008 numbers, beating Bernie Sanders 55 to 41 percent. At the same time, Donald Trump edged out a 40–37 percent win against Ted Cruz, one of several close wins for Trump in the South that kept Cruz from taking advantage of his strongest region.

Source

Shirley, Craig. 2005. *Reagan's Revolution: The Untold Story of the Campaign That Started It All.* Nashville, TN: Thomas Nelson.

North Carolina Primary and Caqucus Results 2000–2016

2000

Democratic primary (5/2)		Republican primary (5/2)	
Gore	70.4	Bush	78.6
Bradley	18.3	McCain	10.9
No Preference	9.1	Keyes	7.9
LaRouche	2.1	No Preference	1.7
		Bauer	1.0

2004

Democratic caucuses (3/9)		Republican caucuses (2/1–3/31)	
Edwards	51.6	**Delegates to national convention**	
Kerry	27.1	Bush	100.0
Kucinch	11.7		
Dean	5.9		
Sharpton	3.2		

2008

Democratic primary (5/6)		Republican primary (5/6)	
Obama	56.1	McCain	74.0
Clinton	41.6	Huckabee	12.2
No Preference	1.5	Paul	7.2
		No Preference	4.0
		Keyes	2.6

2012

Democratic primary (5/8)		Republican primary (5/8)	
Obama	79.2	Romney	65.6
No Preference	20.8	Paul	11.1
		Santorum	10.4
		Gingrich	7.6
		No Preference	5.2

2016

Democratic primary (3/15)		Republican primary (3/15)	
Clinton	54.5	Trump	40.2
Sanders	40.9	Cruz	36.8
No Preference	3.3	Kasich	12.7
O'Malley	1.1	Rubio	7.7

Sources: Federal Election Commission:
https://transition.fec.gov/pubrec/fe2000/2000presprim.htm#top;
https://transition.fec.gov/pubrec/fe2008/federalelections2008.pdf;
https://transition.fec.gov/pubrec/fe2012/2012pres.pdf;
https://transition.fec.gov/pubrec/fe2016/federalelections2016.pdf; also,
https://www.thegreenpapers.com/P04/NC-D.phtml;
https://www.thegreenpapers.com/P04/NC-R.phtml.

2020 Delegate Selection

Democratic

Number of delegates: 122 total delegate votes—72 district, 24 at-large, 14 pledged PLEOs, 12 unpledged PLEOs

Date of 2020 contest: March 3

What week of the delegate selection season: 5

Type of delegate selection event: Semiopen primary (D & I)

Mode of awarding delegates: Proportional representation with a 15 percent threshold

How delegates are chosen: According to the results of the primary, district delegates to the national convention are elected by congressional district conventions and at-large delegates and pledged PLEOs are elected by the state convention

Bound for how many national conventions ballots: One

Source: https://www.thegreenpapers.com/P20/NC-D.

Republican

Number of delegates: 71 total delegates—32 at-large (10 base, 3 party, 19 bonus), 39 in 13 congressional districts

Date of 2020 contest: March 3

What week of the delegate selection season: 5

Type of delegate selection event: Semiopen primary (R & I)

Mode of awarding delegates: At-large: Proportional representation with a 20 percent threshold based on statewide vote. District: Winner-take-most: If a candidate wins more than two-thirds of the district vote, or if only one candidate wins 20 percent or more, that candidate receives all district delegates; otherwise, the top vote-getter receives two delegates and the runner-up receives one

How delegates are chosen: According to the results of the primary, district delegates to the national convention are elected by congressional district conventions and at-large delegates are elected by the state convention

Bound for how many national conventions ballots: One

Source: http://www.thegreenpapers.com/P20/NC-R.

—*Andrew E. Busch and Richard C. Wiltshire-Gordon*

North Dakota

North Dakota is built on a history of reliance on agriculture and community, which gives both political parties opportunities for a foothold. Historically, North Dakota sends its electoral votes to the Republican nominee, but the "social connectedness" of the state, traceable back to prairie populism in the 1890s and the "Nonpartisan League" of the 1920s, has allowed Democrats to win some statewide offices. At the same time, both the state's social conservatism and its reliance on oil and natural gas pushes voters in the Republican direction. Democrats have hopes grounded in the growing tech innovation market catalyzed by Microsoft's acquisition of Great Plains Software in 2000, but those hopes have not materialized so far (Barone and McCutcheon 2014). At the presidential level, no Democratic presidential nominee has won the state since Lyndon Johnson in 1964. In 2016, Donald Trump defeated Hillary Clinton 63 to 27 percent.

North Dakota's first presidential primary was the first presidential primary in the country on March 19, 1912. The state continued holding primaries, always in mid-March, through 1932, when Franklin Roosevelt garnered 62 percent in the Democratic contest. From 1936 until 1984, the state used a caucus-convention procedure for delegate selection. During those years Democratic delegations from North Dakota backed John F. Kennedy in 1960, Hubert Humphrey in 1968, and George McGovern in 1972, while giving Edward Kennedy a bare edge against Jimmy Carter in 1980. Republican delegations gave Robert Taft, Barry Goldwater, and Gerald Ford solid but not overwhelming majorities. Primaries returned from 1984 to 1992, but caucuses were the delegate selection mode from 1996 through 2016. Most of these caucuses were scheduled early in the campaign season, in February or March, though Democratic caucuses in 2016 took place in early June. Democratic caucuses are so-called "firehouse caucuses" in which voters may stop by the caucus location and cast a ballot or may mail in their ballot.

Key North Dakota results have included:

1992: In a sign that political dissatisfaction was surging across the political spectrum, independent Ross Perot won enough write-in votes in the Democratic primary to finish first, outpolling Bill Clinton by a 2–1 margin.

2004: John Kerry won the Democratic caucuses with 51 percent of the vote to Wesley Clark's 24 percent and Howard Dean's 12 percent.

2008: In the GOP caucuses, Mitt Romney came out ahead with 36 percent of the votes. John McCain followed with 23 percent, Ron Paul with 21 percent, and Mike Huckabee with 20 percent. On the Democratic side, Barack Obama's campaign perceived an opportunity in a state seldom given much heed in Democratic presidential politics. Obama ramped up operations in the state as his challengers continued to neglect it. On caucus day (February 5), Obama's attention paid off, as he beat Hillary Clinton decisively. Obama's early North Dakota win showed he could do well in states with few minorities, and served as a template for his subsequent caucus state successes. It also showed Obama's potential to excite and mobilize voters: 19,012 Democrats in the state came to vote, while the Republican caucuses featured only 9,785 voters (Barone and McCutcheon 2014).

2012: Republican Rick Santorum soundly defeated Mitt Romney 40–28 percent, reaffirming the social conservative's strength in caucus settings and his status as Romney's strongest challenger.

2016: Democratic caucuses were held on June 7, one day after Clinton was declared the presumptive nominee by the media. The other contests held on June 7 helped secure Clinton's lead, as she won 254 of California's delegates and 79 of New Jersey's. North Dakota emerged as an exception. Vermont senator Bernie Sanders won nearly two-thirds of the caucus vote, holding Clinton to 26 percent. Including North Dakota, Sanders won every caucus following his February 20 loss in Nevada. On the other side of the aisle, the Republican Party declined to hold a presidential preference caucus or primary. Instead, local caucuses led to the election of delegates to the national convention at a state convention held on April 3. Although delegates were elected as officially unpledged, news reports indicated that most were loyal to Texas senator Ted Cruz (Mattingly and LoBianco 2016). However, Cruz withdrew from the race after the May 3 Indiana primary and North Dakota's delegates ultimately gave 21 votes to Trump, 6 to Cruz, and 1 to Ben Carson.

Sources

Barone, Michael, and Chuck McCutcheon. 2014. *Almanac of American Politics.* Washington, DC: National Journal.

Mattingly, Phil, and Tom LoBianco. 2016. "Cruz Allies Prevail in North Dakota Delegate Race." CNN, April 4. https://www.cnn.com/2016/04/03/politics/north-dakota-gop-delegates-donald-trump-ted-cruz-john-kasich/.

North Dakota Caucus Results 2000–2016

2000

Democratic caucuses (3/7)		Republican caucuses (2/29)	
Delegates to national convention			
Gore	55.0	Bush	75.7
Uncommitted	36.0	McCain	18.9
Bradley	9.0	Keyes	5.3

2004

Democratic caucuses (2/3)		Republican caucuses (2/3)	
Kerry	50.8	**Delegates to national convention**	
Clark	23.7	Bush	100.0
Dean	11.7		
Edwards	9.2		
Kucinich	2.9		

2008

Democratic caucuses (2/5)		Republican caucuses (2/5)	
Obama	61.2	Romney	35.7
Clinton	36.6	McCain	22.8
Edwards	1.5	Paul	21.3
		Huckabee	19.9

2012

Democratic caucuses (6/5)		Republican caucuses (3/6)	
Delegates to national convention		Santorum	39.7
Uncommitted	18.5	Paul	28.1
Available	81.5	Romney	23.7
		Gingrich	8.5

2016

Democratic caucuses (6/7)		Republican caucuses/state convention (4/1–3)	
Sanders	60.9	Unpledged	100.0
Clinton	30.4		
Abstention	8.7		

Sources: https://www.thegreenpapers.com/PCC/Tabul.html;
http://www.thegreenpapers.com/P04/ND-D.phtml;
https://www.thegreenpapers.com/P04/ND-R.phtml;
http://www.thegreenpapers.com/P08/ND-D.phtml;
http://www.thegreenpapers.com/P08/ND-R.phtml;
https://web.archive.org/web/20120307200153/http://www.northdakotagop.org/caucus/
(archived web page of 2016 official results from ND GOP in 2012);
http://www.thegreenpapers.com/P16/ND-D.

2020 Delegate Selection

Democratic

Number of delegates: 18 total delegate votes—9 district, 3 at large, 2 pledged
PLEOs, 4 unpledged PLEOs

Date of 2020 contest: March 10

What week of the delegate selection season: 6

Type of delegate selection event: Open caucus/convention

Mode of awarding delegates: Proportional representation with a 15 percent threshold

How delegates are chosen: District delegates to the national convention are elected by the state convention in accordance with caucus results; at-large delegates and pledged PLEOs are elected by state party Select Committee on Delegates in accordance with caucus results

Bound for how many national conventions ballots: One

Source: https://www.thegreenpapers.com/P20/ND-D.

Republican

Number of delegates: 29 total delegates—26 at-large (10 base, 3 party, 13 bonus), 3 in 1 congressional district

Date of 2020 contest: April 3–5

What week of the delegate selection season: 10

Type of delegate selection event: Closed caucus/convention

Mode of awarding delegates: Delegate selection caucus

How delegates are chosen: The state committee presents a slate of delegate candidates to the state convention for election

Bound for how many national conventions ballots: None—all delegates are free to vote their conscience

Source: https://www.thegreenpapers.com/P20/ND-R.

—Andrew E. Busch and Jacob S. Leischner

Ohio

Ohio was the first American state carved from the Northwest Territory. It was settled by New Englanders in the northeast, Virginians in the south, and the Amish in the middle. These segregated communities created a split between southern- and northern-accented counties. After leaning Republican for decades, Ohio began to lean Democratic during the 1930s as it became the site of class warfare and strikes by industrial unions. However, Republicans such as Senator Robert Taft remained key figures. Since the New Deal, there have been two politically distinct parts of Ohio: the liberal northeast and the conservative southwest (Barone and McCutcheon 2014). Ohio prides itself on being one of the most important swing states in presidential elections. The state has not voted for a presidential loser since 1960; since 1912, no Republican has been elected to the White House without Ohio. In 2016, Donald Trump won Ohio by a surprisingly large margin of 51 to 43 percent by winning over a number of working-class counties that had backed Barack Obama in 2008 and 2012.

Ohio held its first presidential primary on May 21, 1912, and has held a primary election every four years since then. For the next four elections,

Ohio held its primary in late April, then from 1932 to 1992 it voted in early May, except in 1976, 1980, and 1992, when the primary was scheduled in early June. Recognizing that this late date frequently rendered the Ohio vote inconsequential in the nomination race, the state moved its primary to early or mid-March, where it has remained. Ohio law provides for semiopen primaries, meaning independents can vote in either party's primary.

Notable Ohio primaries have included:

1912: Theodore Roosevelt defeated William Taft in Taft's home state of Ohio by 16 percentage points in the Republican primary.

1972: In contrast to four years earlier, when Hubert Humphrey declined to campaign in most primaries, in 1972 Humphrey met the primary challenge head-on. In a showdown against anti–Vietnam War senator George McGovern, Humphrey won with 41 percent of the vote to George McGovern's 40 percent.

1976: In the Republican nomination fight, President Gerald Ford won an important victory against Ronald Reagan, 55 to 45 percent. On the Democratic side, Jimmy Carter crushed his nearest competitor, Morris Udall, by a 52 to 21 percent margin. Senator Frank Church of Idaho, who had made a serious run on Carter in the late primaries, ended with 14 percent. Carter's big win in this key state started a stampede of delegates and Democratic power brokers. Senator Henry Jackson and George Wallace, Carter's rivals for the Democratic nomination, released their delegates to Carter, putting him over the top (Brockell 2019).

1980: Jimmy Carter repeated his Ohio success, defeating Edward Kennedy 51–44 percent in a hard-fought primary held on the last day of Democratic primaries.

1984: Democratic senator Gary Hart of Colorado upset Walter Mondale 42–40 percent despite Mondale's strong labor support. Jesse Jackson finished third with 16 percent.

1996: Republican Bob Dole defeated conservative commentator Pat Buchanan by a 3–1 margin, mimicking his wins in Illinois, Michigan, and Wisconsin in the March 19 "Great Lakes Primary."

2000: George W. Bush won the Republican primary over John McCain, 58 percent to 37 percent. Ten other states held primaries the same day (March 7), and Bush won most of them, cementing his control of the GOP race.

2004: Democrat John Kerry decisively prevailed over John Edwards, 52 percent to 34 percent.

2008: Reversing his 2000 loss, John McCain beat Mike Huckabee in the GOP primary by nearly a 2–1 margin. At the same time, Hillary Clinton won a hard-fought 54–45 percent victory against Barack Obama. Clinton also won Texas, giving her a very good day in a race that went back and forth until June.

2012: In the 2012 Republican primary election, Mitt Romney won but only reached 38 percent of the vote and only won 58 percent of the state's delegates in the winner-take-most primary. Rick Santorum won 37 percent of the vote but failed to submit delegate slates in nine of Ohio's congressional districts, so he was unable to fully capitalize (Green Papers 2012).

2016: Aiming to maximize the state's power at the nominating convention, and to avoid the divisiveness of 2012, Ohio's Republican Party made the primary winner-take-all. This move was also expected to help Ohio governor and 2016 Republican presidential candidate John Kasich. Kasich indeed won, beating Donald Trump 47 to 36 percent. Kasich's win helped him remain in the race for two more months. In the Democratic primary, Hillary Clinton scored another big win, outpolling Bernie Sanders by a 56 to 43 percent margin. A controversy erupted prior to the election when Republican secretary of state Jon A. Husted announced that 17-year-olds who were turning 18 before the November election would be barred from participating in the 2016 primaries. His ruling was challenged in separate lawsuits from nine 17-year-olds and the Sanders campaign, and was ultimately overruled by state courts ("17-year-olds" 2016; Atkinson 2016).

Sources

Atkinson, Khorri. 2016. "Sanders Campaign Praises Ohio Ruling That Allows 17-Year-Olds to Vote." MSNBC, March 12. http://www.msnbc.com/msnbc /sanders-campaign-praises-ohio-ruling-allows-17-year-olds-vote.

Barone, Michael, and Chuck McCutcheon. 2014. *Almanac of American Politics 2014*. Washington, DC: National Journal.

Brockell, Lillian. 2019. "The Last Time the Democratic Field Was So Crowded, a Peanut Farmer Won the White House." *Washington Post*, May 3. https:// www.washingtonpost.com/history/2019/05/01/last-time-democratic -field-was-so-crowded-peanut-farmer-won-white-house/.

The Green Papers. 2012. "2012 Presidential Primaries, Caucuses, and Conventions: Ohio Republicans." http://www.thegreenpapers.com/P12/OH-R.

"17-Year-Olds Shut Out of Presidential Primary." 2016. *Columbus Dispatch*, March 5. https://www.dispatch.com/content/stories/local/2016/03/05/17 -year-olds-shut-out-of-presidential-primary.html.

Ohio Primary Results 2000–2016

2000

Democratic primary (3/7)		Republican primary (3/7)	
Gore	73.6	Bush	58.0
Bradley	24.7	McCain	37.0
LaRouche	1.7	Keyes	4.0

2004

Democratic primary (3/2)		Republican primary (3/2)	
Kerry	51.8	Bush	100.0
Edwards	34.1		
Kucinich	9.0		
Dean	2.5		
Lieberman	1.2		
Clark	1.0		

2008

Democratic primary (3/4)		Republican primary (3/4)	
Clinton	53.4	Romney	38.9
Obama	44.8	McCain	29.7
Edwards	1.7	Huckabee	16.1
		Paul	6.3
		Thompson	3.7

2012

Democratic primary (3/6)		Republican primary (3/6)	
Obama	100.0	Romney	38.0
		Santorum	37.0
		Gingrich	14.6
		Paul	9.3

2016

Democratic primary (3/15)		Republican primary (3/15)	
Clinton	56.1	Kasich	47.0
Sanders	43.1	Trump	35.9
		Cruz	13.3
		Rubio	2.3

Sources: Federal Election Commission:
https://transition.fec.gov/pubrec/fe2000/2000presprim.htm#top;
https://transition.fec.gov/pubrec/fe2004/federalelections2004.pdf;
https://transition.fec.gov/pubrec/fe2008/federalelections2008.pdf;

https://transition.fec.gov/pubrec/fe2012/2012pres.pdf;
https://transition.fec.gov/pubrec/fe2016/federalelections2016.pdf.

2020 Delegate Selection

Democratic

Number of delegates: 153 total delegate votes—89 district, 29 at-large, 18 pledged PLEOs, 17 unpledged PLEOs

Date of 2020 contest: March 17

What week of the delegate selection season: 7

Type of delegate selection event: Semiopen primary (D & I)

Mode of awarding delegates: Proportional representation with a 15 percent threshold.

How delegates are chosen: According to the results of the primary, district delegates are elected by congressional district caucuses, and at-large delegates and pledged PLEOs are elected by the state executive committee

Bound for how many national conventions ballots: One

Source: http://www.thegreenpapers.com/P20/OH-D.

Republican

Number of delegates: 82 total delegates—34 at-large (10 base, 3 party, 21 bonus), 48 in 16 congressional districts

Date of 2020 contest: March 17

What week of the delegate selection season: 7

Type of delegate selection event: Semiopen primary (R & I)

Mode of awarding delegates: Winner-Take-All on basis of statewide primary vote

How delegates are chosen: Presidential candidates approve slates of national convention delegates prior to the primary. The candidate who has the most votes statewide has his or her slate elected

Bound for how many national conventions ballots: One

Source: http://www.thegreenpapers.com/P20/OH-R.

—*Andrew E. Busch and Nandeeni K. Patel*

Oklahoma

Part agrarian prairie, part cowboy West, part Confederate South, and part Indian Territory, home to the tribes relocated by Andrew Jackson along the Trail of Tears (among others), Oklahoma is an eclectic state. Once nearly as reliably Democratic as the Solid South, Oklahoma is now one of the most reliably Republican states in the country. Lyndon Johnson in 1964 was the last Democratic presidential candidate to win the state. In 2016 Donald Trump won 65 percent of the general election vote, his third-highest percentage in the country.

Previously depending on a caucus-convention system, Oklahoma adopted a presidential primary for the first time in 1988 timed to coincide with Super Tuesday. Every Oklahoma primary but two have been held in the first half of March. In 2004 and 2008, at the height of front-loading mania, Oklahoma temporarily moved its presidential primary up a month to the first week of February.

In the caucus-convention era, Oklahoma delegations to the Democratic national convention backed Harry Truman in 1948, Lyndon Johnson in 1960, Hubert Humphrey in 1968, Henry Jackson in 1972, and Jimmy Carter in 1980. In 1984, the delegation was roughly split between Walter Mondale and Gary Hart. Republicans supported Dwight Eisenhower in 1952, Barry Goldwater in 1964, and Ronald Reagan in 1976.

Notable Oklahoma primaries have included:

1988: In the first Oklahoma primary, on a date shared with 15 other primary states, Democrat Al Gore defeated Jesse Jackson by 41 to 33 percent, with Michael Dukakis trailing at 20 percent. Republican George H. W. Bush edged out Bob Dole 37 to 35 percent, with televangelist Pat Robertson gaining 21 percent of the vote, one of his best primary showings of the year.

1992: Democrat Bill Clinton, hailing from neighboring Arkansas and fitting the mold of Oklahoma's moderate Democrats such as Senator David Boren, demolished his primary rivals with 71 percent of the vote. Altogether, Clinton won six of eight primaries that day, taking a big step toward his nomination.

2004: Former NATO commander General Wesley Clark (ret.) won a close Democratic primary with 29.9 percent of the vote to John Edwards's 29.5 percent and John Kerry's 26.8 percent. In the battle of expectations, Edwards needed Oklahoma and (barely) did not get it. Clark got it, but could not use it: Oklahoma was his only primary win of the year and he soon dropped out of the race.

2008: Republican John McCain defeated Mike Huckabee 37 to 33 percent in a state Huckabee thought he could win. At the same time, Hillary Clinton beat Barack Obama 55 percent to 31 percent.

2012: Republican primary winner Rick Santorum won with 34 percent; the tight race for second place was won by Mitt Romney over Newt Gingrich.

2016: In a reversal from eight years before, Bernie Sanders soundly (and surprisingly) defeated Hillary Clinton by 52 to 42 percent in the Democratic primary. Ted Cruz won over Donald Trump, with Marco Rubio nipping at

Trump's heels in third place. Cruz's win in Oklahoma and his neighboring home state of Texas kept him in the hunt.

Oklahoma Primary Results 2000–2016

2000

Democratic primary (3/14)		Republican primary (3/14)	
Gore	68.7	Bush	79.1
Bradley	25.4	McCain	10.4
LaRouche	5.4	Keyes	9.3

2004

Democratic primary (2/3)		Republican primary (2/3)	
Clark	29.9	Bush	90.0
Edwards	29.5	Wyatt	10.0
Kerry	26.8		
Lieberman	6.5		
Dean	4.2		
Sharpton	1.3		

2008

Democratic primary (2/5)		Republican primary (2/5)	
Clinton	54.8	McCain	36.6
Obama	31.2	Huckabee	33.4
Edwards	10.2	Romney	24.8
Richardson	1.7	Paul	3.3

2012

Democratic primary (3/6)		Republican primary (3/6)	
Obama	57.1	Santorum	33.8
Terry	18.0	Romney	28.1
Rogers	13.8	Gingrich	27.5
Richardson	6.4	Paul	9.6
Ely	4.7		

2016

Democratic primary (3/1)		Republican primary (3/1)	
Sanders	51.9	Cruz	34.4
Clinton	41.5	Trump	28.3
O'Malley	2.3	Rubio	26.0
Judd	1.3	Carson	6.2
Steinberg	1.2	Kasich	3.6
Locke	1.0		

Sources: Federal Election Commission:
https://transition.fec.gov/pubrec/fe2000/2000presprim.htm#OK;
https://transition.fec.gov/pubrec/fe2004/federalelections2004.pdf;
https://transition.fec.gov/pubrec/fe2008/federalelections2008.pdf;
https://transition.fec.gov/pubrec/fe2012/federalelections2012.pdf;
https://transition.fec.gov/pubrec/fe2016/federalelections2016.pdf.

2020 Delegate Selection

Democratic

Number of delegates: 42 total delegate votes—24 district, 8 at-large, 5 pledged PLEOs, 5 unpledged PLEOs

Date of 2020 contest: March 3

What week of the delegate selection season: 5

Type of delegate selection event: Semiopen primary (D & I)

Mode of awarding delegates: Proportional representation with 15 percent threshold

How delegates are chosen: Delegates to the national convention are elected by the state convention in accordance with the primary results

Bound for how many national conventions ballots: One

Source: http://www.thegreenpapers.com/P20/OK-D.

Republican

Number of delegates: 43 total delegates—28 at-large (10 base, 3 party, 15 bonus), 15 in 5 congressional districts

Date of 2020 contest: March 3

What week of the delegate selection season: 5

Type of delegate selection event: Closed primary

Mode of awarding delegates: Winner-take-most: District—If a candidate for president wins a majority of the district primary vote, or if only one candidate receives 15 percent or more of the vote, he or she receives all the district's delegates. Otherwise, if two candidates win at least 15 percent of the vote, the plurality winner receives two delegates, the runner-up one; if more than two candidates win at least 15 percent of the vote, the top three vote-getters each receive one delegate

At-large—If a candidate for president wins a majority of the statewide primary vote, he or she receives all the at-large delegates; if not, delegates are allocated proportionally on the basis of the statewide vote with a 15 percent threshold

How delegates are chosen: In accordance with primary results, district delegates to the national convention are elected by congressional district conventions and at-large delegates are elected by the state convention

Bound for how many national conventions ballots: All

Source: http://www.thegreenpapers.com/P20/OK-R.

—Andrew E. Busch

Oregon

A state known for its rugged Pacific coastline, pristine rainforests, earnest environmentalists, "hip" youth culture, and left-leaning urban hub of Portland, Oregon has long had a progressive tilt to its politics. Home to Democrats such as outspoken early Vietnam War critic Wayne Morse and liberal Republicans such as Robert Packwood and Mark Hatfield, Oregon has voted for the Democratic presidential candidate since 1988. While consistently producing a Democratic majority, Oregon is more closely divided than many blue states. In 2016, Hillary Clinton outpolled Donald Trump by 12 percentage points, matching Barack Obama's margin four years earlier. In 2004, though, John Kerry only beat George W. Bush by 4 percentage points, and in 2000 Al Gore's margin of victory was 50 percent to 47 percent.

Oregon was among the first states to adopt the presidential primary in 1912, and has held primaries in every presidential election year through 2016. After its 1912 primary, held on April 19, the Oregon primary has always been scheduled in mid to late May, with one exception—1996, when pressures for front-loading temporarily pushed it up to mid-March. Prior to heavy front-loading, the Oregon primary more frequently had an important impact on nomination races.

Some notable Oregon primaries have included:

1912: In Oregon's first primary, Democrat Woodrow Wilson won with 53 percent while Republican Theodore Roosevelt defeated Robert La Follette and William Howard Taft 40 to 31 to 29 percent.

1948: Republican Thomas Dewey, governor of New York, won a pivotal battle against Minnesota governor Harold Stassen, 52 percent to 48 percent.

Prior to the primary, Dewey and Stassen had engaged in the country's first live presidential debate on radio. The debate had a single issue: Should the Communist Party be banned? Stassen said yes, Dewey no. Dewey would go on to win the GOP nomination and lose the general election to Harry Truman in one of the most shocking political upsets in American history (Busch 2012).

1952: Dwight Eisenhower won the Republican primary 65 to 17 percent over California governor Earl Warren. Ike would later tap Warren to serve as Chief Justice of the United States Supreme Court.

1964: In the lead-up to the crucial California primary, liberal Republican governor Nelson Rockefeller of New York won the Oregon primary with 33 percent. His main rival, conservative senator Barry Goldwater of Arizona, came in third with 18 percent. In second was Henry Cabot Lodge, U.S. ambassador to South Vietnam, whose supporters were touting him although he was not in the country. To some observers, Goldwater's campaign was finished, but he came back to win California against Rockefeller and was also quietly collecting hundreds of committed delegates in the nonprimary states (White 1965, 117–121).

1968: In a showdown between anti-administration Democrats, Eugene McCarthy beat Robert Kennedy 44 to 38 percent. Kennedy would die in California one week later. It was the first time in 28 contested elections that a Kennedy had lost. Both candidates were politically suited for Oregon, but McCarthy's more laid-back style was a better fit. In addition, Kennedy alienated some voters by pointedly refusing to debate McCarthy (Nelson 2014, 102–103).

1972: On his way to the Democratic nomination, South Dakota senator George McGovern confirmed Oregon's leftward bent by beating George Wallace and Hubert Humphrey 50 percent to 20 percent to 13 percent.

1976: In the Republican primary, incumbent president Gerald Ford edged challenger Ronald Reagan by 50–46 percent, stalling Reagan's drive late in the race. Meanwhile, Democratic senator Frank Church of neighboring Idaho held off Jimmy Carter 33 to 27 percent, with California governor Edmund "Jerry" Brown coming in a close third with 25 percent.

1980: Four years later, the losers of the 1976 primaries came back to win important contests. Jimmy Carter, now fighting for his presidency against Edward Kennedy, defeated the challenger decisively, 57–31 percent. Republican Reagan outpolled his main rival, George H. W. Bush, by a 54–35 percent margin. Reagan's win in Oregon helped offset his loss in Michigan the same day, and the delegates Reagan won in the two states put him over the number needed to nominate.

1984: Colorado senator Gary Hart badly needed a victory as the Democratic primaries were nearing completion. He got one, defeating Walter Mondale 59–28 percent. It was not enough, though, and Mondale went on to win the nomination.

1992: Leading but with the race not yet wrapped up, Bill Clinton won the Oregon primary over Jerry Brown, 45 percent to 31 percent—16 years after Brown had last lost a key Oregon primary.

2008: Barack Obama beat Hillary Clinton by an overwhelming 3–2 margin, padding his lead going into the final stage of the Democratic race.

2016: Clinton's fortunes did not improve eight years later, as she lost Oregon again, this time to Bernie Sanders. The senator from Vermont, though not young and hip, won 56 to 42 percent, nearly the same margin Obama had won against Clinton in 2008.

Sources

Busch, Andrew E. 2012. *Truman's Triumphs: The Election of 1948 and the Making of Postwar America.* Lawrence: University Press of Kansas.

Nelson, Michael. 2014. *Resilient America: Electing Nixon in 1968, Channeling Dissent, and Dividing Government.* Lawrence: University Press of Kansas.

White, Theodore H. 1965. *The Making of the President 1964.* New York: Atheneum.

Oregon Primary Results 2000–2016

2000

Democratic primary (5/16)		Republican primary (5/16)	
Gore	84.9	Bush	83.6
LaRouche	10.9	Keyes	13.4

2004

Democratic primary (5/18)		Republican primary (5/18)	
Kerry	78.6	Bush	94.9
Kucinich	16.3	Misc.	5.0
LaRouche	2.3		

2008

Democratic primary (5/20)		Republican primary (5/20)	
Obama	58.5	McCain	80.9
Clinton	40.5	Paul	14.5

2012

Democratic primary (5/15)		Republican primary (5/15)	
Obama	94.8	Romney	70.9
		Paul	12.8
		Santorum	9.4
		Gingrich	5.4

2016

Democratic primary (5/17)		Republican primary (5/17)	
Sanders	56.2	Trump	64.2
Clinton	42.1	Cruz	16.6
		Kasich	15.8

Sources: Federal Election Commission:
https://transition.fec.gov/pubrec/fe2000/2000presprim.htm#OR;
https://transition.fec.gov/pubrec/fe2004/federalelections2004.pdf;
https://transition.fec.gov/pubrec/fe2008/federalelections2008.pdf;
https://transition.fec.gov/pubrec/fe2012/federalelections2012.pdf;
https://transition.fec.gov/pubrec/fe2016/federalelections2016.pdf.

2020

Democratic

Number of delegates: 66 total delegate votes—34 district, 11 at-large, 7 pledged PLEOs, 14 unpledged PLEOs

Date of 2020 contest: May 19

What week of the delegate selection season: 16

Type of delegate selection event: Closed primary

Mode of awarding delegates: Proportional representation with a 15 percent threshold

How delegates are chosen: In accordance with primary results, district delegates to the national convention are elected by congressional district conventions and at-large delegates and pledged PLEOs are elected by the state convention

Bound for how many national conventions ballots: One

Source: http://www.thegreenpapers.com/P20/OR-D.

Republican

Number of delegates: 28 total delegates—13 at-large (10 base, 3 party), 15 in 5 congressional districts

Date of 2020 contest: May 19

What week of the delegate selection season: 16

Type of delegate selection event: Closed primary

Mode of awarding delegates: Proportional representation

How delegates are chosen: In accordance with primary results, district delegates
    to the national convention are elected by congressional district conventions
    and at-large delegates are elected by the state convention

Bound for how many national conventions ballots: Two

Source: http://www.thegreenpapers.com/P20/OR-R.

—Andrew E. Busch

Pennsylvania

As one of the 13 original colonies, Pennsylvania quickly established itself as a center of government, commerce, and culture. In the 19th century, the state became an industrial hub due to its abundance of coal and other key natural resources. For generations after the Civil War, Pennsylvania was heavily Republican-leaning, both out of residual loyalty to the Union cause and for the sake of the steel industry, which was protected by Republican tariffs. In the New Deal, the political climate flipped. Pennsylvania was a crucial swing state from the 1950s to the 1990s. Starting in the 1990s, the affluent east and blue-collar west increasingly traded places politically, with the east trending Democratic and the west Republican (Cohen and Barnes 2018). The state voted for the Republican presidential candidate three times in the 1980s and voted, usually narrowly, for the Democratic candidate from 1992 to 2012, up until Donald Trump won in 2016. Trump's razor-thin margin of victory—48.17 percent to 47.46 percent—attests to Pennsylvania's ongoing status as a swing state.

Presidential primaries for both parties began in 1912 with victories for Theodore Roosevelt and Woodrow Wilson. Pennsylvania has held a presidential primary in every presidential election year since 1912. Starting in 1924, every Pennsylvania primary has been scheduled in April, usually in the third or fourth week of the month. Early Pennsylvania primaries were frequently dominated by favorite-son candidates or write-ins. Today, while all Democratic delegates and at-large Republican delegates are elected as part of a presidential preference primary, Republican delegates elected by congressional district are elected directly by name without any connection or pledge to a presidential candidate.

Pennsylvania has sometimes had an important impact on presidential nomination contests, including these cases:

1968: Eugene McCarthy won the Democratic primary decisively, with 72 percent of the vote, just three weeks after his win in Wisconsin. As write-in candidates, Robert Kennedy got 11 percent and Vice President Hubert Humphrey 9 percent. McCarthy and Kennedy would go on to trade primary victories in upcoming states while Humphrey collected a majority of delegates in the nonprimary states.

1972: Running a full-scale campaign this time, Hubert Humphrey won with 35 percent in a fractured Democratic field. George Wallace, George McGovern, and Edmund Muskie scrambled for second place with between 20 and 23 percent, and finished in that order.

1976: Jimmy Carter won an important Democratic primary victory with 37 percent to Washington senator Henry Jackson's 25 percent and Morris Udall's 19 percent. Jackson soon dropped out of the race. Before the Pennsylvania vote, Carter stirred controversy by declaring that neighborhoods should be able to maintain their "ethnic purity." Carter apologized, but some suspected he was making a not-so-subtle overture to racially intolerant George Wallace voters (Stroud 1977, 277–281).

1980: In the Republican primary, George H. W. Bush defeated Ronald Reagan by a margin of 51 to 43 percent, one of Bush's notable wins of the year. However, Reagan's campaign was too strong elsewhere, and Bush had to settle for the vice presidency, at least for eight years. The Democratic primary saw challenger Edward Kennedy edge President Jimmy Carter by a whisker, 45.7 percent to 45.4 percent. Like the New York primary a month earlier, Pennsylvania gave fresh energy to the Kennedy campaign, which many pundits had once again given up for dead (Busch 2005).

1984: Democrat Walter Mondale, enjoying the support of organized labor, beat Colorado senator Gary Hart 45–33 percent.

1992: Bill Clinton went on to win 56 percent of the vote in the Democratic primary. Jerry Brown won the second most votes while Paul Tsongas placed third.

2008: In a much anticipated primary, Hillary Clinton defeated Barack Obama by a margin of 55 to 45 percent. Though Obama held a narrow lead in the number of delegates, Clinton momentarily took hold of the narrative of the race, having won the big states of Ohio and Texas in addition to Pennsylvania. The importance of Pennsylvania despite its late-April date was a lesson to other states to move their primaries later in the schedule after 2008.

2016: Returning to the scene of her big 2008 win, Hillary Clinton won the Democratic primary against Bernie Sanders with 56 percent of the vote. In the Republican primary, Donald Trump won Pennsylvania 56 percent to 22 percent over Ted Cruz. On the same day, Trump won decisively in four other northeastern primaries. Trump's victory followed by one week his sweep of

New York, and set him up to deliver the coup d'grace against Cruz in the upcoming Indiana primary.

Sources

Busch, Andrew E. 2005. *Reagan's Victory: The Presidential Election of 1980 and the Rise of the Right.* Lawrence: University Press of Kansas.

Cohen, Richard, and James Barnes. 2018. *Almanac of American Politics.* Washington, DC: National Journal.

Kandy Stroud. 1977. *How Jimmy Won: The Victory Campaign from Plains to the White House.* New York: William Morrow.

Pennsylvania Primary Results 2000–2016

2000

Democratic primary (4/4)		Republican primary (4/4)	
Gore	74.2	Bush	72.5
Bradley	20.7	McCain	22.4
LaRouche	4.5	Forbes	2.5
		Bauer	1.4
		Keyes	1.1

2004

Democratic primary (4/27)		Republican primary (4/27)	
Kerry	74.2	Bush	100.0
Dean	10.1		
Edwards	9.7		
Kucinich	3.8		
LaRouche	2.2		

2008

Democratic primary (4/22)		Republican primary (4/22)	
Clinton	54.5	McCain	72.9
Obama	45.4	Paul	15.8
		Huckabee	11.3

2012

Democratic primary (4/24)		Republican primary (4/24)	
Obama	97.0	Romney	57.8
Uncommitted	3.0	Santorum	18.4
		Paul	13.1
		Gingrich	10.4

2016

Democratic primary (4/26)		Republican primary (4/26)	
Clinton	54.7	Trump	56.4
Sanders	42.8	Cruz	21.6
		Kasich	19.4

Sources: Federal Election Commission:
https://transition.fec.gov/pubrec/fe2000/2000presprim.htm;
https://transition.fec.gov/pubrec/fe2004/federalelections2004.pdf;
https://transition.fec.gov/pubrec/fe2008/federalelections2008.pdf;
https://transition.fec.gov/pubrec/fe2012/2012pres.pdf;
https://transition.fec.gov/pubrec/fe2016/federalelections2016.pdf.

2020 Delegate Selection

Democratic

Number of delegates: 177 total delegate votes—100 district, 33 at-large, 20 pledged PLEOs, 24 unpledged PLEOs

Date of 2020 contest: April 28

What week of the delegate selection season: 13

Type of delegate selection event: Closed primary

Mode of awarding delegates: Proportional representation with a 15 percent threshold

How delegates are chosen: District delegates to the national convention appear on the primary ballot and selections are made from the highest vote getters in accordance with the primary results; at-large delegates and pledged PLEOs are elected by the state committee

Bound for how many national conventions ballots: One

Source: http://www.thegreenpapers.com/P20/PA-D.

Republican

Number of delegates: 88 total delegates—34 at-large (10 base, 3 party, 21 bonus), 54 in 18 congressional districts

Date of 2020 contest: April 28

What week of the delegate selection season: 13

Type of delegate selection event: Closed primary

Mode of awarding delegates: At-large: statewide winner-take-all; district: direct delegate election without presidential preference

How delegates are chosen: District delegates are directly elected by voters in the district primaries; at-large delegates are elected by the state committee in accordance with the primary results

Bound for how many national conventions ballots: District delegates are unpledged and unbound; at-large delegates are bound for one ballot

Source: http://www.thegreenpapers.com/P20/PA-R.

—*Andrew E. Busch and Nandeeni K. Patel*

Rhode Island

The smallest state by square miles, Rhode Island long had a rebellious streak. Its promiscuous use of paper money in the 1780s was cited by some Founders as an example of abuses at the state level justifying establishment of the Constitution, and it was the only state not to send delegates to the federal convention of 1787. In the early 20th century it was heavily Catholic and heavily Democratic, and along with Massachusetts was one of only two states outside the Deep South to vote for Al Smith in the 1928 general election. For most of the subsequent century it has remained Democratic and gave Hillary Clinton a 15 percentage point advantage over Donald Trump in 2016. Rhode Island has not voted for a Republican candidate for president since Ronald Reagan in 1984.

Rhode Island began using presidential primaries in 1976, when Democrats gave a slight lead to unpledged delegates over Jimmy Carter and Frank Church. Gerald Ford ran away with the Republican primary by a 2–1 margin over Ronald Reagan. Before 1976, Rhode Island used caucus-convention procedures. Delegates to the Democratic national convention backed Al Smith in both 1928 and 1932, John F. Kennedy in 1960, Hubert Humphrey in 1968, and George McGovern in 1972. Republican delegations supported William Howard Taft in 1912, Dwight Eisenhower over Robert Taft in 1952, and William Scranton over Barry Goldwater in 1964.

The first two Rhode Island primaries were held in early June, then the primary was shifted to early March. In 2012 it was moved back to late April, voting with several other Northeastern states, where it stayed in 2016.

Key Rhode island primaries have included:

1980: Reaching the end of the primary schedule, Rhode Island gave Edward Kennedy a crushing 68–26 percent victory over Jimmy Carter in the Democratic primary. Kennedy's win in five of eight June 3 primaries contributed to suggestions that delegates be freed to vote their current preferences rather than be bound to outdated primary results from months before.

1984: Democrat Gary Hart scored a 45–35 percent win over Walter Mondale two weeks after Hart's New Hampshire win, adding to Hart's apparent momentum.

2000: Arizona senator John McCain outpolled Texas governor and eventual nominee George W. Bush 60 to 37 percent in the GOP primary in one of a handful of states McCain won that day.

2008: McCain again won handily, defeating Mike Huckabee by a 3–1 margin on his way to the nomination. Hillary Clinton also prevailed, defeating Barack Obama 58 to 40 percent.

2016: With both major party nominations still up for grabs, Donald Trump and Bernie Sanders scored major wins. Trump's 64–24 romp over John Kasich (with Ted Cruz trailing at 10 percent) was of a piece with his other Northeastern Republican primary wins that day, setting up a final showdown with Cruz in Indiana a week later. On the Democratic side, Sanders beat Clinton 55 to 43 percent, refusing to go away despite Clinton's large delegate lead.

Rhode Island Primary Results 2000–2016

2000

Democratic primary (3/7)		Republican primary (3/7)	
Gore	57.2	McCain	60.2
Bradley	40.6	Bush	36.5
Uncommitted	1.8	Keyes	2.6

2004

Democratic primary (3/2)		Republican primary (3/2)	
Kerry	71.2	Bush	84.9
Edwards	18.6	Uncommitted	12.4
Dean	4.0		
Kucinich	2.9		
Uncommitted	1.2		

2008

Democratic primary (3/4)		Republican primary (3/4)	
Clinton	58.4	McCain	64.8
Obama	40.4	Huckabee	21.7
		Paul	6.6
		Romney	4.4

2012

Democratic primary (4/24)		Republican primary (4/24)	
Obama	83.4	Romney	63.0
Uncommitted	14.0	Paul	23.9
		Gingrich	6.0
		Santorum	5.7

2016

Democratic primary (4/26)		Republican primary (4/26)	
Sanders	54.7	Trump	63.7
Clinton	43.1	Kasich	24.3
Uncommitted	1.4	Cruz	10.4

Sources: Guide to U.S. Elections, 7th ed., Vol. I;
Atlas of U.S. Presidential Elections,
www.uselectionatlas.org.

2020 Delegate Selection

Democratic

Number of delegates: 30 total delegate votes—14 district, 4 at large, 3 pledged
PLEOs, 9 unpledged PLEOs

Date of 2020 contest: April 28

What week of the delegate selection season: 13

Type of delegate selection event: Semiopen primary (D & I)

Mode of awarding delegates: Proportional representation with a 15 percent
threshold

How delegates are chosen: District delegates to the national convention appear
on the primary ballot and selections are made from the highest vote getters
in accordance with the primary results; at-large delegates and pledged
PLEOs are elected by the state committee.

Bound for how many national conventions ballots: One

Source: http://www.thegreenpapers.com/P20/RI-D.

Republican

Number of delegates: 19 total delegates—13 at-large (10 base, 3 party), 6 in 2 congressional districts

Date of 2020 contest: April 28

What week of the delegate selection season: 13

Type of delegate selection event: Semiopen primary (R & I)

Mode of awarding delegates: District: Winner-take-most: If only one candidate receives 10 percent or more of the district vote, he or she receives all three delegates; if two candidates receive 10 percent or more, the plurality winner receives two delegates and the runner-up one; if three or more candidates win 10 percent or more of the vote, the top three vote-getters each receive one delegate

At-large: Delegates are allocated proportionally based on the statewide primary vote with a 10 percent threshold

How delegates are chosen: Candidates for delegate to the national convention, along with their presidential preference, appear on the primary ballot. The highest vote-getters become delegates in accordance with the primary results.

Bound for how many national conventions ballots: One

Source: http://www.thegreenpapers.com/P20/RI-R.

—Andrew E. Busch

South Carolina

The Civil War began in South Carolina and ultimately devastated the state. Real economic recovery did not fully begin until after World War II. African Americans constituted 43 percent of the state's population in 1940, but this number fell to just 29 percent by 2008. After civil and voting rights legislation passed nationally, voter registration and turnout improved for minority populations in the state, leading even staunch South Carolina segregationists like Senator Strom Thurmond to begin hiring black staffers. Despite these shifts, the state's politics remain conservative, and South Carolina has not voted for a Democrat for president since Jimmy Carter in 1976. President Trump won the state in 2016 by a margin of 55 percent to 40 percent. The state elected its first African American senator, Republican Tim Scott, in a special 2014 election.

The South Carolina primary is most solidly rooted in the Republican Party. It held its first presidential primary in March 1980, an open primary allowing anyone to vote on the Republican candidates. Except for breaks in 1984, 2004, and 2020, when Republican presidents were running for renomination unopposed, Republicans have held a primary every year. Democrats did not hold a presidential primary until 1992, and then not again until 2004. Since 2008, both parties have held primaries early enough in the nominating season to be the second or third primary state. In recent years, the Democratic primary has typically been held one or two weeks after the Republican primary. In 2016, both parties gave South Carolina a privileged position along with Iowa, New Hampshire, and Nevada as one of four states permitted to conduct delegate selection prior to March 1.

Prior to primaries, South Carolina's Democratic delegations supported FDR in 1932, Georgia senator Richard Russell in 1948, Lyndon Johnson in 1960, Hubert Humphrey in 1968, and Jimmy Carter in both 1976 and 1980. In the chaotic postreform year of 1972, Democrats were split into left (McGovern won a small plurality of 10 delegates), center (Henry Jackson and Terry Sanford combined for 15 delegates), and hard right (George Wallace finished with 6 delegates). Republican delegations supported Barry Goldwater and Ronald Reagan.

As the South became increasingly important to Republican fortunes, the South Carolina primary grew to serve as a crucial gateway to the South in the Republican nomination contest. Its early date has also frequently provided an opportunity for candidates to regain their footing after a surprising loss in New Hampshire. Altogether, South Carolina has arguably established itself as the third most important early contest in the country, at least in the GOP, a position enshrined in state Republican Party rules that require the Republican primary to be held no more than two weeks after New Hampshire in order to preserve South Carolina's "first in the South" status.

Significant primary races have included:

1980: Ronald Reagan won the state's first Republican primary contest with 55 percent of the vote, beating the rest of the field by a wide margin. Texas governor John Connally came in second with 30 percent, and George H. W. Bush finished a distant third with 15 percent. Reagan's win decidedly increased his chances of winning the nomination—he had won New Hampshire, but Bush had won Iowa. Connally had pinned his hopes on the Palmetto State, and he dropped out after losing (Busch 2005).

1988: In the Republican primary, Vice President George H. W. Bush's big victory over Bob Dole and Pat Robertson, 49 percent to 21 percent to 19 percent, presaged his decisive sweep of the South four days later on Super Tuesday.

1992: Four years later, President Bush's convincing victory over Patrick Buchanan, 67 percent to 26 percent, undermined the upstart candidate's claim to Southern support and marked a key turning point in the Republican contest (Barone and McCutcheon 2014, 1328).

1996: Bob Dole cemented his front-runner status by beating Pat Buchanan, 45 percent to 33 percent. Buchanan had pulled off an upset in New Hampshire, but Dole regained control of the race in South Carolina (The State).

2000: During the Republican primary campaign, Senator John McCain spoke out against the South Carolina flag and its Confederate design, calling it "a symbol of racism and slavery," but then seemingly reversed his views the next day and called it a "symbol of heritage." George W. Bush won the contest 59 percent to 41 percent, giving the Texas governor a much-needed victory after his loss to McCain in New Hampshire. After his defeat, McCain returned to his initial position condemning the flag, and he apologized for not calling for its removal from the statehouse. The episode damaged the candidate's reputation as a maverick and a truth-teller unconcerned with political self-interest (Holmes 2000).

2008: Senator Barack Obama bounced back from a loss to Hillary Clinton in New Hampshire with a resounding win in the South Carolina primary, 55 percent to 27 percent. North Carolina senator John Edwards, born in South Carolina, finished a distant third with 18 percent of the vote. Over half of Democratic voters were African American, and Obama won 80 percent of them, a key factor in his victory (Zeleny and Connelly 2008). On the Republican side, John McCain managed to put the ghosts of the 2000 South Carolina primary to rest by narrowly prevailing over Mike Huckabee, 33 percent to 30 percent (Cooper and Thee 2008). Huckabee's loss was particularly damaging to his viability because it occurred in a Southern state with a high proportion of evangelical voters.

2012: Republican Newt Gingrich defeated Mitt Romney, indicating that the South would be contested and Romney's road to the nomination would not be an easy one.

2016: Advisers to Marco Rubio outlined the candidate's "3-2-1" plan, wherein Rubio aimed to place third in Iowa, the first contest; second in New Hampshire; and then win the South Carolina primary. While Rubio did indeed finish third in Iowa behind Ted Cruz and Donald Trump, he placed fifth in New Hampshire and second in South Carolina to Trump. What began as a come-from-behind plan to catapult Rubio into front-runner status by the South Carolina primary instead marked an embarrassing missed prediction that did not bode well for the candidate (Alberta 2016). At the same time, Cruz's narrow third-place finish in South Carolina prevented him from consolidating his position as the main alternative to Trump. On the Democratic side, Hillary Clinton bounced back from her 2008 loss in the state to Barack Obama as well as her lopsided defeat to Senator Bernie Sanders in the New Hampshire primary. Clinton won 8 out of every 10 African American voters, boosting her to a wide margin of victory in both the vote and the delegate count (Phillip, Wagner, and Gearan 2016).

Sources

Alberta, Tim. 2016. "Rubio's Team Plots Path to Nomination: Third in Iowa, Second in N.H., First in S.C." *National Review.* https://www.nationalreview.com/2016/01/marco-rubios-south-carolina-strategy/.

Barone, Michael, and Chuck McCutcheon. 2014. *Almanac of American Politics.* Washington, DC: National Journal.

Busch, Andrew E. 2005. *Reagan's Victory: The 1980 Election and the Rise of the Right.* Lawrence: University Press of Kansas, 2005.

Cooper, Michael, and Megan Thee. 2008. "McCain Victory in South Carolina Caps Comeback." *New York Times,* January 20. https://www.nytimes.com /2008/01/20/us/politics/20carolina.html.

Holmes, Steven. 2000. "After Campaigning on Candor, McCain Admits He Lacked It on Confederate Flag Issue." *New York Times.* https://www.nytimes.com /2000/04/20/us/after-campaigning-on-candor-mccain-admits-he-lacked -it-on-confederate-flag-issue.html.

Phillip, Abby, John Wagner, and Anne Gearan. 2016. "Hillary Clinton Easily Defeats Bernie Sanders in South Carolina Primary." *Washington Post.* https://www.washingtonpost.com/politics/hillary-clinton-easily-defeats -bernie-sanders-in-south-carolina-primary/2016/02/27/6e9787fe-dd18 -11e5-891a-4ed04f4213e8_story.html.

The State. "A Quick History: The S.C. GOP Primary." https://www.thestate.com /news/politics-government/politics-columns-blogs/the-buzz/article 60570956.html.

Zeleny, Jeff, and Marjory Connelly. 2008. "Obama Carries South Carolina by Wide Margin." *New York Times,* January 27. https://www.nytimes.com /2008/01/27/us/politics/27carolina.html.

South Carolina Primary Results 2000–2016

2000

Democratic caucuses (3/9)		Republican primary (2/19)	
Gore	91.8	Bush	53.4
Uncommitted	5.3	McCain	41.9
Bradley	1.8	Keyes	4.5
Kreml	1.1		

2004

Democratic primary (2/3)		Republican primary	
Edwards	45.2	No Republican primary	
Kerry	29.8	National Convention delegates	
Sharpton	9.7	Bush	100.0
Clark	7.2		
Dean	4.8		
Lieberman	2.4		

2008

Democratic primary (1/26)		Republican primary (1/19)	
Obama	55.4	McCain	33.2
Clinton	26.5	Huckabee	29.8
Edwards	17.6	Thompson	15.6
		Romney	15.3
		Paul	3.6
		Giuliani	2.1

2012

Democratic primary (1/28)		Republican primary (1/21)	
Obama	100.0	Gingrich	40.4
		Romney	27.9
		Santorum	17.0
		Paul	13.0
		Cain	1.1

2016

Democratic primary (2/27)		Republican primary (2/20)	
Clinton	73.4	Trump	32.5
Sanders	26.0	Rubio	22.5
		Cruz	22.3
		Bush	7.8
		Kasich	7.6
		Carson	7.2

Sources: Federal Election Commission:
https://transition.fec.gov/pubrec/fe2000/2000presprim.htm;
https://transition.fec.gov/pubrec/fe2004/federalelections2004.pdf;
https://transition.fec.gov/pubrec/fe2008/federalelections2008.pdf;
https://transition.fec.gov/pubrec/fe2012/2012pres.pdf;
https://transition.fec.gov/pubrec/fe2016/federalelections2016.pdf.

2020 Delegate Selection

Democratic

Number of delegates: 63 total delegate votes—35 district, 12 at-large, 7 pledged
PLEOs, 9 unpledged PLEOs

Date of 2020 contest: February 29

What week of the delegate selection season: 4

Type of delegate selection event: Open primary

Mode of awarding delegates: Proportional representation with a 15 percent threshold

How delegates are chosen: Delegates to the national convention are elected by the state convention in accordance with the primary results

Bound for how many national conventions ballots: One

Source: https://www.thegreenpapers.com/P20/SC-D.

Republican

Number of delegates: 50 total delegates—29 at-large (10 base, 3 party, 16 bonus), 21 in 7 congressional districts

Date of 2020 contest: April TBD; May 2

What week of the delegate selection season: TBD; 13

Type of delegate selection event: Conventions

Mode of awarding delegates: Congressional district delegates will be elected by district conventions in April; at-large delegates will be elected by the state convention on May 2

How delegates are chosen: Congressional district delegates will be elected by district conventions in April; at-large delegates will be elected by the state convention on May 2

Bound for how many national conventions ballots: One

Source: http://www.thegreenpapers.com/P20/SC-R; South Carolina Republican Party.

—Andrew E. Busch and
Richard C. Wiltshire-Gordon

South Dakota

South Dakota, known for its windswept plains, its bison, and Mt. Rushmore, has been a Republican stronghold for presidential elections ranging back to its inception. Since gaining statehood in 1889 South Dakota has only voted for the Democratic nominee four times, most recently in 1968. The Midwesterners who came to South Dakota early and began to settle the territory brought their Republican ideals with them and catalyzed the tradition (Barone and McCutcheon 2014). In 2016, Donald Trump outpolled Hillary Clinton by a margin of 62 to 32 percent.

Like its namesake to the north, South Dakota got an early start in the presidential primary business, holding its first primary in 1912 (won by Theodore Roosevelt and Woodrow Wilson). Both parties have held primaries ever since, except on a handful of occasions when one party dispensed with its primary because an incumbent president was seeking renomination without opposition—Republicans in 1984 and 2004, Democrats in 1996 and 2012, plus Democrats in 2000 when Vice President Al Gore was treated like an incumbent. Historically, South Dakota's primary was held in May or June until 1988, when lawmakers moved the primary to one week after New Hampshire in a bid to increase the state's influence. After three election cycles, South Dakota moved its primary back to early June, where it has remained from 2000 through 2016.

Some key South Dakota primaries have included:

1952: In a prairie showdown, Ohio senator Robert Taft defeated Dwight Eisenhower 50.3 to 49.7 percent, a fitting launch into a hotly contested Republican national convention (ultimately won by Eisenhower).

1968: As one of only 17 states to host a Democratic primary that year, South Dakota was an important battleground between Robert F. Kennedy and Eugene McCarthy, both of whom were challenging the incumbent Johnson administration (represented by then-Vice President Hubert Humphrey). Kennedy won with 50 percent to McCarthy's 20 percent; Lyndon Johnson also received 30 percent, though he was no longer running. South Dakota was one of four primaries that Kennedy won in 1968. South Dakota's primary was held on the last day of primaries (June 4) along with New Jersey and California. McCarthy won New Jersey, Kennedy California. Celebrating his victories in California, Kennedy was assassinated. Subsequently, South Dakota delegates rallied support for home state senator George McGovern and gave him 24 of 26 delegates at the national convention.

1976: In the epic Ford-Reagan Republican nomination contest, Ronald Reagan beat incumbent president Gerald Ford 51–44 percent. Jimmy Carter strengthened his hold on the Democratic nomination, defeating Morris Udall 41 to 33 percent.

1980: Returning to the scene of his brother's 1968 triumph, Edward Kennedy's slate of delegates defeated Jimmy Carter's slate 48.6 percent to 45.4 percent. Kennedy's South Dakota victory gave Kennedy five wins in eight states holding primaries that day, once again the last day of Democratic primaries, slowing Carter's drive to the nomination.

1984: Democrat Gary Hart beat front-runner Walter Mondale 51–39 percent.

1988: A week after his loss in New Hampshire, Republican Bob Dole put himself back in the chase, at least for a while, by convincingly beating rivals Pat Robertson and George H. W. Bush, 55 to 20 to 19 percent. On the Democratic side, Missouri representative Richard Gephardt defeated Massachusetts governor Mike Dukakis 44 percent to 31 percent, showing continuing Midwestern strength after his own loss to Dukakis in New Hampshire.

1992: Democratic senator Bob Kerrey of neighboring Nebraska beat Tom Harkin of Iowa 40 to 25 percent, with Bill Clinton trailing at 19 percent. Held a week after New Hampshire, South Dakota gave Kerrey a crucial but short-lived boost. He and Harkin were both soon gone from the race. Clinton survived and gained strength, winning the nomination.

1996: For the second time in eight years, Bob Dole took advantage of the South Dakota primary to recover lost ground after a New Hampshire defeat, beating Pat Buchanan 45 to 29 percent. This time, Dole sustained his recovery and went on to win the Republican nomination.

2008: Battling to the end of the primary season, Hillary Clinton defeated Barack Obama 55 to 45 percent. The win proved hollow, however, as Obama gained enough delegates that day in South Dakota, Montana, and among superdelegates to assure convention victory.

2016: Eight years later, Clinton again defeated an insurgent, by the smaller margin of 51 to 49 percent over Bernie Sanders. Clinton had been declared the presumptive nominee the day before. Voting results showed a deep geographical split, with the state's eastern half backing Clinton and its western counties supporting Sanders.

Source

Barone, Michael, and Chuck McCutcheon. 2014. *Almanac of American Politics.* Washington, DC: National Journal.

South Dakota Primary Results 2000–2016

2000

Democratic primary		Republican primary (6/6)	
No primary; Al Gore was the only candidate that qualified to appear on the ballot		Bush	78.2
		McCain	13.8
Delegates to national convention		Keyes	7.7
Gore	68.0		
Uncommitted	32.0		

2004

Democratic primary (6/1)		Republican primary	
Kerry	82.3	*No primary; Bush was unopposed*	
Uncommitted	6.1	**Delegates to national convention**	
Dean	5.7	Bush	88.9
LaRouche	3.5	Uncommitted	11.1
Kucinich	2.4		

2008

Democratic primary (6/3)		Republican primary (6/3)	
Clinton	55.4	McCain	70.2
Obama	44.7	Paul	16.5
		Huckabee	7.1
		Romney	3.3
		Uncommitted	2.9

2012

Democratic primary		Republican primary (6/5)	
No primary		Romney	66.2
Obama was unopposed		Paul	13.0
Delegates to national convention		Santorum	11.4
Obama	90.3	Uncommitted	5.4
Uncommitted	9.7	Gingrich	3.9

2016

Democratic primary (6/7)		Republican primary (6/7)	
Clinton	51.0	Trump	67.1
Sanders	49.0	Cruz	17.0
		Kasich	15.9

Sources: The Green Papers: https://www.thegreenpapers.com/PCC/Tabul.html; https://www.thegreenpapers.com/P04/SD-R.phtml; http://www.thegreenpapers.com/P12/SC-D; Federal Election Commission: https://transition.fec.gov/pubrec/fe2000/2000presprim.htm#SD; https://transition.fec.gov/pubrec/fe2004/federalelections2004.pdf; https://transition.fec.gov/pubrec/fe2008/federalelections2008.pdf;

https://transition.fec.gov/pubrec/fe2012/federalelections2012.pdf;
https://transition.fec.gov/pubrec/fe2016/federalelections2016.pdf.

2020 Delegate Selection

Democratic

Number of delegates: 19 total delegate votes—9 district, 3 at-large, 2 pledged PLEOs, 5 unpledged PLEOs

Date of 2020 contest: June 2

What week of the delegate selection season: 18

Type of delegate selection event: Semiopen primary (D & I)

Mode of awarding delegates: Proportional representation with a 15 percent threshold

How delegates are chosen: District delegates to the national convention are slated by congressional district conventions prior to the primary and are elected according to the primary results; at-large delegates and pledged PLEOs are elected by the state convention and state committee according to the state-wide primary results

Bound for how many national conventions ballots: One

Source: https://www.thegreenpapers.com/P20/SD-D.

Republican

Number of delegates: 29 total delegates—26 at-large (10 base, 3 party, 13 bonus), 3 in 1 congressional district

Date of 2020 contest: June 2

What week of the delegate selection season: 18

Type of delegate selection event: Closed primary

Mode of awarding delegates: Winner-take-all primary based on the statewide primary vote

How delegates are chosen. National convention delegates are elected by the state national delegate selection meeting prior to the primary and are bound to the winner

Bound for how many national conventions ballots: One

Source: https://www.thegreenpapers.com/P20/SD-R.

—*Andrew E. Busch and Jacob S. Leischner*

Tennessee

Tennessee's political history begins with Andrew Jackson, who served as the state's first congressman, representing a large Scots-Irish population. The state featured liberal Democrats like Senators Albert Gore Sr. and Estes

Kefauver in the mid-20th century, but later transitioned to a more centrist political orientation with Senators Al Gore Jr. and Jim Sasser. As of 2019, the state is strongly Republican, with seven of the nine House seats held by Republicans along with both Senate seats, though with a strong representation of moderate Republicans. Tennessee has voted Republican in every presidential election since 2000, when Al Gore's loss in his home state sealed his fate. Donald Trump scored an impressive victory in 2016, defeating Hillary Clinton by 61 percent to 35 percent.

Tennessee has held a presidential primary every election year since 1972. In that first Democratic primary contest, Governor George Wallace won the state with 68 percent of the vote to Hubert Humphrey's 16 percent and George McGovern's 7 percent. Wallace was shot just two weeks after Tennessee's primary, with the wounds eventually forcing him out of the race and leaving him paralyzed from the waist down. Tennessee's primary was held in May every election from 1972 until 1988, when the primary was moved to March (with exceptions in 2004 and 2008, when the primary was held in February). Though initially May was a more advantageous month to hold the primary because many races had still not been decided, as other states moved their elections earlier and earlier, Tennessee's importance to the nomination process waned. By pushing up its primary date to Super Tuesday, Tennessee has regained some clout in the process.

Prior to the advent of primaries, Tennessee's Democratic delegates threw their support to Franklin Roosevelt in 1932, Richard Russell in 1948, Lyndon Johnson in 1960, and Hubert Humphrey in 1968; Republicans backed Robert Taft in 1952 and Barry Goldwater in 1964.

Notable Tennessee primaries have included:

1976: Having completely supplanted George Wallace as the candidate of the South, Democrat Jimmy Carter dominated with 78 percent. Republican president Gerald Ford escaped with a 49.8 to 49.1 percent win against Ronald Reagan two weeks before the end of the primary season, a result indicative of the close national contest between the two.

1980: In the home stretch of their respective nomination races, Jimmy Carter and Ronald Reagan scored nearly identical lopsided victories over their rivals. Carter dispatched Edward Kennedy 75 to 18 percent, while Reagan beat George H. W. Bush 74 to 18 percent.

1984: Walter Mondale won a solid victory against Colorado senator Gary Hart in the Democratic primary, 41 to 29 percent.

1988: Scheduled as part of Super Tuesday, the Tennessee primary featured a 60–22 percent romp by Republican George H. W. Bush against Kansas senator Bob Dole, consistent with Bush wins around the country. On the Democratic side, Senator Al Gore won his home state primary with 72 percent of the vote. Although Super Tuesday was designed by its advocates with candidates like Gore in mind, he could only split the day's winnings with Jesse Jackson and Massachusetts governor Michael Dukakis.

1992: Bill Clinton beat Paul Tsongas 67 percent to 19 percent in the Democratic primary, held on Super Tuesday.

2004: John Kerry won the Democratic primary with 41 percent to John Edwards's 27 percent, part of Kerry's Super Tuesday Southern victory against the North Carolinian.

2008: Mike Huckabee narrowly defeated John McCain in a race that was initially too close to call. The race was an important symbolic victory for Huckabee's struggling campaign, but Huckabee only received six more delegates than McCain, not enough to significantly help him given McCain's delegate advantage (McCain had 689 delegates to Huckabee's 156) ("Primary Results" 2008). On the Democratic side, Hillary Clinton beat Barack Obama 54–40 percent.

2012: Republican Rick Santorum won a tough three-way-race with 37 percent to Mitt Romney's 28 percent and Newt Gingrich's 24 percent. Romney went on to win the nomination anyway, but Santorum remained his closest competitor throughout the primary season.

2016: Donald Trump won Tennessee by a wide margin as part of a larger Super Tuesday rout. Established Tennessee GOP leaders, such as Governor Bill Haslam and Senator Lamar Alexander, threw their support behind Senator Marco Rubio in the week before the election, but excitement about Trump drove record turnout and led to a double-digit victory (Garrison 2016). Rubio finished third, with Ted Cruz in second. On the Democratic side, in another race that was very much alive, Hillary Clinton doubled Bernie Sanders's vote totals. The South would continue being Clinton's strongest region throughout the Democratic primaries.

Sources

Garrison, Joey. 2016. "Donald Trump Wins Tennessee Republican Primary." *The Tennessean*, March 1. https://www.tennessean.com/story/news/politics/2016/03/01/tennessee-republican-primary-super-tuesday/81109798/.

"Primary Results." 2008. *New York Times*, September 22. https://web.archive.org/web/20080916170904/http://politics.nytimes.com/election-guide/2008/results/gopdelegates/index.html.

Tennessee Primary Election Results 2000–2016

2000

Democratic primary (3/14)		Republican primary (3/14)	
Gore	92.1	Bush	77.0
Bradley	5.3	McCain	14.5
		Keyes	6.7

2004

Democratic primary (2/10)		Republican primary (2/10)	
Kerry	41.0	Bush	95.5
Edwards	26.5	Uncommitted	4.5
Clark	23.1		
Dean	4.4		
Sharpton	1.7		

2008

Democratic primary (2/8)		Republican primary (2/8)	
Clinton	53.8	Huckabee	34.5
Obama	40.5	McCain	31.8
Edwards	4.5	Romney	23.6
		Paul	5.6
		Thompson	2.9

2012

Democratic primary (3/6)		Republican primary (3/6)	
Obama	88.5	Santorum	37.1
Uncommitted	11.5	Romney	28.1
		Gingrich	24.0
		Paul	9.0

2016

Democratic primary (3/1)		Republican primary (3/1)	
Clinton	66.1	Trump	38.9
Sanders	32.5	Cruz	24.7
		Rubio	21.2
		Carson	7.6
		Kasich	5.3
		Bush	1.1

Sources: https://www.thegreenpapers.com/P04/TN-R.phtml;
Federal Election Commission: https://transition.fec.gov/pubrec
/fe2000/2000presprim.htm#top;

https://transition.fec.gov/pubrec/fe2004/federalelections2004.pdf;
https://transition.fec.gov/pubrec/fe2008/federalelections2008.pdf;
https://transition.fec.gov/pubrec/fe2012/2012pres.pdf;
https://transition.fec.gov/pubrec/fe2016/federalelections2016.pdf.

2020 Delegate Selection

Democratic

Number of delegates: 73 total delegate votes—42 district, 14 at-large, 8 pledged PLEOs, 9 unpledged PLEOs

Date of 2020 contest: March 3

What week of the delegate selection season: 5

Type of delegate selection event: Open primary

Mode of awarding delegates: Proportional representation with a 15 percent threshold

How delegates are chosen: In accordance with the primary results, district delegates to the national convention are elected by congressional district conventions and at-large delegates and pledged PLEOs are elected by the state executive committee

Bound for how many national conventions ballots: One

Source: http://www.thegreenpapers.com/P20/TN-D.

Republican

Number of delegates: 58 total delegates—29 at-large (10 base, 3 party, 18 bonus), 27 in 9 congressional districts

Date of 2020 contest: March 3

What week of the delegate selection season: 5

Type of delegate selection event: Open primary

Mode of awarding delegates: Winner-Take-Most: District—If a candidate for president wins two-thirds of the district primary vote or if only one candidate wins at least 20 percent of the district vote, he or she will receive all the district's delegates to the national convention; if more than one candidate wins 20 percent of the vote and no one wins at least two-thirds, the plurality winner will receive two delegates and the runner-up one delegate

At-large: If one candidate for presidents wins two-thirds of the statewide primary vote or if only one candidate wins 20 percent of the statewide vote, he or she will receive all the at-large delegates to the national convention; if more than one candidate wins 20 percent of the vote, at-large delegates will be allocated proportionally with a 20 percent threshold

How delegates are chosen: District delegates appear on the primary ballot and are directly elected by primary voters according with the primary results; of the at-large delegates, half are elected directly in accordance with the primary vote and half are appointed by the state executive committee

Bound for how many national conventions ballots: Two

Source: http://www.thegreenpapers.com/P20/TN-R.

—*Andrew E. Busch and Richard C. Wiltshire-Gordon*

Texas

Among states, Texas is the second largest (to Alaska) and second-most populous (to California). Texas sits at the crossroads of the Old South, Old West, and Spanish Southwest, and has developed an independent culture exemplified by the Alamo and the phrase "Don't Mess with Texas." The Lone Star State is conservative but with a rapidly growing Hispanic population. Once home to Democratic leaders such as Sam Rayburn, Lyndon Johnson, and Jim Wright, Texas has been solidly Republican at the presidential level since the 1980s; the last Democratic presidential candidate to win Texas was Jimmy Carter, who narrowly beat Gerald Ford there in 1976. In 2016, Donald Trump won Texas by nearly 10 percentage points; in 2012 Mitt Romney outpolled Barack Obama 57 to 41 percent.

The first Texas primary was held in 1964, when Republicans established a primary in hopes of boosting Barry Goldwater's nomination chances; true to expectation, Goldwater won with 75 percent of the vote. The next Texas primary was for delegate selection separate from presidential preference in 1976. Since 1980, Texas has held a presidential preference primary. The first two were held in early May, the 2012 primary in late May, and the rest in the first half of March.

In years when Texas was not holding a primary, delegates were selected by caucus-convention procedures; until it was banned by party rules in 1968, Democrats typically used the unit rule at the national convention. Prior to the introduction of the primary in Texas, the state's Republican delegation played an important role in Dwight Eisenhower's convention win in 1952, when a credentials dispute between Eisenhower and Taft forces in Texas, Georgia, and Louisiana was resolved in favor of Ike, leading to a stampede that led to his nomination. In 1968, Texas Democrats backed Hubert Humphrey at the contentious national convention. In 1932, 1940, and 1960, they gave their convention votes to home state contenders John Nance Garner and Lyndon Johnson.

From 1976 to 2008, Texas Democrats held both a primary and caucuses later that day. Primary results determined 75 percent of Texas's delegates—those elected at the district level—while caucuses determined the other 25 percent who were at-large. Only those who voted in the primary were eligible to participate in the caucuses, but caucus turnout was generally smaller.

Results often differed substantially between the two modes. In 2012, when Barack Obama was seeking renomination unopposed, Texas Democrats selected all delegates through the caucus process, leaving only an advisory primary. After 2012, the Democratic National Committee Rules and Bylaws Committee declared that the "Texas Two-Step," as the primary-caucus combo was known, was too confusing to voters. State Democrats abandoned the caucus element and in 2016 held a straightforward primary. At the same time, Texas Republicans had hoped in 2016 to institute their own version of the Two-Step, with most delegates elected in a primary and the rest by the state convention, but national Republicans said no ("Texas Democrats" 2016; Mutnick 2015).

Notable Texas primaries have included:

1976: In a major campaign showdown, Republican challenger Ronald Reagan swamped incumbent president Gerald Ford by a 2–1 margin, winning in all 24 congressional districts with the help of Democratic crossover votes. Overall, the Texas Republican primary yielded a 100–0 delegation in favor of Ronald Reagan. Jimmy Carter prevailed in the Democratic primary, outpolling Texas favorite son Sen. Lloyd Bentsen 48 to 22 percent. The Democratic delegation produced 124 first ballot votes for Jimmy Carter at the national convention out of 130 delegates (Texas Almanac).

1980: Democratic president Jimmy Carter walloped challenger Edward Kennedy 56 to 23 percent. At the same time, Ronald Reagan won the pivotal Republican primary with 51 percent to George H. W. Bush's 47 percent, depriving the Texan Bush of a much-needed win along the homestretch of the nomination race.

1988: After eight years as Ronald Reagan's vice president, George H. W. Bush won his home state's Super Tuesday primary decisively over Pat Robertson and Bob Dole, with nearly two-thirds of the vote to Robertson's 15 percent and Dole's 14 percent. Michael Dukakis won the Democratic primary, with 33 percent to Jesse Jackson's 25 percent. Al Gore, the sort of Southern moderate for whom Super Tuesday was designed, came in third with 20 percent. However, Jackson won the caucuses held the same day.

1992: Bill Clinton won a delegate-rich victory with two-thirds of the Texas primary vote.

2008: In a battle between two Texas neighbors, Arizona's John McCain won the Republican primary with a solid 51 percent to Arkansas's Mike Huckabee with 38 percent. Democrat Hillary Clinton also finished with 51 percent in the primary to Barack Obama's 47 percent. Clinton badly needed the win, and got it by running an advertisement asking voters if Obama was prepared to get an emergency phone call at 3 a.m. in the White House. Clinton's victory was blunted, though, when Obama won the caucuses later that day by a lopsided margin, winning 57 percent of the at-large and pledged PLEO national convention delegates (The Green Papers 2008). As a result, Obama ended the night with more Texas delegates than Clinton (Ceaser, Busch, and Pitney 2009).

2016: Home state senator Ted Cruz won an important victory over Donald Trump, 44 percent to 27 percent, keeping him in the Republican race for another two months. On the Democratic side, Hillary Clinton won two-thirds of the vote against Bernie Sanders of Vermont.

Sources

Ceaser, James W., Andrew E. Busch, and John J. Pitney Jr. 2009. *Epic Journey: The 2008 Elections and American Politics.* Lanham, MD: Rowman & Littlefield.

The Green Papers. 2008. "2008 Presidential Primaries, Caucuses, and Conventions." https://www.thegreenpapers.com/P08/TX-D.phtml.

Mutnick, Ally. 2015. "Texplainer: What's the 'Texas Two-Step' and Why Is It Gone?" *Texas Tribune*, July 7. https://www.texastribune.org/2015/07/07/texplainer-whats-texas-two-step-and-why-it-gone/.

Texas Almanac. *Presidential Primaries 1976–2016.* https://texasalmanac.com/topics/elections/presidential-primaries-1976-%E2%80%93-2016.

"Texas Democrats, Republicans Scrapping 'Two-Step' Presidential Primary." 2016. *Austin American Statesman*, September 27. https://www.statesman.com/news/20160923/texas-democrats-republicans-scrapping-two-step-presidential-primary.

Texas Primary Results 2000–2016

2000

Democratic primary (3/14)		Republican primary (3/14)	
Gore	80.2	Bush	87.5
Bradley	16.3	McCain	14.5
LaRouche	3.4	Keyes	6.7

2004

Democratic primary (3/9)		Republican primary (3/9)	
Kerry	67.1	Bush	92.5
Edwards	14.3	Uncommitted	7.5
Dean	4.8		
Sharpton	3.7		
Lieberman	3.0		
Clark	2.2		
Kucinich	1.8		
Gephardt	1.4		

2008

Democratic primary (3/4)		Republican primary (3/4)	
Clinton	50.9	McCain	51.2
Obama	47.4	Huckabee	38.0
Edwards	1.0	Paul	4.9
		Romney	2.0

2012

Democratic primary (5/29)		Republican primary (5/29)	
Obama	88.2	Romney	69.1
Wolfe	5.1	Paul	12.0
Richardson	4.3	Santorum	8.0
Ely	2.5	Gingrich	4.7
		Uncommitted	4.2

2016

Democratic primary (3/1)		Republican primary (3/1)	
Clinton	65.2	Cruz	43.8
Sanders	33.2	Trump	26.8
		Rubio	17.7
		Kasich	4.3
		Carson	4.2
		Bush	1.3
		Uncommitted	1.0

Sources: Guide to U.S. Elections, 7th ed., Vol. I. New York: CQ Press/Sage; Atlas of U.S. Presidential Elections, www.uselectionatlas.org.

2020 Delegate Selection

Democratic

Number of delegates: 262 total delegate votes—149 district, 49 at-large, 30 pledged PLEOs, 34 unpledged PLEOs

Date of 2020 contest: March 3

What week of the delegate selection season: 5

Type of delegate selection event: Closed primary

Mode of awarding delegates: Proportional representation with a 15 percent threshold

How delegates are chosen: In accordance with primary results, district delegates to the national convention are elected by state senate district caucuses and at-large delegates and pledged PLEOs are elected by the state convention

Bound for how many national conventions ballots: One

Source: https://www.thegreenpapers.com/P20/TX-D.

Republican

Number of delegates: 155 total delegates—47 at-large (10 base, 3 party, 34 bonus), 108 in 36 congressional districts

Date of 2020 contest: March 3

What week of the delegate selection season: 5

Type of delegate selection event: Open primary

Mode of awarding delegates: Winner-take-most: District—If a presidential candidate wins a majority of the district primary vote, he or she receives all the delegates from that district; if no one wins a majority and at least one candidate wins 20 percent or more of the vote, the plurality winner receives two delegates, the runner-up one; if no candidate wins 20 percent of the vote, the top three vote-getters each receive one delegate

At-large—If a presidential candidate wins a majority of the statewide vote, he or she receives all at-large delegates; if no candidate wins a majority and at least two candidates win at least 20 percent of the vote, at-large delegates will be allocated proportionally with a 20 percent threshold; if only one candidate wins 20 percent or more of the vote, delegates are allocated proportionally between the top two vote getters; if no candidate wins at least 20 percent of the vote, delegates will be allocated proportionally

How delegates are elected: Delegates to the national convention are elected by the state convention

Bound for how many national conventions ballots: Two

Source: https://www.thegreenpapers.com/P20/TX-R.

—Andrew E. Busch

Utah

Utah joined the Union in 1896, nearly 48 years after the United States was granted the territory from Mexico in the Treaty of Guadalupe Hidalgo. From Brigham Young's term as first governor of the state to Mormons accounting for 75 percent of Utah voters in recent elections, Mormonism has dominated the political culture of the state (Barone and McCutcheon 2014). Utah's electoral votes in the general election have gone to the Republican ticket in every year since 1968. In 2012, Mitt Romney outpolled Barack Obama 73 to 25 percent. Four years later, Donald Trump struggled, but defeated Hillary Clinton 45 to 27 percent. After being trounced in the Republican caucuses by Ted Cruz, Trump had to send running mate Mike Pence to Utah in October to hold down the fort against Evan McMullin, the independent conservative (and Mormon) who had drawn within close range of Trump after release of the *Access Hollywood* tape in which Trump was heard making offensive comments about women. In the end, McMullin won 21 percent, enough for a strong third-place finish and his best showing in the country.

Utah held its first presidential primary in 2000, having used a caucus-convention system before that. The primary system has not put down deep roots since then. In 2004, when George W. Bush was running unopposed for renomination, Republicans did not hold a primary; likewise, in 2012, when Barack Obama was seeking renomination without opposition, Democrats did not hold a primary; and in 2016, both parties reverted to caucuses rather than holding primaries. In contentious races prior to 2000, Utah's Republican delegation to the national convention consistently demonstrated a conservative streak, backing Robert Taft in 1952, Barry Goldwater in 1964, and Ronald Reagan in 1976. Democrats supported Franklin Roosevelt in 1932, John F. Kennedy in 1960, Hubert Humphrey in 1968, George McGovern in 1972, Jimmy Carter in 1980, and Michael Dukakis in 1988. Except in 2012, when Utah's June 26 primary was the last in the country, recent Utah contests have been held relatively early, in February or March. In 2020, Utah will shift again to a presidential primary, scheduled for March 3.

Notable contests have included:

2004: John Kerry defeated John Edwards 55 percent to 30 percent in the Democratic primary, giving the Massachusetts senator a useful win in the final primary before Super Tuesday when nine state primaries would be on the line, including big prizes such as California, New York, and Ohio.

2008: Barack Obama swamped Hillary Clinton 57 to 39 percent on Super Tuesday, as Utah joined 15 other state primaries. Clinton won nine primaries while Obama won seven primaries and six caucus states.

2008 and 2012: In both contests, former Massachusetts governor Mitt Romney, who was Mormon and had headed the 2002 Salt Lake City Olympics committee, easily captured the vast majority of votes (90 percent on Super Tuesday 2008 and 93 percent in June 2012) and all of the state's national convention delegates. The 2012 primary, held after Romney had established himself as the presumptive nominee, saw Romney win up to 97 percent in some counties (Barone and McCutcheon 2014).

2016: In the Republican caucuses, the state delivered Cruz his ninth state victory. The Texan received over 69 percent of the vote share and all 40 of the state's delegates. Ohio governor John Kasich came in second, earning 17 percent of the vote, leaving Trump in third place with only 14 percent of the vote. The progressive left hoped that Utah's caucuses would set the tone for remaining Democratic contests when Bernie Sanders received a landslide 79 percent of the vote to Hillary Clinton's 20 percent (*New York Times*). However, Sanders's success did not translate onto the national scene, with Clinton winning most primaries and ultimately receiving the Democratic Party's nomination.

Sources

Barone, Michael, and Chuck McCutcheon. 2014. *Almanac of American Politics.* Washington, DC: National Journal.
Utah Caucus Results. 2016. *New York Times*, March 22. https://www.nytimes.com/elections/2016/results/primaries/utah.

Utah Primary and Caucus Results 2000–2016

2000

Democratic primary (3/10)		Republican primary (3/10)	
Gore	79.9	Bush	63.3
Bradley	20.1	Keyes	21.3
		McCain	14.0

2004

Democratic primary (2/24)		Republican caucuses (2/24)	
Kerry	55.2	**Delegates to national convention**	
Edwards	29.8	Uncommitted	100.0
Kucinich	7.4		
Dean	3.8		
Clark	1.4		
Lieberman	1.2		

2008

Democratic primary (2/5)		Republican primary (2/5)	
Obama	56.7	Romney	89.5
Clinton	39.1	McCain	5.4
Edwards	2.9	Paul	3.0
		Huckabee	1.4

2012 (June 26)

Democratic caucuses (3/13)		Republican primary (6/26)	
Delegates to national convention		Romney	93.1
Available	85.3	Paul	4.8
Uncommitted	14.7	Santorum	1.5

2016 (March 22)

Democratic caucuses (3/22)		Republican caucuses (3/22)	
Sanders	79.3	Cruz	69.2
Clinton	20.3	Kasich	16.8
		Trump	14.0

Sources: Federal Election Commission:
https://transition.fec.gov/pubrec/fe2000/2000presprim.htm;
https://transition.fec.gov/pubrec/fe2004/federalelections2004.pdf;
https://transition.fec.gov/pubrec/fe2008/federalelections2008.pdf;
https://transition.fec.gov/pubrec/fe2012/federalelections2012.pdf;
https://www.nytimes.com/elections/2016/results/primaries/utah.
Also Green Papers: https://www.thegreenpapers.com/P04/UT-R.phtml;
http://www.thegreenpapers.com/P12/UT-D.

2020 Delegate Selection

Democratic

Number of delegates: 35 total delegate votes—19 district, 6 at-large, 4 pledged
    PLEOs, 6 unpledged PLEOs

Date of 2020 contest: March 3

What week of the delegate selection season: 5

Type of delegate selection event: Closed primary

Mode of awarding delegates: Proportional with a 15 percent threshold

How delegates are chosen: National convention delegates are elected by the state
    convention in accordance with the primary results

Bound for how many national conventions ballots: One

Source: https://www.thegreenpapers.com/P20/UT-D.

Republican

Number of delegates: 40 total delegates—28 at-large (10 base, 3 party, 15 bonus),
    12 in 4 congressional districts

Date of 2020 contest: March 3

What week of the delegate selection season: 5

Type of delegate selection event: Closed primary [pending announcement by state GOP]

Mode of awarding delegates: Winner-take-most: If a presidential candidate wins a majority of the statewide primary vote, he or she will receive all of Utah's national convention delegates; if no one wins a majority but three or more win at least 15 percent of the vote, delegates will be allocated proportionally with a 15 percent threshold; if no candidate wins 15 percent or more of the state-wide votes, delegates will be allocated proportionally among all contenders

How delegates are chosen: National convention delegates are elected by the state convention in accordance with primary results

Bound for how many national conventions ballots: One

Source: https://www.thegreenpapers.com/P20/UT-R.

—Andrew E. Busch and Jacob S. Leischner

Vermont

One of two states that voted against Franklin Roosevelt's reelection in 1936, Vermont is now home to Bernie Sanders and a haven for environmentalists, socialists, and those fleeing Massachusetts because it is too conservative. At the same time, dairy farmers and gun owners are major interests in the rural state. In recent years, Vermont has produced liberal Republicans, who are sometimes elected governor, and more liberal Democrats, and is now a Democratic state in presidential elections. In 2016, Hillary Clinton defeated Donald Trump by nearly 21 percentage points, while third-party candidates Gary Johnson (Libertarian) and Jill Stein (Green) won over 5 percent between them.

Vermont held a presidential primary in mid-May 1916 and 1920, then relied solely on caucuses until it held a primary again in 1980. From 1980 through 2016, Vermont primaries were held every presidential year except 1992, always in the first week of March. During the national Democratic battle over the open primary in the 1980s, Vermont's Democratic primary was an advisory "beauty contest" only, with binding delegate allocation coming through a separate caucus process.

Before 1980, Vermont's Democratic delegations to the national convention backed FDR in 1932, JFK in 1960, and were split evenly between Hubert Humphrey, Eugene McCarthy, and George McGovern in 1968. In 1972, McGovern enthusiasts captured the Democratic caucuses and sent a McGovern delegation to Miami. Republican national convention delegates from

Vermont supported Eisenhower in 1952 and Ford in 1976, but were split between Goldwater, Rockefeller, and Scranton in 1964.

Notable Vermont primaries have included:

1916: In its first presidential primary, Vermont voters supported New York governor Charles Evans Hughes for the Republican nomination and the renomination of Democratic president Woodrow Wilson.

1980: Showing that he could win in New England outside of conservative New Hampshire, Ronald Reagan edged out John Anderson 30 percent to 29 percent in the GOP primary, with George H. W. Bush trailing with 22 percent. Reagan's win in Vermont helped balance a narrow loss in Massachusetts the same day. For his part, incumbent Democratic president Jimmy Carter easily outpaced challenger Edward Kennedy by a margin of 73 to 26 percent.

1984: Democrat Gary Hart buried Walter Mondale 70 percent to 20 percent in the primary, but only led by 6 percent in the caucuses (49–43 percent).

1988: Two weeks after his New Hampshire win and a week after his slate of delegates lost in South Dakota to Bob Dole's slate, George H. W. Bush started a comeback by winning the Vermont primary 49 to 39 percent over Dole. Within a week, Bush had won South Carolina and most of Super Tuesday, gaining a stranglehold over the Republican nomination. On the Democratic side, Michael Dukakis beat Jesse Jackson by 30 points in the primary, but Jackson narrowly won the caucuses. The two candidates split the Vermont delegation 9–9 at the national convention.

1996: Bob Dole came back to win Vermont, beating Pat Buchanan 40 to 17 percent, part of a sweep by Dole of all eight primaries that day.

2000: Capitalizing on his New Hampshire win, John McCain defeated George W. Bush 60 to 35 percent. McCain won four of 11 primary states voting that day, all in New England, but Bush won big prizes in California, New York, and Ohio.

2008: Barack Obama won the Democratic primary decisively over Hillary Clinton, 59 to 39 percent.

2012: In the Republican contest, Mitt Romney beat Ron Paul 40 to 25 percent, with Rick Santorum trailing slightly behind Paul. Vermont was one of four states won by Romney that day versus two for Santorum and one for Newt Gingrich.

2016: Bernie Sanders won his home state decisively, outpolling Hillary Clinton by 86 to 14 percent in the Democratic primary. The Republican primary was won by Donald Trump, who led John Kasich 33 to 30 percent. Marco Rubio trailed at 19 percent. Vermont was one of many primaries where Trump probably benefited from the divided GOP field, as either Kasich or Rubio might have beaten Trump one-on-one.

Vermont Primary Results 2000–2016

2000

Democratic primary (3/7)		Republican primary (3/7)	
Gore	54.3	McCain	60.3
Bradley	43.9	Bush	35.3
		Keyes	2.7

2004

Democratic primary (3/2)		Republican primary (3/2)	
Dean	53.6	Bush	96.7
Kerry	31.6	Write-in	3.3
Edwards	6.2		
Kucinich	4.1		
Clark	3.3		

2008

Democratic primary (3/4)		Republican primary (3/4)	
Obama	59.3	McCain	71.3
Clinton	38.6	Huckabee	14.3
Edwards	1.2	Paul	6.6
		Romney	4.5
		Giuliani	2.3

2012

Democratic primary (3/6)		Republican primary (3/6)	
Obama	98.4	Romney	39.5
Write-in	1.7	Paul	25.3
		Santorum	23.6
		Gingrich	8.1
		Huntsman	2.0

2016

Democratic primary (3/6)		Republican primary (3/6)	
Sanders	86.0	Trump	32.5
Clinton	13.6	Kasich	30.2
		Rubio	19.2
		Cruz	9.7
		Carson	4.2
		Bush	1.8

Sources: Guide to U.S. Elections, 7th ed., Vol. I. New York:
CQ Press/Sage; *Atlas of U.S. Presidential Elections,*
www.uselectionatlas.org.

2020 Delegate Selection

Democratic

Number of delegates: 23 total delegate votes—11 district, 3 at-large, 2 pledged
PLEOs, 7 unpledged PLEOs

Date of 2020 contest: March 3

What week of the delegate selection season: 5

Type of delegate selection event: Open primary

Mode of awarding delegates: Proportional with 15 percent threshold

How delegates are chosen: District delegates to the national convention are
elected by the state convention according to the primary results; at-large
delegates and pledged PLEOs are elected by the district delegates

Bound for how many national conventions ballots: One

Source: https://www.thegreenpapers.com/P20/VT-D.

Republican

Number of delegates: 17 total delegates—14 at-large (10 base, 3 party, 1 bonus),
3 in 1 congressional district

Date of 2020 contest: March 3

What week of the delegate selection season: 5

Type of delegate selection event: Open primary

Mode of awarding delegates: Winner-take-most: If a presidential candidate wins
a majority of the statewide vote, he or she receives all national convention
delegates; if not, delegates are apportioned among the candidates proportionally with a 20 percent threshold

How delegates are chosen: National convention delegates are elected by the state
convention

Bound for how many national conventions ballots: One
Source: https://www.thegreenpapers.com/P20/VT-R.

—Andrew E. Busch

Virginia

From its early beginnings as part of the United States, producing four of the first five presidents, to more recent prominence as a critical bellwether for presidential electoral politics, the Commonwealth of Virginia has a rich political history. While consistently a Democratic state during the years of the "Solid South," Virginia has also always had an independent streak—in 1952, 1956, and 1960 it cast its electoral votes for the Republican presidential candidates, one of only a handful of southern states to flip in those cycles. Once Jim Crow voting restrictions were finally rolled back in the 1960s, African American votes significantly shifted political headwinds in the Commonwealth. Virginia's population has increased dramatically, more than doubling from 1960 to 2017 thanks to a suburban surge around Washington, DC, and steady growth in Richmond and Hampton Roads (United States Census Bureau). Though Virginia voted Republican in presidential elections from 1968 through 2004, it has shifted toward the Democratic Party. As of 2019, Democrats hold the governor's mansion, both of the state's Senate seats, and 7 out of the 11 members of the House delegation. Democrats have won the last three presidential elections, including a 5 percentage point victory by Hillary Clinton over Donald Trump in 2016.

Virginia has held a presidential primary every election year since 1988. In the preceding era the state used a caucus-convention system for delegate selection. During that period, Virginia's Republican delegations favored Robert Taft in 1952 by a narrow margin, Barry Goldwater nearly unanimously in 1964, and Ronald Reagan in 1976 by a 2–1 margin over incumbent president Gerald Ford. Democratic delegations backed Franklin Roosevelt (though not until the fourth ballot) in 1932, Lyndon Johnson in 1960, Hubert Humphrey in 1968, and Jimmy Carter in 1980. George McGovern's movement army took over Democratic caucuses in 1972, and Jesse Jackson won the 1984 Virginia Democratic caucuses in a competitive three-way race, finishing with 36 percent of the vote to Walter Mondale's 30 percent and Gary Hart's 20 percent. Despite his lead in first-round caucus votes, Jackson won fewer delegates from the contest than second-place finisher Mondale (Williams 1988).

The state's first primary, on Super Tuesday (March 8) 1988, was another victory for Jesse Jackson, who won the state's Democratic contest with 45 percent of the vote, defeating Al Gore (22 percent) and the eventual Democratic nominee, Michael Dukakis (21 percent). At the same time, George H. W. Bush notched an important win against Bob Dole, 54 to 26 percent.

Other notable Virginia primaries have included:

2000: George W. Bush's win over John McCain, 53–44, in what was expected to be a much tighter race, foretold Bush's Super Tuesday sweep one week later that knocked McCain out of contention for good. The victory appeared to turn Bush's campaign around after he had lost two contests in Arizona and Michigan the week before (Rothenberg 2000).

2004: Democrat John Kerry defeated John Edwards from neighboring North Carolina by a 2–1 margin, clearly indicating that the Massachusetts senator had national appeal and could beat Edwards in his native South.

2008: Barack Obama crushed Hillary Clinton in the Democratic primary, winning with 64 percent of the vote to Clinton's 36 percent. At the same time, John McCain reversed his 2000 loss to Bush, beating Mike Huckabee 50 percent to 41 percent.

2016: Marco Rubio's campaign banked on a successful performance in Virginia on Super Tuesday as a critical way to gain momentum in the race. Rubio's narrow 35–32 percent loss to Donald Trump instead strengthened Trump's front-runner status and presaged Rubio's exit from the race two weeks later (Schwartzman 2016). On the Democratic side, Hillary Clinton outpolled Bernie Sanders by nearly a 2–1 margin.

Sources

Rothenberg, Stuart. 2000. "Bush Roars Back; McCain's Hopes Dim." *CNN*, March 1. http://www.cnn.com/ALLPOLITICS/analysis/rothenberg/2000/03/01/.

Schwartzman, Paul. 2016. "Clinton Wins Virginia; Trump Defeats a Strong Rubio." *Washington Post*, March 1. https://www.washingtonpost.com/local/virginia-politics/clinton-wins-va-trump-and-rubio-battling-it-out/2016/03/01/19bc609e-df00-11e5-846c-10191d1fc4ec_story.html.

United States Census Bureau. https://www.google.com/publicdata/explore?ds=kf7tggluo9ude_&met_y=population&hl=en&dl=en#!ctype=l&strail=false&bcs=d&nselm=h&met_y=population&scale_y=lin&ind_y=false&rdim=country&idim=state:12000&ifdim=country&hl=en_US&dl=en&ind=false.

Williams, Linda. 1988. "Will Tuesday Be Super for Jesse Jackson?" *Los Angeles Times*, March 6. http://articles.latimes.com/1988-03-06/opinion/op-702_1_jesse-jackson.

Virginia Primary and Caucus Results 2000–2016

2000

Democratic caucus (2/29)		Republican primary (2/29)	
Delegates to national convention		Bush	52.8
Gore	83.0	McCain	43.9
Uncommitted	17.0	Keyes	3.1

2004

Democratic primary (2/10)		Republican caucuses (2/4–4/4)	
Kerry	51.5	**Delegates to national convention**	
Edwards	26.6	Uncommitted	100.0
Clark	9.2		
Dean	7.0		
Sharpton	3.3		
Kucinich	1.3		

2008

Democratic primary (2/12)		Republican primary (2/12)	
Obama	63.7	McCain	50.0
Clinton	35.5	Huckabee	40.7
		Paul	4.5
		Romney	3.7

2012

Democratic primary (3/6)		Republican primary (3/6)	
Obama	100.0	Romney	59.5
		Paul	40.5

2016

Democratic primary (3/1)		Republican primary (3/1)	
Clinton	64.3	Trump	34.8
Sanders	35.2	Rubio	32.0
		Cruz	16.7
		Kasich	9.5
		Carson	5.9

Sources: https://www.thegreenpapers.com/PCC/Tabul.html;
https://www.thegreenpapers.com/P04/VA-R.phtml;
Federal Election Commission: https://transition.fec.gov/pubrec
/fe2000/2000presprim.htm; https://transition.fec.gov/pubrec
/fe2004/federalelections2004.pdf; https://transition.fec.gov/pubrec
/fe2008/federalelections2008.pdf; https://transition.fec.gov/pubrec
/fe2012/2012pres.pdf; https://transition.fec.gov/pubrec/fe2016
/federalelections2016.pdf.

2020 Delegate Selection

Democratic

Number of delegates: 124 total delegate votes—65 district, 21 at-large, 13 pledged PLEOs, 25 unpledged PLEOs

Date of 2020 contest: March 3

What week of the delegate selection season: 5

Type of delegate selection event: Open primary

Mode of awarding delegates: Proportional representation with a 15 percent threshold

How delegates are chosen: In accordance with the primary results, district delegates to the national convention are elected by district conventions and at-large delegates and pledged PLEOs are elected by the state convention

Bound for how many national conventions ballots: One

Source: http://www.thegreenpapers.com/P20/VA-D.

Republican

Number of delegates: 49 total delegates—16 at-large (10 base, 3 party, 3 bonus), 33 in 11 congressional districts

Date of 2020 contest: March 3

What week of the delegate selection season: 5

Type of delegate selection event: Open primary

Mode of awarding delegates: Proportional representation

How delegates are chosen: In accordance with statewide primary results, district delegates are elected by congressional district conventions and at-large delegates are elected by the state convention

Bound for how many national conventions ballots: One

Source: http://www.thegreenpapers.com/P20/VA-R.

—Andrew E. Busch and Richard C. Wiltshire-Gordon

Washington

Washington state is home to venerable economic giants like Boeing aircraft, as well as newer machines of wealth including Amazon, Starbucks, and Microsoft. Divided between a more rural and conservative east and a more populated, urban, and liberal coast, Washington is also one of the most reliably Democratic states. There has been a Democratic governor since 1985 and the state has voted for the Democratic nominee for president consistently since the 1988 election. In 2016, Hillary Clinton beat Donald Trump 53 percent to 37 percent.

Washington held its first presidential primary in 1992, and many Washington primaries have been nonbinding "beauty contests" accompanied by caucuses that allocate delegates. Prior to 1992, Washington's delegations to the Democratic national convention decisively supported FDR in 1932 and Hubert Humphrey in 1968 but were frequently divided more closely. In 1960, John F. Kennedy won a bare majority of Washington's delegates; nearly half were scattered among other candidates. In 1972, George McGovern took 30 delegates to 20 for favorite son Henry "Scoop" Jackson; Jimmy Carter won a solid but unspectacular majority against Edward Kennedy in 1980; and Gary Hart edged Walter Mondale in 1984. Republican national convention delegations solidly backed Dwight D. Eisenhower in 1952, Barry Goldwater in 1964, and Ronald Reagan in 1976 (though first-round caucuses favored Gerald Ford). The Goldwater takeover of the Washington party in 1964 was an archetypical illustration of how conservatives organized in the nonprimary states to give the GOP nomination to the Arizonan (White 1965).

After three presidential primaries, Washington canceled the 2004 presidential primary. The Republican presidential incumbent George W. Bush was unopposed and the Washington State Democratic Party had chosen to utilize a caucus-style election. In 2008, Washington resumed holding its primary and moved the date to February with the goal of being an influential early state. Both Democrats and Republicans held both a primary and a caucus. Republicans chose 19 of their 40 delegates based upon the results of this primary, while the remainder were chosen based on caucus results. State Democrats, on the other hand, held a nonbinding preference primary and selected all of their delegates through caucuses (2008 Results). In 2012, the legislature again canceled the primary, both for budgetary reasons and because the Democratic nominee, incumbent president Barack Obama, was all but decided. Both parties used caucuses only. The 2016 Washington primary featured yet another version of the state's ongoing primary/caucus matrix. As in 2008, the state Democratic Party held a nonbinding primary combined with caucuses, while Washington Republicans held only a primary. In 2020, both parties will once again hold only primaries for binding delegate allocation.

Notable recent contests in Washington state have included:

1988: Republican caucuses were won by televangelist Pat Robertson, who upset Vice President George H. W. Bush. Concern over the ability of a committed movement like Robertson's to control the caucuses led to Washington's adoption of the primary in 1992 (Brunner 2016).

1992: In the first Washington primary, George H. W. Bush and Bill Clinton won their respective parties' contests. However, Clinton came in fourth in the caucuses, which were won by Paul Tsongas. Demonstrating his surprising cross-party appeal, independent Ross Perot finished second in both the Republican and Democratic primaries as a write-in candidate. Perot garnered 20 percent of the Republican primary vote and 19 percent of the Democratic vote.

2000: In the Republican primary, George W. Bush won an important victory against John McCain, 58 to 39 percent, paralleling his caucus win. The same day, Bush won an equally impressive victory in Virginia. The twin primary wins came just before Super Tuesday. For his part, Democrat Al Gore defeated the struggling Bill Bradley 68 to 31 percent in Bradley's last real chance to change the direction of the race.

2004: In the Democratic caucuses held in early February, Massachusetts senator John Kerry outpolled Vermont governor Howard Dean 48 percent to 30 percent.

2008: Both parties demonstrated a political truism: that campaigns built on meticulous organization and ideological intensity frequently do better in caucuses. Barack Obama won the Democratic caucuses 67–31 percent over Hillary Clinton, while defeating her in the primary by the much smaller margin of 51 to 46 percent. On the Republican side, the center-right John McCain won the primary over social conservative Mike Huckabee 50 to 24 percent, but barely held on to beat Huckabee by two percentage points in the caucuses. Both McCain and Obama went on to win their party's nominations.

2012: Mitt Romney won the Republican caucuses with 38 percent to Ron Paul's 25 percent, Rick Santorum's 24 percent, and Newt Gingrich's 10 percent.

2016: In March, Bernie Sanders crushed Hillary Clinton in the Democratic caucuses, 73 to 27 percent. Two months later, when the Democratic primary was held, Clinton turned the tables, beating Sanders 52 to 48 percent. But it was the caucuses, not the primary, that determined Washington's delegates to the Democratic national convention. Donald Trump won the Republican primary with three-quarters of the vote, but already had his nomination wrapped up.

Sources

Brunner, Jim. 2016. "Washington's Caucus History Filled with Surprises." *Seattle Times*, March 25. https://www.seattletimes.com/seattle-news/politics/washingtons-caucus-history-filled-with-surprises/.

"2008 Results." 2008. *New York Times*, February 18. https://www.nytimes.com/2008/02/18/us/politics/18washington.html?ref=politics.

White, Theodore H. 1965. *The Making of the President 1964*. New York: Atheneum.

Washington Primary and Caucus Results 2000–2016

2000

Democratic primary (2/29)		Republican primary (2/29)	
Gore	68.2	Bush	57.8
Bradley	31.4	McCain	38.9
		Keyes	2.4

Democratic caucuses (3/7)		Republican caucuses (3/7)	
Gore	68.4	**State convention delegates**	
Bradley	28.2	Bush	82.2
LaRouche	3.4	McCain	12.9
		Keyes	5.0

2004

Democratic caucuses (2/7)		Republican caucuses (3/9)	
Precinct delegates		**Delegates to national convention**	
Kerry	48.3	Uncommitted	100.0
Dean	30.0		
Kucinich	8.3		
Edwards	6.7		
Uncommitted	3.4		
Clark	3.3		

2008

Democratic primary (2/19)		Republican primary (2/9)	
Obama	51.2	McCain	49.5
Clinton	45.7	Huckabee	24.1
Edwards	1.7	Romney	16.3
		Paul	7.7

Democratic caucuses (2/9)		Republican caucuses (2/19)	
Precinct delegates		McCain	25.7
Obama	67.6	Huckabee	23.9
Clinton	31.2	Paul	20.8
Uncommitted	1.1	Romney	16.7

2012

Democratic caucuses (3/3)		Republican caucuses (3/3)	
Available	87.5	Romney	37.7
Uncommitted	12.5	Paul	24.8
		Santorum	23.8
		Gingrich	10.3
		Uncommitted	3.3

2016

Democratic caucuses (3/25)		Republican primary (5/23)	
Legislative district delegates		Trump	75.5
Sanders	72.7	Cruz	10.8
Clinton	27.1	Kasich	9.8
		Carson	4.0

Democratic primary (5/23)	
Clinton	52.4
Sanders	47.6

Sources: https://transition.fec.gov/pubrec/fe2000/2000presprim.htm#WA;
https://uselectionatlas.org/RESULTS/state.php?year=2004&fips=53&off=0&elect
=1&f=0; https://www.thegreenpapers.com/P04/WA-D.phtml; https://www
.thegreenpapers.com/P04/WA-R.phtml; https://www.thegreenpapers.com
/P08/WA-D.phtml; https://www.thegreenpapers.com/P08/WA-R.phtml; http://www
.thegreenpapers.com/P12/WA-D; http://www.thegreenpapers.com/P12/WA-R; https://
www.thegreenpapers.com/P16/WA-D; https://www.thegreenpapers.com/P16/WA-R.

2020 Delegate Selection

Democratic

Number of delegates: 107 total delegate votes—58 district, 19 at-large, 12
    pledged PLEOs, 18 unpledged PLEOs

Date of 2020 contest: March 10

What week of the delegate selection season: 6

Type of delegate selection event: Closed primary (mail ballot)

Mode of awarding delegates: Proportional representation with a 15 percent
    threshold

How delegates are chosen: In accordance with primary results, district delegates
    to the national convention are elected by congressional district caucuses and
    at-large delegates and pledged PLEOs are elected by the state committee

Bound for how many national conventions ballots: One

Source: https://www.thegreenpapers.com/P20/WA-D.

Republican

Number of delegates: 44 total delegates—14 at-large (10 base, 3 party, 1 bonus),
    30 in 10 congressional districts

Date of 2020 contest: March 10

What week of the delegate selection season: 6

Type of delegate selection event: Closed primary

Mode of awarding delegates: At-large delegates to the national convention are allocated proportionally with a 20 percent threshold based on the statewide vote; district delegates are elected winner-take-most based on the district vote—If a presidential candidate wins a majority of the district vote, or if only one candidates wins at least 20 percent, he or she receives all three delegates; if no one wins a majority and two candidates win at least 20 percent, the plurality winner receives two delegates and the runner-up receives one delegate; if no candidates or more than two candidates win at least 20 percent of the vote, the top three vote-getters receive one delegate each

How delegates are chosen: Delegates to the national convention are slated and elected by the state convention

Bound for how many national conventions ballots: One

Source: https://www.thegreenpapers.com/P20/WA-R.

—*Andrew E. Busch and Jacob S. Leischner*

West Virginia

A mountainous border state that split off from Virginia during the Civil War because it opposed secession, West Virginia emblemizes culturally conservative working-class voters who were the backbone of the New Deal coalition but have felt increasingly uncomfortable with the modern Democratic Party. The state has not voted for a Democratic candidate for president since Bill Clinton in 1996, and it gave Donald Trump his second-highest percentage of any state in 2016, 67.9 percent. Democratic senator Joe Manchin has survived by hewing far to the right of his co-partisans in the Senate, and was the only Senate Democrat to vote for the Supreme Court nomination of Judge Brett Kavanaugh.

West Virginia held its first presidential primary in 1916 and has held a primary every presidential election year since then. After the 1916 vote, held in early June, West Virginia scheduled its primaries for late May and then, from 1932 through 1976, early May. In 1980 and 1984 it shifted back to early June, then back to early May from 1988 through 2016. West Virginia's consistently late primary means it has had limited influence in the front-loaded system of recent decades. In the Democratic primary, the allocation of delegates is determined by the primary vote for candidates. In the GOP primary, on the other hand, delegates are directly elected without connection to the presidential preference vote, which is purely advisory.

Key West Virginia primaries have included:

1928: West Virginia Democrats backed New York governor Al Smith over home state U.S. senator Guy D. Goff 50 to 46 percent. Smith went on to become the first Roman Catholic to be nominated for president by a major party, though he lost the general election to Herbert Hoover.

1960: Trying to prove that his own Catholicism was not a fatal electoral disability, even in heavily Protestant West Virginia, John F. Kennedy fought it out with labor favorite Hubert Humphrey. When Kennedy won 61 to 39 percent in a dramatic primary largely centered around religious liberty, it knocked Humphrey out of contention and seriously damaged the prospects of Kennedy's other rivals including Lyndon Johnson, Stuart Symington, and Adlai Stevenson. West Virginia was a signal of Kennedy's electability to undecided delegates and party leaders that helped assure his nomination (White 1961).

1976: In the contested Republican primary, incumbent president Gerald Ford beat Ronald Reagan 57 to 43 percent, balancing Reagan's win in Nebraska the same day.

1980: In a fight against challenger Edward Kennedy, Democratic president Jimmy Carter won 62 to 38 percent on the final day of primaries, giving Carter a much-needed win on a day when Kennedy won five of the other seven primaries, including California and New Jersey.

1984: With the Democratic nomination outcome still undetermined, Walter Mondale beat Gary Hart 54 to 37 percent. Similar to Carter in 1980, Mondale lost four of the remaining five primaries on the last day of contests. It would be more than two decades before the West Virginia primary took place while a serious nomination race was still undecided.

2008: In the ongoing Democratic contest between Barack Obama and Hillary Clinton, Clinton won with two-thirds of the vote. Though winning West Virginia, she lost Nebraska by a smaller margin the same day.

2016: Bernie Sanders beat Hillary Clinton by a 51 to 36 percentage point margin with a month remaining in the primary season. Sanders's win was predictable in some ways but not others. Throughout the primary season, he did best in areas that were heavily white—like West Virginia—but also affluent and college-educated.

Source

White, Theodore H. 1961. *The Making of the President 1960.* New York: Atheneum.

West Virginia Primary Results 2000–2016

2000

Democratic primary (5/9)		Republican primary (5/9)	
Gore	72.0	Bush	79.6
Bradley	18.4	McCain	12.9
MacDonald	7.6	Keyes	4.8
LaRouche	1.9	Forbes	1.6
		Bauer	1.2

2004

Democratic primary (5/11)		Republican primary (5/11)	
Kerry	69.2	Bush	100.0
Edwards	13.4		
Lieberman	5.5		
Dean	4.2		
Clark	3.6		
Kucinich	2.4		
LaRouche	1.6		

2008

Democratic primary (5/13)		Republican primary (5/13)	
Clinton	66.9	McCain	76.0
Obama	25.8	Huckabee	10.3
Edwards	7.3	Paul	5.0
		Romney	4.4
		Giuliani	2.4
		Keyes	1.2

2012

Democratic primary (5/8)		Republican primary (5/8)	
Obama	59.4	Romney	69.6
Judd	40.7	Santorum	12.1
		Paul	11.0
		Gingrich	6.3
		Roemer	1.0

2016

Democratic primary (5/10)		Republican primary (5/10)	
Sanders	51.4	Trump	77.1
Clinton	35.8	Cruz	9.0
Farrell	8.9	Kasich	6.7
Judd	1.8	Carson	2.2
O'Malley	1.6	Rubio	1.4
		Bush	1.1

Sources: *Guide to U.S. Elections,* 7th ed., Vol. I. New York: CQ Press/Sage; *Atlas of U.S. Presidential Elections,* www.uselectionatlas.org.

2020 Delegate Selection

Democratic

Number of delegates: 30 total delegate votes—16 district, 5 at-large, 3 pledged PLEOs, 6 unpledged PLEOs

Date of 2020 contest: May 12

What week of the delegate selection season: 15

Type of delegate selection event: Semiopen primary (D & I)

Mode of awarding delegates: Proportional representation with a 15 percent threshold

How delegates are chosen: In accordance with primary results, district delegates to the national convention are elected by congressional district caucuses at the state convention and at-large delegates and pledged PLEOs are elected by the state executive committee

Bound for how many national conventions ballots: One

Source: https://www.thegreenpapers.com/P20/WV-D.

Republican

Number of delegates: 34 total delegates—25 at-large (10 base, 3 party, 12 bonus), 9 in 3 congressional districts

Date of 2020 contest: May 12

What week of the delegate selection season: 15

Type of delegate selection event: Delegate selection primary (semiopen)

Mode of awarding delegates: District delegates to the national convention appear on the ballot and are directly elected in the district primary; at-large delegates are directly elected at the state level

How delegates are chosen: District delegates to the national convention appear on the ballot and are directly elected in the district primary; at-large delegates are directly elected at the state level.

Bound for how many national conventions ballots: Unclear

Source: https://www.thegreenpapers.com/P20/WV-R.

—*Andrew E. Busch*

Wisconsin

Justice Louis Brandeis once commented that Wisconsin has been one of America's leading "laboratories of reform" because of its trailblazing public policies. The progressive tendency of government in Wisconsin is heavily influenced by its immigrant culture, especially mass waves of Scandinavians and Germans. Wisconsin was also one of two states, the other being Michigan, that were the birthplace of the Republican Party (Cohen and Barnes 2016). Wisconsin voted Democratic in the seven presidential elections from 1988 to 2012. However, it is a "perennial" swing state, frequently competitive at both the federal and state levels, and it went Republican in 2016 when Donald Trump beat Hillary Clinton by 0.77 percent.

Wisconsin was an early adopter of the presidential primary and has held one every election cycle since 1912. It has held its vote in early April every year except when it joined the national rush to front-loading by scheduling its primary on March 19 in 1996, February 17 in 2004, and February 19 in 2008. Historically, Wisconsin has been proud of its open primary and engaged in a decade-long struggle with the Democratic National Committee when Democrats adopted national reforms banning the open primary for delegate selection. For a time in the 1980s, Wisconsin's Democrats turned their open primary into a nonbinding "beauty contest" and held closed caucuses for delegate selection. After 1984, national Democrats gave up their campaign against open primaries and Wisconsin returned to its traditions (Wekkin 1984).

Wisconsin has frequently been one of the most influential primaries in the nation. Those primaries included:

1944: Wendell Willkie's fourth-place finish in the Republican primary prompted the 1940 GOP nominee to suspend his presidential campaign. The big winner was General Douglas MacArthur, who received 73 percent in a draft campaign while he was commanding U.S. troops in the Pacific.

1948: A second campaign to draft MacArthur in the Republican primary fell short when he was outpolled by Minnesota governor Harold Stassen, 39 percent to 34 percent. The "Draft MacArthur" effort collapsed and third-place finisher Thomas Dewey went on to win the GOP nomination.

1960: In a key test of strength, John F. Kennedy won against Hubert Humphrey 57 to 43 percent on his way to the Democratic nomination. JFK's Wisconsin win was widely thought to have depended heavily on crossover votes from Catholic Republicans, and set the stage for his crucial rematch with Humphrey in West Virginia a month later (White 1961).

1964: On the day of the deadline to put his name on Wisconsin's Democratic primary ballot, Alabama governor George Wallace announced his presidential candidacy. The pro-segregationist Wallace was opposed by his party, clergy, and many prominent media outlets, but shocked the political world by receiving one-third of the Democratic primary vote. Wallace's surprising success in Wisconsin, followed by Indiana and Maryland, presaged his 1968 independent candidacy (Carter 1995).

1968: Richard Nixon won the Republican primary, while anti–Vietnam War candidate Senator Eugene McCarthy won the Democratic primary over Lyndon Johnson, 56 percent to 35 percent. Anticipating defeat, Johnson had already announced two days before the Wisconsin vote that he was dropping out of the race. Robert F. Kennedy, whose campaign materialized two weeks before the primary, garnered 6 percent of the vote (White 1969).

1972: Senator George McGovern of South Dakota, hero of the anti–Vietnam War movement, gained his first primary victory with slightly under 30 percent of the vote. His Wisconsin win arguably saved his campaign and put him on the road to the Democratic nomination.

1976: Democrat Jimmy Carter won a nail-biter against liberal Arizona representative Morris Udall, 37 to 36 percent, thwarting what might have been the favored Udall's best opportunity to break out. In the Republican primary, incumbent Gerald Ford defeated conservative challenger Ronald Reagan by a margin of 55 to 44 percent.

1980: In the Democratic primary election, incumbent president Jimmy Carter defeated Massachusetts senator Ted Kennedy by 26 percentage points. California governor Edmund "Jerry" Brown, who had thrown his hat in the ring late, made a play for Wisconsin and never recovered from his 12 percent showing. Carter's foes complained that he made a presidential announcement regarding the abortive Iranian hostage rescue mission as polls opened in Wisconsin. On the Republican side, Ronald Reagan beat George H. W. Bush 40 to 30 percent, with John Anderson finishing third with 27 percent (Busch 2005).

1984: Colorado senator Gary Hart won the Democratic primary, defeating Walter Mondale by a slim margin. However, Wisconsin's Democratic Party also held caucuses after the primary, which Mondale dominated, enabling Mondale to win the most delegates (Haynen 2016).

1992: Bill Clinton won an important showdown with Jerry Brown, 37 to 35 percent. Paul Tsongas finished third with 22 percent.

2004: Senator John Kerry's win in the February primary led Howard Dean to announce the end of his campaign.

2008: Barack Obama took a big step toward the Democratic nomination by beating Hillary Clinton with 58 percent of the vote. The 646,851 votes Obama received were the most by any candidate in Wisconsin primary history (Haynen 2016). Obama's victory provided early evidence that he could do well in a heavily white electorate.

2012: Former Massachusetts governor Mitt Romney beat former senator Rick Santorum 44–37 percent. One week after Romney won Wisconsin, Santorum suspended his campaign.

2016: Texas senator Ted Cruz won the 2016 Republican primary by 48–35 percent. It seemed for a moment that Cruz might have found the formula for consolidating the conservative anti-Trump forces. However, he was unable to sustain his momentum. Vermont senator Bernie Sanders won the Democratic primary by 14 percentage points over Hillary Clinton, who lost Wisconsin for the second time. In November, she would lose it a third time.

Sources

Busch, Andrew E. 2005. *Reagan's Victory: The Presidential Election of 1984 and the Rise of the Right*. Lawrence: University Press of Kansas.

Carter, Dan T. 1995. *The Politics of Rage: George Wallace, the Origins of the New Conservatism, and the Transformation of American Politics*. New York: Simon & Schuster.

Ceaser, James W., Andrew E. Busch, and John J. Pitney Jr. 2017. *Defying the Odds: The 2016 Elections and American Politics*. Lanham, MD: Rowman & Littlefield.

Cohen, Richard E., and James A. Barnes. 2016. *The Almanac of American Politics 2016*. Washington, DC: National Journal.

Haynen, Nick. 2016. "Here Are the Winners of Every Wisconsin Presidential Primary Since 1968." *Wisconsin State Journal*, April 6. https://madison.com /wsj/news/local/govt-and-politics/here-are-the-winners-of-every-wiscon sin-presidential-primary-since/collection_75367382-e757-5d96-a57b -5177b923b60b.html#26.

Wekkin, Gary D. 1984. *Democrat versus Democrat: The National Party's Campaign to Close the Wisconsin Primary*. Columbia: University of Missouri Press.

White, Theodore H. 1961. *The Making of the President 1960*. New York: Atheneum.

White, Theodore H. 1969. *The Making of the President 1968*. New York: Atheneum.

Wisconsin Primary Results 2000–2016

2000

Democratic primary (4/4)		Republican primary (4/4)	
Gore	88.6	Bush	69.2
Bradley	8.8	McCain	18.1
LaRouche	1.0	Keyes	9.9
		Forbes	1.1

2004

Democratic primary (2/17)		Republican primary (2/17)	
Kerry	39.6	Bush	99.1
Edwards	34.3		
Dean	18.2		
Kucinich	3.3		
Sharpton	1.8		
Clark	1.5		

2008

Democratic primary (2/19)		Republican primary (2/19)	
Obama	58.1	McCain	54.7
Clinton	40.8	Huckabee	37.0
		Paul	4.7
		Romney	2.0

2012

Democratic primary (4/3)		Republican primary (4/3)	
Obama	97.9	Romney	44.0
		Santorum	36.8
		Paul	11.2
		Gingrich	5.8

2016

Democratic primary (4/5)		Republican primary (4/5)	
Sanders	56.6	Cruz	48.2
Clinton	43.1	Trump	35.0
		Kasich	14.1

Sources: Federal Election Commission:
https://transition.fec.gov/pubrec/fe2000/2000presprim.htm#top;
https://transition.fec.gov/pubrec/fe2004/federalelections2004.pdf;
https://transition.fec.gov/pubrec/fe2008/federalelections2008.pdf;
https://transition.fec.gov/pubrec/fe2012/2012pres.pdf;
https://transition.fec.gov/pubrec/fe2016/federalelections2016.pdf.

2020 Delegate Selection

Democratic

Number of delegates: 90 total delegate votes—50 district, 17 at-large, 10 pledged PLEOs, 13 unpledged PLEOs

Date of 2020 contest: April 7

What week of the delegate selection season: 10

Type of delegate selection event: Open primary

Mode of awarding delegates: Proportional representation with 15 percent threshold

How delegates are chosen: According to the primary results, district delegates to the national convention are elected by congressional district caucuses and at-large delegates and pledged PLEOs are elected by the state party administrative committee

Bound for how many national conventions ballots: One

Source: http://www.thegreenpapers.com/P20/WI-D.

Republican

Number of delegates: 52 total delegates—28 at-large (10 base, 3 party, 15 bonus), 24 in 8 congressional districts

Date of 2020 contest: April 7

What week of the delegate selection season: 10

Type of delegate selection event: Open primary

Mode of awarding delegates: At-large: Winner-Take-All based on statewide primary vote; District: Winner-Take-All based on district primary vote

How delegates are chosen: District delegates to the national convention are elected by congressional district conventions according to the district primary results; at-large delegates are selected by the candidate who won a plurality of the statewide vote and are ratified by the state executive committee

Bound for how many national conventions ballots: All

Source: http://www.thegreenpapers.com/P20/WI-R.

—*Andrew E. Busch and Nandeeni K. Patel*

Wyoming

Sparsely populated Wyoming still embraces the individualistic frontier ethic. Farming, ranching, mining, tourism (especially in Yellowstone and Grand Teton National Parks), and the Union Pacific Railroad rumbling through Cheyenne help define the state, which is now solidly Republican. A significant pocket of Mormon voters in the southwest corner of the state add to the state's conservatism. No Democrat has won Wyoming in a presidential race since Lyndon Johnson in 1964; when Donald Trump defeated Hillary Clinton by a margin of 68.2 percent to 21.9 percent, Wyoming edged out West Virginia as the state with the highest Trump percentage in the country.

Wyoming relies on caucus-convention procedures to select its national convention delegates. Republican delegations from Wyoming split equally between Eisenhower and Taft in 1952, backed Goldwater in 1964, and gave Reagan a modest edge over Ford in 1976. Democratic delegations supported

Roosevelt in 1932, Kennedy in 1960, Humphrey in 1968, Carter in 1980, Dukakis in 1988, and Bill Clinton in 1992. Democrats split closely between Henry Jackson and George McGovern in 1972 and between Walter Mondale and Gary Hart 12 years later.

Democratic caucuses were held in March in 2000–2008 and in the first half of April in 2012–2016; Republicans have held their county conventions in early January (2008), February (2004 and 2012), and early March (2000 and 2016). In 2000 and 2004, both parties' caucuses were lopsided affairs, with Al Gore and George W. Bush sweeping in 2000 and John Kerry and George W. Bush sweeping in 2004. The statewide popular vote in Democratic caucuses is sometimes reported, but results for both parties are more often reported in terms of delegates won to the state convention or even the national convention.

Notable recent caucuses and conventions in Wyoming have included:

2008: Barack Obama defeated Hillary Clinton 61 to 38 percent. On the Republican side, Mitt Romney won Wyoming's early county conventions decisively, getting two-thirds of the national convention delegates to Fred Thompson's 25 percent. By scheduling their county conventions two days before the Iowa caucuses, Wyoming Republicans violated national GOP rules prohibiting delegate selection prior to February 5 and were deprived of half of their delegates to the national convention.

2012: Republican country conventions were competitive, with Mitt Romney winning 39 percent of the caucus vote to Rick Santorum's 32 percent and Ron Paul's 21 percent.

2016: As was the case in Democratic caucuses across the country, Bernie Sanders defeated Hillary Clinton by 57 to 43 percent. Also typical in 2016, Ted Cruz dominated the Republican caucus/convention system, beating Marco Rubio 69 percent to 14 percent in the county conventions. Donald Trump finished in fourth place at 7 percent, behind the vote for "uncommitted."

Wyoming Caucus/Convention Result 2000–2016

2000

Democratic caucuses (3/25)		Republican county conventions (3/10)	
State convention delegates		**Delegates**	
Gore	85.4	Bush	77.6
Uncommitted	7.3	Keyes	11.7
Bradley	5.0	McCain	10.3
Others	2.3		

2004

Democratic county conventions (3/6–3/20)		Republican county conventions (2/3–2/29)	
State convention delegates		**Delegates to national convention**	
Kerry	77.4	Uncommitted	100.0
Uncommitted	8.4		
Kucinich	6.1		
Edwards	4.2		
Dean	3.1		

2008

Democratic caucuses (3/8)		Republican county conventions (1/5)	
Obama	61.4	**Delegates to national convention**	
Clinton	37.8	Romney	66.7
		Thompson	25.0
		Hunter	8.3

2012

Democratic county caucuses (4/14)		Republican county conventions (2/29)	
Delegates to national convention		**Delegates**	
Available	81.2	Romney	39.0
Uncommitted	18.2	Santorum	31.9
		Paul	20.8
		Gingrich	7.8

2016

Democratic caucuses (4/9)		Republican county conventions (3/12)	
Sanders	56.7	**Delegates**	
Clinton	43.1	Cruz	68.8
		Rubio	14.1
		Uncommitted	7.6
		Trump	6.8
		Kasich	2.6

Sources: https://www.thegreenpapers.com/P04/WY-D.phtml;
https://www.thegreenpapers.com/P04/WY-R.phtml;
https://www.thegreenpapers.com/P08/WY-D.phtml;
https://www.nytimes.com/elections/2008/primaries/results/states/WY.html;
http://www.thegreenpapers.com/P12/WY-D;
http://www.thegreenpapers.com/P12/WY-R;
https://uselectionatlas.org/RESULTS/.

2020 Delegate Selection

Democratic

Number of delegates: 17 total delegate votes—8 district, 3 at-large, 2 pledged PLEOs, 4 unpledged PLEOs

Date of 2020 contest: April 4

What week of the delegate selection season: 9

Type of delegate selection event: Closed caucus/convention

Mode of awarding delegates: Proportional representation with a 15 percent threshold

How delegates are chosen: Delegates to the national convention are elected by the state convention

Bound for how many national conventions ballots: One

Source: http://www.thegreenpapers.com/P20/WY-D.

Republican

Number of Delegates: 29 total delegates—26 at-large (10 base, 3 party, 13 bonus), 3 in 1 congressional district

Date of 2020 contest: March 14

What week of the delegate selection season: 6

Type of delegate selection event: Closed caucus/convention

Mode of awarding delegates: Delegates are selected without formal connection to presidential preference, though candidates for delegate are required to state their preference (including undecided)

How delegates are chosen: 12 delegates to the national convention will be elected by county conventions; the remaining 17 delegates will be elected by the state convention

Bound for how many national conventions ballots: Delegates are required to state a presidential preference before being elected, though it may be uncommitted. The three party delegates are automatically unpledged

Source: http://www.thegreenpapers.com/P20/WY-R.

—Andrew E. Busch

U.S. Territories and Americans Abroad

Although the national convention for presidential nominations was built around state representation, U.S. territories were first granted delegates to the national convention by Republicans in 1868, when Colorado, Idaho, Montana, Nevada, and Dakota sent delegations. Democrats were more concerned with respecting state prerogatives, but began following the Republican practice in 1884. Gradually, the western territories of the mid-19th century transformed into states.

As a result of the Spanish-American War in 1898 and other efforts to extend the strategic reach of the United States, a new set of territories outside of continental North America were acquired. Over time, these too were incorporated into the national convention system of each party.

Two such territories were granted delegates for a time, but no longer are because their international status has changed. The Philippine Islands, acquired in the war with Spain, sent delegates to the Republican national convention from 1904 to 1944 and to the Democratic national convention from 1912 to 1944. After World War II, the Philippines became an independent country. Also, from 1920 to 1944, Democrats allotted delegates to the Canal Zone. That practice was also discontinued after the war, though the canal was not returned to the control of Panama until December 31, 1999.

Four or five additional delegations are recognized by the Republican and Democratic parties:

Puerto Rico began sending delegations to the Democratic national convention in 1916 and the Republican national convention in 1920. At varying times it has used both a primary and a caucus/convention system.

The U.S. Virgin Islands sent its first delegates to the 1924 Democratic convention. Republicans followed in 1952. Caucuses have been the mode of delegate selection.

Guam began receiving delegates from Democrats in 1968 and Republicans in 1972. As in the Virgin Islands, caucus/convention processes have been used.

American Samoa was first allocated delegates to the national convention by Democrats in 1984 and Republicans in 1992, and has always used caucus/convention processes to choose those delegates.

The Northern Marianas were allocated national convention delegates starting in 2008 by Republicans and 2012 by Democrats.

Finally, Democrats established a process for Democrats living outside the United States and its territories to participate in their nomination process. "Democrats Abroad" have sent delegates to the Democratic convention since 1976. They have used regional caucuses and, in 2012 and 2016, a "global primary." As Democrats Abroad described the process in 2016, "Ballots were cast by email, fax, post, or in-person at Voting Centers in countries around the globe," followed by a combination of local, regional and worldwide caucuses, culminating in a Global Convention in Berlin to choose delegates to the Democratic National Convention (Democrats Abroad).

As a general rule, the territories and Democrats Abroad possess a small number of delegates and their results are rarely noticed by the American media. In 2020, American Samoa, Guam, the Northern Marianas, and the U.S. Virgin Islands are allocated 9 delegates each by Republicans; Democrats give 11 delegates each to Samoa, Guam, and the Marianas, 13 to the Virgin Islands, and 17 to Democrats Abroad. Puerto Rico represents an occasional exception, as it has a more significant delegate catch (in 2020, 59 for Democrats and 23 for Republicans), sometimes holds a primary rather than caucuses, and has a longer history of participating in the nominating process. In 2016, for example, Marco Rubio won some positive press for his victory in the Puerto Rico Republican primary, one of his few wins of the year (O'Keefe 2016).

Political parties in U.S. territories have a strong tendency to align themselves with their party's mainland establishment. In the last five election cycles, one might identify the "establishment" favorites as Gore and Bush in 2000; Kerry and Bush in 2004; Clinton and McCain in 2008; Obama and Romney in 2012; and Clinton and anyone but Trump (including uncommitted) in 2016. Measured that way, over the last five elections, American Samoa backed the establishment choice nine times out of 10, as did Puerto Rico. Guam aligned with the Democratic establishment choice four of five times (with the exception being a 50.1 percent to 49.9 percent win by Obama in 2008), and the Republican establishment another four of five times. The Northern Marianas hewed to the establishment preference three in four contests. Only Democrats in the U.S. Virgin Islands showed a rebellious streak, veering from the "insider" choice half the time. Altogether, the four territories endorsed the establishment pick in 33 cases out of 43 since 2000, and in seven of those cases the leading vote-getter was "uncommitted" or "available." Only three times out of 43 did a territorial vote give first place to a candidate who could be considered an "outsider"—Barack Obama in 2008 in Guam and the Virgin Islands, and Donald Trump in 2016 in the Northern Marianas Islands. For their part, Democrats Abroad has leaned to the left, preferring Obama over Clinton in 2008 and Sanders over Clinton in 2016.

Sources

Democrats Abroad. "The 2016 Delegate Selection Plan for Democrats Abroad." https://www.democratsabroad.org/global_presidential_primary.

O'Keefe, Ed. 2016. "Marco Rubio Wins the Puerto Rico Primary." *Washington Post*, March 6. https://www.washingtonpost.com/news/post-politics/wp/2016/03/06/marco-rubio-wins-the-puerto-rico-primary.

American Samoa

Caucus/Convention Results 2000–2016

2000

Democratic convention (3/7)		Republican caucuses (2/26)	
Gore	84.0	**Delegates to national convention**	
Bradley	16.0	Bush	100.00

2004

Democratic convention (3/8)		Republican caucuses (2/28)	
Kerry	83.0	**Delegates to national convention**	
Kucinich	17.0	Bush	66.7
		Uncommitted	33.3

2008

Democratic caucuses (2/5)		Republican caucuses (2/23)	
Clinton	57.2	**Delegates to national convention**	
Obama	42.5	McCain	66.7
		Uncommitted	33.3

2012

Democratic caucuses (3/6)		Republican caucuses (3/13)	
Delegates to national convention		**Delegates to national convention**	
Obama	50.0	Uncommitted	100.0
Uncommitted	50.0		

2016

Democratic caucuses (3/1)		Republican caucuses (3/22)	
Clinton	68.4	**Delegates to national convention**	
Sanders	25.7	Uncommitted	100.0
Guerra	5.9		

2020 Delegate Selection

Democratic

Number of delegates: 11 total delegate votes—6 at-large, 5 unpledged PLEOs

Date of 2020 contest: March 3

What week of the delegate selection season: 5

Type of delegate selection event: Open caucus

Mode of awarding delegates: Proportional representation with 15 percent threshold

How delegates are chosen: At-large delegates to the national convention are elected in the territorial caucus in accordance with caucus results

Bound for how many national conventions ballots: One

Source: http://www.thegreenpapers.com/P20/AS-D.

Republican

Number of delegates: 9 total delegates—9 at-large (6 base, 3 party)

Date of 2020 contest: March 24

What week of the delegate selection season: 8

Type of delegate selection event: Open caucus

Mode of awarding delegates: Delegates are not bound to presidential candidates

How delegates are chosen: Delegates to the national convention are elected by the territorial caucus

Bound for how many national conventions ballots: Delegates are unbound

Source: http://www.thegreenpapers.com/P20/AS-R.

Democrats Abroad

Primary and Caucus Results 2000–2016

2000

Local caucuses (3/10)
Delegates to national convention
Gore   100.0

2004

Local caucuses (2/6–2/9)	
Kerry	56.0
Dean	18.8
Clark	10.1
Edwards	9.4
Kucinich	4.8

2008

Local caucuses (2/5–2/12)	
Obama	65.9
Clinton	32.5

2012

Global primary (5/1–5/6)	
Obama	99.1

2016

Global primary (3/1–3/8)	
Sanders	68.8
Clinton	30.9

2020 Delegate Selection

Number of delegates: 17 total delegate votes—12 at-large, 1 pledged PLEO, 4 unpledged PLEOs

Date of 2020 contest: March 3–March 10

What week of the delegate selection season: 5–6

Type of delegate selection event: "Global primary" (open caucus with multiple remote voting options)

Mode of awarding delegates: Proportional representation with a 15 percent threshold

How delegates are chosen: 9 delegates to the national convention will be elected in three regional caucuses according to the results of the global primary; 3 at-large delegates and 1 pledged PLEO will be elected by a global convention

Bound for how many national conventions ballots: One
Source: http://www.thegreenpapers.com/P20/DA-D.

Guam

Caucus and Convention Results 2000–2016

2000

Democratic caucuses (convention 3/18)		Republican caucuses (convention 2/26)	
Delegates to national convention		Delegates to national convention	
Gore	100.0	Bush	100.0

2004

Democratic convention (4/24)		Republican caucuses (2/21)	
Kerry	77.0	Delegates to national convention	
Write-in/others	23.0	Bush	66.7
		Uncommitted	33.3

2008

Democratic caucuses (5/3)		Republican caucuses (3/8)	
Obama	50.1	Delegates to national convention	
Clinton	49.9	Uncommitted	100.0

2012

Democratic caucuses (5/5)		Republican caucuses (3/10)	
Obama	100.0	Romney	100.0

2016

Democratic caucuses (5/7)		Republican caucuses (3/12)	
Clinton	59.5	Delegates to national convention	
Sanders	40.5	Uncommitted	100.0

2020 Delegate Selection

Democratic

Number of Delegates: 11 total delegate votes—6 at-large, 5 unpledged PLEOs

Date of 2020 contest: May 2

What week of the delegate selection season: 13

Type of delegate selection event: Closed caucus

Mode of awarding delegates: Proportional representation with 15 percent threshold

How delegates are chosen: At-large delegates to the national convention are elected by the territorial caucus

Bound for how many national conventions ballots: One

Source: http://www.thegreenpapers.com/P20/GU-D.

Republican

Number of delegates: 9 total delegates—6 base at-large, 3 party

Date of 2020 contest: March 14

What week of the delegate selection season: 6

Type of delegate selection event: Closed caucus

Mode of awarding delegates: Election of delegates is not formally connected to presidential preference

How delegates are chosen: Delegates to the national election are elected by the territorial caucus

Bound for how many national conventions ballots: Both elected delegates and automatic party delegates are unbound

Source: http://www.thegreenpapers.com/P20/GU-R.

Northern Mariana Islands

Caucus Results 2008–2016

2008

Republican convention (2/23)	
McCain	91.3
Huckabee	4.4
Paul	4.4

2012

Democratic caucuses	Republican convention (3/10)	
None	Romney	87.3
	Santorum	6.3
	Paul	3.3
	Gingrich	3.2

2016

Democratic caucuses (3/12)		Republican convention (3/15)	
Clinton	54.0	Trump	72.8
Sanders	34.4	Cruz	24.0
Uncommitted	11.6	Kasich	2.1
		Rubio	1.1

2020 Delegate Selection

Democratic

Number of delegates: 11 total delegate votes—6 at-large, 5 unpledged PLEOs

Date of 2020 contest: March 14

What week of the delegate selection season: 6

Type of delegate selection event: Closed caucus/convention

Mode of awarding delegates: Proportional representation with 15 percent threshold

How delegates are chosen: At-large delegates to the national convention are elected by the territorial convention in accordance with the caucus vote

Bound for how many national conventions ballots: One

Source: http://www.thegreenpapers.com/P20/MP-D.

Republican

Number of delegates: 9 total delegates—6 base at-large, 3 party

Date of 2020 contest: March 17

What week of the delegate selection season: 7

Type of delegate selection event: Closed caucus/convention

Mode of awarding delegates: Winner-take-all

How delegates are chosen: Delegates to the national election are elected by the territorial convention in accordance with the presidential preference result

Bound for how many national conventions ballots: One
Source: http://www.thegreenpapers.com/P20/MP-R.

Puerto Rico

Primary and Caucus Results 2000–2016

2000

Democratic caucuses (4/2)		Republican primary (2/27)	
Delegates to national convention		Bush	94.2
Gore	87.9	McCain	5.3
Uncommitted	12.1		

2004

Democratic caucus cancelled		Republican caucus cancelled	
Delegates to national convention		Delegates to national convention	
Kerry	89.5	Bush	100.0
Uncommitted	10.5		

2008

Democratic primary (6/1)		Republican caucus (2/24)	
Clinton	68.4	McCain	90.4
Obama	31.6	Huckabee	4.8
		Paul	4.3

2012

Democratic caucuses (6/3)		Republican primary (3/18)	
Delegates to national convention		Romney	82.6
Available	89.6	Santorum	8.2
Uncommitted	10.5	Roemer	2.2
		Write-in	2.1
		Karger	1.5
		Paul	1.2

2016

Democratic primary (6/5)		Republican primary (3/6)	
Clinton	61.1	Rubio	70.2
Sanders	37.9	Trump	13.3
		Cruz	8.8
		Kasich	1.4

2020 Delegate Selection

Democratic

Number of delegates: 59 total delegate votes—33 district, 11 at-large, 7 pledged PLEOs, 8 unpledged PLEOs

Date of 2020 contest: March 29

What week of the delegate selection season: 8

Type of delegate selection event: Open primary

Mode of awarding delegates: Proportional representation with 15 percent threshold

How delegates are chosen: District delegates appear on the ballot and are elected in accordance with primary results in each Senate district; at-large delegates and pledged PLEOs are elected by the Assembly of the Democratic Party of the Commonwealth of Puerto Rico in accordance with the commonwealth-wide primary vote

Bound for how many national conventions ballots: All

Source: http://www.thegreenpapers.com/P20/PR-D.

Republican

Number of delegates: 23 total delegates—10 base at-large, 3 party

Date of 2020 contest: March 8

What week of the delegate selection season: 5

Type of delegate selection event: Open primary

Mode of awarding delegates: Winner-take-most: If a presidential candidate wins a majority of the commonwealth-wide vote, he or she receives all delegates to the national convention; if not, delegates are allocated proportionally with a 20 percent threshold

How delegates are chosen: Delegates appear on the ballot and are directly elected according to the results of the primary

Bound for how many national conventions ballots: One

Source: http://www.thegreenpapers.com/P20/PR-R.

U.S. Virgin Islands

Caucus and Convention Results 2000–2016

2000

Democratic convention (1/1)		Republican caucuses (2/26)	
Delegates to national convention		Delegates to national convention	
Gore	100.0	Bush	100.0

2004

Democratic convention (4/17)		Republican caucuses (2/28)	
Delegates to national convention		Delegates to national convention	
Kerry	50.0	Uncommitted	100.0
Uncommitted	50.0		

2008

Democratic convention (2/9)		Republican caucuses (4/5)	
Obama	90.0	**Delegates to national convention**	
Clinton	7.6	Uncommitted	100.0
Uncommitted	2.5		

2012

Democratic convention (6/2–6/3)		Republican caucuses (3/10)	
Delegates to national convention		Uncommitted	33.6
Available	53,9	Paul	29.2
Uncommitted	46.1	Romney	26.3
		Santorum	6.0
		Gingrich	4.7

2016

Democratic caucuses (6/4)		Republican caucuses (3/10)	
Clinton	87.1	Uncommitted	65.3
Sanders	12.9	Cruz	11.7
		Rubio	9.9
		Carson	6.6
		Trump	6.4

2020 Delegate Selection

Democratic

Number of delegates: 13 total delegate votes—7 at-large, 6 unpledged PLEOs

Date of 2020 contest: June 6

What week of the delegate selection season: 18

Type of delegate selection event: Closed caucus/convention

Mode of awarding delegates: Proportional representation with 15 percent threshold

How delegates are chosen: At-large delegates are elected by the territorial convention in accordance with the caucus voting results

Bound for how many national conventions ballots: One

Source: http://www.thegreenpapers.com/P20/VI-D.

Republican

Number of delegates: 9 total delegates—6 base at-large, 3 party

Date of 2020 contest: March 12

What week of the delegate selection season: 6

Type of delegate selection event: Closed caucus/convention

Mode of awarding delegates: The territorial convention includes a presidential preference vote, and delegates may announce a preference, but the two are not formally connected

How delegates are chosen: Delegates to the national convention are elected by the territorial caucus

Bound for how many national conventions ballots: One, except for the 3 party delegates, who are unpledged

Source: http://www.thegreenpapers.com/P20/VI-R.

Sources: 2000–2016 Results: The Green Papers, Primary, Caucus, and Convention Results:
https://www.thegreenpapers.com/PCC/Tabul.html;
https://www.thegreenpapers.com/P04/CO-D.phtml;
https://www.thegreenpapers.com/P08/;
http://www.thegreenpapers.com/P12/;
https://www.thegreenpapers.com/P16/.

—*Andrew E. Busch*

Appendix

2020 Primary, Caucus, and National Convention Calendar (as of September 1, 2019)

February 3	Iowa caucuses
February 11	New Hampshire primary
February 22	Nevada D caucuses
February 29	South Carolina D primary
March 3	Alabama primary
	Alaska R district conventions
	American Samoa D caucuses
	Arkansas primary
	California primary
	Colorado primary (D binding, R advisory)
	Maine primary
	Massachusetts primary
	Minnesota primary
	North Carolina primary
	Oklahoma primary
	Tennessee primary
	Texas primary
	Utah primary
	Vermont primary
	Virginia primary
	Democrats Abroad begin global primary

March 7	
March 8	Puerto Rico R primary
March 10	Hawaii R caucuses
	Idaho primary
	Michigan primary
	Mississippi primary
	Missouri primary
	North Dakota D primary
	Washington primary
March 12	Virgin Islands R caucuses
March 14	District of Columbia R convention
	Guam R caucuses
	Northern Marianas D convention
	Wyoming R county conventions
March 17	Arizona D primary
	Florida primary
	Illinois primary
	Northern Marianas R convention
	Ohio primary
March 21	Kentucky R caucuses
March 24	American Samoa R caucuses
	Georgia primary
March 29	Puerto Rico D primary
April 3–5	North Dakota R convention
April 4	Alaska D primary
	Hawaii D primary
	Louisiana primary
	Wyoming D caucuses
April 7	Wisconsin primary
April 11	Colorado R state convention
April 28	Connecticut primary
	Delaware primary
	Maryland primary
	New York primary
	Pennsylvania primary
	Rhode Island primary

May 2	Guam D caucuses
	Kansas D primary
	South Carolina state convention
May 5	Indiana primary
May 9	Kansas R state convention
May 12	Nebraska primary
	West Virginia primary
May 19	Kentucky D primary
	Oregon primary
June 2	District of Columbia D primary
	Montana primary
	New Jersey primary
	New Mexico primary
	South Dakota primary
June 6	Virgin Islands D caucuses
July 13–16	Democratic national convention
August 24–27	Republican national convention

For postpublication updates, check FrontloadingHQ, "The 2020 Presidential Primary Calendar," http://frontloading.blogspot.com/p/2020-presidential-primary-calendar.html; RealClearPolitics, "2020 Election Calendar," https://www.realclearpolitics.com/elections/election_dates/2020/; The Green Papers, "2020 Presidential Primaries, Caucuses, and Conventions Chronologically," https://www.thegreenpapers.com/P20/events.phtml?s=c.

Index

About the Editor

Andrew E. Busch is Crown Professor of Government and George R. Roberts Fellow at Claremont McKenna College, where he serves as director of the Rose Institute of State and Local Government. Busch is author, coauthor, or editor of 16 books on American politics, including *Defying the Odds: The 2016 Elections and American Politics*, *The Front-Loading Problem in Presidential Nominations*, and *Outsiders and Openness in the Presidential Nominating System*.